SĪBAWAYHI'S PRINCIPLES

RESOURCES IN ARABIC AND ISLAMIC STUDIES

series editors

Joseph E. Lowry
Devin J. Stewart
Shawkat M. Toorawa

international advisory board

Maaike van Berkel
Kristen Brustad
Antonella Ghersetti
Ruba Kana'an
Wen-chin Ouyang
Tahera Qutbuddin

Number 5
Sībawayhi's Principles:
Arabic Grammar and Law in Early Islamic Thought

SĪBAWAYHI'S PRINCIPLES

ARABIC GRAMMAR AND LAW IN EARLY ISLAMIC THOUGHT

Michael G. Carter

LOCKWOOD PRESS
Atlanta, Georgia
2016

SĪBAWAYHI'S PRINCIPLES
ARABIC GRAMMAR AND LAW IN EARLY ISLAMIC THOUGHT

All rights reserved. No part of this work may be reproduced or transmitted in any form or by any means, electronic or mechanical, including photocopying and recording, or by means of any information storage or retrieval system, except as may be expressly permitted by the 1976 Copyright Act or in writing from the publisher. Requests for permission should be addressed in writing to Lockwood Press, P.O. Box 133289, Atlanta, GA 30333, USA.

© Lockwood Press

ISBN: 978-1-937040-58-1

Library of Congress Control Number: 2016958226

Cover design by Susanne Wilhelm.

Cover image: Sibawayhi, Kitab, MS no. C-272, folio 1b, courtesy of the Institute of Oriental Manuscripts, Russian Academy of Sciences.

Printed in the United States of America on acid-free paper.

Contents

Series Editors' Preface

Michael Carter has had a long and very distinguished career as an Arabist. His first published article was the still much-cited 'The Kātib in Fact and Fiction' (1971); in 2006, a bibliography of his work appeared in a collection honoring him, and another appeared in 2009 in a special issue of the *Journal of Arabic and Islamic Studies* dedicated to him. Remarkably, in the seven years since, his work rate has not diminished. He has written on ʿAbd al-Qādir al-Baghdādī, on Andalusian grammarians, on Sufi commentary, and on much else besides; in 2013, the text of his Presidential Address to the American Oriental Society appeared, exhibiting his characteristic humor, incisiveness, and erudition. But, as the editors of his Festschrift note, Michael Carter's name "will always be most strongly linked with Sībawayhi." We are delighted, therefore, that he agreed to let us publish his 1968 Oxford doctoral thesis, "Sībawayhi's Principles of Grammatical Analysis," in our series.

Sībawyhi's Principles: Arabic Grammar and Law in Early Islamic Thought is a corrected version of the thesis, updated with copious Addenda after each chapter. It systematically argues that the science of Arabic grammar owes its origins to a special application of a set of methods and criteria developed independently to form the Islamic legal system, not to Greek or other foreign influence. These methods and criteria were then adapted to create a grammatical system brought to perfection by Sībawayhi in the late second/eighth century. It describes the intimate contacts between early jurists and scholars of language out of which the new science of Arabic grammar evolved, and makes detailed comparisons between the technical terms of law and grammar to show how the vocabulary of the law was applied to the speech of the Arabs. It also sheds light on Sībawayhi's method in producing his magisterial *Kitāb*. Although Professor Carter first formulated the arguments in his thesis fifty years ago, and although many of the ideas found their way into his formidable scholarly output thereafter, there is still an enormous amount to be learned and gleaned from this defining study.

We are grateful to: Mike Carter for his careful corrections and addenda and we crave his and the reader's indulgence for any errors that crept in when we converted the text; Susanne Wilhelm for the splendid book design; Ian Stevens for making RAIS books widely available; and publisher Billie Jean Collins for untiringly helping us promote Arabic and Islamic Studies.

Joseph E. Lowry
Devin J. Stewart
Shawkat M. Toorawa

Preface

In writing this thesis I have always been conscious of the warning of Māzinī: Whoever intends to perform a great deed in grammar after the *Kitāb* of Sībawayhi, let him be humble.[a] If in the pages below I appear to have reserved my humility for the *Kitāb*, and shown less regard for the opinions of other scholars, I hope that my intemperance will be taken as a sign of zeal and not of rancour. Writing a thesis is rather like piercing a silk handkerchief in the air with a sword: the necessary violence of the manoeuvre leads one into some pretty strange postures.

My object throughout has been to remove the patina of critical misrepresentation which overlays the *Kitāb*, by presenting an account of the various ways in which Sībawayhi's grammar differs from what is generally regarded as typical Arabic grammar. By thus returning directly to the *Kitāb*, and discounting the prejudices of the later grammarians, it is hoped that Sībawayhi's achievement will at last be discovered.

As a matter of convenience, the narrow transcription of Arabic has been used only in the bibliography, and, with one exception, page [210], no diacriticals or quantity marks are employed in the text.[b] I feel I ought to apologise to the professional linguists for the brief use I have made of the method of Immediate Constituent Analysis; this short excursion across the boundaries of academic disciplines will surely be excused for the light it throws on Sībawayhi's methods.

I do not know whether to believe Ibn Jinnī, who regarded the study of grammar as something to learn to like and to exercise one's mind upon,[c] or Kramers, who reports the view of another Arab, that too much grammar [ii] drives one mad.[d] I have, however, been guided between these two extremes by my supervisor, Professor Beeston. The hard work of producing the thesis was largely done by my wife, who alone knows how grateful I am. I would also like to thank the Principal and Librarian of Manchester College, who generously put at my disposal the Carpenter Library of Comparative Religion, and thus afforded me that rarest of commodities for the Oxford student, simple privacy.[e]

The work completed, I am more than ready to echo the plea of Labīd:[f]

قُلْتُ هَجِّدْنِي فَقَدْ طَالَ السُّرَى

Addenda to the Preface

(a) Reported in Sīrāfī, *Aḫbār al-naḥwiyyīn* 50.

(b) When this thesis was typed there were no diacritics or quantity marks available, but they have now been inserted in the present version. The digraphs *dh, gh, kh, sh, th* are replaced by *ḏ*, *ġ*, *ḫ*, *š* and *ṯ* , but reproduced as printe din book title (see further in the second Preface).

(c) Strictly speaking he is referring to *taṣrīf*, those morphological games which test the student's mastery of conjugation, of which Ibn Jinnī remarks, *Ḫaṣā'iṣ* 2, 487, that "their only goal is that you should become familiar with the process and exercise your mind on it", *innamā l-ġaraḍu fīhi l-ta'annusu bihi wa-i'māl ul-fikrati fīhi.*

(d) "He who occupies himself much with grammar becomes unhinged thereby," attributed by Kramers, *Analecta Orientalia* 2, 167, to Ibn 'Abd Rabbihi (d. 328/940).

(e) The reference is to the married graduate student, a social category which at the time was scarcely acknowledged by the Oxford system.

(f) See Fischer/Bräunlich 1945, 175, rhyme غَفْل, for the edition of the *Dīwān*: it is quoted by Ibn Qutayba, *Adab al-Kātib* 483. The original هجّدنا has here been adapted to هجّدني.

Preface to This Edition

It is customary for an academic career to begin with a thesis and end with a festschrift. In my case the sequence, albeit not the chronology, has been reversed.

It is an honour to have been invited to issue the thesis in this Series, and I thank the editors and the publishers, all of whom have had to deal with more than the usual range of technical difficulties. My special gratitude goes to Shawkat Toorawa, who spent so much time and energy on the preparation of the final version that his name should appear on the title page, not as editor, but as co-author.

The text of the thesis has been left unaltered, apart from the correction of typographical errors and a few minor emendations, and some long paragraphs have been broken up. In a number of cases (indicated in the Addenda) outright mistakes of fact or interpretation have been corrected. As for my frequent intemperate critical outbursts, there was nothing to be done except to apologise in situ and leave them as they stand, to be a lesson to others.

The discursive and often speculative Addenda make few concessions to the non-specialist reader, and most of the evidential material is untranslated. Every effort has been made to paraphrase recent work in the field accurately and justly. Two things will be obvious: there has been an enormous output of research on Sībawayhi in the last few decades, and we are still a long way from understanding him completely.

The linking of the Addenda is not always ideal, and sometimes the reference is in a footnote rather than the body of the text. In their apparent randomness the Addenda mimic the non-linearity of Sībawayhi's thought, with which readers of the *Kitāb* are familiar.

The bibliographical conventions of the thesis are preserved, but the Addenda and its supplementary bibliography refer to Author, year and page. Given the semi-antiquarian nature of this publication, it was decided not to venture into the world of the Internet.

Although the thesis did generate a number of articles, which are mentioned in the Addenda, presenting the full form of the arguments here will have a greater impact than their less detailed abridgements, whereby this work may acquire a usefulness beyond a simple contribution to the history of scholarship.

Michael G. Carter

Chapter One
The Background of the *Kitāb*

It goes without saying that a work of the size and scope of the *Kitāb* cannot be without antecedents. Unfortunately no authentic work survives of any grammarian before Sībawayhi, the *Muqaddima* of his elder contemporary Ḫalaf al-Aḥmar being most probably spurious.[1] There remain two sources through which the earliest history of Arabic grammar may be glimpsed, one, much used and much to be mistrusted, the Arabs' own accounts, and one scarcely appreciated until recently, the contents of the *Kitāb* itself.

We need not doubt that all the various tales of the grammatical activities of Abū al-Aswad al-Du'alī are useless as evidence for the beginnings of grammar, through they may conceal the first rumblings of the purist reaction, about which we shall speak later. As assembled by Zubaydī,[2] whose list is longer than that offered by Flügel,[3] the stories involving Abū al-Aswad as a grammarian fall fall into three groups: the first consists of mispronunciations, e.g., ضالع for ظالع , جامس for جامد, presumably a relic of the traditional Arab contempt for those who could not pronounce their language properly, the second consists of grammatical mistakes emanating from the same sort of people, e.g., تُوُفِّي ابانا وترك بنون which is emblematic rather than a *verbatim* report of actual errors, and the third consists of such grammarians' [2] frivolities as ما أشدَّ الحرِّ \ ما أشدُّ الحرَّ and هلمّ اقاربْك, perhaps echoing the more feeble erudite jokes going the rounds of the *majālis*. The reliability of the Arab historians on the origins of Arabic grammar may be gauged from the story of Ibn al-Nadīm in which he describes an autograph manuscript by Yaḥyā ibn Ya'mar of Abū al-Aswad's grammatical treatise. It was written, thought Ibn al-Nadīm, "on Chinese paper."[4] Since Chinese paper did not reach even the easternmost part of Islam until A.H.

1. See below p. [2].
2. Zubaydī, *Ṭabaqāt* 13–19[(a)].
3. Flügel, *Gram. Schulen* 17–26.
4. Ibn al-Nadīm, *Fihrist* 67, Flügel, *Gram. Schulen* 24–26.

134,[5] and Yaḥyā died in A.H. 129 it seems clear that, if Ibn al-Nadīm was right about the paper, the manuscript must have been a forgery. Finally we may observe that the surviving poetry of Abū al-Aswad reveals no particular reason why he should be regarded as the founder of Arabic grammar. Occasional lines of his *Dīwān* where the subject of speech crops up are better evidence for that ingrained habit of the Arab mind which expresses man's conduct through the metaphor of movement towards or away from the good, than as proof that Abū al-Aswad was even remotely interested in grammar. That he is quoted several times by Sībawayhi in the *Kitāb* as a poet[6] but never mentioned as a grammarian is perhaps all the confirmation we need to assert with Aḥmad Amīn that this whole matter is nothing but a "fairy tale."[7]

The only other serious contender for an important place in the history of Arabic grammar is Ḫalaf al-Aḥmar, whose claim is based on the existence of an abridged grammar attributed to him, the attribution [3] being stoutly, but somewhat vainly defended by his editor 'Izz al-Dīn al-Tanūḫī. There are three reasons why the authenticity of the manuscript is to be denied. The editor publishes as part of his preface the opinions of several Arab scholars, of which I give here the essence:[8] the terminology and topics of the *Muqaddima* do not differ from those of the Baṣrans, and so there is nothing to prevent it from being Ḫalaf's work (Muḥammad al-Fahhām); it represents grammar of the time "before they philosophised it" (Aḥmad Ḥasan al-Zayyāt); the Ḫalaf of the manuscript is not the 'Alī al-Aḥmar with which he is often confused (Muḥammad 'Alī al-Najjār); finally Muḥyī al-Dīn 'Abd al-Ḥamīd declares, "I agree with the opinion of my friend Dr. Fahhām... this is one of the simplest grammars ever composed, resembling the Ājurrūmiyya for students." The accumulation of these evasive remarks has, if anything, the opposite effect to that intended by the editor: if so many eminent scholars are anxious not to confirm the authenticity of the work, who will dare contradict them?[(a)]

Secondly, the internal evidence makes it difficult to believe that this work was written before, or even contemporaneously with the *Kitāb*. I will not stress the inadequacy of the editor's own view that the short introductory prayer and formula قال عزّ وجلّ before Qur'anic quotations are "signs of antiquity,"[9] but I would point out that the manuscript evinces a technical knowledge of purely grammatical causes (علل) and grammatical principles [4] (اصول النحو) which one would not expect in a work of this putative date.[10] There is a curious inconsistency in terminology which the editor takes as proof of antiquity but which could equally well betray a clumsy attempt to give the work the character of a

5. *EI*[2] art. Kāghad.
6. *Kitāb* 1, 16/21, 60/71, 72/85, 125/149.
7. A. Amin, *Ḍuḥā al-Islām* 2, 285: "خرافة."
8. Ḫalaf, *Muqaddima* 5–6.
9. Id. 7.
10. Ḫalaf, *Muqaddima* 33, 34, 100.

grammar composed before the rival schools became rigidly distinct. If this is so, the author of the *Muqaddima* should not have shown such a concern to give explicitly "Kūfan" and "Baṣran" equivalents on two minor occasions[11] if he is supposed to be writing in a period when the two schools did not exist.[12]

The third reason for dismissing the work as spurious is a more general one. The editor admits that Ḫalaf is not credited with any grammatical works by the biographers, and we might well ask what would be the reason for composing an abridged text-book of a discipline which did not yet formally exist. The second century A.H. is too early for such manuals of instruction, for the subject itself has yet to be fully explored and defined. Even the *Kitāb* is primitive enough not to recognise the academic independence of the system it describes, in marked contrast with such third century works as the *Muqtaḍab* of Mubarrad, to which the *Muqaddima* is much closer in spirit. For this and other reasons mentioned above it can safely be said that the *Muqaddima* is neither a work of Ḫalaf's nor of the second century A.H., which leaves us with no material evidence for the forerunners of Sībawayhi outside his own acknowledgements or refutations in the *Kitāb* itself.

[5] Not only do we lack direct evidence of grammatical activity before Sībawayhi, we are also likely to find, on examining the works of the Arab biographers, that there are no books before Sībawayhi which, from their titles at least can with certainty be said to be grammatical treatises in the way that the *Kitāb* is a grammatical treatise. Ḫalīl, *pace* Reuschel,[13] is a case in point. His works increase in number with the date of the biographer, so that in the earliest he is credited with nothing more than the *Kitāb al-'Ayn*,[14] which is shortly increased by the addition of prosodic works,[15] until we reach the time when he is given the authorship of grammatical works with suspiciously sophisticated titles such as *Kitāb al-'awāmil*.[16] These, one feels, would surely have been mentioned by Sībawayhi if they had existed, or at the very least some reference would be found in the biographers closest to him in time.[(a)]

Two other works reputedly written before the *Kitāb*, and indeed said to be included in the *Kitāb* itself, are the *Jāmi'* and the *Ikmāl* of 'Īsā ibn 'Umar. Having no corroboration in the form of quotations or surviving fragments it is impossible to invalidate the account or to make any use of it in the study of early Arabic grammar. There is, however, a disparity between 'Īsā's relatively early date of death (149 A.H.) and the assumption that he was a direct influence upon Sībawayhi, who would have been somewhat young (not more than 14 years old) for the supposed speculations of 'Īsā. Since the latter is only rarely [6]

---

11. Id. 53, 80.
12. Cf. Anbārī, *Inṣāf*, intro. 61, and below pp. [28] and [35].
13. Reuschel, *Ḫalīl* 8.
14. Ibn al-Nadīm, *Fihrist* 70, Abū Ṭayyib, *Marātib* 30f., Sīrāfī, *Aḫbār* 38.
15. Zubaydī, *Ṭabaqāt* 291.
16. Flügel, *Gram. Schulen* 38 (Suyūṭī and Ibn Ḫallikān).

quoted in the *Kitāb*[17] and mostly via Yūnus, the incongruity of the fact that Sībawayhi never refers to any book of ʿĪsā's is increased, and the likelihood of ʿĪsā's being the author of any grammatical work in such an early period correspondingly decreases.

The same might be said of Yūnus, whose idiosyncrasies in the matter of grammatical technique have been pointed out more than once without, to my knowledge, ever having been substantiated.[18] They may be based on nothing more than the impression that Sībawayhi often quotes Yūnus in order to disagree with him,[19] which could account for the desire of the later biographers to father upon Yūnus the work bearing the title *Kitāb al-qiyās fī l-naḥw*,[20] which is significantly absent from the list of Yūnus's works in the *Fihrist*. In addition, the source of Yūnus's reputation for individual *qiyās*, namely Sīrāfī, does not mention any works with which to support the assertion: it seems that Flügel has misunderstood Sīrāfī's phrase وله قياس في النحو as meaning "he is the author of a book *Qiyās fī l-naḥw*," which throws enough doubt on the matter to enable us to feel certain that Yūnus did not write any grammatical works, even though he may have produced several lexicographical and dialectal treatises or, more likely, compilations.

Perhaps these alleged early works are the kind described by Abū Ṭayyib when discussing ʿAbdullāh ibn Abī Isḥāq, another of Sībawayhi's sources: "He had so much to say about *hamz* that a book on that subject [7] was made up from what he dictated."[21] It is possible that Ibn Abī Isḥāq knew enough about *hamz* for this to happen but that is no proof that it did. It is extremely doubtful, on the other hand, whether we can accept as genuine a work of his entitled *Šarḥ al-ʿilal* on such a late attribution as Suyūṭī, in the absence of any corroboration from the earlier sources.[22]

Other older contemporaries of Sībawayhi, such as Abū Zayd al-Anṣārī and Abū ʿAmr ibn al-ʿAlāʾ can claim authorship only of marginal works, i.e., of lexical and dialectal content, and by the time we reach the period of Aṣmaʿī with his *Kitāb uṣūl al-kalām*, Kisāʾī with his *Kitāb al-fayṣal*, Quṭrub with his *Kitāb al-ʿilal fī l-naḥw* and so on, the moment has passed when we can consider any of these as forerunners of Sībawayhi, who in any case predeceased even some of the earlier "grammarians" such as Yūnus, Ibn Abī Isḥāq and Kisāʾī. The old tale that the *Kitāb* is a result of the labors of forty-two scholars[23] is not only meaningless on the grounds that there were scarcely more than a handful of scholars who could assist Sībawayhi, it is made meaningless by its lack of precision: we do not know whom Ṯaʿlab means and how he understands them to have contributed to the

17. Reuschel, *Ḫalīl*, 10: 13 times, but see Troupeau, *Arabica* 8, 309–312[(a)].
18. E.g., Flügel, *Gram. Schulen* 35, Weil, *Inṣāf*, intro. 71 .
19. See below, p. [34].
20. Only in Flügel, loc. cit.
21. Abū Ṭayyib, *Marātib* 12.
22. Suyūṭī in Flügel, *Gram. Schulen* 29[(a)].
23. Ibn al-Nadīm, *Fihrist* 82.

Kitāb. Most likely it is a mere attempt on the part of the fanatical "Kūfan" to belittle the achievement of the greatest "Baṣran" grammarian.

Everything points to the absence of any formal predecessor for the *Kitāb*, in the sense that Sībawayhi was probably the first person to [8] treat this relatively new subject (which even then did not have a name) in a comprehensive, unified and consistent way. But it should not be supposed that the lack of technical literature before the *Kitāb* is evidence for the absence of discussion of Arabic grammatical problems. This had obviously been going on ever since the poetic *koine* of pre-Islamic Arabia achieved a recognisable form: with the standardisation of such an artificial language inevitably came the awareness of divergences from it. Thus the poet Nābiġa al-Ḏubyānī, who died shortly before the advent of Islām, though near enough to meet the *muḫaḍramī* poet Ḥassān ibn Ṯābit, offers an example of the sort of criticism current among poets at that time: in response to the verses of Ḥassān ibn Ṯābit quoted in support of his claim to be a superior poet to Nābiġa and Ḫansā' who was also present, Nābiġa says, "You would certainly be a poet if you did not give جفان the plural of paucity and did not boast of your offspring instead of boasting of your forebears."[24] Other criticisms are given in an alternative *riwāya*, mainly concerned with pointing out Ḥassān's ineptitude in choice of vocabulary for the verses. The awareness of the difference in meaning between the two plurals of جفان (if the story is genuine) must not be taken, however, as proof of any "grammatical" speculations at so early a date.

Similarly the famous poem by Ḥuṭay'a, which was apparently composed with a quiescent rhyme-letter, but which can be vocalised throughout in the "nominative" form without breaking the rules of grammar or of [9] rhyme is not evidence for any knowledge of the nature and functions of the "nominative" as such, which is what Ibn Fāris seems to imply when he says that "if Ḥuṭay'a had not knowingly done this, it is most probable that the endings would all have differed, because for them all to have the same single vowel by accident and without intention can scarcely be."[25] Ibn Fāris' implications are, for this period of Arabic, less probable than the chance agreement of restored vowels in a quiescent rhyme. A recent attempt to revive this belief has been made by Nāṣir al-Dīn Asad, who uses Ibn Fāris's story of Ḥuṭay'a for the same purpose.[26] It cannot be said that either has proved the specific point for which the poem was adduced, namely that the early Arabs were familiar with the skill of writing, for the prosodic ambiguity of rhyme would not show in writing anyway. Both scholars may well be right in asserting that the Arabs of the Jāhiliyya were not as "ignorant" as they were made out to be, but nor were they as sophisticated as Ibn Fāris and Asad would have us believe. The true picture is more likely to be that painted by Abū 'Alī al-Fārisī, who explained that the Bedouin Arabs were prone

24. Iṣfahānī, *Aġānī* 8, 195, in Krenkow, *JRAS Centenary Supplement* 1924, 255.
25. Ibn Fāris, *Kitāb al-Ṣāḥibī*, 37, Suyūṭī, *Muzhir* 2, 345.
26. Nāṣir al-Dīn Asad, *Maṣādir al-Ši'r al-Jāhilī* 47f.

to make mistakes "because they had no (grammatical) principles to refer to and no rules to resort to."[27] At least this view is founded on common sense, in spite of the fallacy (still current, alas) that native speakers of any language ever make conscious reference to a body of abstract rules.

[10] A more useful example for Asad's case, and one which also serves our purposes equally well, is the answer given by Ayesha in response to a query about the grammar of Sūra 4, 162:[(a)] "It is reported from Ayesha that she was once asked about this place, and she said, 'It is a mistake of the scribe's'."[28] All we need to know is that was possible in those days to distinguish between right and wrong language, and we must beware of assuming that the ability to do so is testimony to the existence of a conscious "grammar." Even as late as Farazdaq, who was reputedly very sensitive to criticisms of his language, there is still no evidence of specifically grammatical awareness. We might go as far as to claim that no "grammar" is involved even when Farazdaq's target is a grammarian, for example his well-known satire on ʿAbdullāh ibn Abī Isḥāq,[29] or when, in a mellower mood, he praises Abū ʿAmr ibn al-ʿAlāʾ.[30] Perhaps it may be taken as a further sign of the absence of grammatical speculations that, on another occasion, Farazdaq absolutely refused to consider an alternative case-ending in one of his verses, where it is astonishing that Ibn Abī Isḥāq's discussion of the problem is completely devoid of grammatical terms. Instead he says "if you were to say فعولَيْن instead of فعولان" etc., which suggests that he, at least, could not provide any grammatical descriptions of the words whose grammar he could nevertheless discuss in lay fashion.[31]

[11] This seems to have been the normal state of affairs in Umayyad times: many examples are to be found in Fück's *Arabīya*[32] both from the Umayyad and early Abbasid periods, from which we may at least grant that the wealth of evidence precludes the spuriousness of the entire collection of stories, and reveals the genuine acuity of Arab *Sprachgefühl* which was later channelled into the construction of a grammar of the language.[(a)]

This ability to sense mistakes of language, however, is not by any means unusual, being essentially an intuitive grasp of the mother tongue, and far from needing the support of an abstract system, it could not possibly devise one as long as the reasons for the awareness of speech mistakes remained intuitive. The Arabs thus found themselves in the situation described by Bloomfield:

27. Ibn Jinnī, *Ḫaṣāʾiṣ* 3, 273, Suyūṭī, *Muzhir* 2, 494.
28. Anbārī, *Inṣāf* 195, cf. Sezgin, *GAS* 1, 3.
29. *Kitāb* 2, 53/58.
30. *Kitāb* 2, 150/148.
31. Zajjājī, *Majālis* 85.
32. Op. cit. chs. 2 and 3.

> There are some circumstances, however, in which the conventionally educated person discusses linguistic matters. Occasionally he debates questions of "correctness" ... If possible he looks to the conventions of writing for an answer ... Otherwise he appeals to authority: one way of speaking, he believes, is inherently right, the other is inherently wrong.[33]

It is certain that Bloomfield had never read any of the accounts of the *majālis* in the second century A.H., which makes it all the more significant that his words should apply so aptly to most of the contents of these Arab *causeries*. Unfortunately, for the reason I have already [12] given, such academic conversations could not provide a satisfactory explanation for the origins of Arabic grammar. The purist is seldom an innovator: his energies are directed towards the preservation of the *status quo* and the rejection of alien elements both lexical and grammatical. His contribution to a scientific study of his language would always remain within the limits described by Bloomfield, which in the particular case of Arabic characteristically led to the adoption of the *isnād* as a formalised "authority" for the purist's judgements, just as the *isnād* was used to authenticate tradition of every kind in Islām, in which linguistic behavior was only one of many aspects of the *sunna*. This is probably the stage reached by the immediate predecessors of Sībawayhi, and we can be sure that Abū ʿAmr ibn al-ʿAlāʾ, ʿAbdullāh ibn Abī Isḥāq, ʿĪsā ibn ʿUmar, Yūnus and Ḫalīl all had a highly developed sense of linguistic correctness, a nose for anomalies and suffie cient personal authority to give prescriptive force to their utterances. Whether they also had a technical vocabulary is a point I shall deal with in due course, but it will be enough for the present to say that only Yūnus and Ḫalīl of the above show signs of any systematic abstraction of grammatical phenomena. The others must be regarded as highly observant purists whose principal contribution to Arabic grammar lay in detecting, and perhaps discussing, lines of poetry, verses of the Qurʾān etc., which attracted their attention simply on the grounds that their language seemed different from the expected standard. In this they reached a point which had already been accurately described by Flügel in his [13] assessment of the earliest grammarians:

> We may expect to find in them no system, no closely-knit paragraphs, strictly ordered and conforming to a doctrine, for which all those poetic fragments and quotations could serve as examples: instead they were scattered grammatical or linguistic studies and observations as they occurred in isolation to every compiler, lacking inner consistency and rational treatment.[34]

33. Bloomfield, *Language* 3.
34. Flügel, *Gram. Schulen* 35.

It is time now to turn to the *Kitāb*, which as well as providing valuable evidence for early Arabic grammar, will, I hope, also reveal itself to be conspicuously closely-knit and well ordered in contrast with the kind of works Flügel described.

The *Kitāb* itself is the earliest source of information about the history of Arabic grammar, and both in its construction and in its allusions it reveals that there was certainly some sort of grammatical speculation in progress during the time of its composition, although it offers no conclusive evidence for such activities before that time. The mere fact that the arguments of Sībawayhi sometimes take for granted theorems which have yet to be established is clear proof that the *Kitāb* is an apology for ideas already well-known to its intended readership. This and other features of the work will be dealt with in later chapters.

Following the negative tone which I have so far maintained, let me [14] reiterate that Abū al-Aswad al-Du'alī is never mentioned in the *Kitāb* as a grammarian, but only as a poet. Conversely, Ru'ba the poet is occasionally cited as the authority for certain prose constructions, in every case but one on the authority of Yūnus.[35] This is a particularly important fact for the history of Arabic grammar, and one which Reuschel characteristically dismisses as irrelevant.[36] It shows us that at least by A.H. 149 (the date of Ru'ba's last datable poem[37]) and probably earlier, the "grammarians" were beginning to cross-examine the poets about their usage. But significantly Ru'ba is not quoted as having any grammatical opinions of his own: that is exclusively Yūnus's occupation. Equally significantly Ru'ba is never directly quoted by Sībawayhi, which affords a little certainty amidst the confusion of Sībawayhi's dates, for it suggests that Ru'ba's death and Sībawayhi's birth must have been fairly close, i.e., about A.H. 150. Curiously enough, 'Īsā ibn 'Umar died at about the same time and he, too, is mostly transmitted through Yūnus. Thus Yūnus himself provides, as it were, an *ante quem non* for the beginnings of Arabic grammar. This can be supported by examining the use Sībawayhi makes of 'Īsā ibn 'Umar in the *Kitāb*: of the fourteen occasions[(a)] when Sībawayhi refers to 'Īsā, two are simply poetic quotations transmitted by 'Īsā,[38] one gives [15] his manner of reading a Qur'anic verse,[39] four concern 'Īsā's way of expressing himself without implying that he could formulate in grammatical terms the peculiarities of his speech,[40] three refer to 'Īsā's report of other people's usage,[41] and only four are remotely connected with the "verdict" (*qawl*) of 'Īsā as a grammarian.[42] But it is almost certain that 'Īsā's "grammatical" views are merely his lay

35. *Kitāb* 1, 19/25, 206/241, 263/304, 2, 49/54, 209/201, 348/395, no attribution: "it has reached us."
36. Reuschel, *Ḫalīl* 11.
37. *EI*[1], art. Ru'ba by F. Krenkow[(b)].
38. *Kitāb* 1, 72/85, 213/250.
39. *Kitāb* 2, 170/165.
40. Id. 1, 168/199, 2, 7/7, 68/73, 134/132.
41. Id. 1, 318/363, 366/412. 2, 302/278.
42. Id. 1, 194/228, 232/272, 2, 6/7, 38/42.

opinion translated into the technical language of his transmitter, Yūnus, or by Sībawayhi himself in discussing the problems raised. The same is true of the five[(a)] occasions on which Sībawayhi quotes ʿAbdullāh ibn Abī Isḥāq: three are concerned only with the non-grammatical facts that he "allows" a verse of poetry to be read in a certain way or reads and speaks in a particular manner.[43] The remaining two cases reveal unmistakably amateur philology in the garb of intricate grammatical reasoning. When Sībawayhi says that

> Yūnus ... (dealing with) مررت به المسكين used to correlate the 'nominative' with the 'nominative,' 'genitive' with 'genitive' and 'accusative' with 'accusative.'[(b)] He claimed that the 'nominative' as we have explained it was erroneous even though this was the opinion of Ḫalīl and Ibn Abī Isḥāq.[44]

there is nothing which compels us to believe that the last-named authority had any idea of what was meant by "nominative" etc.

[16] Likewise in the discussion of the verse[(a)]

ما بالدينة دارٌ غيرُ واحدةٍ   دارُ الخليفة إلا دارُ مروانا [45]

it would seriously affect the history of Arabic grammar if Ibn Abī Isḥāq's "*qawl*" had been as Sībawayhi reports it, viz.

> They have made غير an adjective in the status of مثل, and whoever makes it an exceptive will have no alternative but to put one of two (excepted words) in the "accusative."

Such grammatical sophistication from a man who died in A.H. 127 is not to be expected. At the very least it would suggest that he was as familiar with grammatical terminology as Ḫalīl or Yūnus, thereby entailing the heresy that Ḫalīl, Yūnus and Sībawayhi found their entire system already worked out for them and fully developed, having been so since as far back as the end of the reign of Caliph Hišām (125 A.H.). It is much more sensible to assume that Ibn Abī Isḥāq was aware that the use of غير in the line in question brought about differences of meaning,[(b)] which he may have pointed out to Yūnus (who was evidently a pupil and admirer of his) and that this observation was then transmuted into grammatical form by Yūnus and Sībawayhi. The same strictures apply to the other grammarians whom Sībawayhi mentions by name, Abū al-Ḫaṭṭāb, Hārūn and Abū ʿAmr ibn al-ʿAlāʾ, this last (who died in 154 A.H.) probably being available to Sībawayhi only through Yūnus and, rarely, Ḫalīl.[46] For the purposes of the history of Arabic grammar

43. Id. 1, 118/141, 379/426, 2, 458/410 respectively.
44. Id. 1, 218/256.
45. Id. 1, 325/373.
46. Reuschel, *Ḫalīl* 10.

the absence in the *Kitāb* [17] of any references to the first two *ṭabaqāt* of the traditional Arab scheme (which led Ibrāhīm Muṣṭafā to suppose that the founder of Arabic grammar must therefore be ʿAbdullāh ibn Abī Isḥāq, who belongs to the third *ṭabaqa*[47]), and the likelihood that Sībawayhi received his tuition almost exclusively from Ḫalīl and Yūnus, together imply that there was no grammar before Sībawayhi encountered his two great masters. As we shall see later, Sībawayhi did not even come to Baṣra to study grammar in the first place, which is quite consistent with the impression created by the references in the *Kitāb* to other so-called "grammarians."[(a)]

Yet other "grammarians" there must have been, for Sībawayhi refers on a variety of occasions to *naḥwiyyūn*. Since he does not name them, even when he says, for example, "Yūnus and some of the grammarians,"[48] it seems likely that the term *naḥwī* had not yet acquired its academically defined sense usually rendered in English as "grammarian." Very probably, judging from the way Sībawayhi disagrees with them more often than not, their name has something of a pejorative quality once inherent in such English nicknames as "Methodist" and "Quaker," which have long since lost their original opprobrium, just as *naḥwiyyūn* now applies to perfectly respectable scholars. Their name is evidently derived from their frequent use of the term *naḥw*, about whose meaning I shall have more to say below.[(b)]

I shall now follow, as briefly as possible, the arguments of the "grammarians" in the *Kitāb*. It need not be stressed that these [18] disagreements are probably the only reliable, direct evidence for the state of grammar in Sībawayhi's time. For that reason I shall supplement the overt arguments with certain examples of dispute between unnamed opponents, either unspecified "people" or merely "those who say" (من قال, من زعم) and the like.

1) 1, 140/167-8. Jahn translates the last part of the title of this chapter wrongly as "Ueber diejenigen Constructionen, welche die Grammatiker als incorrect für hässlich halten, und anders beurteilen als die Araber"[49] (my emphasis). It should read, "Concerning what the grammarians detest as bad Arabic, for they put such words in a position that the Arabs do not," taking الكلام فيه to mean "words in the *bāb* under discussion." This is the only way to make sense out of the fact that Sībawayhi defends the natural unassimilated form ويحٌ له وتبًّا against the form devised by "the grammarians," ويحٌ له وتبٌّ, and for the fact that he dismisses تبًّا لك وويحًا as "bad Arabic," because the "grammarians" have put ويحًا in a position where it is not used by the Arabs. If they insist on putting it there, says Sībawayhi, it has to take direct[(a)] form to account for its apparent isolation. All "grammarians" agree that تبًّا (with its complementary idea له) takes the direct form. It is not at all clear, however, whether Sībawayhi counts himself among the *naḥwiyyūn* in thus saying. [19]

47. *Actes du XXe Congrès des Orientalistes*, Paris 1948[(c)].
48. *Kitāb* 2, 160/157.
49. Jahn, *Kitāb* §69.

2) 1, 164/194-5. When the types اما العلمَ فذو علم and اما العبيدُ فذو عبيد are conjoined the "grammarians" assimilate them into اما العلمَ والعبيدَ فذو علم وذو عبيد, thereby relating عبيد to a verbal noun like علم. This is regarded by Sībawayhi as bad Arabic and the objection is supported by a reference to the false assimilation in the previous case of ويحٌ له وتبٌ, emphasising that the conjunction of the two constructions, wrong in itself, leads to further mistakes of theory.

3) 1, 184/216. To say مررت برجل أسد شدةً وجراةً when all you mean is "like a lion" is both feeble and bad Arabic, being nothing but the "grammarians'" invention from a false comparison with مررت بزيد أسدًا شدةً in which أسدًا is rightly considered to be a *ḥāl*, but from which it has been falsely deduced that أسد may be an adjective. This is denied by Sībawayhi.

4) 1, 190/223. Because the emphatic and generalising words like كله , كلهم etc. follow the inflections of the words they qualify, the "grammarians" have wrongly assumed that they must be adjectives.

5) 1, 193/227-228. Here for the first time Sībawayhi seems to ally himself with the "grammarians," though with reservations. The case arises out of the claim (ان زعم زاعم) made by an anonymous adversary of Sībawayhi that is is possible to distinguish between the meaning of مررت برجل مخالط بدنه داءٌ and مررت برجل مخالط بدنَه داءٌ where مخالط with *tanwīn* would give present and future meaning, and without *tanwīn* past meaning. Sībawayhi implies that the unknown critic must fall foul both of the "grammarians" and of the Arabs if [20] he persists in his erroneous view. The point is argued at some length by Sībawayhi, in the true Socratic dialectic of obtaining step by step the agreement of his adversary until the latter has talked himself into the opposite of his original claim. It is an interesting coincidence, but scarcely proof of any Greek influence, that the debate should be conducted in this way, the typical antiphony of the *majlis*.[(a)]

That this is a dispute of considerable importance is shown by the subsequent digression in which Sībawayhi expounds, without apparently sharing, the views of 'Īsā ibn 'Umar and Yūnus on an even more subtle distinction. The root of the difficulty is in the borderline cases where adjectives become *ḥāl*s, typified in the sentence مررت برجل قائمًا. The quality of an adjective is that it is identical with the word it describes and therefore takes identical form, while the characteristic of the *ḥāl* is that it is expressly not identical with the term it qualifies, and so takes an explicitly different form. This latter situation is exemplified in عشرون درهمًا, for a discussion of which see Chapter Six. When we encounter mixed forms such as مررت برجل قائمًا, where strictly speaking a *ḥāl* should not qualify an undefined[(b)] term, we realise that the Arab grammarians had already firmly established their principles, and so were very likely to differ profoundly on marginal cases such as those in this chapter. What they are trying to solve is the problem of the adjective which has verbal (participial) form, and threfore brings in difficulties of temporal connotation which should not be present in true adjectives [21] but which are inherent in *ḥāl* situations, and which also has a double reference (i.e., the *sabab* of improper *iḍāfa*) both backwards to the noun it qualifies, and forwards to its verbal complements. It may not make the problem any easier to discuss it in these terms, but we must assume that those were the considerations which brought about the difference of views we are trying to analyse. It will be perhaps simpler to treat this issue as two distinct questions: when Sībawayhi talks about concordance he is trying to unravel the confusion of *ḥāl* and adjective, and when he talks about *tanwīn* he is concerned with the difference in meaning (which he does not himself fully accept) between participial adjectives with or without *tanwīn*. The two problems combine in the sentence به داءٌ مخالطَه/مخالطُه, but I hope that by now there will be no need to point out the easiest way to approach such a rebarbative specimen.

It only remains to tabulate the views of the "grammarians" on the meaning of the *tanwīn*:

Yūnus believes that as well as the difference effected by the presence or absence of *tanwīn*, there is a further subdivision of forms without *tanwīn*, namely the type of action which has no perceptible execution, e.g., لازم , آخذ etc., and that which has, e.g., كاسر, ضارب. The first type, somewhat unexpectedly, is always treated as a *ḥāl* and given direct form (cf. به داءٌ مخالطَه) while the second, which might seem to us to be more suitable for *ḥāl* status, is always independent and adjectival.

'Īsā ibn 'Umar proposes a different scheme for the two types of [22] meaning when there is no *tanwīn*. The first, treated as *ḥāl*s and therefore direct in form, are the words which denote actions that have occurred, while those which denote actions which have not (yet) occurred are treated as independent adjectives.

Needless to say, these are wanton speculations based on an apparent inconsistency in Arabic usage, and Sībawayhi presents them only as examples of an approach he certainly deplored. We have here an interesting example of the capabilities of the early "grammarians" but it is also significant that such a complex dispute is rare in the *Kitāb*.

6) 1, 206/242. The "grammarians" wrongly suppose that adjectives may be freely inverted. If this were so, "a great deal of what people say would be corrupt." The point is proved by *reductio ad absurdum*: the inverted form of مررت برجل حسن الوجه حميلَه/جميله would be nonsense if the pronoun of جميله preceded its noun, and equally nonsensical is the transformation of جميله into a dependent *ḥāl* جميلَه, both on grounds of meaning and of the unsuitability of the undefined term (رجل) for qualification by خبر المعرفة, i.e., *ḥāl*.

7) 1, 219/257. Although the personal pronouns are normally used instead of the name of the person whose identity they denote, there is one case, e.g., انا عبد الله فاخرًا, where the pronoun can be qualified by its proper noun as a form of emphasis. The situation in which this occurs is described by Sībawayhi as cases of "threatening, boasting and self-abasement," which makes the rhetorical nature of this [23] construction pretty clear. On the other hand it is quite wrong to do as the "grammarians" do and make the pronoun into a subject and the proper noun into its predicate, as in انا عبد الله منطلقًا, when the emphasis is only on the going away, not, as in the correct usage, on the fact that a named person is in a certain state or condition.

8) 1, 335/383. The suffixed pronouns have a natural order of attachment corresponding to our 1st, 2nd and 3rd person. In doubly transitive verbs the second object may be suffixed (أعطانيه) or take the disjunctive form (أعطاني اياه). The forms of the type أعطاهوني are

"bad Arabic not spoken by Arabs, but the 'grammarians' have derived them by analogy" (قاسوه).[(a)]

9) 1, 345/393. The use of the independent pronouns as adjectives is likened by Sībawayhi to the use of نفس, كل etc. (cf. example no. 4 above), but they are not true adjectives, contrary to the assumption of the "grammarians."

10) 1, 347/395. When the independent pronouns are used to separate the two parts of a sentence, they do not affect the behavior of either part. Thus لـ may be prefixed to them at will, leaving the predicate unchanged, which is the practice of "the Arabs and all the grammarians." This is only the second case among those cited here, where the Arabs and "grammarians" agree, cf. example no. 5 above.

11) 1, 369/414-415. When using حتى with the independent form, i.e., denoting a definite temporal connection between the main and [24] subordinate verbs, it makes no difference if the main verb refers to continuous past action (كنت سرت) or to an isolated past action (سرت مرّة في الزمان الاول): in either case the verb of حتى will be independent. "To say that there is a difference is only what the 'grammarians' say on feeble grounds. They say that if no change of meaning (قلب) is allowed [after قد] we use the direct form. This, if they are right, would oblige them to say قد سرت حتى ادخلَها in the direct form, and yet there is not an Arab in the world who says سرت حتى ادخلُها without also saying قد سرت حتى ادخلُها."

This is a difficult argument to grasp. Jahn, in following Sīrāfī, missed the point completely by taking قلب to mean syntactical inversion.[50] It is better to take قلب as meaning change in meaning, cf. the لم قلب معنى المضارع الى الماضي [51] and note also that Sībawayhi elsewhere expresses syntactical inversion in connection with قد by تقديم وتأخير.[52] Whether قلب in this rarer meaning is Sībawayhi's own term or whether he is quoting it as part of the usage of his opponents is not clear, though the latter seems more likely.

At all events, as the preceding and subsequent passages show, Sībawayhi is at pains to prove that no modification of the verb, either through قد or additions such as إنما, أني, كنت and negative particles, affects the form of the verb after حتى [25]. The "grammarians," on the other hand, distinguish between simple سرت and modified قد سرت etc., on the grounds that after modified verbs the connection between the main and subordinate verbs is then of the kind which requires a direct form after حتى. Thus they contrast سرت حتى ادخلُها "I travelled and now I have entered it" with قد سرت حتى ادخلَها "I once travelled and at that time entered it." This contrast is rejected by Sībawayhi, who turns the argument of the "grammarians" against them by saying that if قد always has to mean the same thing they would always have to use direct verbs after it whereas, in fact, you can say قد سرت حتى ادخلُها if the entry is regarded in the present, which is confirmed by Arab usage. As always the semantic argument is much more difficult than the formal one.

---

50. Jahn, *Kitāb* §239 and notes.

51. Reckendorf, *Arab. Syntax* 46.

52. *Kitāb* 1, 39-40/50–51.

12) 1, 385/433. Regarding the connection between interrogative and conditional particles, which has been over-generalised by the "grammarians," Sībawayhi says, "As for the opinion of the 'grammarians' that everything which can be used as an interrogative can also be used as a conditional particle, it makes no sense (لا يستقيم) by virtue of the fact that you can use حيثما إن and اذ ما as conditionals, but not as interrogatives." Though it is not our purpose to criticise the validity of Sībawayhi's objections to the "grammarians," it must surely seem from the naïve logical fallacy this argument contains, that Sībawayhi was scarcely an Aristotelian!

[26] 13) 1, 386/434. A verse adduced to illustrate the independent form of an inverted object after اذا ما viz.

اذا ما الخبز تأدمه بلحم　　　فذاك أمانة الله الثريد

receives the well-deserved qualification: "it is said that the grammarians forged it."(b) The expression is in brackets, and presumably was not written by Sībawayhi, but by Jarmī when he attributed all the verses quoted anonymously by Sībawayhi.(b)

14) 2, 18/18. If masculine sound plural or dual nouns were to be used as proper names they would keep their original inflections, but some "grammarians" give them partial inflection by saying هذا رجلانُ by analogy with عثمانُ, in which case, Ḫalīl points out, they would also be obliged to say مسلمينُ, by analogy with سنينُ.

15) 2, 106/107. Concerning the formation of the diminutive of quinquiliterals a purely theoretical observation is attributed to Ḫalīl: "If I were to make diminutives of these nouns without eliding any part of them as some of the 'grammarians' say, I would say سفيرجل as you can see, so that it took the pattern of دُنَيْنير, which is nearer [to the normal usage] even though it is not part of the Arabs' speech."

16) 2, 160/157. A case of over-enthusiastic analogising is attributed to "Yūnus and certain grammarians (Kūfans according to Sīrāfī[53])." They form non-existent energetic imperatives [27] اضربان and اضربنان for the dual and feminine plural respectively. The Arabs do not say this, nor are there any similar examples in their speech.

17) 2, 343/315. In a chapter-heading there is a reference to "what the 'grammarians' call التصريف والفعل." This would seem to mean the process of deriving from the triliteral root all the nominal patterns, though as such it is hardly ever used.(a) I have found it once in Ibn Jinnī, where he says that the تصريف of the word لغة is the form فُعْلة from the verb لغوت.[54] From the occasions when the expression occurs in the *Kitāb*[55] it is not quite clear whether they cover all the nominal derivatives of the verb or merely the verb's powers of full con-

53. Jahn, *Kitāb* 2, 478 adds the parenthetical comment.

54. Ibn Jinnī, *Ḫaṣāʾiṣ* 1, 33.

55. *Kitāb* 2, 421/380, 432/388, 432/389, 474/423 *et passim*.

jugation. Perhaps, if the latter is more likely, the observation that the "grammarians" had a term التصريف والفعل may be nothing more than a later addition to the text.

Significantly, Sībawayhi invariably quotes the "grammarians" in order to refute them. Disregarding the occasion on which they are accused of forging a verse of poetry (example no. 13) the disputed fall into three main types, viz. the group of wrong assumptions alleged to have been made (nos. 6, 7, 11), two cases where Sībawayhi and the "grammarians" seem to align themselves against the opinions of a third, unnamed critic (nos. 5 and 10) and all the rest, which deal, as might be expected, with the exaggerated or mistaken analogies drawn by the [28] "grammarians."

The very existence of methodological disputes points to more than just the "*qawl*" of the named grammarians in the *Kitāb*, which, as we have seen, may mean nothing more than an uncritical observation decked out in technical jargon by a later scholar. These "grammarians," on the other hand, are clearly specialists and capable of going beyond the appeal to authority, into the realm of systematic speculation. Against this, however, we must set the fact that there is no suggestion of any "Kūfan"or "Baṣran" schools—indeed we would not expect to find any in this period. The anonymity of the "grammarians" perfectly reflects the inchoate state of their science, and, incidentally, confirms that the conventional history of grammar at this stage is necessarily based, as it so obviously betrays itself as being, on mere guess-work and legend. It is thus possible to discern in the background of Sībawayhi's speculations a well-informed but unidentifiable body of specialists in refutation of whom, and indeed for the enlightenment of whom the *Kitāb* was written.[56] The "grammarians" are perforce the audience and public at which the *Kitāb* was aimed, and the old Newtonian principle of action and reaction is seen to apply here as well as to the mechanics of the universe: there must have been at least as much grammatical "action" to provide the springboard for Sībawayhi's grammatical "reaction." I find myself agreeing with Fück (though for entirely different reasons), that the *Kitāb* is a reactionary work, but whereas Fück regards as the most noteworthy feature of the *Kitāb* the fact that Sībawayhi relies almost exclusively [29] on Bedouin Arabs and dead poets for his material,[57] I would regard it of fundamental importance that the *Kitāb* would have been literally incomprehensible if it were not the product of a climate of intense technical discussion against which, as I have shown, it was a reaction. This interpretation imposes a certain modification of the usual history of Arabic grammar, for it follows that anything which Sībawayhi does not undertake to refute can be assumed not to have been within his knowledge: I need not enlarge on the effect of this view upon the theory that Arabic grammar owes its origins to Greek logic!

56. Cf. Ḥadīṯī, *Abniyat al-ṣarf* 64.
57. Fück, *Arabīya* 29–30.

So much for explicit references to "grammarians." Of the many occasions when there is obviously a debate in progress between Sībawayhi and unnamed opponents, here follow some characteristic examples:

1) 1, 169/199. In the expression هذا بُسْرًا أطيب منه رَطبًا the direct forms are explained by Sībawayhi as denoting a state (*ḥāl*). Other "people," however, try to connect their direct form with the elision of اذا كان or اذ كان, which Sībawayhi does not accept.

2) 1, 227/266. There is disagreement over nouns which are composed of ابن followed by a word of the pattern أفعل. If this word denotes only a common noun then, according to Sībawayhi, the combined expression ابن أفعل can become defined only by prefixing the article to the second term, whereas there are some who erroneously maintain that all nouns composed of ابن and أفعل are defined. They base their claim on the fact that أفعل is not fully declinable and must therefore always be defined, a claim which is quickly dismissed [30] by Sībawayhi with the example احمرُ قمدٌ and a verse of D̲ū al-Rumma in which أولاد أحقبَ is qualified by the undefined adjective صيام.

3) 1, 341/389. In order to explain the forms لولاي and عساني where the personal suffixes are independent in function and respectively oblique and direct in form some "people" draw a parallel between the real double functions of ه and ك (oblique and direct) and a hypothetical double function in ـي (independent and oblique) and ـني (independent and direct). This is called a "disgraceful way of arguing" (وجه رديء) by Sībawayhi, who goes on to say, in a most interesting statement of his principles, "You have no right to violate a grammatical category when it is uniformly consistent and when you can find a valid alternative argument. There are indeed times when one thing is determined by something remote if nothing else can be found, and this often happens in their speech."

4) 1, 357/403. In *ḥikāya* the words may be left in their original form (Ḥijāzī usage) or restored to their independent form (Tamīmī usage). Thus from the statement رأيت زيدًا the Ḥijāzī would ask من زيدًا while the Tamīmī would ask من زيدٌ. When more than one word is to be repeated it is general in both dialects to restore them to the independent form, but some "people" by applying analogy arrive at such forms as من عمرًا وأخا زيد. This is described by Sībawayhi as "better Arabic" than the type من عمرٌو وأخو زيد suggested by Yūnus.

5) 1, 237/277. قائمًا فيها رجل is just not said, according to Sībawayhi, though he allows it in poetry. If anyone says (إن قال قائل) [31] let it have the status of راكبًا مرّ زيدٌ, the answer is that, although فيها has enough resemblance to a verb for these two sentences to be analogical in form, it has not the *taṣarruf* of a verb[(a)] and so cannot exercise all the functions of a verb, i.e., in this case to allow the *ḥāl* to precede it.

6) 1, 252/293. The كم that is equivalent to رُبَّ prompts the question: what business has this predicative كم assuming the status of a noun without *tanwīn*? Sībawayhi's not very convincing answer is that since كم has two functions it is given the status of the numerals, i.e., it can be followed either by direct or oblique forms just as the numerals are.

7) 1, 383/430. It is not a little disturbing to find in the next argument both the terms سبب and علة in the meaning of "cause." Fortunately they are not used to mean grammati-

cal cause, and they are furthermore used as synonyms, which is scarcely precise enough for philosophy.

The dispute concerns the unusual direct verb in Sūra 2, 282: أنْ تَضِلّ إحْداهُما فَتُذَكِّرَ إحْداهُما الأُخْرَى. If somebody (! انسان) asked why أن تضل is read as though to mean "in order that (one of the two female witnesses) should go astray" when it obviously does not mean that, Sībawayhi would give the following somewhat odd answer: "أن تضل is only mentioned as the cause (سبب) of reminding, as a man says, 'I prepared it that the wall might lean (أن يميل) and I might prop it up.' Here he is [32] not, by the act of preparation, requiring the wall to lean, but he is simply stating the reason (علة) and cause (سبب) of the propping up." The likelihood that the explanation is an interpolation is suggested by the fact that we do not find it in one place where we might expect it, namely in Farrā''s discussion of the same verse.[58]

There are many other such examples, illustrating a kind of permanent opposition from the critics of Sībawayhi's theories. Sometimes the tone of an entire chapter is contentious in the extreme, as for instance chapters 250 and 251, where the phrase ألا ترى occurs with almost rhetorical frequency. And even Ḫalīl is not always accepted by Sībawayhi as infallible, witness the occasion where an opinion of Ḫalīl's is declared to be "bad Arabic, feeble and inadmissible except in cases of necessity," and in another place, "that first explanation of Ḫalīl's is far-fetched and only allowed in poetry or necessity."[59] To these we can add the following as evidence of Sībawayhi's independence from Ḫalīl: the attraction of the type هذا جحرُ ضب خرب is allowed by Ḫalīl only when the number and gender of the two terms are the same, but not when they are different (هذان جحرا ضب خربان) of which Sibawayhi says, "This is what Ḫalīl says, but in my opinion the two expressions are identical."[60] Similarly, when Ḫalīl explains أمس as a contraction of بالأمس, Sībawayhi says that "what Ḫalīl says is not a strong argument, for you can say ذهب أمس بما فيه"[61] in [33] which أمس is the subject of ذهب. Ḫalīl's etymology of لن from لا أن is disallowed by Sībawayhi on the grounds that "if it was as Ḫalīl says, you would not be able to say أما زيدًا فلن اضرب, since ان and its verb constitute a noun in which the verb is a *ṣila*, which would be like saying (wrongly) أما زيدًا فلا الضرب له."[62] On another occasion Ḫalīl's explanation of إن لقيت أفضلهم, namely that افضلهم is dependent upon لقيت and not إن, described by Sībawayhi as "in this respect not good Arabic in speech, because all that is meant is إنه إياك لقيت with the *hā'* left out, although it is permissible in poetry."[63] One final example, in which Sībawayhi actually rejects Ḫalīl's argument in favour of Yūnus's, will suffice to demon-

58. Farrā', *Ma'ānī* 1, 184.
59. *Kitāb* 1, 151/181 and 351/398 respectively, in Mubārak, *Rummānī* 127.
60. Id. 1, 185/217.
61. Id. 1, 254/294.
62. *Kitāb* 1, 361/407.
63. Id. 1, 333/381.

strate the independence of the pupil from the master: when the conjunction أو joins a verb of independent form with one of apocopated form, as in(a)

إن تَرْكبوا فَركوبُ الخيلِ عادتُنا   أو تَنْزِلون فإنّا معشرٌ نُزُلُ

Ḫalīl can only explain it as "association" (اشتراك) of two meanings just as in the verse(b)

بدا لي أنّي لستُ مدرِكَ ما مضى   ولا سابقٍ شيئًا اذا كان جائيا

where لا سابق is oblique in form by analogy with the meaning of a predicate of ليس using بـ. By the same token أو تنزلون is independent because it relates to the equivalent of a question, i.e. أتركبون, which is identical in meaning with إن تركبوا. Yūnus's "easier" explanation is simply that أو تنزلون begins a new [34] sentence, and Ḫalīl's "association" is discounted by Sībawayhi as "farfetched.[64]

This brings us to the problem of Yūnus's role in the *Kitāb*, where he is quoted 201 times.[65] In contrast with his relatively rare disagreements with Ḫalīl, Sībawayhi frequentt ly disagrees with Yūnus. Often the disagreement is merely implied by reporting first the acceptable ideas of Ḫalīl and only then the dissenting opinion of Yūnus, prefaced by "as for Yūnus" (أما يونس) or "Yūnus claimed" (زعم يونس).(a) When more positive rebuttal is necessary, Sībawayhi discusses the weak points of Yūnus's argument in detail, e.g., 1, 303/347, or dismisses Yūnus's claims with such verdicts as "not allowed" (1, 217/255 لا يجوز), "bad Arabic" (1, 233/273 قُبْح), "bad Arabic and feeble grounds" (1, 111/132 ضعيف قبيح), "far-fetched" (1, 232/272, 1, 356/402 بعيد) and even "rarely used and abominably bad Arabic" (1, 164/194 قليل خبيث). If anything, the fact that Sībawayhi can be so critical of a man whose views he is nevertheless prepared to accept when they seem better than Ḫalīl's, is excellent proof of Sībawayhi's fundamental independence from all his mentors. The study of this particular problem by Reuschel tends to obscure Sībawayhi's independence by demonstrating that Ḫalīl was familiar with everything which Sībawayhi discusses. This has the effect of depriving Sībawayhi of any originality whatsoever, which, if this were the case, would leave unanswered the vital questions of why Ḫalīl is never [35] crede ited with any specifically grammatical works and why all the hostility in the historical accounts is directed towards Sībawayhi.

I am afraid that it is impossible to reconcile Reuschel's implications with the physical presence of a work which Ḫalīl could not possibly have written. Sībawayhi self-consciously seeks to overcome objections to his ideas, whether they emanate from his two masters, from unnamed "grammarians," or merely from "people" who disagree with him, so much so that the *Kitāb* depicts, as it were, a running battle between Sībawayhi and his opponents. This is the true state of affairs of which the accounts of his bicker-

64. *Kitāb* 1, 382/429.

65. Reuschel, *Ḫalīl* 10, but v. Troupeau, *Arabica* 8, 310, 311(b).

ings with Kisā'ī and Farrā' are nothing but distorted reflections. Moreover, if we were to take the trouble to extract and classify all the points of diagreement, we would almost certainly arrive at the interesting conclusion that the disputes between Sībawayhi and his opponents are altogether different in subject matter from those between the "Kūfans" and the "Baṣrans," thereby confirming what has recently been claimed, that the two schools of grammar are not primitive, but are merely the product of rivalries at the court of Baghdad[66] with Kisā'ī and Farrā' as the ring-leaders.[67] This helps to account for the fact that Sībawayhi never refers to Kūfans except with regard to their Qur'anic "readings" and never to Yūnus as a protagonist of Kūfan views.[(a)] Yūnus, of course, was long regarded as the founder of the Kūfan school[68] in the sense that his method appeared to contain individual features foreign to the Baṣran approach. But [36] this fact provides only a negative reason for Yūnus's alleged Kūfan bias, and it is more than likely that his name was attached to the Kūfan school by default.

It is even possible to suspect that he was pushed into the Kūfan camp by the mere fact that Sībawayhi appears to disagree with him so often. Certainly the *Kitāb* itself does little to confirm long-held beliefs on this subject: it is nonsense to assert that when Sībawayhi quotes an unnamed Kūfan he means Ru'āsī[(a)], for Sībawayhi never mentions Kūfan "grammarians" as such, and the references to Kūfan "readings" are surely not sufficient to justify Ru'āsī's claim, as one recent scholar seems to believe.[69] Yūnus's connection with the Kūfans may, in fact, be nothing more than the result of a chance remark of his about 'Īsā ibn 'Umar, that "he is not the sort of person to relate what he had not heard".[70] This would immediately make Yūnus a likely candidate for founder membership of a school of grammar noted for its emphasis on سماع. But we should also note that Sībawayhi himself runs the risk of being associated with the Kūfans by declaring, in connection with the problem of the *mamdūd* and the *maqṣūr*, "They say رضا with *kasra* of the *r* just like شبَع and do not pronounce it on the pattern of the words to which it is [most] similar, but they only dare to do this sort of thing on the basis of what they hear (سماع) ... and there are many cases in speech where it is not known whether the word is defective until you find out that the Arabs speak it, and if they do you will then know [37] that the word ends in *y* or *w* preceded by a *fatḥa*."[71] The obvious willingness of Sībawayhi to accept evidence, which, though authentic, is incompatible with theory, seems to be more Kūfan in spirit than Baṣran, if we are to believe Weil's grim portrait of Baṣran hyper-rationalisation.

66. Mubārak, *Rummānī* 28f.
67. Maḫzūmī, *Madrasat al-Kūfa* 65–67 and 74.
68. Anbārī, *Inṣāf*, intro. 71.
69. Ḥadīṯī, *Kitāb Sībawayhi* 40.
70. *Kitāb* 1, 366/412.
71. *Kitāb* 2, 166/162.

The last major matter I propose to deal with in this section, since we are looking in the *Kitāb* for evidence of the earliest state of Arabic grammar, is the way in which Ḫalīl seems to favour grammatical arguments based on phonological rather than syntactical considerations. We shall thus be able to suggest that, to judge from the type of analysis favored by Ḫalīl at least, the first enquiries in Arabic grammar may have been largely phonologically inspired, thereby laying to rest an ancient ghost which evidently haunted Jahn to the extent of frightening away common sense, when he wrote, of the structure of the *Kitāb*:

> The Arab grammarians conclude with phonology (as the most difficult), with which our grammarians begin.[72]

There must be a better reason than that: I would like to think that the arrangement of the *Kitāb* (which was, of course, slavishly followed by every subsequent Arab grammarian), reflects Sībawayhi's priority of interest in syntax and a deliberate change from the mode of thought in which he first developed his ideas.[a] By following some of Ḫalīl's arguments we may gain an impression of the background of Sībawayhi's speculations.

[38] It has already been pointed out that one effect of Reuschel's study of Ḫalīl is to obliterate any difference which might have been discernible between master and pupil, even as far as ignoring instances where Sībawayhi declares his disagreement with Ḫalīl, with one exception.[73] Yet many of the arguments put forward by Ḫalīl are notably phonological in character. I shall list the most interesting of them in order of their occurrence:

1) 1, 185/217. Of the attraction in هذا جحر ضب خرب, Ḫalīl offers two explanations, one of which is that "they have made oblique (جر) follow oblique just as they make *kasra* follow *kasra* in the words بهم , بدارهم etc." Note here, too, the use of جر in a phonological sense.[a]

2) 1, 252/293. Sībawayhi asks Ḫalīl about the expression على كم جذع بيتك مبني, to which he replies, "Most people say جذعا in the direct form, which is the correct analogical form. Those who make it oblique wish to give it the meaning of من, but they elide من here to make it easier for the tongue, and على compensates for من." This kind of elision is then compared with elisions in oaths beginning with الله, shortened from لا والله and the like.

3) 1, 253/294. Ḫalīl explains لاه ابوك and أمس as contractions of لله ابوك and بالأمس with elisions "to make it easier for the tongue," which Ḫalīl qualifies with the general statement that "they often suppress and elide the preposition (جار) in expressions which occur frequently in their speech because they have most need to make easier that which is in most use." [39]

72. Jahn, *Kitāb* §565, n. 1.
73. Reuschel, *Ḫalīl* 24.

[39] 4) 1, 269/310. The word اللهمّ is explained as having a *mīm* at the end to replace the *yā* of the vocative, except that "in this case the *mīm* is part of the word just as *nūn* is in مسلمين."

5) 1, 277/320. Ḫalīl explains the لام الاستغاثة as follows: "This *lām* is a substitute for what is added to the end of the word when *yā* if prefixed, e.g., يا بكراه ، يا عجباه , when you call for help or express surprise. Each one of these (*yā-lām* and *yā-āh*) is equivalent to the other, just as the *ḥā'* of جحاجحة is equivalent to the *yā'* of جحاجيج, or the *alif* of يمان to the *yā'* in يمني. This sort of thing is common in their speech, as I hope you will see."

6) 1, 281/323. On this occasion we find Ḫalīl using an argument which is peculiar to him, though Sībawayhi makes use of his own development of the idea in the *Kitāb*. Ḫalīl regards the second part of *iḍāfa* as equivalent to the "completion" of a single word, hence the *muḍāf ilayhi* can be considered as equivalent to the *tanwīn* on a single word.[a] In this case the criterion is used to distinguish between وا أمير المؤمنيناه, whose form tells us that it is being treated as a single word, and such pairs as وا زيد الظر يف, where as Ḫalīl says, the suffixing of the *-āh* is prevented by the fact that the second word is not part of the vocative expression in the way that the *muḍāf ilayhi* is in the first example.

7) 1, 282/325. The same argument is used to account for يا ضاربًا رجلاً, i.e., that "the *tanwīn* remains because it is the middle of the word and رجلا is the completion of the word." The whole group, which can be paraphrased by an *iḍāfa* (ضاربُ الرجل), is therefore [40] treated as equivalent to a single word just as a true *iḍāfa* is considered syntactically and phonologically to be a single word.

8) 1, 298/341.[a] To form the shortened vocative (ترخيم) of compound nouns Ḫalīl dee clares that the second part of the compound should be left off, it being, in his opinion, "of the same status as the *hā'* of feminine nouns." This also includes the numerals 11–19.

9) 1, 306/350. Using the same principle as set out in no. 6 above, the combination of لا and the *manfī* is treated as a single noun in which the *tanwīn* (e.g., لا خيرًا منه لك) marks the middle of the word. The explanation is expressly connected with the case of the vocative (no. 7 above).

10) 1, 338/386. Two different explanations of the formation of لَعَلّي from لَعَلّني are given. In the first case, لَعَلّي is grouped with similar words of common occurrence, such as ولكنّي,إنّي etc., where their frequency makes the full form of the suffix (e.g., ولكنّني) seem too "heavy," hence the reduction to ولكني etc. In addition, to those who suggest that in any case لَعَلّي contains no *nūn* in the suffix, Ḫalīl replies that the *nūn* has been assimilated to the adjacent *lām* "which is the nearest to *nūn*" phonetically.

11) 1, 343/391. It is bad Arabic to say مررت بك انت وزيد "because the verb is self-sufficient with its agent, but the *muḍāf* is not self-sufficient with the *muḍāf ilayhi* because the latter is in the status of *tanwīn*." That is to say the verb and the pronoun it contains, although they are parts of one word, make a self-sufficient unit [41] comparable to, as Ḫalīl says, the initial term and predicate of a sentence. The parts of an *iḍāfa*, on the other hand, are like the components of a single word (with the *muḍāf ilayhi* as the *tanwīn*) and such a single word cannot make a self-sufficient utterance. Applied to the sentence in question

this means that انت وزيد are both *muḍāf ilayhi* and cannot therefore stand without a *muḍāf*, while in the permissible sentence قمتَ انت وزيدٌ the substitute terms انت وزيدٌ are equivalent to independent parts of the construction. It may be worth noting that Ḫalīl concentrates on self-sufficiency (استغناء), which is a structural feature, and leaves intelligibility (استقامة) out of account.

12) 1, 361/407. This is Ḫalīl's famous etymology of لن from the reduction of لا أن, which he compares with the similar reduction in وَيْلُمِّه. It is clever of Ḫalīl to prove in addition the fact that Arabic does contain compound words, by giving يومئذ and هلاّ as examples. Sībawayhi rejects this with some vigour, but Ḫalīl at least has Reckendorf on his side.

13) 1, 385/433. On the etymology of مَهْمَا Ḫalīl explains that it is the particle ما with the neutralised suffix ما which is also found in اينما, متى ما etc., and that the *hā'* has been inserted "because they think it is bad to repeat the same sound and say ما ما, so they changed the *alif* of the first ما to *hā'*.

14) 1, 423/474. Ḫalīl derives كأنّ from the *kāf* of comparison and the particle إنّ, they then acquiring the status of one word. Ḫalīl shrewdly backs this up with a reference to such compounds as [42] كأيّ رجلاً and كذا وكذا درهمًا, where the accompanying dependent terms are formal proof that the preceding compounds are complete single words. As with عشرون درهمًا, the completion of the first word brings about the dependent form in the second.[(a)]

15) 2, 1/2. The absence of *tanwīn* in the words of أفعل pattern is first explained on the grounds that they resemble verbs, after which Ḫalīl makes it a general principle that *tanwīn* in verbs and verb-like words is "regarded as too heavy."

16) 2, 12/12. By an argument which is inevitably circular (cf. no. 8 above), Ḫalīl treats the suffixed *hā'* of the feminine as having "the status of a noun combined with another, and together they are made into one noun like حضرموت."

17) 2, 39/43. If by any chance the expression ذو مال were to be used as a man's name, the first part of the name would decline fully in its *muḍāf* form (بذي مال etc.) because the second part is a correct *muḍāf ilayhi*, as is proved by the real name ذو يَزَن. The point of Ḫalīl's argument is that if the second term were not a correct *muḍāf ilayhi*, then ذو would have to behave as though it were the end of the word itself. But since the *iḍāfa* is sound, ذو can behave like أبو in *iḍāfa* (and not like أب). Once more the emphasis is on the unity of two words bound together in *iḍāfa*. Perhaps the best way to appreciate the consequences of this argument is to compare ذو مال with فيّ زيد in the somewhat hypothetical meaning of "the 'in' of Zayd," where if في is to retain its meaning of "in" it must be made "heavy" (فيّ) in order to distinguish it from [43] the word في meaning mouth.[74]

18) 2, 62/66. If such pairs as ضاربٌ رجلاً , خيرٌ منك were to be made into names they could not be separated because the second word in each pair has the status of *tanwīn*. This is the same argument as is used in no. 7 above.

74. *Kitāb* 2, 62/66.

19) 2, 84/87. To form what are now known as *nisba* adjectives (but are always called *iḍāfa* by Sībawayhi) from compound nouns, including feminine ncuns ending in suffixed *-hā'*, the second component is rejected and replaced by the *yā'* of the *nisba*.[(a)]

20) 2, 136/134. The diminutives of the compound nouns are formed by altering only the first part, and the second being regarded as having the status of the *muḍāf ilayhi*, i.e., ultimately of *tanwīn*.[(b)]

21) 2, 162/158. When the last radical of a doubled verb has a vowel "the Arabs are unanimous in assimilating the two radicals, for that," according to Ḫalil, "is more suitable because when the radicals are both in the same place they find it heavy to raise their tongues once and then return them to the same place." This is an example of the principle of economy of effort which Sībawayhi frequently applies without attributing it to Ḫalīl, who is certainly the originator of the idea. A good example is Chapter 470 (2, 252/270), which deals with the effect of the six gutturals on the medial vowel of the verb: it is explained in some detail that the gutturals bring the vowel down from *kasra* to *fatḥa* for reasons of economy of effort, and we can [44] be quite sure that this explanation derives from Ḫalīl, because it was Ḫalīl who first classified the consonants in order of place of articulation.[(a)]

22) 2, 433/390. When asked to explain why the forms قوّة and جوّ can be regarded as equivalent to the forms غَزْوَةٌ and غَزْوٌ, but that no verbs of the form يَقْوُو قَوَوْت, can be formed by analogy with such forms as يَغْزُو, غَزَوْت, Ḫalīl answers "That is because in قووت there are two *wāws*, so the speaker would have to raise his tongue once and then raise it again, whereas in قوّة he raises his tongue only once. This is permissible as with سآل and رآس, for where he raises his tongue only once, the sound has the status of cnly a single *hamza*."

These arguments can be put into four categories. On the simplest level Ḫalīl uses the idea of phonetic attraction, e.g., examples n. 1, 32, and the second part of n. 10. For the second category, elision for the sake of ease of pronunciation as in examples nos. 2, 3, and 12 can be grouped with other cases based on economy of effort, i.e., nos. 13, 15, 22 and the first part of n. 10. The third class contains those examples where he favors the principle of phonological equivalence (nos. 4 and 5), which is a kind of analysis below word-level which Sībawayhi does not practice. The fourth type embraces a substantial group of arguments—nos. 6, 7, 8, 9, 11, 14, 16, 17, 18, 19, and 20, in which Ḫalīl develops his own unusual line of enquiry. I think I am right to say that it is the sort of interpretation which would only occur to someone whose inclinations favored phonology rather than syntax, [45] morphophonology rather than grammar, since it is quite obvious that Ḫalīl, in pursuing his investigations, was striving to identify and define what would nowadays be called, perhaps, the morphological word.[(a)] For Ḫalīl, the formal sign of a morphologically complete word was the *tanwīn*, and he seems to have made a simple equation between *tanwīn* and any attachment to a word (by <u>any</u> syntactic device) from which the resultant pair of terms acquire the same limited status as a single word. This extends from the feminine singular to the *iḍāfa* and pseudo-*iḍāfa* combinations, all of which have no more power to stand alone (i.e., make sentences by themselves) than any isolated noun. That may be regarded as a percipient analysis by Ḫalīl: certainly it is one which simplified Sībawayhi's task considerably, and he developed it in his own way in his establishment of the phrase عشرون درهمًا as an important *locus probans* in the *Kitāb*, which I shall discuss in due course.(b)

We are left with a strong impression that Ḫalīl's interest in Arabic was concentrated on the word and its parts, whether as a phonetician and lexicographer, of which the arrangement and composition of *Kitāb al-ʿAyn* provide excellent evidence for his capacity in those fields or as a thing to be isolated from the chain of speech, of which the arguments I have selected above will supply the proof. It is a pity that Reuschel overlooked this most important aspect of Ḫalīl's contribution to the *Kitāb*, for it masks the originality both of Ḫalīl and of Sībawayhi. The failure to notice this quality of Ḫalīl's share in Sībawayhi's work, however, is far from unusual in studies of the [46] *Kitāb*, as we shall see when we turn to examine the present state of criticism of this much misunderstood work. To conclude this chapter, here are a few miscellaneous items of interest.

Despite his apparent reliance on Bedouin informants, Sībawayhi only ever mentions one by name. He is Abū Murhib,[75] and I can find no information at all about him. His name, therefore, adds nothing to our knowledge of Sībawayhi's sources.

Another name without a background is Abū Rabīʿa, who is quoted as a grammatical authority by Abū al-Ḫaṭṭāb.[76] Like Abū Murhib, he is unknown to the biographers and commentators, and for that reason of little help to us.(a) The obscurity of these two may, however, be some indication of their authenticity, though this is vitiated by the self-same obscurity.

It is worth recording, if only for its negative value, that nowhere in the *Kitāb* does Sībawayhi refer to Abū Zayd al-Anṣārī by name. It has already been suggested that this man's claim to be Sībawayhi's anonymous "reliable" informant[77] is false, nothing more than historical opportunism.[78] This is rendered more likely by the fact that Abū Zayd himself does quote Sībawayhi in his *Kitāb al-nawādir*, but he also quotes such grammarians as Aḫfaš the Least, Riyāšī and Aṣmaʿī, all of whom were much later than Sībawayhi. Despite Abū Zayd's longevity it seems probable that he was not active during Sībawayhi's lifetime: by the names he drops he betrays himself as belonging to a later period. It is also hardly to be expected that Sībawayhi should omit his name from the *Kitāb* when he is careful to mention other, less well-known grammarians. [47]

Aṣmaʿī is referred to on two occasions in the *Kitāb*.[79] One would not expect to find him there, as he was so much younger than Sībawayhi. They did meet once, if we are to

75. *Kitāb* 1, 137/165.
76. Id. 135-6/163.
77. Cf. Zubaydī, *Ṭabaqāt* 67 and Sirāfī, *Aḫbār* 49 for two early versions.
78. Krenkow, *EI*[1], art. Sībawaihi(b).
79. *Kitāb* 1, 388/437, 396/446. Not noted by Troupeau, *Arabica* 8, 309-312(b).

believe the biographers,[80] but nothing of any consequence was exchanged in the inteview, nor are Aṣmaʿī's contributions to the *Kitāb* of any importance. On the first occasion he attributes a verse, and on the second he actually recites two lines to the author (أنشدنيهما)[(a)] but in both instances the mention of Aṣmaʿī's name is almost certainly due to the editorial efforts of Jarmī.

One line of verse is attributed to Marwān al-Naḥwī.[81] He is known to the biographers as a descendent of Muhallab ibn Abī Ṣufra and a pupil of Ḫalīl,[82] in which case one might have expected him to make a little more éclat. An attempt to make him a grammarian was evident in the records of his discussions with Yūnus and Aḫfaš,[83] but, as we have seen with Abū al-Aswad and Ru'ba, Sībawayhi takes grammatical data from poets and quotes only the poetry of those who are alleged dubiously to be grammarians. We may conclude, then, that Marwān is a name added somewhat loosely to the *Kitāb*, backed by an apologetic rather than a factual biography.

Another name which tells us little is Ibn Marwān, who apparently attracted the censure of Abū 'Amr ibn al-'Alā' for a solecism.[84] He is presumably a Reader, possibly of Medinese provenance, since the grammar [48] in question is associated a line or two above Ibn Marwān's name with "the people of Medina."

The *Kitāb* makes strange bedfellows of two well-known Islamic figures: ʿAlī is mentioned indirectly in the proverbial expression قضيةٌ ولا أبا حسن,[85] while Musaylima is mentioned by chance in a chapter on diminutives, in the sentences كان مُسَيْلَمَةُ نُبَيْءَ سوء and تَنَبَّأَ مُسَيْلَمَةُ,[86] which are designed to shed light on the diminutive of نَبِيّ but not of مسلمة!

There remains a sizeable body of people whose names are given in the *Kitāb*, with which I may include their collective title, for they are all "Readers." In this connection it is remarkable that no mention is made of Ḥamza, Kisā'ī or Farrā', although Sībawayhi is said to have had frequent altercations with these last two. It is, therefore, difficult to believe the stories in the *majālis* literature, which often centre around exegetical disputes, when no trace of them is found in the *Kitāb*. A case in point is Sūra 54, 49, which according to the grammatical interpretation attributed by Māzinī to Sībawayhi,[87] entailed a simple choice between orthodox and Qadarite theology. On this verse the *Kitāb* itself is silent, and, with the absence of all reference to Farrā' and Kisā'ī, suggests that the rivalry of these grammarians is a historical fabrication, probably an exaggeration of a brush or two in the short time when Sībawayhi was in Baghdad.

---

80. Zubaydī, *Ṭabaqāt* 68, 185, Anbārī, *Nuzha* 122.
81. *Kitāb* 1, 39/50. Not noted by Troupeau, loc. cit.[(c)].
82. Suyūṭī, *Buġya* 2, 284, Baġdādī, *Ḫizāna* 1, 447.
83. Sīrāfī, *Aḫbār* 34, Zajjājī, *Majālis* 76–77, 87, 244, 323 6.
84. *Kitāb* 1, 349/397[(d)].
85. *Kitāb* 1, 310/355[(a)].
86. Id. 2, 128/126.
87. Zajjājī, *Majālis* 294.

To return to the Readers in the *Kitāb*, they are, of course, mentioned collectively as قرّاء and their Readings as قراءة on [49] numerous occasions.[(a)] More specifically there are references to the people of Mecca (2, 321/294, 457/408, 459/410), of Medina (1, 244/283, 381/429, 411/463, 2, 157/154) and of Kūfa (1, 350/397, 383/430, 2. 476/426) but never of Baṣrans, perhaps because there was no need to point out the origins of such Readings. Of named Readers Sībawayhi mentions Ubayy (1, 38/49, 340/481), Aʿraj (1, 264/305, 416/467, 2, 321/294), Abū ʿAmr (1, 204/238, 2, 316/289, 395/358, 467/417), Ibn Masʿūd (1, 220/258, 420/471, 2, 260/244), Mujāhid (1, 371/417) and one "Ḥasan" (1, 73/87, 2, 459/410), possibly Ḥasan al-Baṣrī. In addition there are references to *mufassirūn*, e.g., 1, 250/290, 413/464, 418/469, 2, 22/23 and the term *tafsīr* is occasionally used of Qur'anic exegesis, though its main use is to denote grammatical explanations.

One of the outstanding features of Sībawayhi's treatment of Qur'ān problems is his obvious indifference to the doctrinal implications of textual criticism. The situation described by Pellat still must have obtained when Sībawayhi wrote, i.e., that an official Uthmanic recension was in competition with various private copies.[88] That it was the private copies which Sībawayhi meant by *muṣḥaf* is clear from his reference to "the *muṣḥaf* of Ubayy"[89] and to "one of the *maṣāḥif*" بعض المصاحف.[90] These references clearly prove that there was a disagreement among the *maṣāḥif*, which is a point that has been discussed by Beck. On the basis of four references to *maṣāḥif* in the *Kitāb* he concludes that by "the *muṣḥaf* of Ubayy" and "in one of the *maṣāḥif*" Sībawayhi means [50] an ausserutmanischer Kodex,[91] while the one reference to "*al-muṣḥaf*" means "der utmanische Kodex als Einheit gefasst."[92] This seems a little forced. Certainly Beck was right in pointing out that Sībawayhi knew no non-Baṣran codexes, which suggests to me that in the case of *al-muṣḥaf* Sībawayhi meant only the Baṣran codex *sui generis*, especially as the verse which prompts the allusion is one which raises the problem of the Ḥijāzī/Tamīmī dialect cleavage. For it is still too early, witness the continued textual disputes which Beck himself describes, for *muṣḥaf* to have taken on its later, specialised meaning of Uthmanic recension pure and simple.

In conclusion we may also note that Sībawayhi distinguishes between the *qur'ān*, to which he frequently refers, and the *maṣāḥif*. It would seem that by *qur'ān* he understood the original, revealed text, the word of God, while by *muṣḥaf* he understood those various families of manuscripts in which it was extant. There is no indication that he regarded the Uthmanic codex as any more authoritative than the others, unless it can be the version for which he reserves the name "*qur'ān*." In view of his patently lukewarm attitude

88. Pellat, *Milieu Baṣrien* 73f.

89. *Kitāb* 1, 430/481.

90. Id. 1, 365/411, 376/422.

91. Beck, *Orientalia* (NS) 14, 357[(b)].

92. Id. 360.

to dogmatic and sectarian issues we can assume that this aspect of textual criticism had no interest for him. He uses the Qur'anic text, official or otherwise, only to illustrate or confirm points of purely grammatical import.[a]

We shall now turn to examine the curious and varied prejudices to which the *Kitāb* has fallen victim at the hands of Western critics, often totally obscuring Sībawayhi's intentions.

Summary

[325] Traditional and contemporary accounts of early grammar are unreliable. A work attributed to Ḫalaf al Aḥmar is certainly spurious and the grammatical works listed in the biographies of Sībawayhi's early masters are not to be credited. Sībawayhi was a genuine innovator.

But grammatical sensibility existed long before Sībawayhi: Nābiġa, Ḥuṭay'a and Farazdaq showed a highly developed purism, but they could have nothing more than personal authority on grammatical questions. Sībawayhi's authority, on the other hand, is in the strength of his grammatical arguments.

The *Kitāb* is the only reliable source of evidence for early grammar. There we find no mention of Abū al-Aswad as a grammarian, and only modernised accounts of the views of the so-called early grammarians.

But 17 references are made to "grammarians" and these are examined. They show that there was a body of grammatical opinion, and the *Kitāb* must have been composed for these "grammarians." Evidently Sībawayhi was sure enough of his own views to disagree with others, even with Ḫalīl and frequently with Yūnus.

Ḫalīl's own interest in language was primarily phonological, and 22 examples from the *Kitāb* are given. They suggest that Sībawayhi's interest in grammar led him to extend Ḫalīl's less advanced theories.

A list of the the historical people mentioned in the *Kitāb*, and of the Qur'ān readings and readers, concludes this chapter.

Addenda to Chapter One

Since this thesis appeared a great deal of work on the early history of Arabic grammar has been done. One of the most useful publications (still valuable in our computerised age) is Troupeau 1976: his *Lexique-index* has served to refine a number of references to the location and frequency of names and terms in the *Kitāb*, as will be obvious below. The other enormous contribution to our access to early grammatical terms is Kinberg on Farrā', 1996, see [303] (c), (d).

The appearance of vols. 8 and 9 of Sezgin's *GAS* (1982, 1984) has immensely increased our knowledge of the early period.

Parts of this chapter dealing with the lack of historical precedents for the *Kitāb,* in Arabic and especially in Greek, were used in Carter 1972a; much the same ground is covered by Baalbaki 1995, with additional comparisons with the work of Mubarrad.

The topic of early schools was taken up by Belguedj 1973, and Talmon, particularly 1982, 1984, 1985a, 1985b, 1987a, 1987b, 1990, 1997, 2003, has added a vast amount of detail to our knowledge of the earliest stages of grammar. Versteegh 1990b, 1993, has literally rewritten the history of pre-Sībawayhian grammar, see under the individual issues below. Larcher 2007 re-examines the conventional account of the origins of grammar as related in some detail by the 4th/10th century grammarian al-Zajjājī, and concludes that, while Sībawayhi was describing a fully inflected classical language, the inflections had begun by Zajjājī's time to lose their functions with the emergence of the uninflected neo-Arabic dialects. Zajjājī's narrative, then, reflects an attempt to legitimise the reconstruction of the "classical" form of the language which had existed side by side with the "neo-Arabic" dialects, but these now threatened to replace it.

[1] (a) Zubaydī was chosen as one of the early sources: as time goes by the narrative increases in length but not in comparable authenticity.

[3] (a) Ḫalaf's *Muqaddima* is the topic of Talmon 1990, where he argues confidently, on the basis of its arrangement and contents, that it is indeed one of the most ancient grammatical texts we have. Furthermore, he sees enough biographical evidence to suggest that there was a Ḫalaf al-Aḥmar, who sided with Kisā'ī against Sībawayhi, and who could have been the author of the *Muqaddima.*

[5] (a) A *Kitāb al-Jumal* has been falsely ascribed to Ḫalīl (noted by Sezgin, *GAS* 9, 47), and see Carter 1974 for another work wrongly attributed to Ḫalīl, also Carter 1998a for a portrait of Ḫalīl constructed retrospectively by the biographers, depicting him as a kind of saintly figure.

[6] (a) Troupeau, in both 1961 and 1976, lists 20 occurrences of 'Īsā's name against the 13 stated by Reuschel, but this latter number is also an error, as Reuschel has miscounted his own list, which contains 14 occurrences.

[7] (a) The Suyūṭī source is not named, but Flügel seems to have misunderstood *Buġya* 2, 2 as referring to a book title, where Suyūṭī says that Ibn Abī Isḥāq *šaraḥa l-'ilal.* No such work is mentioned in Sezgin, *GAS* 9, 36f.; it may be compared with the attribution of a book on *qiyās* to Yūnus above, [6].

[10] (a) The issue is of a false coordination in *yu'minūna bi-mā unzila ilayka wa-mā unzila min qablika * wa-l-muqīmīna l-ṣalāti* (* marks the syntactical boundary, see further [205] (a) on internal *waqf*), "they believe in what has been sent down to you * and in what has been sent down before you * and [we praise] those who perform the prayer" misunderstood as "they believe in what has been sent down * and [believe] in those who perform the prayer." This verse attracted Sībawayhi's attention twice in the *Kitāb*, 1, 78/94, (as part of the *tanwīn-naṣb* topic) and 1,212f/248f, where *wa-l-muqīmīna* is explained as a laudatory expression, hence its dependent form. It is certainly an anomaly, and Ayesha could have been right: the less problematical *wa-l-muqīmūna* certainly exists as a variant.

[11] (a) One early "*naḥwī*" who is known only by name is the Persian Biškasṭ (thus transcribed by Fück 1950, 38, n. 5, correcting Brockelmann's Šikast. Talmon 1985a regards him as authentic and therefore evidence of a "Medinan" school (see [17] (a) on "schools"). But we lack precise information about his grammatical ideas.

[14] (a) The number fourteen is an error; see [6] (a) for the correct figure of 20.

[14] (b) The *EI*² art. Ru'ba (W. Heinrichs) does not raise this issue, but gives a possible death date of 145/762.

[15] (a) Troupeau 1976 has seven occasions. However, the two additional cases do not change the picture: in one (2, 281/261) there is an indirect report from Ibn Abī Isḥāq of an unusual ā vowel raising (*imāla*) by a certain tribe, in the other (2, 22/23) he is credited, along with Abū 'Amr (and again indirectly) with the observation that when fully declinable masc. personal names are applied to females they become semi-declinable.

[15] (b) The case names are in quotations marks because their conventional translations are not those favoured by this thesis, see [298].

[16] (a) The poet is Farazdaq, lit. "There is not in the city any dwelling other than a single one, the dwelling of the Caliph, [that is] except for the dwelling of Marwān." The issue is the case of *ġayru* and of *dāru* after *'illā*: all the printed editions have both in independent form, but the dependent form of *dāra* is proposed as an alternative by Mubarrad, *Muqtaḍab* 4, 425. See Fischer/Bräunlich 1945, 279 and Ya'qūb 1992, 970 for references.

[16] (b) For "brought about differences of meaning" it now seems better to say "could be used in different meanings."

[17] (a) For obvious reasons "grammarians" must be in quotation marks here and in the ensuing discussion. See further also [303] (c).

The works of Talmon have now advanced and deepened this field. Among his many articles Talmon 1982 takes a critical view of the sections below on *naḥwiyyūn*, arguing that they were more systematic than they have been portrayed, and indeed may be considered "grammarians" in the full sense; nor were they truly anonymous, as Yūnus and Abū 'Amr are named as *naḥwiyyūn* (1982, 30). In 1984 and 1985a Talmon reviews the evidence of early grammatical activities with a view to showing that they were highly elaborate even before Sībawayhi's time, and he detects the existence of a Medinan school.

In 1985b and 1987b Talmon returns to the question of who was the first grammarian, concluding there were pre-Sībawayhian "schools," at least in Iraq and the Hijaz, determined by the scholar's location rather than his doctrine (à la Schacht), and that the first "grammarian" was indeed 'Abdullāh ibn Abī Isḥāq, as already proposed by Ibrāhīm Muṣṭafā in 1948. Again following Schacht, the Abū al-Aswad claim is dismissed as a later imposition on the tradition, once the Baṣrans had achieved ideological dominance in grammar.

Two monographs add massive amounts of data, paintakingly collected and classified. Talmon 1997 is focussed on Ḫalīl, and so presents a great deal of grammatical information from Ḫalīl's *Kitāb al-'Ayn*, while Talmon 2003 explores an "Old Iraqi School," as he terms it.

No-one has discovered more material about early Arabic grammar than Talmon, some of it used as evidence against the position of this thesis. This is not the place for a refutation of what is essentially a disagreement in the interpretation of the same data. It is better to look for common ground: we both agree that the *Kitāb* is the only comprehensive and reliable source of information about the "grammarians" of Sībawayhi's time and before, supplemented by the *Ma'ānī* of al-Farrā', who died more than two decades after Sībawayhi.

The irony of Talmon's position is that, while he concedes (1985, 142) "the absolute absence of any details in the authentic sources from the 2nd/8th century concerning *awā'il* information," i.e., on the first grammarian(s), he then uses the same data as the Muslim sources to reconstruct his own version of events. It may be worth noting that the Muslims themselves were well aware of their predicament, that their reliance on undocumented transmission meant that the objective truth about the past was inaccessible to them (see Brown 2009 on this issue in the Ḥadīṯ: he points out that the true text of the Gettysburg Address is equally impossible to establish).

One invaluable result of Talmon's researches is the abundant disagreement among the early "grammarians" which he uncovers: while he goes too far in regarding them as "schools" (see further [303]), he does give an account of the reactions of their curious minds to a linguistic situation in which "Classical Arabic" was still being formalised. Many of their arguments are a reflection of the instability and incompatibility of the data, which is still clearly visible in the *Kitāb*. We can be grateful to Talmon for giving us the most thorough survey we are ever likely to have of this primitive stage of pre-scientific linguistic speculation. However, the one reference to "Kūfans" (*Kitāb* 2, 438/393) on the pattern *fay'il* is too isolated (if not an interpolation) to justify a "Kūfan" school.

All the above issues are reviewed by Versteegh 1990b and expanded in 1993, where an entirely new approach is set out, namely that early grammar was heavily dependent on the first exegetes as they struggled with the linguistic problems of the Qur'ān. In the process they developed a fairly advanced technical vocabulary, and, being for the most part Kūfans, inevitably they became the founding fathers of the Kūfan "school" when it finally emerged. While there can be no doubt that Muqātil and his contemporaries had an elaborate specialist vocabulary for linguistic phenomena, the same objections apply here as to Talmon, that it is not possible to prove that a Kūfan "school" existed before the *Kitāb*.

[17] (b) See ch. 4.

[17] (c) This conclusion is strongly supported by Pellat, *Milieu baṣrien* 130, n. 5.

[18] (a) Here and elsewhere "direct" should be read as "dependent," see discussion at [298] (a).

[20] (a) In other words the "Socratic" style attributed here to Sībawayhi is by no means intended to suggest any direct Greek influence, cf. [268] (a) on Bezirgan's 1979 claim that Sībawayhi used syllogistic arguments.

[20] (b) The preference here and in the following pages is now for "indefinite" rather than "undefined," see [250] (a).

[23] (a) An extreme case, *'ajibtu min i'ṭā'ihi hāhu* [sic] "I was amazed at his giving her it," is attributed to Ibn Qutayba in a late and inauthentic-looking manuscript, Carter 1979, 271.

[26] (a) The anonymous passive *yuqālu* of Būlāq is preferred here, as it is not clear who is speaking from Derenbourg's *qāla waḍa'ahu l-naḥwiyyūn*.

[26] (b) This silly verse is quoted again in the *Kitāb*, 2, 147/144, to which we can respond in kind by quoting Howell's pompous translation, "Whenever thou seasonest the bread with meat, then that, (I swear by) God's trust, is the dish called *ṯarīd*." See Fischer/Bräunlich 1945, 56, Ya'qūb 1992, 228 for other locations of this still as yet unattributed line.

[27] (a) The term *taṣrīf* occurs twice more, alone, in 1, 297/341, 409/460 (see Troupeau 1976, s.v.). The original metaphor is "putting [a coin] into circulation."

The same metaphor is seen in the cognate term *taṣarruf* in [31], i.e., "circulating freely" in all syntactic environments.

Another cognate, *ṣarf* "free circulation" denotes the possession of full inflection by nouns, specifically marked by *tanwīn*, hence (a fourth cognate!) such fully inflected nouns are called *munṣarif* "being circulated freely," see [262] (b).

Ṣarf also acquired (but not in the *Kitāb*) the specific sense of "morphology" in contrast to *naḥw* "syntax," see [154].

Our notion of the "currency" of a coin expresses a similar concept.

[31] (a) For *taṣarruf* "circulating freely," see [27] (a).

[31] (b) Lit. "that one of them should mistake, so the other will remind her," with a problematical *an* "that" where *in* "if" would be expected.

[33] (a) The poet is A'šā, see Fischer/Bräunlich 1945, 186, Ya'qūb 1992, 691: "If you ride [to battle], then riding horses is our custom [too], or you dismount, well, we are a people who [also] dismount [to fight]."

[33] (b) The poet is Zuhayr, see Fischer/Bräunlich 1945, 288, Ya'qūb 1992, 1066: "it appeared to me that I shall not catch up with what has already passed, nor outpace anything when it is coming."

[34] (a) One wonders whether *za'ama* is used slightingly here, cf. the Ḥadīṯ *bi'sa maṭiyyatu rajuli za'amū*, and the more prosaic *za'amū kunyatu l-kiḏb*, and similar sentiments in *Tāj al-'arūs* under *za'ama*. [Ibn] al-Anbārī, *Asrār* 157, observes that *za'ama* introduces "a statement of something unsound" *al-qawl 'an ġayr ṣiḥḥa*. See also Iványi 1991, 201–3 on levels of reliability in Sībawayhi's data.

[34] (b) Troupeau 1976, 230 retains his revised figure of 217 times.

[35] (a) In fact there is one reference to Kūfans in a purely morphological context, see [17] (a) at end. For further comments on the "Baṣrans" and "Kūfans" see [303] (c).

[36] (a) Notwithstanding that Farrā', *Ma'ānī* 1, 9, does identify Ru'āsī as *rajul min al-naḥwiyyīn* (unless this is a gloss), but in any case it involves a Qur'ān reading. Baalbaki

1981a argues that a work attributed to Ru'āsī under the title *al-Fayṣal* may in fact have been a version of the *Kitāb* that he was working on, and on which he was consulted by no less than Ḫalīl. This certainly muddies the waters about the pre-history of the *Kitāb*, while going some way to justify the scepticism of Talmon, cf. [17] (a).

[37] (a) This is a very immature judgement, for a number of reasons. First of all, the sequence syntax-morphology-phonology is appropriate for describing the language to native speakers: Western critics start from a pedagogical perspective designed for non-native speakers who must begin with the sounds. Secondly the amount of space Sībawayhi devotes to morphology is about as much as he gives to syntax, and this is hardly good evidence of a prejudice agains morphology. Thirdly a phoneme inventory, unlike a morpheme inventory or set of syntactic structures, is very limited, so that the number of variants and combinations can be covered in a much smaller space. The fact that this thesis gives so little attention to these last two is partly due to a personal preference, partly to the belief that Sībawayhi's originality lay in his perception of the language as following the same principles at all levels. See further [179] (a).

[38] (a) See [164](a).

[39] (a) Sībawayhi seems to be applying this principle in his own way when invoking the complementary distribution of *alif-lām* and *tanwīn* below, see [260] (b).

[40] (a) The topic is discussed at considerably more length in 1, 298-299/342.

[42] (a) Here the term "dependent" for "direct" has inexplicably crept in, see [298] (a). Ḫalīl does not himself quote *'išrūna dirhaman* in his argument, though he would have been aware of the issues, see below [262]–[263]. Note also that variations in the syntax of *kaḏā wa-kaḏā dirhaman* were linked with the Ḥanafī legal school by one late commentator on Ibn al-Mu'ṭī (d. 628/1231), see Carter 2003, 180f.

[43] (a) Thus *ḫamsī* as the *nisba* of *ḫamsata 'ašara*.

[43] (b) Thus *'ubaydu llāhi* as diminutive of *'abdu llāhi*.

[44] (a) Ḫalīl's views on the short vowels should be added here, though they are not prominent in Sībawayhi's own analysis, namely (2, 342/315) that the short vowels *a*, *i*, *u* are augments (*zawā'id*) to the consonants required to enable the consonant to be pronounced (*al-takallum bih*), and that they are derived from *alif*, *yā'* and *wāw* respectively. The former part of this formulation obviously underlies Quṭrub's claim that inflectional vowels are meaningless and serve only a phonological purpose, where he may have over-interpreted Ḫalīl's term *zawā'id*, here denoting "augments," not "redundant elements," see Versteegh 1981 (1983) for a detailed survey of Quṭrub's position and Nasser 1993, 20 for a brief reference to the origins of the short vowels: neither work acknowledges Ḫalīl as the originator of these concepts.

[45] (a) To this extent we can agree with the findings of W. Fischer, 1985, 100, that "al-Ḫalīl's approach to linguistics was morphophonemic."

[45] (b) See Chapter Six. See also [181] on the syntactical units treated as single words by Sībawayhi.

He was certainly aware of the *kalima* as a unit of discourse, without troubling to define it explicitly, though Levin 1986, 426, sees *Kitāb* §508 as a *de facto* definition of *kalima,* since it lists all the possible forms of the consonantal roots from biliteral to quinquiliteral. This is in keeping with Sībawayhi's practice of defining by enumeration, as he does from the very first lines of the *Kitāb*. Levin's exhaustive account of the *kalima* shows above all how sensitive Sībawayhi was (following Ḫalīl) to the status of compound free morphemes, notably with the distinction between the etymological consonants (radicals) and augments, as well as between stems and inflections. We can certainly agree that our term "morpheme" does not map exactly on to Sībawayhi's analysis: elswhere in the *Kitāb* Sībawayhi does provide an empirical definition of the phonological unit (of any size) by observing that all utterances begin with a vocative element (which may be omitted) and end in a pausal form, see below [204]f.

[46] (a) Abū Rabīʿa is mentioned as a lexicographer and linked with Ḫalīl in Sezgin, *GAS* 8, 29, but not listed among the grammarians in *GAS* 9. Whether he is the Rabīʿa al-Baṣrī, a sedentarised Bedouin mentioned in Ibn Nadīm, *Fihrist* 80 (reproduced in Ibn al-Qifṭī, *Inbāh* 2, 9, with one further reference to Ibn Maktūm) remains to be confirmed.

[46] (b) This view is preserved implicitly in *EI*[2], art. Sībawayhi, without discussion.

[47] (a) To put this more clearly, *Kitāb* 1,396/446 reports that Ḫalīl said Aṣmaʿī recited to him two lines of verse by an Asadī poet, on the authority of Abū ʿAmr ibn al-ʿAlāʾ. This elaborate *isnād* has the effect of removing Aṣmaʿī from Sībawayhi's direct acquaintance. It is not insignificant that the older "grammarians" cited in the Kitāb are mostly known indirectly to Sibawayhi, often through Yūnus.

[47] (b) But he is picked up in Troupeau 1976, 228.

[47] (c) The name given here must be corrected to Ibn Marwān al-Naḥwī, listed in Troupeau 1976, 232 as a poet. This creates a new problem, as we end up with two different people with very similar names, (1) Ibn Marwān al-Naḥwī the poet and (2) an Ibn Marwān listed as a grammarian in Troupeau 1976, 227 and connected with Medina.

Both have to be left here with the problem unsolved, as there is not enough biographical information to separate them. No "Ibn Marwān" is listed in Sezgin *GAS* 8 or 9 as a lexicographer or grammarian, and Talmon 1990, 227, can add nothing to the little we know. The remote chance that one of them bears the title *Naḥwī* as a simple tribal *nisba* (cf. Ibn Durayd, *Ištiqāq* 512f) cannot be ruled out, but again we are no wiser.

[48] (a) This might be translated "What, a case [in law] and no ʿAlī to judge it!?" The ensuing discussion identifies "Abū Ḥasan" here with the fourth Caliph. The grammatical anomaly is that his original *kunya* Abū al-Ḥasan has to become formally indefinite in order to be categorically negated by *lā*. The expression is quoted again below, [150], as evidence of Sībawayhi's use of legal material.

[49] (a) See now Troupeau 1976, 227–231 (Grammarians and Readers). The page references following have not been checked against Troupeau's list, and may not be exhaustive.

[50] (a) As stated, Sībawayhi was not interested in the theological consequences of Qur'anic usage or establishing the superiority of one version over another. More significantly, he had no desire to set up the Qur'ān as a model for perfect Arabic: he parades its anomalies with the same impartiality as those of the poets. He reveals his personal position in a remark about the Ḥijāzī dialect as being "good old Arabic." (*Kitāb* 2,474/424), quoted below, see [291] (a), with the implication that it is not the variety favoured in the urban centres of the East. However, he also makes it clear that the language of the Qur'ān is that of the ordinary people: "God's servants were spoken to in their own speech and the Qur'ān came down in their language and according to what they mean" (*Kitāb* 1, 139/167).

For studies of Sībawayhi's use of the Qur'ān see Anṣārī 1972, Baalbaki 1985 and Brockett 1988. This last tabulates all the verses quoted, both in page order and by Sūra, concluding that "it is as though [Sībawayhi] studiously avoided readings with bearing on *fiqh*, *kalām* or *ta'rīkh*, perhaps to preserve as much objectivity as possible." (207, n. 7). In this light it is worth noting that on two occasions readings are attributed to anonymous Bedouin, viz. *al-ḥamdu l-llāhi rabba l-'ālamīn* (for *rabbi*, Sūra 1,2, *Kitāb* 1, 221/248) and *iḏan lā yalbaṯū* (for *yalbaṯūna*, Sūra 17, 56, *Kitāb* 1, 365/411). This is astonishing in itself but seems to pass without comment in Brockett, although it would certainly strengthen our general impression that Sībawayhi was not unduly concerned with questions of personal textual authority, see Carter 2015, 58.

A chapter in a work attributed to Zajjāj, *I'rāb al-Qur'ān* (§87, pp. 45-935), is entitled *Mā jā'a fī l-tanzīl min al-qirā'āt allatī rawāhā Sībawayhi fī Kitābih*. This is not the place to explore it in detail (not least because the attribution to Zajjāj is itself challenged), but the chapter needs further study.

[50] (b) Beck's statements can be translated "an extra-Uthmanic codex" and "the Uthmanic codex considered as a single entity" respectively.

Chapter Two
The State of *Kitāb* Criticism

There seems to be a quite irrational reluctance on the part of Western scholars to accept Arabic grammar as a truly native invention. For Goldziher, in an uncharacteristic generalisation, "*Fiqh* is just as little a product of the Arab mind as grammar (*naḥw*) or dogmatic dialectic (*kalām*),"[1] while one less reluctant to generalise roundly declares:

> Although Arabic philology undoubtedly arose out of the Koran, it has been clearly demonstrated that it was systematised, as it developed in Baṣra under the influence of the eclectic school of Jundishāpur, on a totally different basis, the principle agent of which was the Aristotelian logic.[2]

This "dogma" of Hellenism, as it has aptly been called,[3] constitutes the most severe hindrance of our understanding of the *Kitāb* in particular and probably of Arabic grammar in general, which shows relatively little interest in the Greek sciences even after they had penetrated Islam. It is sufficient to point to the heated argument between Sīrāfī and Abū Bišr,[4] the historical *raison d'être* of which is to symbolise the hostility between grammarians and philosophers, to have evidence that the Arabs themselves did not wish to acknowledge any conscious debt to the Greeks as far as grammar was concerned.[(a)] This dislike of philosophical [52] interference in Arabic grammar resulted in a malicious slander of one grammarian, Rummānī, for his alleged leanings towards philosophy. It is said of him that the grammarians disowned him with the words "His business with grammar is not our business,"[5] but in the same passage he is rejected both by theologians and

1. Goldziher, *Muh. Stud.* 2, 76.
2. Gibb, *Arabic Lit.* 52.
3. Weiss, *ZDMG* 64, 349 .
4. Ed. Margoliouth, *JRAS* 1905, 79ff, also in Tawḥīdī, *Imtā'* 1, 107ff, Yāqūt, *Iršād* 3, 105ff, Tawḥīdī, *Muqābasāt* 68.
5. Tawḥīdī, *Baṣā'ir* 141, cf. also Mubārak, *Rummānī* 42, n. 4.

by logicians. A cursory examination of his main work, the *Šarḥ Kitāb Sībawayhi*, reveals only a very modest attempt to introduce some philosophical order into his speculations, the predominant tone being more of common sense than of logic, and it is clear that Rummānī has been the victim of a plot to blacken his reputation.[(a)]

Consider, too, the *Īḍāḥ* of Zajjājī,[(b)] which is a defence of grammatical argument against philosophical methods: unless we are to assume that the Arabs borrowed philosophical ideas into grammar without knowing, and moreover did not recognise those ideas when their Greek original became known,[(c)] we must believe that Zajjājī's disclaimer is honestly meant when he declares:

> (The logicians) say that a noun is a conventional sound accidentally denoting a meaning and unconnected with time. This is not the terminology nor the conventions of the grammarians, but it is merely the logicians' way of talking, although a number of grammarians have taken it up. It is true according to the conventions and system of the logicians, because their aim is not our aim, and their purport is not our purport"[6]

The refusal of Zajjājī to accept the logicians' definition of a noun, a definition which is not, in any case, found anywhere in the *Kitāb*, strikes [53] at the very root of the argument of a misguided article recently written by J. Fischer.[(a)] There he offers us at one point Aristotle's definition of the noun and then requires us to accept that, because the examples (man, horse) are the same in the *Kitāb*, Sībawayhi must have borrowed the definition of Aristotle.[7] If it is not a coincidence that "man" and "horse" are used both by Aristotle and by Sībawayhi, what else can the fundamental dissimilitude of their defnitions mean but that Sībawayhi either rejected, or, more likely, knew nothing about Aristotle's definition? In an alleged "borrowing" of this kind partial congruence is not enough to prove a connection which may with equal probability be fortuitous.

Part of Fischer's argument is based on the assumption that the Arabic version of Aristotle's *Poetics*, from which he tries to show that the principal concepts of Arabic grammar were borrowed, was a "popular" work.[8] This raises a general issue which it would be as well to dispose of before replying to various points of detail in Fischer's case. Apart from the fact that the earliest extant translation of the *Poetics* in Arabic, that of Abū Bišr (died A.H. 328) is about one hundred and fifty years too late to have any direct bearing on the *Kitāb* (which vitiates almost the whole of Fischer's introductory discussion), it is also extremely pertinent to ask why a borrowing of the kind assumed by Fischer would ever be made by the Arabs in the first place. It seems an obvious way to approach the problem, but one [54] which those blinded by the dogma of Hellenism perhaps cannot understand.

---

6. Zajjājī, *Īḍāḥ* 48.
7. Fischer, *JQR* (NS) 54, 152.
8. Id., *JQR* (NS) 53, 20 and *JQR* (NS) 54, 159.

For them it is unquestionable that all that is best in the culture of the Arabs must have been borrowed from the Greeks. As one who has achieved the difficult feat of reading less of Aristotle than Fischer has read of Sībawayhi (he has read the first and third chapters of the first volume, a total of sixteen lines in the Būlāq edition), I would be the first to dissent from his confident opening salvo:

> It is generally accepted that the tripartite division of speech was adopted by Hebrew grammarians from Arabic and that the Arabs have followed in this formulation the Greek pattern.[9]

The question begged by this challenging assertion is the question I have just posed: why would the Arabs want to borrow their grammatical system from the Greek? Fischer's case does not require merely that similarities of terminology be pointed out, nor that it should be shown that the opportunity existed for the borrowings to occur; as a matter of fact Fischer scarcely achieves even this limited aim by his arguments. What is needed is to prove beyond all reasonable doubt that a motive for such borrowing existed at the same time as the means and the opportunity, which is a side of the question which, as far as I can judge, never even occurred to Fischer at all. For my part, rather than answer the question directly, thereby running the risk of making ethnic generalisations which are both irrelevant and absurd, I would prefer to let the *Kitāb* be its own witness. The chapters below, in which I have tried to characterise Sībawayhi's work in the spirit [55] in which I believe it was composed, should be read as a general demonstration of Sībawayhi's independence from the Greek cast of thought, and of his radically different intentions from those which, if my slight acquaintance with Aristotle does not mislead me, informed the minds of the Greek speculators. "Aristotle," it has been written, "relies greatly on linguistic facts, but his aim is to discover truths about non-linguistic items."[10] This is a succinct statement of an attitude which even the most bigoted Hellenist would find it impossible to discern in the *Kitāb*. What interested Sībawayhi is not the way reality is ordered but simply the way language works, and I hope by elucidating this aspect of the *Kitāb* to demonstrate beyond the power of mere polemic how utterly unconnected the Greek and the Arab motives are.

Having declared my prejudice, I hope now to substantiate it with some evidential details.

The "popularity" of Aristotle's *Poetics* in Arabic during the crucial period of the second century A.H. appears not so plausible when we read in Jāḥiẓ ("cet homme dont l'esprit est attiré par toutes les nouveautés")[11] that although the Greeks were the acknowledged masters in philosophy and logic, they were thought to be undistinguished

9. Fischer, *JQR* (NS) 53, 1.
10. Ackrill, *Categories* 71.
11. Pellat, *Milieu Baṣrien* 68.

in matters of rhetoric and oratory.[12] Brockelmann, of course, can be quoted to support any theory,[13] but I believe he was on safe ground, with his vast knowledge of Arabic literature, when he declared that the [56] *Naqd al-šiʿr* of Qudāma, based as it was on Greek logical methods, made little headway in the Islamic world.[14] This goes to confirm what Jāḥiẓ had to say about Greek rhetoric, and seriously affects the validity of Fischer's claim that the popularity of the *Poetics* is "historically confirmed"[15] during the period which interests us. Another place where we might expect to find evidence of Greek borrowing into Arabic grammar is the *Mafātīḥ al-ʿulūm* of Ḫwārizmī. He scrupulously acknowledges Greek influence where it is discernible, but we note that traditional Arabic grammar is not ascribed to any Greek sources. In fact, as the exception to prove the rule, Ḫwārizmī does include a special section on what he calls the "modes of inflection according to the method of the Greek philosophers,"[16] but it seems to be based on a misapprehension: it deals with the theory that the short vowels 'a,' 'i' and 'u' are really defective semi-vowels (i.e., the consonants *alif*, *yā'* and *wāw*), or, alternatively, that the long vowels are "satiated" (مشبع) forms of the short vowels. This peculiar analysis may owe its origin to the writings of Ibn Jinnī.[(a)] At least Ḫwārizmī's intentions, namely, to preserve a clear distinction between Arab and Greek grammatical methods, are quite plain.[(b)]

An interesting way to assess the effect of Greek logic upon Arabic grammar is to examine a genuine example of such influence. A good specimen is a short work by Fākihī (d. 972/1546) entitled *Ḥudūd al-naḥw*.[(c)] In passing it is worth noting that the *ḥudūd* of Fākihī's title are certainly logical "definitions," as may also be true of the *ḥudūd* works attributed to [57] Farrā', although none survives to confirm it, But *ḥadd* in the *Kitāb* is used exclusively in the sense of "normal way of speaking," and there is no justification for claiming, as Beck did, that it is a philosophical term.[17] With Fākihī we find that logical methods have penetrated into his grammatical analysis so much that *iḍāfa*, for instance, is described as the *isnād* of one noun to another,[18] i.e., a "relation" in the logical sense, using *isnād* as a term of logic and not in its more usual grammatical meaning of what we might loosely call "predication." Elsewhere Fākihī speaks somewhat obscurely of three kinds of verb, the transitive, the intransitive and the "middle" (متوسّط), which is presumably a borrowing from the Greek idea of the Middle Voice.[19] One last example will show how alien Arabic grammar strikes the eye when it is in a Greek disguise: as well as the usual types of sentence, (nominal, verbal, prepositional etc.) which are found in Arabic

12. Jāḥiẓ, *Bayān* 3, 27f.
13. E.g., J. Fischer, op. cit. 1, n. 1.
14. Brockelmann, *GAL*, S 1, 407[(d)].
15. J. Fischer, op. cit. 20.
16. Ḫwārizmī, *Mafātīḥ* 46.
17. Beck, *Orientalia* (NS) 29, 353.
18. Fākihī, *Ḥudūd al-naḥw*, 12.
19. Id. 7.

grammar after Sībawayhi but never in the *Kitāb* itself, Fākihī defines simple sentences as "minor" (صغرى) and complex sentences as "major" (كبرى) sentences.[20] The extent to which *isnād* as a logical term has replaced *isnād* as a grammatical concept, however, is clear from the way Fākihī resorts to the old notion of *binā'* for sentence structure, and does not use *isnād* at all in that context.

All this goes to show that the borrowings that the Arabs did make from Greek sources are conspicuously different from the grammar [58] developed long before such borrowings were made. It is even possible to take the view that the old stand-by, Jundishapur, cannot uncritically be evoked as the source of all early Greek influence on the Arab sciences.[(a)] It was, after all, primarily a medical school, not a universal academy of all the sciences, and it has recently been suggested that its connection with Islamic learning is not to be taken for granted.[21] At all events, it seems that the influence of Jundishapur was chiefly upon Baghdad, which makes it too late to have affected Sībawayhi in quite the simple and direct way that was claimed by Fleisch.[22]

The effect of Greek thought can be monitored in a striking way by following the notion of sentence-types, which is characteristic of the Greek approach. In Syriac grammar a classification of undoubted Greek provenance is offered by Thomas the Deacon (died ca. 600 A. D.):

> Aristotle said wisely that there are five signs of discourse: interrogative, calling, persuading, commanding, breaking off.[23]

These we might compare with Ibn Maḍā''s list of verb-types: denying, asserting, prohibiting, commanding, conditional, depending on a condition, predicative and interrogative,[24] or Ibn Fāris' classification of sentences into giving and seeking information, commanding and forbidding, praying and demanding, proposing and inciting,[(b)] hoping and marvelling.[25] They do not necessarily correspond exactly to any Greek model, but in spirit they are apparently Greek.[(c)] What is important for the history [59] of Arabic grammar is that these categories are not found in the *Kitāb*, which implies either that they were not available to be borrowed, or that they were rejected as being unsuitable for Sībawayhi's purpose. The former seems more likely, partly because Arab interest in semantics is a relatively late development, where, however, it was probably the Hellenistic mentality which spurred the Arabs to such enquiries rather than the Greeks' own system of semantics, i.e., the Aristotelian logic.[(a)]

---

20. Id. 2[(a)].
21. *EI*[2], art. "Gondēshāpūr."
22. Fleisch, *Arabica* 4, 4.
23. Segal, *The Diacritical Point*, 120.
24. Ibn Maḍā,' *Radd*, 156[(d)].
25. Ibn Fāris, *Ṣāḥibī*, 179.

I have so far given general reasons why it is unlikely that any of the earliest Arabic grammar was derived from Greek sources, and have promised to let Sībawayhi speak for himself in due course. As far as I know, the hypothesis of Greek influence has never been tested against the whole of the *Kitāb*, but has been taken for granted on the minimum of evidence—in Fischer's case apparently on the basis of the first and third chapters of the *Kitāb* and no more. I have confessed to having read less Aristotle than Fischer's sixteen lines of Sībawayhi, but I may plead that if my attempts to find a connection between Greek notions and the principles of the *Kitāb* are unsuccessful, it will not be due to my ignorance of Greek, but to the fact that no connections exist. Nothing else matters but that Sībawayhi should be seen to have nothing in common with Greek attitudes: not all the efforts of Fārābī, of Abū Bišr, of Averroes, of Avicenna, of the Hebrew grammarians, and of the numerous unnamed grammarians whom Fischer parades before us in support of his case will alter the fact that Sībawayhi was dead decades and even centuries before any of these figures came upon the scene. [60] Unfortunately, Fischer's thesis, apart from being founded on the feeble claim of *post hoc propter hoc*, is characterised by a resolutely *hysteron proteron* approach, with the result that my most difficult task is not that of refuting his argument, which could be blown over by a puff of common sense, but of keeping my patience.

There is a lesson to be learned from the fact that it is so very difficult to equate Arabic with Greek terms satisfactorily, and from the fact that so many have to be left without Greek equivalents. "Sporadic congruences, be they never so complete, in no way justify the conclusion that borrowing has taken place,"[26] is a warning from more than half a century ago. What is so damaging for Fischer's case is not so much that he did not heed this warning, but that he did not read at all the article in which it was written. Weiss's article is one of the few clear-sighted examinations of the problem of Arabic grammatical origins, and offers by itself a perfectly adequate refutation of many of Fischer's arguments, which I hope to supplement with my own observations.

We could not do better than to start with a fundamental term, that of "grammarian." It is important to remind even the Hellenists that *grammatikós*[(a)] implies quite a different type of learning from that of the *naḥwī*. I find it astonishing that Abū Bišr, of whose ability as a translator Fischer seems entirely confident,[27] was floored by the word *grammatikós* in his Greek text, so that Fischer is [61] obliged to point out that

> Abū Bišr often transcribes Greek words for which he had no Arabic equivalent ... words like *sígunon, auletikès, grammatikós* (غرماطيكوس).[28]

26. Weiss, *ZDMG* 64, 389.
27. Fischer, *JQR* (NS) 54, 133.
28. Ibid. 134 and n. 8. Read غراماطيقوس.

It is difficult to believe that *grammatikós* was untranslatable unless it was not felt by Abū Bišr to correspond to the Arabic *naḥwī*, in which case it hardly seems reasonable to press the claim that the Arabs borrowed Greek grammar. The fact is that *grammatikós* and *naḥwī*, of course, do not correspond. A Greek "grammarian," according to Liddell and Scott, is primarily one who knows his letters and is a good scholar, and secondarily one who occupies himself with literary texts, hence a grammarian. He is, then, the *kātib* of Arab culture, and *dapīr* of the Sassanians, and his interest in language is certainly not that of the *naḥwī*. This latter person is concerned with the way people speak, hence his *nisba* title, but the way, *naḥw*, is expressed in the *Kitāb* by so many synonyms that it would be quite out of the question to suggest that it alone is either a translation or a cultural equivalent of *grammatikós*. The Arabs, on the other hand, seem to have been quite aware that *grammatikè* was to do with writing, witness the translation of *kaì epì tès grammatikès tà stoikheîa prótera tòn sullabòn* into Arabic as وفي الكتابة حروف المعجم متقدمة للهجاء.[29] Where we do find *grammatikè* translated as *naḥw* is in those authors who are known to have been influenced by [62] Greek, e.g., Fārābī[30] and Qudāma,[31] neither of whom were grammarians. Or in such later scholars as Ṯa'lab, who uses the following rather un-Arab mode of expression:[32]

لا يصح الشعر ولا الغريب ولا القرآن الا بالنحو. والنحو ميزان هذا كله وقال تعلّموا النحو فإنه أعلى المراتب

where *naḥw* seems to be used in the meaning of grammar *sui generis*. But not a trace of this attitude is discernible in the *Kitāb*. There *naḥw* is to all intents and purposes identical in meaning with what the Greek word *trópos* implies, as any lexicon will show.

The failure to distinguish between *naḥw* as a purely Arab concept and *grammatikè* as an equally pure Greek concept led Fleisch to admit that he did not know how a word meaning "direction, voie, chemin, également intention" came to denote grammar: "Ceci reste obscur."[33] If he had counted all the thousands of occasions where *naḥw* occurs in the *Kitāb*, often with the meaning of "kind" or "sort," which Fleisch overlooked, he would have seen that Sībawayhi uses it predominantly in the natural metaphor of the "way you speak," even, on one occasion, with reference to the way birds "speak" قال الغراب هذا النحو.[34] The same salutary exercise would have forestalled Troupeau's attempt to render *naḥw* by "la Méthode,"[35] which is far less apt than "manière" or "façon" in this particular

29. Weiss, *ZDMG* 64, 360[(a)].
30. Fārābī, *Iḥṣā' al-'ulūm* 15.
31. Qudāma, *Naqd al-ši'r* 189.
32. Ṯa'lab, *Majālis* 1, 375[(b)].
33. Fleisch, *Arabica* 4, 3.
34. *Kitāb* 2, 49/53, quoting Ḫalīl.
35. Troupeau, *Arabica* 5, 170.

context.[a] We can attribute to the same [63] error among modern Arabs the praiseworthy attempt of Māzin Mubārak to remind his readers that for Sībawayhi the term *naḥw* covered a much wider range of subjects than is subsumed by the term in modern Arabic.[36] We might point out, however, that Mubārak is not correct in including rhetoric (*balāġa*) under *naḥw*: while it is probably true to say that Sībawayhi was conscious that style often dictates grammatical form, it is also to be taken into account that he uses neither rhetorical terminology nor rhetorical criteria in his explanations of grammatical phenomena.

The prejudice, Hellenistic or Arab, which obscures the attempt to understand what *naḥw* means in the *Kitāb* can easily be dispelled by the simple realisation that the *Kitāb* itself constitutes an exhaustive definition of the significance of the term *naḥw*. But I suppose it has always been easier to perpetuate the facile Hellenistic view than to undertake the labour of testing it against the *Kitāb*. The unfortunate result of this mixture of inertia and arrogance is that the native concepts of Arabic grammar have been forced into pigeon-holes which are intrinsically inappropriate, on the strength of mere partial and always coincidental resemblances with Greek.

Nowhere is this plainer than in the question of the tripartite division of speech. It has never been explained why, if the Arabs had up to eight parts to choose from in the Greek, they only chose three. Such a choice would, to my mind, call into play considerably more grammatical finesse than an outright comprehensive borrowing. Fischer [64] has tried to explain this by adjusting the arrangement of the "parts" to suit his argument. In the *Poetics* some eight "parts" are listed, vis. letter, syllable, conjunction, article, noun, verb, case and diction. For Fischer, it is a simple matter to declare that the first two and last three of these are not grammatical "parts" at all, leaving him very conveniently with three for his thesis.[37] What he has not proved, however, is that any Arab grammarian ever went through the same process of selection. Neither do I find in Abū Bišr's translation anything to support the claim that he has "preserved the interpretation inherent in the original text,"[38] nor could I say with the same degree of certainty as Fischer deploys what, if anything, is "inherent" about Abū Bišr's translation. To group the "parts" together as Fischer does is an arbitrary manipulation of the facts. In passing, it is worth comparing Fischer's emphasis on the progressive arrangement of topics from letter to diction, which he regards as important,[39] with the fact that Sībawayhi and every other Arab grammarian reverse this order in their treatment of Arabic. This being so, it is not easy to see how the Greek arrangement could have anything to do with the Arabic unless some Humpty Dumpty principle of contrariety is assumed to operate.

36. Mubārak, *Rummānī* 110, 112.
37. Fischer, *JQR* (NS) 54, 135.
38. Ibid. 135.
39. Ibid. 135.

To return to the "parts" of speech, just as Fischer takes it for granted that the Arabs borrowed them from the Greeks, so he also takes it for granted that Arabic has exactly three parts of speech in any [65] case. I will not dwell here on the likelihood that Fischer's article might never have been written if he had read Weiss's excellent reply to Praetorius, but I will revive, for it has been neglected for too long, Weiss's interesting conjecture that Arabic grammar recognised only <u>two</u> parts of speech.[40] Like Roman law, Arabic grammar admitted no third parties,[41] and so, after the identifiable categories of "noun" and "verb" there was left "alles übrige ohne technische Bezeichnung,"[(a)], i.e., the *ḥarf*. This classification, which Weiss arrived at by noting the numerous non-grammatical meanings of *ḥarf* in the *Kitāb* (e.g., to denote a passage of the Qur'ān, etc.) and in Arabic generally, is amply borne out by the multiplicity of functions covered by the term *ḥarf* in the *Kitāb* when it does refer to grammatical entities. Needless to say, these functions are far wider than mere "joining," which is all Fischer can think about in this case.[42] The word that all the Hellenists would dearly like to see in place of حرف is رباط , but unfortunately even Praetorius had to admit that it never caught on Arabic grammar. This prompted Weiss to make the very pertinent enquiry:

> One might well ask where and when رباطات was at all available. For the ancient Arab philologists must have been very strange people indeed if, instead of adopting the convenient expression which was at hand, they tormented themselves for years with circumstantial paraphrases. (i.e., حرف جاء لمعنى).[43]

[66] The answer lies in the fact that Sībawayhi had no use for a third category in his system, as Weiss has shown. But it presents a formidable obstacle to Fischer's case, and one which his own arguments do little to obviate. For example, he claims that the wide range of the Greek term *súndesmos* is to be "compared" with Sībawayhi's "sweeping statement" (I cannot forbear to interject here that all definitions are necessarily sweeping. This is a gratuitous slur by Fischer) that "the particle is what is not a noun or a verb."[44] Now it is good that Fischer is prepared to take Sībawayhi at his word, but it is bad that he should make no further attempts to find out exactly how Sībawayhi uses *ḥarf* in the *Kitāb*, all the more so because Abū Bišr's translation of *súndesmos* is not حرف but رباط. Nor is it surprising that *ḥarf* should cover a wide range of meanings in the *Kitāb* since it includes everything outside the noun and verb, but can the same truly be said of *súndesmos*? It seems to mean "conjunction," as the Arab translation رباط recognises, and I cannot accept that this function, which in any case is rendered by عطف in the *Kitāb*, is either as wide as, or intrin-

40. Weiss, *ZDMG* 64, 379.
41. Nicholas, *Roman Law* 199.
42. Fischer, *JQR* (NS) 54, 150 and n. 71.
43. Weiss, loc. cit. 379.
44. Fischer, *JQR* (NS) 54, 148.

sically similar to the numerous functions designated by the term *ḥarf*. Likewise *áthron* (which presumably is also a *ḥarf*, though Fischer is silent on that point) is a joining word with a specific function that was clearly not recognised by the Arabs as belonging to any Arabic class of functions, if we are to believe the translators. In truth, the only similarity between *ḥarf* and *súndesmos/áthron* is that they are neither nouns nor verbs, but that does not suffice [67] to make them equivalent. Yet another barrier to the belief that *ḥarf* equals *súndesmos* is the occurrence of the phrase جاء لمعنى after Sībawayhi's definition of *ḥarf*. There is an astonishing claim by Fischer that جاء لمعنى "is apparently a translation of *pephukuìa suntithéstai*,"[45] which I can only assume is wishful thinking. Equally unlikely is Merx's supposition that جاء لمعنى represents the Greek *phônè ásèmos*, thus transforming a "meaningless sound" into a meaningful one.[46] This kind of equationeering is on a level with the medieval etymology which produced such gems as "*gladius dicitur quasi gulam dividens*."[47] Both Merx and Fischer seem compelled to find connections at all costs,[(a)] without pausing to ask themselves whether the attitude underlying the Greek classifications is remotely consonant with the system of analysis developed by Sībawayhi, i.e., a system in which form and function determine membership of two main classes, with a third class for those words which have a specific function but no special form: they are then designated by *ḥarf*, followed by the name of their function, e.g., *ḥarf istifhām*, *ḥarf nidā,'* and so on.

The chief objection to Fischer's attempt to prove that *ism* equals *ónoma* is not that this is unlikely, for it is an obvious but banal possibility which even Weiss admits.[48] In his argument, however, Fischer adduces evidence which fails on the simple detail that none of it applies to the *Kitāb*. Thus it is essential for him to prove that the two terms *ism* and *ónoma* had identical technical use, but this [68] is scarcely substantiated by Fischer's observation that Arabic grammar developed such noun types as حقيقي (proper noun), بسيط (simple noun) and مضاعف ("double noun," whatever that may be)[49] for the earliest Arab grammarian, Sībawayhi, does not use these terms at all. To be sure he does make a distinction between defined and undefined nouns,[(a)] but his word for "defined" is معرفة, not معروف as Fischer has it, and as for نسبة as "*nomen relativum*," it is called إضافة throughout the *Kitāb*, the only approach to the later term being a solitary occurrence of the phrase النسب في الاضافة which only proves my point.[50] Only نكرة is left from what Fischer blithely calls a "pleiad" of terms related to *ism* and *onoma* which he regards as "identical."[51] It is a pretty

45. Fischer, *JQR* (NS) 54, 150.
46. Merx, *Hist. Art. Gram.* 143 and cf. Fischer, loc. cit. 149 n. 7 and Praetorius, *Gött. gel. Anz.* 9, 706.
47. Thurot, *Notices et extraits* 147[(b)].
48. Weiss, *ZDMG* 64, 380, 381.
49. Fischer, *JQR* (NS) 54, 153.
50. *Kitāb* 2, 85/88[(b)].
51. Fischer, loc. cit. 153.

poor pleiad, short of its customary complement by one star even before the glimmer of the remaining six is dimmed by the elementary observation that as evidence for Greek borrowing they are entirely irrelevant to the earliest Arabic grammar. Against what is left of the similarities claimed by Fischer we must set his own admission that "it is true that these are exceptions compared with other grammatical terms which show no relation whatsoever to Greek terminology."[52] It is indicative of his curious approach that he tries to turn even this piece of contrary evidence into an argument *e silentio*, which I will pass over in the same.

Merx was perceptive enough to recognise that no amount of critical subtlety could make *fiʿl* into *rhèma*, an act of wisdom which Fischer [69] reports but fails to learn from.[53] In grammar the verb, both as an entity and as a concept, is always called *fiʿl*, a word which is semantically quite unconnected with *rhèma* as is evident from the fact that *rhèma* is invariably translated into Arabic as كلمة. This is no deterrent to Fischer, who argues *hysteron proteron* that Avicenna uses كلمة and فعل for *rhèma*, that Saadia uses both *kalima* and *afʿāl*, as does Ḥayyūj, and that Ibn Ezra used *millā*.[54] Interesting though all this is, it is difficult to see what it has to do with the *Kitāb*. As for the Syriac evidence, which to have been chosen to imply that *rhèma* could be translated at will into كلمة or فعل, the fact that Sībawayhi only ever speaks of *fiʿl* goes to show that his choice of term was probably not made under Syriac influence, unless we are to assume that he deliberately selected the less accurate rendering.[(a)] To do that he must have had sound reasons for rejecting the term which every European nation, imitating the Romans, has forced into its language in the guise of "verb," and Sībawayhi's choice then appears as a superbly defiant gesture of independence, rather than, as Fischer would clearly like to prove, an unimaginative and servile borrowing. Fischer's own imagination can be seen at work in what he calls his "hypothesis" that the term *fiʿl* is related to كلمة and *rhèma* by the same antithesis which exists between the "word" (*lógos/poíesis*) and the "deed" (*érgon/pràxis*).[55] He does not, mercifully, try to connect this with the *Kitāb*; if he had looked there he would have found that the antithesis in Arabic is between كلام and عمل.[(b)]

[70] It is plain that Fischer has fallen into the error he himself describes when alluding to the "strange results achieved when preconceived grammatical formulations are imposed on another language."[56] Although by far the clumsiest, however, he is not alone in his adherence to the dogma of Hellenism, nor is he the only inheritor of the Merxist dialectic, as we shall see.

52. Ibid.

53. Merx, *Hist. Art. Gram.* 148, in J. Fischer, op. cit. 155.

54. Fischer, op. cit. 156.

55. Id. 156–157.

56. Fischer, *JQR* (NS) 54 154, n. 89.

All those numerous scholars who suppose that *isnād* is the main designation of nominal sentence structure and that it is a Greek notion, are wrong on both counts as far as the *Kitāb* is concerned.[(a)] Sībawayhi uses the idea of *isnād* on only four occasions, each time as a paraphrase of his principal structural concept of *binā'*. The notion that *isnād* is a Greek idea overlooks the fact that Arabic sentences are not analysed into "logical" subjects and predicates but into structural and functional subjects and predicates. There has been some pretty confused thinking in this connection: Reuschel declares that "language is applied logic; every sentence contains a judgement (Urteil) and therefore contains a subject and a predicate."[57] This is ludicrous; it is barely applicable to the Arabic nominal sentence, but what kind of "Urteil" does the verbal sentence contain? And what are we to make of Fischer's argument? He frankly admits that the Arabs used a different term for logical subject, *mawḍū'*, and quotes Maimonides to prove it.[58] Nevertheless he then tries to convince the reader that *fā'il* stands for the "subject" of a verbal sentence, when it is abundantly clear that it really stands for the "agent" of the verb, [71] and was never intended to suggest that the verb ever stood in any predicative relation to it as a subject, no matter how the meaning of verbal sentences may lend itself to this interpretation.[(a)] Both Fischer and Reuschel have noticed, indeed, who can fail to notice, that every Arabic sentence falls neatly into two parts, but it is not much to their credit that they immediately jumped to the conclusion that the two parts must correspond to the two parts of a Greek logical proposition. Their views on the Arabic sentence are pursued, I think it is fair to say, in defiance of the facts. It is certainly difficult to account for the presence of the term *mawḍū'*, which is at least a recognisable translation of *hupokeímenon*, if at least two other terms for "logical subject" were already available, as Fischer seems to imply. Against this is the fact that *isnād* belongs by meaning to the same domain as *binā'* and is similar to various other grammatical terms in this respect, e.g., *naṣb*, *imāla*, *i'timād*, etc., which I shall discuss in due course.

A comprehensively Hellenistic interpretation of Arabic grammar is tersely given by Beck in his review of Reuschel, which, if it could be substantiated, would revolutionise the study of the subject. For him the terms *ḥadd*, *ma'nā*, *awwal*, *fā'il*, *fi'l*, *na't* "and others," are all identical in meaning with the terms as used in the translation of the *De Anima*.[59] It is, of course, heretical to suggest that chance congruences of this sort might well be due to borrowing by the translators of terms which had already been coined by the grammarians![(b)] [72] It is surprising that Beck, who is one of the few people to have made any extensive study of the *Kitāb* in recent years, should not have been struck by the totally non-philosophical import of the terms he lists; *awwal*, for example, is never used in the meaning of "Prinzip" given to it by Beck, *ḥadd* never as "definition," *fā'il*, *fi'l* never

57. Reuschel, *Ḫalīl* 15.
58. Fischer, loc. cit. 154.
59. Beck, *Orientalia* (NS) 29, 353.

in any abstract sense, and so on. Once again it seems as if the hypothesis has been uttered without any test of validity.

From what I have said about the absence of sentence categories in the *Kitāb*[60] it follows that, for example, the list given by Trumpp[61] and other such lists found in all European grammars cannot shed any light on the earliest stage of Arabic grammar, though they undoubtedly reflect the proclivities of the later grammarians. Even here, however, it is possible that the Arabs derived only the taste for abstraction from the Greeks, and not any specific logical categories: one thinks immediately of the absence in Arabic of a concept of grammatical passivity. In the *Kitāb* even the elementary categories of, the general and the particular are used in a manner which could never be described as rigorous, suggesting that they did not mean a great deal to Sībawayhi.

In Massignon we can observe the partial triumph of an erroneous academic prejudice over a very sound instinct which rightly seized upon the binary structure of the Arabic sentence:[(a)]

> Avant d'adopter la division tripartite grecque des parties du discours (*ism*, *fi'l*, *ḥarf*), elle avait imaginé une division [73] bipartite, conformeé a sa dialectique sémitique (*aṣl*, *far'*; *'umda*, *faḍla*; *mubtada'*, *ḫabar*).[62]

The same critic also hovered between error and right intuition when he wrote:

> Le premier vocabulaire technique (grammaire) en arabe fut un vocabulaire de noms d'instruments.[63]

It is scarcely conceivable that the law should fail to develop a technical vocabulary before what is, after all, a very servile science, but it is perceptive of Massignon to have grasped the functional nature of Arabic grammar and not to be distracted by the false scent of semantic categories.

Kramers, on the other hand, allows his opinions to be formed entirely by Merx and Praetorius, and the following two quotations will show that his understanding of Arabic grammar was superficial, verging on the flippant:[(a)]

> Half a century ago, however, Merx has clearly demonstrated that the (tripartite) division, which fits the Semitic languages rather well, must have come about through foreign influence ... in the course of time (grammar) owed much to a better acquaintance with the grammatical concepts taught by the Greeks.[64]

60. See above p. [57].
61. Trumpp, *Sitzungsber. d. bayr. Ak.* 1879, 310.
62. Massignon, *Arabica* 1, 6.
63. Id. *REI* 8, 509.
64. Kramers, *Analecta* 2, 155 and 93.

Whether the tripartite division "fits" the Semitic languages is immaterial, even if ascertainable, and as for the second of Kramers' views, I share the opinion of Weiss, that any effect of Greek on Arabic grammar was never on more than a very modest scale.[65]

[74] Merx and Fischer between them are also responsible for a series of equations between Greek and Arabic terms which I have not thought fit to criticise in detail. Most of them fail on the cardinal objection that the Arabic terms are not literal enough to justify the claim of translation, and at the same time are too disparate in underlying meaning to be accepted as cultural borrowings from the alleged originals. Thus *hellènizein* and أعرب, *sèmantikon* and مفيد, *kinèsis* and حركة are close in meaning but refer to entirely different processes in their respective grammars, while such words as *phôné, lógos, léxis,* and لفظ قول , كلام are inevitable parallels in view of the nature of the subject, and probably could not be recognised as translations even if they were. With such terms as *héxeis/diáthesis* and حال, *stoicheîon/árthron* and حرف it is quite clear that no lexical similarity exists, neither are the words used with the same connotations in their respective tongues.[(a)] If the supposed similarities were genuine, it is surely a matter for concern that the word *kanôn* is prominently absent from the grammatical vocabulary until well after the *Kitāb* was written. We find it in grammatical contexts in Fārābī,[66] as well as Ibn Jinnī,[67] Ibn Ya'īš[68] and Ibn al-Anbārī,[69] where it clearly represents a trivial influence from Greek sources. But of قانون in the *Kitāb* there is not a trace. We would not, of course, expect to find it in a time when the subject of grammar had not yet reached the level of abstraction implied by the term قانون.

[75] In general the assumption of Greek influence is a superficial one, though it can yield bizarre names, or Fisher's excursion into the problem of *rhéma* and *fi'l*. The sanest verdict I have so far found in recent times is that of Afnan, who, having examined the philosophical terminology of the Arabs, concluded that

> there is not enough evidence to suppose that Arabic grammar is actually based on Greek logic, as some have claimed. In fact Aristotelian logic cannot be fully applied to other languages besides Greek.[70]

Modern Arab criticism is, on the whole, disinclined to allow that the Arabs borrowed their grammar from the Greeks. A discussion of this, and a refutation of a recent attempt by an Arab to prove Greek influence, is set out in the work of Maḫzūmī on Ḫalīl, especially pp.74–62. It is remarkable for the fact that, unlike some critical works recently

65. Weiss, *ZDMG* 64, 357.
66. Fārābī, *Iḥṣā' al-'ulūm* 15.
67. Ibn Jinnī, *Ḫaṣā'iṣ* 3, 273.
68. Ibn Ya'īš, *Šarḥ al-Mufaṣṣal* 1, 17.
69. Anbārī, *Inṣāf* 211.
70. Afnan, *Philosophical Terminology* 37.

published in the Middle Fast, the author does not stop within the bounds of the classical biographies. Maḫzūmī's strongest point is his observation that logical *qiyās* and grammatical *qiyās* are two entirely different processes,[71] and he comes tantalisingly close to the views presented in this thesis when he speaks of the "juridical analogy" (قياس فقهي) applied by Ḫalīl.[72] To Maḫzūmī's credit he does not fall into the error made by Fauré, who described the grammar of the Baṣrans as representing

[76] l'esprit rationaliste par son goût pour la systématisation et la méthode de déduction syllogistique (*qiyās*) appliquée à la philologie.[73]

In a surprising lapse Pellat compounds the error by adding his own commentary that the tendency described by Fauré is embodied in the *Kitāb* and Ḫalīl's *Kitāb al-'Ayn*. This claim will scarcely survive being tested against the *Kitāb*. As for the "logic" of Sībawayhi and Ḫalīl it may well be that Fauré and others like him have been beguiled by the manifestly systematic nature of their works into the false belief that "system" is the same as "Aristotelian logic."[74] This is a pitfall which all, noticing how systematic these two earliest monuments of Arab philology are, find difficult to avoid unless they are fortunate enough to approach them without the dubious benefit of a Hellenistic background! Just how pervasive this Greek influence on the critics can be is seen in Arnaldez' profound and revealing study of Ibn Ḥazm. It is a minor detail, but nonetheless misleading, to accuse the Arab grammarians as a whole of "introducing into their description and classification of the morphemes of Arabic foreign categories which they adapted more or less happily to the demands of their undertaking."[75] Without wishing to labour the point, I would say that one of the most striking features of the *Kitāb* is the patent absence of "foreign categories," so much so that a great deal of ingenious but complicated periphrasis has to be devised to express [77] what would go (and later often did) very neatly into some "foreign category" of the type meant by Arnaldez. The problem of the *Kitāb*, if I may distort Oscar Wilde, is whether the critics are really blinded by the Greeks, or only pretending to be. There is no doubt that Fischer is not pretending: he devotes a special section to a discussion of *ptôsis* without once attempting to relate it to Arabic grammar,[76] and on another occasion he adduces the phonetic topic of "formulations designating the consonant as the 'substance' and the vowel as the 'accidens' in plain terms of Aristotelian logic"[77] in spite of the uncomfortable fact that nowhere in the *Kitāb* does Sībawayhi

71. Maḫzūmī, *Ḫalīl* 63 and 224.
72. Id. 72.
73. Fauré, in Pellat, *Milieu Baṣrien* 124.
74. Id. 133.
75. Arnaldez, *Ibn Ḥazm* 14.
76. Fischer, *JQR* (NS) 54, 158.
77. Id. 146.

discuss phonetics in these terms. But Fischer's case is neither true to the Greek ideal of lucidity, nor founded on any great knowledge of Arabic; it might be unfair to say that the following passage is typical, but at least we can say that it is characteristic: having discussed *léxis/lógos* and قول/كلام, mostly in post-Sībawayhian terms, he then declares bluntly and with a bold *non sequitur*:

> It is in this form that the concepts of 'language' and 'speech' passed into Arabic terminology, and Sībawayhi opens the *Kitāb* with فالكلام اسم وفعل وحرف, which became in later grammars a traditional way of introducing the three parts of speech.[78]

The punctuation precludes the possibility that the two ideas in the [78] above sentence are unrelated, and I can only assume that Fischer has committed the gross error of mistaking كَلِم for كَلام. As an example of scholarly reasoning Fischer's article is quintessentially medieval, that is to say, he displays no sense of time or physical possibility of the exchange of ideas; instead the evidence is merely culled from one book or another to fit the theory, rather in the way that Virgil was interpreted as prefiguring the coming of Christ.

It is almost with relief that one turns to another source of inspiration which critics have tried to thrust upon Arab grammarians, namely Latin. Setting aside the fact that limited borrowing of the kind advocated would imply either considerable sophistication or crass ignorance on the part of the borrowers, objections can also be sustained on the by now tedious, grounds that the "borrowed" words do not accord with the use of the corresponding term in the *Kitāb*. The classic case is *regere* and *regens*,[(a)] which were put forward as the origin of the idea of the *ʿāmil* by Praetorius,[79] and amply confuted by Weiss, together with another of Praetorius's suggestions, that *ḥarf* corresponds to *terminus*.[80] Although *jins* had already been equated with Greek *génos*,[81] it was Kramers who somewhat optimistically suggested that the Arabs borrowed both "the notion of gender, and also the word for it, from Latin."[82] This assumption appears somewhat trite when we observe that Sībawayhi, although he uses the term *jins* to mean, roughly, species, never uses it to denote gender. The proposal to derive *bināʾ* [79] from *aedificare*[83] is sound enough on lexical and technical grounds, but to be fully credible Praetorius ought to account for the presence in the *Kitāb* of synonyms such as *isnād* and *iʿtimād*, as well as other grammatical terms such as *naṣb*, *imāla*, *iḍāfa* etc., all of which share the curious common property that their literal meanings are closely related. Thus the metaphor in *aedificare* is unique in

78. Id. 140.
79. Praetorius, *ZDMG* 63, 495–505.
80. Weiss, *ZDMG* 64, 349–390.
81. Merx, *Hist. Art. Gram.* 145 and 151.
82. Kramers, *Analecta* 2, 166 [(b)].
83. Praetorius, *Gött. gel. Anz.* 9, 705.

Latin, while in Arabic it has been extended, obviously not under Latin influence, to cover a wide range of grammatical situations. It remains an interesting coincidence. Latin is not a source one would expect the Arabs to make use of, and the few congruences which have been posited are insufficient as evidence for any borrowing.

Now it is time to examine the views of those critics who, while granting that Arabic grammar owed nothing to the Greeks, were moved to pass judgement on the crudeness and inadequacy of the poor structure erected by the Arabs' own efforts.[(a)] The presumptuousness of the Hellenists is now about to be exchanged for the arrogance of the Occidentals. I can think of no finer example of what can only be described as academic racialism, than the following superbly confident nonsense which forms part of Dieterici's introduction to his edition of Ibn 'Aqīl's commentary on the *Alfiyya*. It must be quoted *in extenso* for the full flavour to be appreciated:

> Lassen has called attention, in his *Indian Archaeology*, to the fact that the calm objectivity of the Indo-Germanic mind contrasts with the easily excitable subjectivity of the Semites. [80] Nowhere does this difference show itself more clearly than in language; the short, disconnected sentence of the Semites, put together without any fully developed phrase structure, is far outstripped by the well-constructed Indo-Germanic sentence, the product of pure cogitation (*Denktätigkeit*). If even the native Indian and Greek grammarians never succeeded in establishing a system with a language organised with such pure cogitation, how are we to expect it from the original grammarians of the Semitic languages?[84]

The future editor of Fārābī is only a ridiculous extremist among many who were unable to admire the grammatical accomplishments of the Arabs.[(a)] Ewald, although he is at least categorical that Arabic grammar was not externally influenced, and that "Greek influence among the Arabs has only been suspected out of ignorance,"[85] comes to the curious conclusion that not only the Arabs, but also the Chinese and Indian grammarians failed to learn the "true laws and inner causes" of their languages because their enquiries were inadequate and deficient.[86] Even if Ewald had been competent in all the languages necessary to arrive at such a judgement, it would still not have been possible for him to assess the efficiency and achievement of the grammarians without first taking account of their own motives. This brings him into a more specialised error when he says of the *Kitāb* that, while it certainly contains definite and settled technical terms it "has not yet any fixed system and no conclusive explanations."[87] Even if this opinion was based on more than [81] just the fragment Ewald was reviewing from de Sacy's *Anthologie grammaticale*,

84. Dieterici, *Ibn 'Aqīl* xxii.
85. Ewald, *Gött. gel. Anz.* 1830, 801.
86. Id. 802.
87. Id. 806.

it would never stand up to a close examination of the *Kitāb* in its entirety. Probably such verdicts reflect the critic's personal taste, rather than an attempt to arrive at the absolute truth, witness the opinion of Flügel concerning the *Kitāb*:

> Other writings, such as the *Alfiyya* with Ibn 'Aqīl's commentary, proceed with far more prudence and exactitude in the treatement of grammatical material than happens in the *Book* of Sībawayhi.[88]

Here we may record the evident disappointment of Besthorn that the *Kitāb* did not yield what he was looking for; he describes Sībawayhi's definitions of the parts of speech as "very unclear and very vague,"[89] which is another way of saying that they did not match up to the stern requirements of Aristotle, and somehow implying that they should have done.

Perhaps one of the most repugnant expressions of this Occidental hauteur, because it is so recent, is the question posed by Beck: "What is for us still important and worth investigating in Sībawayhi's *Kitāb*?" One thing which interests Beck is precisely the problem where the *Kitāb* could be of no help, i.e., as evidence for the Greek influence which Beck wrongly supposes he can discern in the *Kitāb*. "The other side of the *Kitāb* which still interests us is not the explanations of linguistic phenomena, which are clever in themselves but mostly gained in the airless space of unobjective abstraction, but only the material, [82] the pattern sentences…."[90] Beck's opinion and the burden of my thesis are in direct contradiction. I do not share his view that the value of Sībawayhi's grammatical explanations is inversely proportional to their ingenuity,[91] I believe that such an opinion betrays a total failure to understand Sībawayhi's purpose. It also follows, if I am right, that a true understanding of the motives of the *Kitāb* will dispel forever the myth that it is based, as Beck assumes, on Greek sources.

From another quarter comes the surprising condemnation that Ḫalīl and Sībawayhi "worked without rising above the subject, staying at the level of the facts, a labour which must needs remain superficial,[92] in other words, the *Kitāb* is too descriptive. But, I need not stress, no comprehensive grammar can be too descriptive, and Fleisch's criticism is too loosely thought out to be effective. He might correctly have claimed that the *Kitāb* does not go as far in its speculations as the works of later grammarians, but that is not a fault, merely a difference. Fleisch's attitude is complicated by the fact that he regards the *Kitāb* as a normative work,[93] an aspect of Arabic grammar which, I would have thought,

88. Flügel, *Gram. Schulen* 43.
89. Besthorn, *Festskr. til V. Thomsen* 170.
90. Beck, *Orientalia* (NS) 29, 353 (my emphasis).
91. Ibid.
92. Fleisch, *Arabica* 4, 5.
93. Id., *Oriens* 16, 134 and *passim*.

became increasingly obvious in every grammarian after Sībawayhi! I hope to show that the *Kitāb* is far from superficial, and far from normative except within the limits [83] explicitly laid down by Sībawayhi. In the meantime, I would suggest that no grammar can be simultaneously normative and too descriptive, which seems to be Fleisch's standpoint.

A similar condescension moved Trumpp to remark that, while the Arabs certainly understood how sentences were constructed, they lacked an overall concept of the sentence.[94] Clearly Trumpp is only reacting to a difference in the way Arabs and Europeans view the same subject. As a matter of fact his work takes no account of what Sībawayhi understood by *kalām* in the absence of the word *jumla* in the meaning of sentence in the *Kitāb*. The definition of a sentence is something which still gives trouble (nor does Trumpp allude to this problem), and it is obvious that Sībawayhi unconsciously avoided it by treating speech (*kalām*) as a chain of indeterminate length, its beginning and end marked by structural and semantic features to which he gives a great deal of attention. It is, therefore, misleading to treat this difference of approach as a failing, not only because it is patronising, but also because it usually stops people from looking any further into the problem.

We constantly encounter cases where an item of Arabic grammar is censured not on the grounds that it is inconsistent with its own system, but because it does not fit into some Western scheme. Fleischer has this to say about the alternation of apposition and *iḍāfa* in the type خاتم فضة: "apposition is more rational (!) than genitival [84] attraction, the latter, however, more frequent."[95] In another occasion he stigmatises the use of أنْ and the independent verb after cognitive verbs as "unlogisch,"[96] which is tantamount to saying that it does not accord with his own ideas on how Arabic should behave. Rabin, to give a more recent example, decides that Sībawayhi's explanation of certain phenomena connected with أنّا is "far from clear and operates with logical categories which seem to have little bearing on the syntactical distinctions."[97] I hope to be able to set this particular problem in its proper context in due course;[98] at the moment it is enough to suggest that the fault may not always lie with Sībawayhi, but with those who measure him against standards that he knew nothing of. An amusing illustration of this attitude is the way Brockelmann held that a disputed work by Kisā'ī could be regarded as genuine because of the "lack of any systematic subdivision."[99] A rigorous application of such a criterion

94. Trumpp, *Sitzungsber. d. bayr, Ak.*, 1879, 309.
95. Fleischer, *Kl. Schr.* 2, 33.
96. Id., *Kl. Schr.* 1, 530$^{(b)}$.
97. Rabin, *Anc. West Arabian* 183.
98. See below p. [306].
99. Brockelmann, *ZA* 13, 29.

would immediately invalidate the *Kitāb*, which is far too well-ordered to pass Brockelmann's test of authenticity.[(a)]

It is an easy transition from those who did not wish to give the Arabs credit for their own grammar, to those who thought they could put the Arabs right where they went wrong. Jahn's translation is a sustained exercise in just this technique, and we may as well discuss here the usefulness of his undertaking. Though it was apparently [85] received with some indifference by the public, Jahn's translation remains an indispensable guide to Sībawayhi's often labyrinthine style. By the idiosyncrasies of his method, however, Jahn has unwittingly ensured that his advice to read both the Arabic and the German together will always have to be followed. For it is not so much a translation as a re-interpretation of Sībawayhi through the medium of Sīrāfī. Jahn came to the *Kitāb* in the conviction that it was "grossenteils unverständlich"[100] and that the only way to make sense of it was by using Sīrāfī's commentary.[101] In this curiously anti-historical approach he was only perpetuating an error disseminated with disastrous results by Fleischer, and reproduced by Jahn as follows:

> Der Aufbau der arabischen Grammatik müsse vom kritischen Stadium der einheimischen Grammatiker ausgehen, aber so, dass man nicht mit den früheren, sondern mit den späteren beginne: denn erst durch Ibn Ja'îsch würden wir den Sībawayhi verstehen lernen.[102]

It will readily be seen that Merx and Fleischer between them have much to answer for! The anti-historical approach accounts for the preposterous suggestion of Fleischer that Sībawayhi and Ḫalīl used the terms *musnad* and *musnad ilayhi* "in reverse" (umgekehrt).[103] It accounts for Jahn's obstinate and thoroughly unjustifiable insistence that "Sībawayhi setzt statt نسبة durchweg إضافة,"[104] whereupon Jahn proceeds to distort إضافة into "Nisbe" throughout his translation. It accounts for Hartmann's assertion that the best way [86] to tackle Sībawayhi is through the *Ājurrūmiyya* (!)[(a)], *Mufaṣṣal*, *Alfiyya* and Ibn Ya'īš.[105] Perhaps it also accounts for the fact that Hartmann "improves" on Sībawayhi's speech criteria by inventing a sixth category, "*mustaqīm, kaḏib, qabīḥ*," merely for the sake of schematic symmetry of his own which was certainly not in Sībawayhi's mind.[106] In a general way Fleischer's appalling *dictum* accounts for all the mistakes which arise when it is tacitly assumed that Sībawayhi cannot possibly mean what he appears to be trying to say. It is

100. Jahn, *Kitāb* 2, preface v[(a)].
101. Jahn, *Zum Verständnis* 8 *et passim* (cf. Jahn, *Kitāb*, §16, n. 3).
102. Ibid. 2[(b)].
103. Fleischer, *Kl. Schr.* 1, 583.
104. Jahn, *Kitāb*, ch. 318, n. 1[(c)].
105. Hartmann, *ZA* 11, 65.
106. Ibid. 75, and cf. below p. [218].

an article of faith with Jahn that Sībawayhi often did not know what he was trying to say: his terminology is "thoroughly hesitant"[107] and marked by "uncertainty of meaning,"[108] which only Sīrāfī can resolve. We shall have occasion to see how trustworthy Sīrāfī is in due course, and, too, how Jahn's translation falls into the same errors. Jahn's liberties with the text are a constant source of annoyance; it is misleading to reverse the ideas in Sībawayhi's باب ما يضاف إلى الأفعال من الأسماء and write "Ueber die Nomina, von welchen Verba (virtuell) im Gen. abhangen"[109] for at least two reasons. Firstly Sībawayhi distinctly says that it is the nouns which are *muḍāf* to the verbs, and not *vice versa* as Jahn makes it; secondly the interpolation of "virtuell" is not necessary because nowhere in the chapter does Sībawayhi ever consider whether the verb is felt to be in any particular case, beyond mentioning the "latitude" by which verbs are allowed to behave as nouns in this [87] construction. To take another example, Jahn regularises into "Ṣifa" every instance where Sībawayhi says *waṣf*.[110] That is scarcely a translation, and since it is not clear exactly what was the difference between *waṣf* and *ṣifa* for Sībawayhi, it is high-handed to obliterate it altogether. How far apart Jahn and Sībawayhi were is succinctly illustrated by this translation:[(a)] "Ueber die Verba, von deren 1. Form das Passiv vorkommt, ohne dass das Activum gebräuchlich ist," which is supposed to render Sībawayhi's هذا باب ما جاء فُعِلَ منه على غير فَعَلْتُهُ, but which obscures the formal approach of Sībawayhi beneath a clutter of inappropriate Latin jargon.[111] Another trivial but typical case of interference is the way Jahn uses the word "Darg" to render Sībawayhi's word "*ṣila*," for this is neither a translation nor a transliteration.[112] Other examples could be found—one thinks of the terrible tangle Jahn and Sīrāfī get into over what Sībawayhi calls the "*iḍāfa*" of اثنا عشر. This Jahn properly recognises as a *nisba*-problem, but when he comes to the phrase لا يضاف ولا يضاف إليه he follows Sīrāfī into the trap where the latter's over-refined subtlety often leads him, and makes a false *distinctio* between لا يضاف meaning the *status constructus* and لا يضاف إليه meaning the *nisba*.[113] This leads Jahn to complain that "it seems as though [Sībawayhi] was deliberately seeking enigmatic and misleading expressions,"[114] when, in fact, all he wanted [88] to say was that اثنا عشر as a numeral "neither forms the base for a *nisba* ending, nor is the *nisba* ending attached to it, (i.e., it is not something to which anything could be *mansūb*)." Sībawayhi is guilty not of obscurity but of over-emphasis, for he has simply said the same thing twice.[(a)] To search for more of Jahn's blunders would not do more

107. Jahn, *Zum Verständnis* 3.
108. Ibid. 7.
109. *Kitāb* 1, 409/460, Jahn §260[(b)].
110. E.g., *Kitāb* 1, 230/269, Jahn 124.
111. Id. 2, 253/238, Jahn §447.
112. Id. 2, 90/92, Jahn §343.
113. Id. 2, 84/87, Jahn §336 and n. 7.
114. Jahn, loc. cit.

than exaggerate the deficiencies of the translation which are already enough to cloud its reputation. The chief objection to the undertaking is that it is a misrepresentation of Sībawayhi which has gravely hindered any understanding of his motives. Partly through Jahn's avowed prejudices and partly through his gratuitous alterations, Sībawayhi has become unrecognisable; no sense of the primitive and exploratory stage represented by the *Kitāb* comes through the ordeal by Jahn. The effect is as misleading as Weil's portrait of Arabic grammar in the introduction to Anbārī's *Inṣāf*, for Weil only offers a very good portrait of what Anbārī must have conceived to be grammar, but throws little light on what other grammarians may have thought. Jahn's efforts were noble but misguided; we may best sum up his achievement by using, his own words, in which the *hysteron proteron* speaks for itself:[(b)]

> The literal construction of the original will become clear to everyone who compares the original with the translation. From such passages it becomes clear how little fruitful (مفيد) it would be to translate Sībawayhi literally. One would be exchanging an incomprehensible German sentence for an incomprehensible Arabic one.[115]

[89] This thesis may be considered as the prolegomena to just such a literal translation which any reader can make for himself, armed by the conclusions of the chapters to come. There we will find, I hope, that the unaptness of the critics' estimations will need no pointing out. Most of what has been written about Arabic grammar in general does not apply to Sībawayhi in particular. The whole of Weil's introduction to the *Inṣāf* (the only comprehensive study in a European language), the entire band of Fleischer disciples, including Fück and Reuschel, and numerous peripheral figures, all are very unsure guides to Sībawayhi's work. Glazer writes of Arabic grammar that it "had very early been equated with absolute reason,"[116] which is certainly not true of Sībawayhi. De Sacy wrote perceptively that

> ... les grammairiens arabes, comme ceux de tous les pays, discutent parfois très-sérieusement des questions assez futiles ...[117]

which admirably characterises the contents of the *Inṣāf* but not the *Kitāb*. The same author describes Sībawayhi's concept of the sentence in a way that catches the spirit remarkably accurately but completely misleads through its anachronistic terminology:

115. Jahn, n.13 to §255.
116. Glazer, *JAOS* 62, 106.
117. De Sacy, *Anthol. gram.* v.

> Le grammairien Sībawayh n'exige, pour autoriser l'usage d'un inchoatif indéterminé, qu'une seule condition; c'est حصول الفائدة, c'est-à-dire que la proposition offre un sens intelligible[118]

The word *fā'ida* is one of the numerous terms regarded as typical of Arabic grammar and which are conspicuously absent from the *Kitāb*.[(a)]

[90] One W. Fischer complains that the names of the Arabic case-endings "contain nothing which says anything about their function,"[119] which is the result of much confusion. Fischer apparently believes that the European case names really do denote functions, though what kind of function "genitive," "accusative," "nominative" etc. are supposed to denote I cannot guess from the actual terms – "accusative" in any case is the result of a mistranslation from the Greek![120] But even if the Latin case names (for it is a matter of debate whether the European languages need be bound by Latin terminology) did denote functions, it does not follow that the Arabic case-names must do the same. What they do describe is the form of the word (*marfū'*, *majrūr*, *manṣūb*) with reference to some purely grammatical function (*raf'*, *jarr*, *naṣb*) which does not base itself, like Latin, on any semantic notion of the order of "being the recipient" (dative) or "being in a place" (locative) and so on.[(a)] By his prejudice Fischer has admirably illustrated just how different the Arabic and Latin systems are. He is also wrong to restrict the case names to nouns,[121] evidently another by-product of the same prejudice. Likewise Praetorius, noting that Arabic grammar definitely recognised the effect of one word upon another, jumped to the conclusion that "there is no doubt that the grammar of the Arabs knows the concept of rection."[122]

Reuschel is the most recent scholar to tackle the *Kitāb* directly,[(b)] [91] and it is clear from his preamble that his approach is steeped in misconception. It must be confessed that his pompous chapter-heading, "Die sprachtheoretischen Grundsätze der arabischen Nationalgrammatiker," makes for a most resounding bathos when the contents are read. Because the *Kitāb* is long, comprehensive and exhaustive, it has given Reuschel the impression that for Sībawayhi language was "a rigid system, incapable of further development, of symbols which can be put together according to fixed rules to make meaningful sentences."[123] In other words the success of Sībawayhi in finding a consistent explanation for every item he touched upon (which surely must have been his ambition in going to such lengths), has been turned into a fault through the failure of one critic to understand the *Kitāb*. Reuschel also seems to believe that the *Kitāb* is a normative, deductive

118. Ibid. 331.
119. W. Fischer, *ZDMG* 113, 283.
120. Robins, *General Linguistics* 292.
121. W. Fischer, loc. cit. 282.
122. Praetorius, *ZDMG* 63, 495.
123. Reuschel, *Ḫalīl* 15.

work: "the task of the grammarian, then, is to teach how people should speak, not how any particular people actually do speak."[124] It has evidently escaped Reuschel's notice that every principle of language that Sībawayhi was able, inductively, to establish, is so hedged about with exceptions and legitimate alternatives, that it would take a first-class grammarian to infer what was the way to speak. Sībawayhi describes, very fully, all the different ways it is possible to speak, and so normatively the work is virtually useless, as we can easily see from the fact that the *Kitāb*, in a nation of voracious students of books telling them how to speak Arabic, is far and away the least read of all the grammatical works! It is not even true of the *Kitāb* to say that one of the [92] grammarian's tasks was to "elucidate difficult (!) passages of the Qur'ān and to unveil the deep meaning which lay hidden behind the words of the divine book."[125] That opinion is not worth the paper it is written on, and its nuisance value is doubled by the need to say so here.[(a)] As a *tafsīr* the *Kitāb* is almost useless, and Reuschel might just as well have tried to convince us that it was also part of the grammarian's task to comment on all the difficult lines of poetry in the *dīwāns* of the hundreds of poets cited in the *Kitāb*.

Reuschel is only Weil carried to ridiculous extremes, but Weil is no sure guide to Sībawayhi either. What I have tried to show in this chapter is that with friends like those I have mentioned, Sībawayhi had no need of enemies. He has been variously misrepresented according to the inclinations of the critic, and we may say that three principal kinds of bias have operated. The first is the Hellenistic bias, represented by Merx and J. Fischer, the second is the arrogance of the European represented by Dieterici, Fleischer, Kramers (and, incidentally the Reckendorfs and Blochs,[(b)] who make their analysis of Arabic in the terms laid down by the Arabs but without taking any of their views into account), and the third is the bias caused by neglect of and indifference to the value of the Arabs' own achievements, represented by Jahn, Weil, Reuschel, Fleisch and so on. The task of this thesis is to silence the Hellenists by showing that Sībawayhi drew his inspiration from an entirely different source, and to reinstate the [93] *Kitāb* from the oblivion into which it has been thrust by the ill-founded misapprehensions of the critics, both of those who read it and those who did not trouble to.

Summary

[325] All study of Arabic grammar is hampered by the "dogma of Hellenism" which denies that Arabic grammar is an independent development. But there is historical evidence for the Arabs' refusal to accept Greek ideas.

A recent attempt by J. Fischer to prove Greek influence is refuted at length. On general grounds it is objected that no reason for the borrowing has ever been shown. It is

124. Ibid.

125. Reuschel, *Ḫalīl* 15.

also true that Aristotle's logic is inherently unrelated to the purposes of Arabic grammar. As for his "Poetics," it is doubtful whether this was a "popular" work in Islām, as Fischer claims. We can see from the works of Ḫwārizmī and Fākihī that foreign elements in Arabic grammar are conspicuously different from native ones. The basic meaning of *naḥw* has nothing to do with grammar in the Greek sense.

The tripartite division of speech is not borrowed from Greek. Arabic grammar probably started started with only two divisions and a third for all the other forms. It is impossible to find satisfactory correspondences between the individual terms *ḥarf, ism, fiʿl*, or any other terms, and their alleged Greek equivalents.

Various critics of the Hellenistic persuasion are shown to be mistaken, and also those who see an influence of Latin upon Arabic grammar.

[326] Others wrongly assume that Arabic grammar is primitive, crude and inadequate, which will be shown to be false in later chapters.

A third body of opinion believes that the Arab grammarians did not know what they were trying to say. Jahn's "translation" is discussed. The most recent work on Sībawayhi, by Reuschel, is briefly touched upon in order to reveal its weaknesses.

The thesis will attempt to re-establish Sībawayhi's Arabic grammar in its own right.

Addenda to Chapter Two

The position of this thesis, as reformulated in Carter 1972a, remains unchanged, and it would be inappropriate to offer a detailed rebuttal here of Rundgren 1976, Versteegh 1977, 1993, of Haldar 1973 (who relies on the same secondary sources as are rejected in this chapter), Troupeau 1981, Macuch 1982, 28–30. The lack of textual evidence of the transmission of Greek methods into Arabic before Sībawayhi, compared with the abundance of evidence for the period after Sībawayhi, is not itself the sticking point: there was no need to borrow a foreign system, because ethico-legal reasoning already provided one, as will be argued in Chapters Three and Four below.

It will be noted that whatever happened <u>after</u> Sībawayhi, the *Kitāb* contains hardly any terminology which can only have entered as a borrowing, because, as Guillaume 1986, 61 points out, Sībawayhi strictly speaking had no metalanguage except his everyday discourse; see further [154] (a).

The only solution for the lack of documentation was to assume a "voie diffuse" of transmission of ideas, a variant of the *post hoc ergo propter hoc* argument. As Versteegh 1993, 35 concedes "we know next to nothing about the early stages of grammar;" nevertheless he reaffirms the originality of Sībawayhi in bringing a new approach (id. 244f) in which the aim was the "analysis and explanation of linguistic facts" and not simply the discussion of the Qur'anic text as heretofore.

[51] (a) This debate has attracted considerable attention. An important survey is Versteegh 2000, 301f, drawing on Mahdi 1970 (now in Baalbaki 2007) and Endress 1986, as

well as a number of other studies. Since these issues are not essential for the present thesis they will not be explored here.

[52] (a) Rummānī may in fact have earned his reputation in ways not appreciated at the time when this thesis was written. His short books of "definitions" certainly reveal a familiarity with logical categories not found in orthodox grammar, such as "form" and "substance," see Sezgin, *GAS* 9, 111, and Troupeau 1985 for a general treatment and 148 n. 19 for his translations of Rummānī's works.

[52] (b) See the copiously annotated translation of Versteegh 1995. For our purposes Zajjājī may be considered as one who advanced the systematisation of grammar while remaining firmly within the Islamic intellectual framework. See also [292]–[293] on the *Risāla* of Sībawayhi, which is held to be the starting point of Zajjājī's *Īḍāḥ*.

[52] (c) My underlining. The purpose of the emphasis is to contrast the overt borrowings which occurred during the translation movement (when the Greek originals would have been known to at least some of the participants) and the fully developed indigenous technical vocabulary which was already in place and deployed by Zajjājī.

[53] (a) In my treatment of Fischer's argument I have fallen well below the standards of academic courtesy. Instead of an apology and some remedial editing. I have chosen to let the text stand unaltered as an example for others of how not to conduct a scholarly polemic. Although I see no reason to retract any of the criticisms and refutations, I cannot justify the rancour and arrogance with which they were formulated.

[56] (a) Similar ideas are credited to Ḫalīl, see above [44] (a), but need not be of Greek origin: they have a firm link with Arabic orthography, where the long vowels are represented as extensions of the short vowels through their homorganic consonants, thus *ī* = *i*+*y*, *ū* = *u* + *w* (*ā* is a special case but historically it is still a closed syllable like *iy*, *uw*). Arabic prosody (which is of course closely connected with Ḫalīl) is clearly independent of Greek influences: see further [179] (a) on prosody and Arabic syllable structure.

[56] (b) Ḫwārizmī also preserves a well developed set of phonetic terms which are not touched upon in this thesis, partly because they do not directly affect the vocabulary of the *Kitāb*. They have been discussed by W. Fischer 1985. See also [164] (a).

[56] (c) To adduce such a late work is not a very strong argument against Beck, but its anachronism is no less striking than Beck's own retrospective imposition of the Greek concepts.

[56] (d) The lack of impact of Greek ideas in this domain was stated long ago, and with some authority, by Grunebaum 1961, 325, "In the field of literary theory, borrowings from the classics remained ineffective," and the same can be said *a fortiori* for linguistic theory.

[57] (a) This division into major and minor sentences is found long before Fākihī, e.g., Ibn Hišām (d. 761/1360), though its origins are not known. A "major" sentence is one in which the predicate is a "minor" sentence, e.g., *zaydun abūhu qā'imun* "Zayd, his father is standing" (better known as the *jumla ḏāt wajhayn*).

[58] (a) Jundishapur is no longer as significant as it used to be in the trail from Greek to Arabic, and Gutas 1999 proposes a different source of inspiration, the royal Persian

libraries. But no matter what pathways we assume for the transmission of ideas, the fact remains that hardly any appear in the *Kitāb*, see [51] (a).

[58] (b) The original thesis has "specifying" here, i.e., *taḫṣīṣ*, a misreading of the Arabic *taḥḍīḍ* in the *Ṣāḥibī*.

[58] (c) This assertions may well be false. The similarity with the Greek categories is patent, but it is also the case that Sībawayhi, seemingly independently, divided utterances formally into assertive (*wājib*) and non-assertive (*ġayr wājib*) in a way not found in Aristotle. Without troubling to alert us, Sībawayhi lists examples of five types of non-assertives in *Kitāb* 1, 399/449: *amr, nahy, istifhām, tamannī, 'arḍ*, which clearly form the basis of the more elaborate scheme of Ibn Maḍā' and Ibn Fāris cited here. See Guillaume 1985, Carter 2012a, and especially Ayoub 2015 for a thorough treatment of the phenomenon in the *Kitāb*.

This distinction was carried into legal theory where it served to identify and interpret the function of performative utterances, see Larcher 2014.

The term *wājib* is worth a comment: it has been occasionally mistranslated as "positive" as opposed to "negative," but many *ġayr wājib* sentences are positive, so this cannot be correct. The nearest context is that of the law, where *wājib* denotes that a contract is "binding." If we transfer this idea to utterance types, *wājib* easily maps onto our "assertive" category in the sense that such utterances bind the speaker to convey information (cf. [222] etc., on the obligation upon the speaker to be *mustaqīm*), which is precisely what the *ġayr wājib* utterance can never do. See Carter 2012a, 322.

[58] (d) See p. [289] (b) on Ibn Maḍā' and language reform.

[59] (a) The possibility of Indian influences has been explored by Danecki 1985 and Law 1990, cf. also Versteegh 1993, 27f. While conceding that there is no formal evidence of contact, Danecki argues that the similarities between the two systems are so striking that some Indian influence on Arabic must be presumed: Sībawayhi would have had access to Indian ideas when at the Barmakid court in Baghdad. But Law 1990 shows that, although there are inevitable parallels between the observations of Indian and Arab phoneticians, both using similar articulatory phonetics, there are no significant correspondences at the systematic level (i.e., theories of articulation), therefore no influence can be assumed.

[60] (a) In the original thesis the Greek words were inserted by hand in original characters. With modern word processors it would be simple to enter them likewise, but this seems rather pretentious, and so the Greek has been transliterated here and henceforth, following the convention of Versteegh 1977, because the vocabulary involved is all more or less covered there.

[61] (a) Lit. "and the 'elements' (i.e., letters) of grammar are prior to the syllable," see Weiss, loc. cit. for the source, Aristotle's *Categories*.

[62] (a) In fact Troupeau was intuitively right, but mainly because he chose a strictly literal translation for all Arabic grammatical terminology: he might also have been aware (see 1976, 19) of the suggestion put forward some time ago by Machuel 1908, 4, n. 2 to

"comparer le sens de نَحْو avec celui du mot *méthode* (meta *vers*, odos *chemin, voie*)." This metaphor can be traced back to the Middle Ages in European literature. What definitely needs to be followed up is the use of *methodikē* in Syriac sources to denote "technical grammar," whatever that may mean: see Watt 1993, 50, 55.

[62] (b) Freely translated as "Poetry, lexical rarities and the Qur'ān are only properly maintained by grammar, for grammar is the scale in which all are weighed, so learn grammar, because it is the highest of the sciences in rank."

[65] (a) Weiss op. cit. 379: "everything else with no technical designation." The only reason why there has been so much discussion of *ḥarf* in Western secondary sources is that it cannot be mapped onto the Graeco-Latin system; Weiss's default definition exactly reflects the vagueness of its use in grammatical theory. Some of these are illustrated in [212]. (b) Levin 2000b briefly reviews the Western scholarly tradition, with objections to errors in Diem's 1974 (2007) interpretation, to which one might respond that Levin's decision to frame his enquiry in terms of the *kalima* is not in the least necessary to understanding what Sībawayhi meant by *ḥarf jā'a li-ma'nan.*

[65] (b) *Ribāṭ* and cognates acquired great prominence in later grammar in reference to the class of conjunctions, and particularly to denote the copula element in equational sentences, but there is no trace of this in the *Kitāb*. See Carter 1997.

[67] (a) I may be doing an injustice to Fischer and Merx here, though neither provide conclusive evidence that Sībawayhi's definition of the *ḥarf* has Greek origins. The passage from the *Poetics* is itself problematical, and beyond the present writer's powers to pass judgement on, though it is clear that Abū Bišr struggled with it too. But if Fischer is claiming that Sībawayhi's *jā'a li-ma'nā* is directly connected with the Greek *pephukuìa suntithésthai* "[a sound without meaning] which has the natural capacity of making a meaningful combination [of several meaningful sounds]," as it has been translated by others, then we can only disagree, and reaffirm that *ma'nā* here has the sense described in the rest of the current paragraph, on which see further [210]–[212].

[67] (b) That is "a sword is called *gladius* because it, so to speak, 'divides your gob'" with *gulam* providing the initial letters *gl-* and *dividens* the *-dius* element (= *divs*). For what it is worth, our "caesarian" operation may be due to a similarly fanciful etymology, as Julius Caesar is said to have been so named because he was "cut" *caesus* from his mother's womb.

[68] (a) Better "definite" and "indefinite," see [250] (a).

[68] (b) Thanks to Troupeau 1976 we now know that the notion occurs altogether seven times in the *Kitāb*, but in every case it refers to the process of expressing a relationship or kinship, and not the formal grammatical category of words bearing the gentilic suffix *-ī*.

[69] (a) The Syriac connection can never be discounted but alas nor can it be documented. King 2012 shows in detail how much contact there was between Arabic and Syriac scholars of all kinds in the centuries before Sībawayhi, but of scientific borrowing by Sībawayhi we have no certain knowledge. Paradoxically it is easier to prove influence

in the other direction after Sībawayhi, perhaps because Arabic grammar in the 'Abbāsid period now had a prestige which eclipsed that of the Greeks.

The letter of Patriarch Timothy, composed in A.D. 785, on the other hand, offers an exciting new perspective (King 2012, 199–201), for he displays an awareness of and admiration for the advanced state of Arabic grammar in his time. Alas we do not know the contents of that grammar, which would have been that developed by the generation(s) immediately preceeding Sībawayhi (d. ca. 793 or later). Since we have Sībawayhi's own evidence of the state of grammar which he inherited (cf. [17]–[29] above), this may have been what Timothy had in mind.

As for his plan to produce a new grammar, we note that he proposed to base it on Aristotelian principles, effectively distancing himself from the methodology of the *Kitāb*. It was, as King, 201 puts it "a particularly busy time in the history of Syriac grammar," but what concerns us here is that there is so little reflection in the *Kitāb* of the enthusiastic pursuit of Greek ideas to which the Syriac scholars devoted their energies in that crucial period.

Nevetheless, we cannot rule out some interaction, but such evidence of parallels as presented by King 202f, and the general observation that the medium of contact was the works of late Antiquity rather than Aristotle directly, still leaves the case unproven; King himself (ibid.) concedes that Sībawayhi's approach was quite different from that of Syriac and Hebrew.

[69] (b) The refutation offered here is superficial and unconvincing; however, the antithesis of word and deed is a commonplace of ethics, and we find *qawl* opposed to *fi'l* in *Kalīla wa-Dimna* (ed. Cheikho) 55 alongside *qawl* v. *'amal* and *kalām* v. *fi'l* in the same work (Beirut ed. 106). Al-Farrā,' *Ma'ānī* 1, 1 opposes *qawl* and *'amal* purely conventionally, "in word and deed." There is no doubt that this ethical dimension contributed to the grammatical terminology, but not in the precise way that Fischer argues here.

[70] (a) This topic has generated considerable comment, restarting briefly with Mosel 1975, 1, 221–23 and thoroughly explored by Levin 1981 (1998), Guillaume 1986, 2004, Talmon 1987a and Goldenberg 1988 (2007). Three main issues are: (i) is this a borrowing from Greek?, (ii) what is it doing in the *Kitāb*?, (iii) why did later grammarians reverse Sībawayhi's explicit order of *musnad* (Subj.) – *musnad ilayhi* (Pred.)?

(i) For the first question, there is evidence that the concept of *isnād* was in circulation before Sībawayhi, in a logical work attributed to Ibn al-Muqaffa' of *Kalīla wa-Dimna* fame, or possibly by his son, but there is no indication that it has foreign origins (see Talmon 1987a, 215–7). Troupeau 1981, while accepting that the author was Ibn al-Muqaffa' senior (d. 757), is positive that the work has no significant connection with Sībawayhi's later system.

(ii) The concept of *isnād* is mentioned on only four occasions in the *Kitāb*, see the full text below, [305], in contrast with more than three hundred instances *in toto* of the notion of the *mabnī 'alayhi* and *ḫabar* as predicate. This has not been satisfactorily accounted for: Talmon 1987a, 217f speculates that *isnād* is rarely referred to in the *Kitāb* because Sībawayhi was not very interested in that aspect of predication.

Guillaume 2004 takes up an often overlooked fact, previously picked up by Levin 1981, that instead of *musnad*, the term *sanad* is ascribed to Ḫalīl in a non-*Kitāb* source (the *Lisān al-ʿArab*, see Levin, op. cit. 150f for details), producing the apparent inconsistency that now *musnad* refers to the second member of the predication construction, i.e., (1) *sanad* – (2) *musnad*, instead of Sībawayhi's (1) *musnad* – (2) *musnad ilayhi* (see below, p. [165] on the underlying "building" metaphor here). For Guillaume the main issue is to determine what is "leaning" on what (bearing in mind that Sībawayhi's terms were reversed by later grammarians), and how this relates to the strictly logical terminology seen in *mawḍūʿ/maḥmūl*, not found in the *Kitāb* but seen in the work of Ibn al-Muqaffaʿ alongside *musnad* and cognates (more details in Talmon, loc. cit.). Guillaume concludes that there was a common vocabulary shared by grammarians and logicians, from which Sībawayhi developed a specific use of *isnād* for the abstraction of predication regardless of structure (cf. above), while the logicians confined it to the simple Aristotleian proposition. Furthermore, the proposition as such was always a verbal sentence.

(iii) This is a problem for the later history of grammar and not for us here: it has been explored in great detail by Levin 1981. Goldenberg 41–51 is a useful survey, building on Levin and Talmon, without modifying the latter's conclusions, including his views on the early history of the term.

The perceptive studies of Guillaume raise issues of the nature of predication, and again, the pre-history of the term *isnād* is not his prime interest, which is to establish exactly what Sībawayhi did with the concept in the *Kitāb*. He interprets *isnād* as denoting the unrealised concept of a predicative relationship, constrasting with *ibtidā,'* which is the linguistic act of predication in whatever form the syntax prescribes. The problem is thus one of metalanguage.

An agnostic position on the *isnād* set seems appropriate: the existence of three sets of terms for predication might be easier to account for as an unresolved eclecticism in the *Kitāb*, where Sībawayhi was drawing on the expertise of different masters from different backgrounds. This would match certain other terminological duplications, such as *ṣifa/naʿt* for adjectival qualification (see [301]) and the parallel terms for the vowels and the case/mood inflections, cf. [164]f, [298].

Among related topics are: the role of the listener's expectations, see [249] (b); obligatory definiteness of the first element (usually the subject), cf. [123] (a); the linking of the predicate to the subject by means of a referential pronoun, see [65] (b); locative predicates, see [270] (a).

On the absence of the term *jumla* in the meaning of "sentence" in the *Kitāb* see 202 (a).

[71] (a) This failure to distinguish between *fāʿil* "agent" and *mubtada' [bihi]* "topic, subject" pervades the entire field of Arabic grammar studies (a notable exception is Levin 1985, 124–8). It seems to spring from a conviction that there is no alternative to the Greek notion that predication is only possible by means of verbs. Sībawayhi was per-

fectly aware that verbs are inherently predicates (or better, attributes): his explanation for semi-declinables (*ġayr munṣarif*) such as *aḥmaru* is based not only on their formal resemblance to verbs (*afʿalu*) but to their common semantic function of denoting attributes (*waṣf*), unlike nouns such as *afkalun, Kitāb* 2, 1/2). The same similarity, but in reverse, allows verbs to occur in annexation (e.g., *yawma jāʾa*) because they, like adjectives, can occur as attributives (*ṣifa*), i.e., in relative clauses, *rajulun jāʾa*, 1, 409/460.

But even as predicates/attributes there is always a structural difference between "subject" and "agent," hence in *ḍaraba zaydun* we have the verbal sentence Verb-Agent, while in *zaydun ḍaraba* we have a complex nominal sentence, Subject – [Verb + Agent], where the Agent (our "logical Subject") does not even have to be the same as the grammatical Subject, e.g., *zaydun ḍarabat ummuhu* and so on. To mask this distinction by calling all Agents "Subjects" is a gross confusion between predication and agency.

Only one exception can be entertained, the special case of the topic noun in *kāna*-type verbs, called *ism kāna*, see below [220] (a), but even here *kāna* is seen as a normal transitive verb.

[71] (b) There has been one such suggestion for pre-Sībawayhian grammar, namely that the concept of *isnād* in Ibn al-Muqaffaʿ was borrowed from grammar, but it has not taken root, see Talmon 1985a, 221 and Guillaume 2004, 74 for references to Zimmermann.

[72] (a) See [179] (a) and [209]ff.

[73] (a) The second adjective in the comment is unwarranted.

[74] (a) *Stoicheîon* was in fact borrowed, but in its entirety, as *usṭuqus*, and retaining its original sense of "element." Versteegh 1977, 47, regarded Arabic *ḥarf* as "an ideal *calque* of the Greek *stoicheîon*, sharing all its extensions of meaning from "letter" to "particle," though he does not say how Sībawayhi might have come across the term. His position is unchanged in Versteegh 1993, 25f, though with less insistence on a direct and formal borrowing process.

[78] (a) Along with the confusion of "topic/subject" and "agent" (see [71]), the insistence that *ʿamila fī* is identical with *regere* is surely the most intrusive element in Western studies of Arabic grammatical theory: cf. Carter 1989, where also appear references to the term *tasallaṭa* "rule over" in relatively early grammar, a marginal curiosity whose historical connection with *regere* is quite unknown.

There is no need to repeat the contents of the argument, as the position has not changed, but some additional remarks and data will be presented. The topic was discussed in general in Carter 1973a, 151f., later by Peled 1992 (*ibtidāʾ* as an *ʿāmil*), Talmon 1993b (similar range of topics to Peled but focussing on the theory of his "Old Iraqi School," q.v. [17] (a) above), and Levin 1995 (1998 and in Baalbaki 2007) on *ʿamal* in general. Of all these it can be said that they start from the position advocated in this thesis, that *ʿamal* is an internal innovation which has nothing to do with the Latin idea of "governing."

It may be useful here to add a few references from the *Kitāb* which illustrate an important characteristic of *ʿamal*, that it refers to "operation" at all linguistic levels. Troupeau 1976 distinguishes three uses of the term, albeit with a degree of subjectivity which leaves us free to debate his classficatory choices. They are (i) literal, e.g., performing an action which is not necessarily linguistic, e.g., *Kitāb* 1, 217/255, where the dependent form of *al-miskīna* in *marartu bi-'Abdillāhi l-miskīna* is accounted for on the grounds that "passing by" is an "action" *'amal* which the speaker has kept in mind (*aḍmara*) as the cause of the inflection of *al-miskīna*. (ii) It can also denote a linguistic operation, e.g., in words of the pattern *fa'āli* ending with *r*, speakers raise the *ā* even though *r* would normally prevent it "so that the action will be in a single mode" *li-yakūna l-'amalu min wajhin wāḥidin* (2, 37/41). Likewise the lengthening of short vowel before *w/y* (so **uw* > *ū*, **iy* > *ī*) is explained as "raising the tongue only once because it as a single operation (*al-'amal wāḥid*) for two sounds in the same position." (2, 439/395). (iii) *'amal* is regrettably labelled by Troupeau as "rection" in spite of his policy of literal translation. One example which deserves to be taken seriously is 1, 55/67 where *musta'mal* is used to indicate "regarded as an operator;" admittedly the passage is obscure, see Jahn's notes on this: he chooses the variant *ġayr mu'mal* "not made to operate," which itself hints at confusion about the text. However Weiss 1910, 383 is content to mention that *ista'mala* in its estimative sense occurs in the *Kitāb*, i.e., not in the sense of "use," so the matter needs to be explored further.

The other important feature of *'amal* is that there is no clear boundary between the concept of a speech element being an operator, and the speaker himself operating on speech elements, see [154] (b).

[78] (b) The attribution of Latin origins to Arabic terminology merely adds confusion to the proposed Greek etymology.

[79] (a) Here too, cf. [53] (a), there is a deplorable lack of good manners in refuting the ideas of my predecessors.

[80] (a) He is far from the last: Haldar 1973, 175, observes that the Arabic and Syriac speakers of the region had no need for any abstract vocabulary before they encountered Greek philosophy.

[84] (a) There are enough forward and backward references within the *Kitāb* to assure us that Sībawayhi always had the whole contents in his mind: see further [289] (a).

[84] (b) This is undoubtedly an over-simplification of Fleischer's treatment of a complex syntactical anomaly to which he considerable space, pp. 525–532, though still from the perspective of European logical categories.

[85] (a) "mostly incomprehensible."

[85] (b) "The structure of Arabic grammar should proceed from the critical study of the native grammarians, but in such a way as to begin not with the earlier grammarians but with the later ones, for only through Ibn Ya'īš will we learn to understand Sībawayhi."

[85] (c) "Instead of *nisba* Sībawayhi consistently puts *iḍāfa*."

[86] (a) The exclamation mark is from the original thesis, reflecting that fact that this grammar, originally written for children, had been the leading authority for Western students of Arabic since it was first printed and translated in 1592.

[86] (b) "Concerning nouns on which verbs depend in the (virtual) genitive." My comment on this could be put more clearly as follows: Jahn inverts the syntactical rela-

tionship of the Arabic *iḍāfa*, in which the first element is dependent upon the second, not, as he puts, the second dependent upon the first.

[87] (a) "Concerning verbs of whose Stem I form the passive occurs, without the active being in use."

[88] (a) The point Sībawayhi is discussing is that when "12" becomes a personal name (see [181] (a) below) it follows the rules for compound nouns, so the second element is dropped, giving *ṯanawī* or *iṯnī*, but when it is a pure numeral, no *nisba* forms of any kind are possible (unlike English, where we can invoke "duodecimal," but that is not what is at issue here). This rule seems to have lapsed in post-Classical Arabic, where we find that the numeral *iṯnā 'ašara* does indeed form a *nisba*, e.g., in the name al-Iṯnā'ašariyya by which the followers of the occluded Twelfth Imam are known.

[88] (b) Here is a good place to apologise posthumously to Jahn, whose judgement is often completely sound, and who scarcely deserves the hostile criticisms expressed in this thesis. As already mentioned, [85], his translation is indispensable to our reading and understanding of the *Kitāb*. Moreover, his reliance on Sīrāfī is tempered by a healthy scepticism which this thesis does not adequately acknowledge.

[89] (a) See [293].

[90] (a) Later, in 1985, W. Fischer produced an interesting account of the case names used by Ḫalīl, which differ considerably from those in the *Kitāb*, see [165] (c).

[90] (b) Once again it is necessary to apologise for the lack of respect shown to a fellow scholar who was a genuine pioneer in *Kitāb* studies.

[92] (a) Sībawayhi's only interest in the Qur'ān was in its grammar, not its interpretation: his appetite extended to all possible utterances in every kind of discourse, see [50] (a).

[92] (b) That is Alfred Bloch, not his more recent namesake Ariel Bloch. For Reckendorf this is another case where the verdict has been unjustly critical: we owe him a great deal for his collection of real data rather than relying on the made-up or inherited examples of the Arab grammarians.

Chapter Three
Grammar and Law

The *Kitāb* is silent on virtually everything which would support the belief that Sībawayhi based his grammar on any form of Greek model. But it also offers proof that grammatical debate had reached a point of some sophistication before the *Kitāb* was written. We must therefore look for some other inspiration, for nothing can come of nothing, and there are nearly a thousand printed pages of closely argued, highly systematic reasoning to account for. I suggest that it was the principles of Islamic law which Sībawayhi took as a model for his grammar.

This is not a new idea, though I may claim some originality in applying it so radically to the problem of Arabic grammatical origins. It is evident from the lengthy discussion of Ibn Jinnī as to whether grammatical reasons (*ʻilal*) are closer to those of law or theology (*kalām*)[1] that the resemblance between legal and grammatical methods must have been recognised in the 4th century A.H. A work in which this is axiomatic is the *Lumaʻ al-adilla* of Anbārī, which expounds grammatical principles purely to show that they are identical with those of the law. Suyūṭī writes that both law and grammar are "the rationalisation of transmitted material" (المعقول من المنقول)[2] and, even more explicitly, "the principles of grammar are based on the principles of the *Šarīʻa*."[3]

[95] Some Western scholars have come to the same conclusion, or approached it, without, however, connecting it with the all-important problem of the origins of grammar. Thus Loucel writes (of the origin of language):

> To better understand Suyūṭī one ought to consult the jurists and see how our problem insinuates itself little by little into their researches ...[4]

1. Ibn Jinnī, *Ḫaṣāʼiṣ* 1, §§7 and 14.
2. Suyūṭī, *Iqtirāḥ* 3.
3. Id. in Zakī, *Al-Ḥayāt al-adabiyya* 188[(a)].
4. Loucel, *Arabica* 11, 72.

but the same notion could better have been applied to the very beginnings of Arabic grammar. In the same way Pellat suggests that

> The parallel between the methods of investigation of the jurists and linguists could be extended considerably further: to the fundamental criteria of the former, the Qur'ān, tradition, *consensus omnium*, analogy and personal opinion, there corresponds among the latter the study of the vocabulary of the Qur'ān, of the traditions and of ancient poetry, usage, and reasoning by analogy.[5]

It will be seen that Pellat is impressed by the external uniformity of the two disciplines, which I suspect, he would attribute mainly to a coincidence of the Arab mentality rather than to any influence of one upon the other. The same is true of Goldziher, who wrote that in the field of lexicography

> we often see jurisprudence enter into a union with philology, to which Arabic linguistics owes many a noteworthy advance[6]

i.e., the cooperation between the two sciences is secondary and does not suggest to Goldziher any more primitive connection of the sort I wish to establish.

[96] An even earlier link between law and grammar is mooted, without the implications being pursued, by Maḫzūmī, who points out that Ḫalīl and Abū Ḥanīfa both applied similar methods in their respective fields but that "there is no priority of time between them which would enable us to say that one influenced the other."[7] This is not a strong argument: surely it is extremely likely that the influence will follow the precedence of the disciplines they practised, i. e. law, which came first, will be assumed to have influenced grammar. What Maḫzūmī says about Ḫalīl, that he regarded language as a social phenomenon,[8] would apply better to Sībawayhi, but is at least a correct appreciation of the attitude out of which the *Kitāb* grew. Weil, on the other hand, seems to delight in coming within a hair's breadth of the truth while missing by a mile the spirit of the earliest grammar: his article in the festschrift for E. Sachau is saturated with legal metaphors, as he refers to the "canonical community" which produced an "imperative," "prohibitive" and "permissive" grammar in which the "rights and duties" of every word in the sentence were evaluated in the belief that Arabic was (amongst other things) the "mirror of divine justice," with the grammarian acting as a "judge" applying his reason and moral consciousness to everyday life.[9] This is only a repeat performance of his excursion

5. Pellat, *Langue et litt. arabes* 32.
6. Goldziher, *Sitzungsber. d. Ak. Wien*, 1871, 212.
7. Maḫzūmī, *Ḫalīl* 235.
8. Ibid. 159.
9. Weil, *Festschrift für E. Sachau, passim.*

into judicial metaphor in his introduction to the *Inṣāf* of Anbārī,[10] and the effect is to [97] tantalise rather than to instruct the unfortunate seeker after the true origins of Arabic grammar. We shall assume that all these half-truths point to the possibility that it was law which gave Sībawayhi his pattern for grammar.[(a)]

There is an impressive similarity between the set of terms used in the *Kitāb* to describe linguistic behaviour and those used in Arabic to describe human behaviour. They will be discussed in more detail later in this chapter; here it suffices to say that the literal meanings of Sībawayhi's technical terms are such that we can regard his grammatical system as a sustained metaphor based on the idea that linguistic items and human conduct can both be judged by the same standards. It is, of course, inevitable that the metalanguage of any grammatical work should require such transference of meaning: nineteenth century European linguistics relied heavily upon Darwin's theories for the source of its metalanguage in comparative philology, and twentieth century linguistics applies algebraic and pseudo-scientific methods in its attempt to account for the peculiarities of language. What is particularly striking about Sībawayhi's analysis is its homogeneity and thoroughness: to match the ethical criteria by which linguistic behavior is judged, the parts of speech have all been personified – they are "mothers," "sisters" and "daughters" of each other and they act upon and with each other in ways hitherto peculiarly human – and the transposition from the domain of ethics to the domain of grammar is thus complete, all-embracing and, without doubt, deliberate.

[98] It is probable that the congruity of ethical and grammatical terminology, though it was intentionally exploited by Sībawayhi, was not the result of his own initiative but something which was latent in the period immediately before Sībawayhi. This is most clearly seen in the works of Ibn al-Muqaffaʿ, whose discussions of ethics always include some considerations of the part played by speech in the conduct of man. It will be noticed that I have so far spoken only of ethics, although it is law which I wish to show to be the source of Sībawayhi's metalanguage. I should, perhaps, make it clear that I do not mean by ethics that curious Greek pastime which resembles nothing so much as an algebra of the emotions, for the Arabs had no direct knowledge of this discipline during the period which concerns us. I am using it in a wider meaning embracing all speculations about human conduct, particularly those which relate to the problem of man's good and bad actions in society. Ibn al-Muqaffaʿ is, by this definition, an ethical writer *par excellence*, since most of what he wrote would appear pointless if it were not taken as an attempt to lay down rules of behaviour in a highly practical and didactic manner. But in any case, there seems to be some confusion over whether law and ethics share common criteria. Thus it is implied by Fyzee that legislation has an explicitly ethical purpose:

10. Esp. 9, 15, 27–28.

> Good and Evil, technically as the Muslim doctors have it *ḥusn*, beauty and *qubḥ*, ugliness, are to be taken in the ethical acceptation of the terms. What is morally beautiful, that must be done....[11]

[99] This is a somewhat condensed idea, which could easily be invalidated by the old claim that law does not enforce morals, even in the special case of Islām, but it is also true to say that all laws strive towards more than mere legality, to the ethical good that is the absolute by which even they themselves are judged. Islām has always had a pecuh liar solicitude for the ethical content of legally controlled actions,[12] and it is this special characteristic which enables me to treat ethics and law as identical for my immediate purposes, although subsequently I shall distinguish between their separate criteria. The confusion between the two receives critical confirmation in the fact that Schacht does not hesitate to use Ibn al-Muqaffaʿ as a source for legal history, though it is certain that Ibn al-Muqaffaʿ, when he touches upon legal matters, is dealing with them from an ethical standpoint. An example from Schacht is his observation that Ibn al-Muqaffaʿ sanctioned the manipulation of the *sunna*.[13] We find, on examining the text, that this recommendation is inspired not by jurisprudence but by political expediency.[14] We learn from this apparent fusion of legal and ethical reasoning that in early Islām the two were not kept clearly apart, and moreover, subsequent legal theory bears a remarkable resemblance in its vocabulary and methods to the ethical theory expounded in the works of Ibn al-Muqaffaʿ. There is scope here for a study of Ibn al-Muqaffaʿ's sources, particularly with reference to Greek and Sassanian theories of ethics, which should lead to the interesting conclusion that the elements of *fiqh* are derived (not necessarily directly) from the [100] model of ethical reasoning represented in Ibn al-Muqaffaʿ's writings, and even those of ʿAbd al-Ḥamīd, who reveals an attitude which is basically similar to, though much less developed than that of Ibn al-Muqaffaʿ. The evidence that follows is not adduced to prove that point, but to show that the inherent similarities of law and ethics in Islām are matched by inherent similarities of law and grammar, the common element most likely being due to that ethical mentality which Gibb regarded as characteristic of the early Muslims.

One of the fundamental ideas both of Islamic ethics and law is that a person is defined by his status and this status determines what functions he shall exercise. "Status" is denoted by منزلة and "function" by موضع, and these are two terms which no-one who has read more than sixteen lines of Arabic grammar will fail to recognise. I think it is fair to say that without these two concepts the entire analogical structures of ethics, law and grammar would collapse into meaninglessness. For there can be no analogy between two

11. Fyzee, *Outlines* 14.
12. cf. Gibb, *MW* 38, 186f.
13. Schacht, *Origins* 58–59.
14. Ibn al-Muqaffaʿ, *Ṣaḥāba* 37.

items until their status or function have been agreed: this forms the basis for those interminable grammatical debates between "Baṣrans" and "Kūfans" and between the lawyers of the various schools. It is a great disservice to Arabic grammar to have relegated *mawḍiʿ* and *manzila* to a mere footnote as Weil has done,[15] thereby throwing undue emphasis upon the more notorious feature of Arabic grammar, *qiyās*. Parity of *manzila* and identity of *mawḍiʿ* are the twin pillars of Arabic grammar, as they are effectively of ethics and law too.

[101] *Mawḍiʿ* is extensively used in early writings to denote the right "place" for an action much in the same way that English uses such expressions as "this is no place for levity" and the like. ʿAbd al-Ḥamīd includes among the qualifications of the *kātib* that he should be

> forebearing in the place (موضع) of forebearance, understanding in the place (موضع) of judgement, forthcoming in the place (موضع) for stepping forward, restrained in the place (موضع) of restraint ... putting all things in their places (مواضعها) and all eventualities in their positions (أماكنها).[16]

Ibn al-Muqaffaʿ says much the same in more general terms:

> "Spare your wit and words but for when you hit on the right place (إصابة الموضع). For not every right thing is good on every occasion, and perfect accuracy of opinion and speech lies in hitting on the right place.[17]

No doubt this is what was meant, too, by ʿAbd al-Ḥamīd when he transmitted Marwān's advice to his son that his advisers should know "when to express their opinion," مواضع الرأي.[18] It is a perfectly familiar attitude to the English reader, and our proverb "a place for everything and everything in its place" might well serve to translate Ibn al-Muqaffaʿ's *sententia*:

> وإما البصر بالموضع فإنما تصير المنافع الى وضع الأشياء مواضعها. [19]

[102] The lawyers are also found to use *mawḍiʿ* in this sense. Šaybānī describes the case of the executor who has been accused of misappropriating the funds in his trust in these words:

> If he has been wronged, and has really put the legacy in its proper place (وضع التركة موضعها) as is right for it, he has the latitude to swear an oath while in-

15. Anbārī, *Inṣāf*, intro. 24, n. 3.
16. ʿAbd al-Ḥamīd, *Rasāʾil* 535.
17. Ibn al-Muqaffaʿ, *Al-adab al-Kabīr* 86.
18. ʿAbd al-Ḥamīd, Id. 481.
19. Ibn al-Muqaffaʿ, *Al-adab al-Ṣaġīr* 14.

> tending something other than what he has been asked to swear. But if he is a wrong-doer who has not put things in their places (لم يضع الأشياء مواضعها) he has no latitude to swear to any of it.[20]

We may compare this with Abū Yūsuf's comment on money captured in battle or conm quest:

> This has the status (منزلة) of money which belongs to no-one and has no inheritor. It is up to the just Imām to decide how much is lawful and to give it to those in Islām who most need it, and impartially to put it in the right place (يضع ذلك موضعه).[21]

As a last example from law there is Šaybānī's explanation that the expression *labbayka* must only be uttered "in its proper place" (في موضعها).[22] Sībawayhi offers several examples of the same usage, but since it is the further developments of the idea of *mawḍiʿ* which interest us, one example will suffice. Speaking of the construction known as *taʿẓīm*,[(a)] Sībawayhi says:

> [103] Know that it is not permitted to use *taʿẓīm* in every place (موضع), nor is every adjective good for use in *taʿẓīm* ... As for the place (موضع) in which *taʿẓīm* is not good, it is that you should mention someone who is not famous to people and not known to be exalted, then exalt him with *taʿẓīm* as you would a famous person.[23]

This is clearly an attempt to define the propriety and social context which determine the grammatical situation, and as an example of the primitive connection between what men say and when they ought to say it, may fruitfully be compared with this *dictum* of Ibn al-Muqaffaʿ:

> To speak well is better than to do so in the wrong place, and a single right word which hits on the proper place (تصيب موضعها) is better than a hundred words spoken inopportunely and out of place.[24]

A more important use of *mawḍiʿ*, however, is in its extended meaning of "function." In Arabic grammar this idea is developed as far as it will go in treating the behaviour of words, for which we almost surely have to thank Sībawayhi. I need not illustrate here how Sībawayhi describes and analyses the functions of Arabic words, as this forms the

---

20. Šaybānī, *Maḫārij* 51–52.
21. Abū Yūsuf, *Ḫarāj* 32.
22. Šaybānī, *Muwaṭṭaʾ* 191.
23. *Kitāb* 1, 214/251. Other examples, 1, 73/87, 191/224; 2, 334/307.
24. Ibn al-Muqaffaʿ, *Al-adab al-Kabīr* 77–78.

subject of a later chapter, but it is worth looking at the same notion in the lawyers and other early writings in order to see how firmly based it is on ethical foundations.

There is, as we have seen, "a place for everything," in purely ethical terms: the rich man, according to Ibn al-Muqaffaʿ, should [104] spend generously in four "places," in giving alms, in time of need, on his children, and on his wives.[25] These "places" simply denote where actions occur and it is by no means a far cry from the notion of such "places" to that of the "functions" with which, in grammar at least, they are always associated:

> The positions in which a form can appear are its functions or, collectively, its function.[26]

This is exactly what Sībawayhi means when he says "كان actually has another function (موضع) in which it is restricted to its agent as when you say قد كان عبدُ الله,"[27] or when he says "كم has two functions (موضعين); one them is interrogation where كم is the interrogative particle in the status of كيف and أين, and the other function (موضع) is predicative, where it has the meaning of رُبّ."[28] On countless occasions Sībawayhi uses *mawḍiʿ* in the meaning of function in the strictly modern connotation,[(a)] and this has often been obscured by translators: Jahn, for example, in both the above cases uses "Gebrauchsweise" for موضع, which quite destroys Sībawayhi's meaning.[(b)]

The lawyers use the idea of function as the inseparable companion of the notion of status, but the term *mawḍiʿ* itself is less common in that meaning. Šaybānī writes of the blind man whose scrutiny of goods in a sale is necessarily by feeling them with his hands (جسّ) that

> [105] Abū Yūsuf said that the blind man is in the position (موضع) of one who if he were sighted would see the goods and having said 'I am satisfied' would not be entitled to hand them back.[29]

To paraphrase this as "the blind man functions as a sighted man"[(a)] would not, I feel, be stretching the meaning too far, though it might possibly be going further than was intended by Abū Yūsuf, if we could ascertain just what he meant by *mawḍiʿ*. It is worth noting, however, that *manzila* "status" would have done equally well for the legal position of the blind man, and, since status and function are aspects of the same problem we may feel justified in assuming that Abū Yūsuf chose the term *mawḍiʿ* deliberately to express the identity of functions within the contract of sale. This is probably true of the use of *mawḍiʿ* in the rebuke of ʿAbdullāh ibn ʿUmar to his father:

---

25. Ibn al-Muqaffaʿ, *Kalīla* 188 (Y. 244)[(c)].
26. Bloomfield, *Language* 185.
27. *Kitāb* 1, 17/21.
28. Id. 1, 251/291.
29. Šaybānī, *Jāmiʿ* 81.

> O Commander of the Faithful, is it in the extent of God's grace to you and the place God has put you in (موضعك الذي وضعك الله فيه) that your rage should carry you to such extremes?[30]

for this appears to be a cliché in which موضع is interchangeable with منزلة, cf. Marwān's complaint that if our educators had learnt everything from themselves alone, with no outside sources, "we would put them in the status of their Creator" (وضعناهم بمنزلة خالقهم).[31]

Abū Yūsuf uses *mawḍiʿ* in a sense which comes near to "function" when he says that the *ḫums* which is extracted from booty for distribution [106] is that part which is disposed of "in the places of the alms tax" (يوضع فيه مواضع الصدقات).[32] This at least shows that there were certain "places" for the *ṣadaqa* and *ḫums*, which is confirmed by the Qur'anic verse which directs precisely where such money should go, "to the Prophet, to his relatives, to orphans, to the poor and to the wayfarer." (Sūra 8, 41). Later Abū Yūsuf says that every product of mining is liable for the *ḫums*, "and this is not in its capacity as *zakāt* but in its capacity as *ġanīma*" وليس هذا على موضع الزكاة إنما هو على موضع الغنائم[33] which seems to confirm that *mawḍiʿ* was not far from meaning "function." On another occasion Abū Yūsuf recommends that the *ḫarāj* and the *ṣadaqa* should be administered separately, otherwise the *ʿušr*, which is part of the *ṣadaqa*, will become confused with the *ḫarāj*, for the tithe is levied upon movable goods "and all that is the place (موضع) of *ṣadaqa*."[34]

Although the lawyers do not use the term *mawḍiʿ* nearly so much as the grammarians, they are nearly as liberal with its concomitant term, *manzila*. In its non-technical but still metaphorical meaning it is found in the *Kitāb* in the example هو منّي منزلة الشغاف and so on,[35] and its meaning of "status" shares with English that strange development into an unqualified "high status," as when Ibn al-Muqaffaʿ says that the rich man must spend his money properly "if he wants status in this world" (إن أراد المنزلة في الدنيا).[36] The purely [107] grammatical meaning of the term is so common in the *Kitāb* that it needs no illustration here.[(a)] But it is worth noting that Sībawayhi also uses it in a non-grammatical way which is very close to its legal application. Thus he explains the difference between temporary and the permanent qualities by saying that

> the voice is a temporary quality (علاج) while knowledge has acquired, for speakers of Arabic, the status (منزلة) of a hand or a leg.[37]

30. Abū Yūsuf, *Ḫarāj* 10.
31. ʿAbd al-Ḥamīd, *Rasāʾil* 475.
32. Abū Yūsuf, *Ḫarāj* 12.
33. Ibid.
34. Id. 46.
35. *Kitāb* 1, 174/205.
36. Ibn al-Muqaffaʿ, *Kalīla* (S) 187.
37. *Kitāb* 1, 152/181.

This parity of status is naturally the principle concern of legal speculation, for the body of general laws could only achieve extension to particular new cases if the subject of the extension could be shown to have parity of status with some item already covered by the law. A very telling example of the change from what one might call an "oral" society to a "literate" one is the way in which care is taken to point out that documents have the same status as their corresponding verbal declarations: we find this set out as follows in Šaybānī's discussion of the clearance of debts:

> And likewise if he gives a written clearance to one of the two (debtors) it has the same status as if he had said "You are clear with me from all the money in everything I have described."[38]

This, incidentally, somewhat modifies Vesey-Fitzgerald's claim that

> writing hardly occupies any place at all in the pre-Ottoman Islamic Law. Every act-in-law ... must be done by word of mouth,[39]

[108] which is seen to be an oversimplification. It would appear that, in financial matters at least, writing occupied a significant place, and the *mukātaba* type of contract may go to confirm this.[40] In addition we may adduce the growing practice of remitting money by cheque[41] as evidence for the increasing role of writing in commerce and hence in law.

Legal status is, of course, only a specialised form of social status, the sort of status which is made the subject of numerous observations in ʿAbd al-Ḥamīd and Ibn al-Muqaffaʿ.

> God in His grace, when He blessed me with (high) status with the Commander of the Faithful, also joined with it my gratitude for it,

writes ʿAbd al-Ḥamīd to Marwān,[42] and Ibn al-Muqaffaʿ uses the same idea more than once:

> "If you know that you have the status of confidence with your governor ..."[43]

> "If you attain an agreeable status with the ruler ..."[44]

Kalīla wa-Dimna is full of descriptions of status, of which I give here a few instances:[(a)]

38. Šaybānī, *Amālī* 35.
39. Vesey-Fitzgerald, *LQR* 1951, 99.
40. Cf. Šaybānī, *Jāmiʿ* 105f.
41. Cf. *ṣakk* in Šaybānī, *Maḫārij* 79, and Mez, *Renaissance* 476.
42. ʿAbd al-Ḥamīd, *Rasāʾil* 554.
43. Ibn al-Muqaffaʿ, *Al-adab al-Kabīr* 71.
44. Ibid. 79.

اعلم أن لكل إنسان منزلةً وقدرًا . . . إن المنازل متنازعة على قدر المروءة فالمرء ترفعه مروءته من المنزلة الوضيعة الى المنزلة الرفيعة ومن لا مروءة له يحط نفسه من المنزلة الرفيعة الى المنزلة الوضيعة [45]

[109] إن الرجل ذا العلم والمروءة يكون خامل الذكر خافض المنزلة فتأبى منزلته إلا أن تشبّ وترتفع [46]

أنا موليك من عملي جسيما ورافعك الى منزلة شريفة[47]

رأي الحزم للملك معرفة أصحابه وإنزالهم منازلهم على طبقاتهم[48]

A not unfamiliar picture is painted of court life in which the flatterers and fawners regard any friend of the ruler with envy and hostility, "and compete with him for his status, coveting it from him and opposing him for its sake."[49]

The impression is thus gained from ʻAbd al-Ḥamīd and Ibn al-Muqaffaʻ that the notion of status was firmly established in the ethical terminology of Arabic, and it might be proper here to give some more examples from law and from the *Kitāb*, to show that the term was used in an identical way in these two fields as well.

In law the gesture indicating safe-conduct is held by Mālik to have the same status (منزلة) as the verbal expression.[50] In the execution of the *ḥadd* punishments "the woman is in the same status (منزلة) as the man because she is struck sitting fully clothed," according to Abū Yūsuf.[51] Šaybānī states that if an accused refuses to give an oath of innocence "this has the status (منزلة) of a confession by the accused of what he has been accused of."[52] If two men stand bail for a person and one of them [110] pays off the debt, the other surety is not obliged to deliver up to the debtor to the claimant because this type of bail "has the same status (منزلة) as when two men stand bail for a fixed sum of money" which, when paid, releases both the sureties.[53] As far as the *ʻušr* and *ḫarāj* are concerned, wild honey is not liable, having "the status (منزلة) of dates growing in the mountains and valleys," according to Abū Yūsuf.[54] Two examples from the *Kitāb* will serve to show that this legal use of *manzila* is identical with Sībawayhi's:

The *tanwīn* is omitted from nouns after لا because the combination of لا and its noun have been given "the status (منزلة) of one word, like خمسة عشر."[55] On another occasion إنّ is said to have "the status (منزلة) of a verb, just as عشرون درهمًا and ثلاثون رجلاً have the status of

45. Ibn al-Muqaffaʻ, *Kalīla* 75 (S. 56, Y 98).
46. Ibn al-Muqaffaʻ, *Kalīla* 79 (S. 59, Y. 103).
47. Ibid. 213 (S. 219, Y. 272).
48. Ibid. 217 (S. 223, Y. 278).
49. Ibid. 213 (S. 220, Y. 273).
50. Ṭabarī, *Iḫtilāf* 25.
51. Šaybānī, *Jāmiʻ* 68.
52. Šaybānī, *Amālī* 16.
53. Šaybānī, *Amālī* 61.
54. Abū Yūsuf, *Ḫarāj* (2) 55.
55. *Kitāb* 1, 300/345.

ضاربون عبدَ الله without being either verbs or participles."[56] Other examples are to be found on almost every page of the *Kitāb*, all involving the concept of status, adapted for the specific idea of grammatical status but otherwise indistinguishable from the lawyers' use of the same term.

What makes it more than a mere coincidence that ethics, law and grammar should use *mawḍiʿ* and *manzila* in their abstract vocabulary, is the fact that so many identical terms are used in conjunction with them in all three fields.

The obvious term to examine in this light is *qiyās*, for this is generally held to be the characteristic feature of both legal and grammatical reasoning in Islām. But it, too, is found in ethical contexts:

> [111] The most just conduct is by comparing (أن تقيس) other people with yourself.[57]
>
> Comparison (قياس) is a guide by which one can find the way to good actions.[58]
>
> The wise man organises things and compares them (يقيسها) before he tackles them.[59]

All these are from Ibn al-Muqaffaʿ[(h)]; there is only one case in ʿAbd al-Ḥamīd, and that is doubtful. He advises ʿAbdullāh ibn Marwān, on behalf of his father, to

> compare (قِسْ) the stations (منازل) of the virtuous in religion, sagacity, opinion, wisdom, organisation and reputation among the commonality, and the stations (منازل) of the insufficient people in the classes (طبقات) and circumstances of virtue.[60]

With this use of *manzila* we may compare the use of *mawḍiʿ* in a similar context by Abū Yūsuf; when choosing a judge (*ḥakam*) from among conquered peoples

> (The Governor) must look for the best and seek people of sound judgement, religion, virtue and position (موضع) with regard to Muslims,[61]

where the ethical import of *mawḍiʿ* is unmistakable in view of the terms associated with it. To that extent *mawḍiʿ* and *manzila* seem to have been synonymous, cf. Ibn al-Muqaffaʿ, who uses both موضع ثقة and منزلة ثقة in the *Adab al-Kabīr*.[62]

---

56. Id. 38/49.
57. Ibn al-Muqaffaʿ, *Al-adab al-Ṣaġīr* 35.
58. Id., *Ṣaḥāba* 38.
59. Id., *Kalīla* 113 (Y. 147).
60. ʿAbd al-Ḥamīd, *Rasāʾil* 494.
61. Abū Yūsuf, *Ḫarāj* 125.
62. Op. cit. 81 and 71.

[112] The word قسْ in the quotation from ʿAbd al-Ḥamīd is also read as فَبَيِّنْ, which is equally plausible on grounds of sense. Note, however, the connection between منزلة and طبقة, which we have already seen in Ibn al-Muqaffaʿ above, p. [109]. But if ʿAbd al-Ḥamīd does not use the word *qiyās*, he certainly believed in applying the analogical method to human conduct:

للأمور أشباه فبعضها دليل على بعض فاستدلّوا على مؤنف أعمالكم بما سبقت إليه تجربتكم ثم اسلكوا مسالك التدبير أوضحها محجّةً وأحمدها عاقبةً [63]

This passage clearly embodies the same principles that Ibn al-Muqaffaʿ expressed through the idea of *qiyās*.

For the lawyers both the idea of analogy, denoted simply by كذلك or the verb شبّه on many occasions, and the technical term *qiyās* are used throughout their legal speculations. Thus a man who entrusts another with money now in dispute may swear before a *qāḍī* that the agent has received it, in which case judgement goes against the agent. If the man swears before someone other than a *qāḍī*, then no judgement against the agent can be given. This is the preferred verdict (*istiḥsān*), but the proper analogy (*qiyās*) according to Abū Yūsuf, is that an oath before a *qāḍī* or anyone else is equally valid.[64] A well-known example of *qiyās* is in the penalties for inflicting wounds, where a strictly analogical tariff of compensation is laid down:

> Whoever is wounded in a manner for which there is a right of retaliation, and proof is furnished, his wound is compared (قيس) and retaliation carried out."[65]

[113] Abū Ḥanīfa is reported as saying that it is not permissible to free captured slaves before they have been shared out, even after the *ḫums* has been levied. If, after sharing, the distribution is one or two slaves to each man in a regiment of not more than one hundred soldiers, any individual soldier may free one or all of the slaves simply by guaranteeing their value to his associates. Whether he is rich or poor is, according to Abū Ḥanīfa, theoretically of no consequence (سواء في القياس) for if the man is too poor to compensate his partners, "others will strive to make up their share."[66]

There is scarcely any need to show that *qiyās* was well-known to Sībawayhi, who uses the term itself upwards of two hundred times,[(a)] with the distribution roughly three times as frequent in the second volume. The method itself, of course, is used on every page of the *Kitāb*. Of *qiyas* itself here is an interesting example in which the term is used seven times in the space of ten lines of Arabic:

63. ʿAbd al-Ḥamīd, *Rasāʾil* 538.
64. Šaybānī, *Jāmiʿ* 96.
65. Abū Yūsuf, *Ḫarāj* 89–90.
66. Ṭabarī, *Iḫtilāf* 165.

> "The dropping of هو with أيّهم is allowed, like the dropping which occurs in the lightened expression لا عليك but it is only allowed rarely and on weak grounds with the sisters of أيّ. As for those who give it direct form, they have derived it by analogy (قاسوه), saying that it has the status of our expression اضرب الذين أفضلُ which we could say if we preferred, in which no-one would use the independent form. And those who say امْرُرْ على أيّكم أفضلُ also say امْرُرْ بأيّهم أفضلُ for these are identical. [114] And if أيّهم occurs in a place where its sister forms can also occur correctly and frequently do, they return it to its basic and analogical forms (إلى الأصل وإلى القياس)[(a)] as they return ما زيد إلا منطلقٌ to its basic and analogical form (قياس) .... Ḫalīl and Yūnus also say اضربْ أيٌّ أفضلُ, but others say اضربْ أيًا أفضلُ, forming it by analogy (يقيس) with الذي and the like, and causing the *ḍamma* to be preserved only in *iḍāfa* because that is how the Arabs say it, and they give أيّ its correct analogical form (قياس); if the Arabs said اضربْ أيٌّ أفضلُ you would say so too, for one is bound to follow them. You ought not to make analogies (تقيس) on rarities which have no known analogical forms (الشاذّ المنكر في القياس)[(b)] just as you do not make analogies (تقيس) like أمْسَكَ from أيقول , أمْس from أتقول and all the other patterns of speech, nor آنَكَ from الآنَ."[67]

As well as leaving no doubt as to the familiarity of the term *qiyās* to Sībawayhi, this passage also shows that the word itself had come to denote more than just the application of analogy. It has acquired the additional meaning of "the product arising from the use of analogy," i.e., the resultant form, which confirms an idea borrowed by Reuschel[68] from Weil, independently of Weil's much later source, Anbārī.[69]

At all events *qiyās* is a well-known term in all three of the areas we are examining, and indeed may be one of the oldest words in this type [115] of vocabulary if the letter of 'Umar to Abū Mūsā al-Aš'arī is genuine. The letter, accepted by Margoliouth as authene tic, though it seems to be a somewhat precocious document, not only contains the term *qiyās*, but direct instructions to "study the theory of analogy" as Margoliouth prefers to render اعرف الأشباه والأمثال.[70] This would place the use of analogical methods well into the period before even Abū al-Aswad could claim to be the originator of Arabic grammar, but even if the document is a later forgery (Schacht, *Origins* 104, is sceptical),[(a)] there is nothing in it which affects the already familiar knowledge that *qiyās* is a legal term of great antiquity.

Still older than *qiyās*, which is a loan-word,[71] are the two terms *ḥasan* and *qabīḥ* which are used in ethics to denoted "good" and "bad," occasionally in law in the same sense,

---

67. *Kitāb* 1, 351/398.
68. Reuschel, *Ḫalīl* 16, n. 2.
69. Anbārī, *Inṣāf*, intro. 27, n. 1.
70. Margoliouth, *JRAS* 1920, 312 and 320.
71. Ibid. 320[(c)].

and occur in the *Kitāb* as a fundamental and well-defined pair of grammatical criteria. The transposition from ethics to grammar is easily made. In English we find ethical terms (that is, terms normally used of human conduct) freely applied to linguistic situations; the editors of *Fragments from the Cairo Geniza* describe the language of some of the specimens as "slovenly."[72] The late Sir Ernest Gowers, editor of Fowler, once called journalistic English "depraved,"[73] and many other examples could be furnished of what is evidently a natural tendency to judge what people say as though that were part of their morals.

Arabic is no exception to this: Sūra 17, 53 says[(b)]

قُلْ لِعِبادِي يَقُولُوا الَّتِي هِيَ أَحْسَنُ

[116] and while I do not believe that this represents anything quite so lofty as "the ideal type of relation between man in social intercourse,"[74] there is no doubt that it is an injunction to speak in a way that is *ḥasan*, though the commentators can only guess at the practical significance of the word.

It is a commonplace in Arabic that "good" speech is part of the equipment of the "good" man, the assumption being that words are as much a part of behaviour as deeds are. They are subordinate to deeds, however, in the sense that

good speech is only perfected by good action[75]

with the emphasis in this case clearly on truthfulness. But truth alone will not elevate speech to the level of the *ṣawāb* defined by Ibn al-Muqaffa‘ in these terms:

> The root of the matter in speaking is that you should be free from lapses of memory, and then, if you are capable of perfect correctness (بارع الصواب), that is best of all.[76]

In addition to the accuracy described here, appositeness has also been mentioned above, p. [103], as an element in the *ḥusn* of speech. To these we may then add an extremely interesting piece of advice from ‘Abd al-Ḥamīd to the son of Marwān:

> You should be firm in the way you speak, dignified in your assemblies, calm of mood, refusing to pad out what you say, abandoning excessive discourse and undue desire for superfluous speech and repetition of such words as: اسمع, افهم عنّي, يا هناه and ألا ترى.[77]

72. Gottheil and Worrel, op. cit. xvi.
73. In a television interview.
74. Izutsu, *Ethico-religious Concepts* 222.
75. Ibn al-Muqaffa‘, *Kalīla* 152 (S. 137, Y. 202).
76. Id., *Al-adab al-Kabīr* 58.
77. ‘Abd al-Ḥamīd, *Rasā’il* 491–92.

[117] The presence of ألا ترى among the undesirables is very interesting, since it has been noted by Schacht as a feature of Abū Ḥanīfa's style![78] We are left with the impression that the early ethical writers had a firm concept of how people should speak, but that their concern was entirely for the timing, content, and relevance of speech, which may explain why they used ethical criteria to evaluate speech. Ibn al-Muqaffaʿ warns that "hypocrisy is the corruption of the tongue,"[79] that it is no use indulging in prolonged rhetorical and eloquent speech (التطاول في البلاغة والفصاحة) before people who are neither rhetoricians nor eloquent themselves,[80] and ʿAbd al-Ḥamīd instructs Marwān's son to avoid the mention of bad things (ما يقبح ذكره).[81] On another occasion Ibn al-Muqaffaʿ says that in order to be virtuous one needs "to straighten one's deeds, thoughts and speech" (تقويم أيديهم ورأيهم وكلامهم)[82] where تقويم both by its etymology and its context comes very close to the idea of *istiqāma* which we find not only in ethics and law but in the grammar of Sībawayhi. No doubt speech is one of the items implied by آداب when Ibn al-Muqaffaʿ says that

> the people have a greater need to straighten their manners and behaviour (تقويم آدابهم وطرائقهم) than they have for the food they live on,[83]

for one of Ibn al-Muqaffaʿ's main concerns is to set down the way a courtier should speak. One way he should not speak, for example is with "frivolous words and too long a tongue with neither reflection nor good judicious management."[84]

[118] Judicious management (التقدير) is a central theme in Ibn al-Muqaffaʿ, and, knowing that one of the consequences of judicious management is bound to be "hitting on the right place" (إصابة الموضع) we might regard Sībawayhi's use of *mawḍiʿ* and Ibn al-Muqaffaʿ's use of judicious management as expressions of an identical attitude. This will become clearer if I say that Sībawayhi would call a word *ḥasan* if it were in its correct *mawḍiʿ* and appropriate form: the striking thing is that Ibn al-Muqaffaʿ would call an action *ḥasan* for precisely the same reasons. In this respect Sībawayhi's system is only a specialised use of the one already found in Ibn al-Muqaffaʿ. There is an extremely interesting passage on speech in the *Adab al-Ṣaġīr* in which impatience is stigmatised as feeble-mindedness (سخافة). When someone cannot wait for someone else to finish, and interrupts, "he has not done well to speak" (لم يُحْسن الكلام).[85] This is the same type of criticism as underlies Sībawayhi's verdict that

78. Schacht, *Origins* 105.
79. Ibn al-Muqaffaʿ, *Al-adab al-Ṣaġīr* 31.
80. Id. *Al-adab al-Kabīr* 114.
81. ʿAbd al-Ḥamīd, *Rasāʾil* 493.
82. Ibn al-Muqaffaʿ, *Ṣaḥāba* 29.
83. Ibid. 45.
84. Id., *Al-adab al-Kabīr* 66.
85. Ibn al-Muqaffaʿ, *Ṣaḥāba* 45, and cf. *Al-adab al-Kabīr* 112.

> If you said أخذتُه بصاعد it would be bad Arabic (قبيحًا) because it is an adjective and should not be in the place (موضع) of the noun.[86]

The legal occurrence of such value-terms as *ḥasan*, *qabīḥ* etc., follows, as we might expect, the pattern laid down in ethical writings. The most obvious example, and one which I do not propose to deal with here, is *istiḥsān*, which figures prominently in Ḥanafī legal reasoning[87] as a device for over-ruling strict *qiyās* in favour of considerations of expediency.

[119] Of *ḥasan* itself, Abū Ḥanīfa's instructions for the muezzin contain several instances: it is "good" even if he does not stop his ears with his fingers, "good" if he turns round in the minaret instead of merely moving his head, and "good," too, is the addition of the sentence "Prayer is better than sleep" in the morning only.[88] If a pilgrim omits to throw at the first *Jamra* on the first day (of the *tašrīq*), but throws at the second and third *Jamras* on their days, it is as "good" if he makes up the first throw subsequently as if he had thrown at them in their correct order.[89] These all go to show that *ḥasan* could be used in law to denote a "good," i.e., legally valid action, but because of its ethical overtones it is naturally far less common than *jā'iz* and *mustaqīm*, for the lawyers were not concerned to pass judgement on the form of human behaviour, which is what *ḥasan* and *qabīḥ* patently describe. Nevertheless we do find it in Šaybānī where the ethical side of a problem seems to overshadow the merely legal:

> This is good (حسن) and this is how one should do it.[90]
>
> Washing on the day of the *'īd* is good (حسن) but not obligatory (واجب), said Abū Ḥanīfa.[91]
>
> To walk in front of the coffin is good (حسن) but to walk behind it is better.[92]

and we even find that prayer in the Ka'ba is called "good and beautiful" (حسن جميل),[93] which is interesting because Sībawayhi also uses the same pair of terms in the same way.[94]

[120] The other principle value-term which occurs in ethics, law and grammar is *mustaqīm*. There is no need to emphasise that this is a very hallowed term indeed in ethical contexts occuring as it does in the *Fātiḥa* as الصراط المستقيم and in several other places in the Qur'ān. In the next chapter I shall have occasion to relate the term *mustaqīm* to the

86. *Kitāb* 1, 122/147.
87. v. Schacht, *Origins* 111–112 *et passim*.
88. Šaybānī, *Jāmi'* 6.
89. Ibid. 31.
90. Šaybānī, *Muwaṭṭa'* 48 and cf. 225, *ḥasan* but not *wājib*.
91. Ibid. 75.
92. Ibid. 164.
93. Ibid. 223 and also 355.
94. See below p. [236].

concept of linear motion which seems to provide the main Arabic metaphor for human conduct; at present it is sufficient to point out that the phrase الصراط المستقيم fully illustrates that aspect of the Arabic vocabulary.

We have already met the phrase تقويم أيديهم ورأيهم وكلامهم and one closely resembling it, تقويم آدابهم وطرائقهم. The moral implications are clear, and the connection with *mustaqīm* is secured beyond doubt by the sentence

[95] لا تلتمس تقويم ما لا يستقيم ولا تعالج تأديب ما لا يتأدّب

Elsewhere Ibn al-Muqaffa' speaks of[96] الاستقامة في الطريقة and recommends to the ruler to surround himself with wise counsellors because

> that is the right and proper way (وجه) and only way (سبيل) through which his action will be right (يستقيم العمل).[97]

and this may be compared with 'Abd al-Ḥamīd's words to the effect that it is the secretaries who see that "the affairs of the Caliphate are right" (تستقيم أمورها).

[121] For ethical writers such as 'Abd al-Ḥamīd and Ibn al-Muqaffa' the notion of *istiqāma* is obviously bound up with "ways" of behaving, whether they be a طريقة, as above, or the very "sunna" of the Prophet, as when 'Abd al-Ḥamīd speaks of استقامة سنّته.[98]

The ethical teachings which abound in *Kalīla wa-Dimna* often use the notion of *istiqāma*, generally in a purely secular sense[99] but once, apparently in paraphrase of the Qur'ān, as يهتدي إلى صراط مستقيم in a religious context.[100] That this term, which is so clearly an ethical term, should appear in the *Kitāb* representing one half of Sībawayhi's criteria of correctness, is a fact of the utmost importance for understanding the *Kitāb*, as we shall see when we come to examine just how it is used in a purely grammatical sense.

The lawyers' use of the term seems to retain a sense of "right," perhaps with some leaning towards "just," though justice, in the Islamic view, evidently has more to do with equity (عدل) than the straightness implied by our word "just." Perhaps the terms have become confused in translation. At any rate Abū Yūsuf offers several examples in which the term *mustaqīm* is explicitly conjoined with the term *jā'iz*, e.g.,

> If the Imam gives that man permission to reclaim the land then it is up to him to do so, and the permission to do it is both lawful and just. (جائزًا مستقيمًا).[101]

95. Ibn al-Muqaffa', *Kalīla* 114 (S. 94, Y. 149).
96. Id., *Al-adab al-Kabīr* 99.
97. Id., *Al-adab al-Ṣaġīr* 23.
98. 'Abd al-Ḥamīd, *Rasā'il* 541.
99. Op. cit. (C) 48, 49, 94, 223.
100. Ibid. 234.
101. Abū Yūsuf, *Ḫarāj* 36.

> [122] If the Imām leaves the prisoners alone, frees them and has mercy on them, leaving their land and property alone, he is within his latitude[(a)] and this is lawful and just.[102]

> The best I have heard (in the settlement of shared irrigation) is that all (the different legal interpretations) are lawful, just and sound (جائز مستقيم صحيح).[103]

This last combination of *mustaqīm* and *ṣaḥīḥ* reminds one of the identical phrase in Šaybānī.[104] The same author also used the ideas of *jawāz* and *istiqāma* together: a client (in the modern sense of the word) enquiries of Šaybānī how he can bend the law by renting out one piece of land in return for the cultivation of another piece of his own land. "Is there a device (حيلة) for this whereby it will become lawful and just?" (حتى يجوز ويستقيم), is the question, and a suitably ingenious answer is forthcoming. By way of contrast, Šaybānī provides an example of the negative of *mustaqīm* together with *qabīḥ*: the case concerns the sale and receipt of a property which is then immediately re-sold. The payment of the second purchase is made through an agent, but a litigant intervenes with a claim of pre-emption (شفعة). Abū Yūsuf says that he would not decide the case in the absence of the second purchaser, because it would be "bad and not right" (قبيح لا يستقيم) to assign the purchase to one who was absent.[105] It is, perhaps, interesting to observe that this example does not contain the [123] idea of lawfulness (جواز) but only two ethical ideas of goodness and rightness, though naturally it is implied clearly enough that the "bad and not right" is unlawful as well. We also note here that the criteria refer to the *qāḍī*'s course of action and not that of the litigants: this is just as true of the prescriptions contained in the *Kitāb*, and an element of grammar which has been overlooked by those who see nothing but normative and prohibitive sentiments in the *Kitāb*. When Sībawayhi uses *mustaqīm*, for example, he does so in the knowledge that, having already defined the term, its force will seem to come not from him but from the nature of communication. This being a social act it is not inappropriate that it should be judged by social standards: it is, according to Sībawayhi, only "right" (*mustaqīm*), to speak in a way that your listener will understand, as we shall see.[(a)] In the meantime one example will show how *istiqāma* is used in the *Kitāb*:

لا يستقيم أن تُخبر المخاطب عن المنكور وليس هذا بالذي يَنزِل به المخاطبُ منزلتَك في المعرفة [106]

It would scarcely seem necessary to give any instances of the term *jā'iz* as it occurs in the works of the lawyers or in the *Kitāb*. As with Abū Yūsuf's "bad and not right" above, we

102. Abū Yūsuf, *Ḫarāj* 38.
103. Ibid. 50.
104. Šaybānī, *Maḫārij* 37, 84.
105. Šaybānī, *Amālī* 82.
106. *Kitāb* 1, 17/22[(b)].

should note, however, that *jā'iz* also occurs with reference to the legitimacy of a *qāḍī*'s action. In the *Ḫarāj* it is stated that when an arbitrator is agreed between Muslims and the inhabitants of a conquered fortress, his verdict (حكم) is lawful (جائز) even when, as in the case in question, [124] that verdict requires the taking prisoner or killing of the combatants.[107]

The ethical writers are as little concerned with the permissibility of behaviour as the lawyers are with its form, so that *jā'iz* is even less frequent in their writings than *ḥasan/qabīḥ* are in legal contexts. The relative distribution of *jā'iz* in legal writings on the one hand, and *ḥasan/qabīḥ* in ethical writings on the other is a good proof of their divergent preoccupations, and can be compared with the extreme frequency of the terms *jarā* and *majrā* in the *Kitāb* against its relative rarity in ethics and law. The reason is that, while all three disciplines are concerned with the behaviour of one kind or another, the linguistic behaviour which is the concern of the *Kitāb* requires a suitable term, *jarā*, which is not applicable to the mostly human behaviour dealt with by the other disciplines. Even these, however, use *jarā* on occasions, as when Abū Yūsuf, describing the freedom from *ḫarāj* in the Prophet's home territory and its extension into "Arab lands," says

> Do you not see that Mecca and the Ḥaram have no *ḫarāj* on them, and they have treated all the Arab lands in the same way (أجروا ... هذا المجرى).[108]

On the whole, however, *jarā* is too specialised to be found abundantly in all three fields.

Not so *wajh*, which seems to me to conceal a profound secret of Arabic vocabulary in that its simple meaning of "face" takes on such an [125] important metaphorical sense in law and ethics. This was recognised by Goldziher when he gave as the translation of على وجهها "as it ought to be,"[109] and it is not difficult to see that *wajh*, the way things ought to be seen to be done, and *ḥusn* and *qubḥ*, the beauty and ugliness of man's actions, are two branches of the same metaphor. It would be no exaggeration to say that Sībawayhi shares with the ethical writers a deep concern for the way behaviour appears to other people, in his case linguistic behaviour, in the case of ethics, all behaviour including language. And, like the lawyers, Sībawayhi is aware that the regulation of behaviour is also subject to the same rules of propriety, so that legal and grammatical arguments must themselves submit to the rule of what is fitting and seeming. It is, therefore, not altogether unexpected that the phrase على وجهه should occur as an amplification of another ethical phrase في موضعه, when Ibn al-Muqaffa' says that

107. Abū Yūsuf, *Ḫarāj* 124.
108. Abū Yūsuf, ibid. 33.
109. Goldziher, *Muh. Stud.* 2, 51.

> Whoever takes from someone else a good utterance and speaks it at the right place and in the right way, on no account will you consider that a triviality on his part.[110]

We have already met one example of this latter use of *wajh*, where Sībawayhi stigmatises the argument of his opponents as "a disgraceful way of arguing" (وجه رديء).[111] A good example from a lawyer is the case of stray camels. Up to the time of ʻUmar these were left free until claimed by their owners; ʻUṯmān instituted the practice of [126] capturing and marking them, selling them, and compensating the owners if they appeared. According to Šaybānī "both of these practices are good" (كلا الوجهين حسن), and the Imām may follow either course.[112]

In its broader sense of the proper way to do something *wajh* is used on numerous occasions in the works of Ibn al-Muqaffaʻ. In the following specimen it is set among several other ethical terms which we have encountered already:

> If the rich man spends his money in the wrong way (في غير وجهه), puts it in the wrong place (وضعه في غير موضعه), or pays the wrong amounts when they fall due (مواضع استحقاقها), then he will have the status (منزلة) of a poor man who has no money at all.[113]

This is as clear a declaration as one could wish for that status, *manzila*, and function, *mawḍiʻ*, are interdependent, as well as showing the use of *wajh* to mean proper procedure. We may also take as an example the passage already used above (p. [120]), to illustrate *istiqāma* where both *wajh* and *sabīl* occur in their ethical meanings. Of the many other possible examples perhaps the most interesting is this from *Kalīla wa-Dimna*. Ibn al-Muqaffaʻ warns the reader not to take the work at its face-value, but to treat it like a nut which must first be cracked in order to be appreciated. Otherwise the reader will find himself in the position of

> [127] the man who desired the knowledge of eloquence and whose friend drew up for him on yellowed paper[(a)] the wordings and turns of expression of eloquent speech (فصيح الكلام وتصاريفه ووجوهه). The pupil departed to his house and began to read a great deal without being aware of the true meanings. Later he was sitting one day in an assembly of learned and cultured people, and began to converse with them. He let slip a word in which he had made a mistake, and one of the group said to him "You have just made a mistake. The proper way (وجه) is

110. Ibn al-Muqaffaʻ, *Al-adab al-Ṣaġīr* 13.
111. *Kitāb* 1, 341/389, see above p. [30].
112. Šaybānī, *Muwaṭṭa'* 363.
113. Ibn al-Muqaffaʻ, *Kalīla* 70 (Y. 93).

> not the way you have just spoken." The man replied, "How can I make a mistake when I have read those yellowed pages and have them at home?" [114]

Needless to say, *wajh al-kalām* is a phrase which occurs innumerable times in the *Kitāb*, which makes the above, non-technical occurrence of the same idea all the more interesting. In its meaning of "the proper way to speak" it thus corresponds not only to the basic meaning of the word *naḥw* itself, but to all the other synonyms of *naḥw*. It has already occurred as the synonym of *sabīl*, and we find in ʿAbd al-Ḥamīd the expression وجه النصيحة ومذهب الشفقة, where it is equated with *madhab*.[115] In law it likewise denotes a way of behaving, as, for example, in various features of the *ḥiwāla*-contract, which are termed *wajh* by Šaybānī,[116] and the same author offers several examples of the question "is there a way out of that?"(هل في هذا وجه؟) when a legal, though not necessarily ethical device is sought to encompass some particular legal trick.[117] The [128] last examples may well be compared with a remark of Sībawayhi's which seems to preserve that legalistic flavour of the word very well:

ليس شيء يُضطرّون إليه إلا وهم يحاولون به وجهًا [118]

which may be translated

> They are never forced into a poetic licence without trying to find some legitimate explanation for it.[(a)]

So far I have tried to show that the three disciplines ethics, law and grammar share a certain body of technical terms without which any one of them could not function. These terms, *mawḍiʿ*, *manzila*, *qiyās*, *ḥasan*/*qabīḥ*, *mustaqīm* and *wajh* are only the most important of a much larger group. It could be shown, at the risk of tedium, that such terms as *fāsid*, *bāṭil*, *aṣl*, *umma*, *jins*, *ḍarb*, *ṣinf*, *nawʿ*, *ḥadd*, *ḥujja*, *dalīl*, *tafsīr* and *niyya*, to mention only purely theoretical terminology, are commonly used by all three in more or less the same sense. Even on the descriptive side of vocabulary there are numerous common terms, of which *ism* and *ḥarf*[119] deserve special mention.

In particular there is a group of terms which must reveal a more than fortuitous connection between grammar and law: the idea of option, expressed as *ḫiyār* or through the verb *šāʾa*, occurs if anything more frequently in the *Kitāb* than in any single book of law. The same might be said of *sabīl* which, though it also occurs in ethical contexts in its

---

114. Ibn al-Muqaffaʿ, *Kalīla* 44 (S. 47, Y. 58).
115. ʿAbd al-Ḥamīd, *Rasāʾil* 488.
116. Šaybānī, *Amālī* 33–37.
117. e.g., *Maḫārij* 12, 44, 71.
118. *Kitāb* 1, 9/13.
119. Cf. Ibn al-Muqaffaʿ, *Al-adab al-Ṣaġīr* 12.

usual sense of "way " (Ḥasan al-Baṣrī warns ʿUmar II not to "follow the path of wrongdoers," سبيل الظالمين),[120] it developed a more [129] restricted meaning of legal way, amounting to a legal right when it occurs in the negative. An example of the latter use is found in Šaybānī: where a creditor settles with a debtor but for a few dirhams outstanding, and receives proof of quittance, the heirs of the creditor after his death have "no claim and no legal right"[(a)] (لا حجّة ولا سبيل) against the debtor.[121] One of innumerable examples from Sībawayhi illustrates exactly the same sense of *sabīl*:

> There is no legitimate way (سبيل) for a noun to be partly oblique and partly independent at the same time.[122]

We shall also see in the next chapter that *sabīl* in its first sense, practically as a synonym for *wajh*, is common in both law and grammar.

Another idea which appears to forge a special link between law and grammar is the notion of *laġw*. In law it is defined as "eine nichtige Erklärung, belanglos"[(b)] by Bergstrasser,[123] which serves very well for the grammatical nullity implied by Sībawayhi, who often uses *laġw* in the *Kitāb*—particularly to denote what was only subsequently termed the ما الكافّة.

There is another concept which is particularly legalistic and yet which forms part of Sībawayhi's system. It is the idea of latitude, *ittisāʿ* and *saʿa*. This forms a significant element in the question of the avoidance of perjury in Šaybānī's *Maḫārij*, where often the deciding factor is simply whether the person can claim the necessary latitude to swear an ambiguous or misleading oath.[124] There is an interesting [130] phrase سعة في اليمين [125] which can be taken as equivalent in legal practice to the سعة الكلام which Sībawayhi so often calls upon in grammar. The presence both in grammar and law of a notion of latitude may be accounted for by the fact that, unlike ethics, they are not exact sciences, despite the reputation of Arabic grammar for being just that. Thus the law describes the greater and lesser pilgrimages as "each one good and up to individual latitude" (كل هذا حسن واسع)[126] and likewise it is open (واسع) to the faster in Ramaḍān to break his fast before or after prayer, as he pleases.[127] This last example is chosen to confirm that it is latitude rather than capability which is implied by واسع , for only the choice of pilgrimage is being discussed in

120. In Ṣafwat, *Rasāʾil* 2, 380.
121. Šaybānī, *Maḫārij* 86.
122. *Kitāb* 1, 210/246.
123. Bergsträsser, *Grundzüge* 32, n. 1.
124. E.g., Šaybānī, op. cit. 24, 40, 44, 52, 72, 78, 79.
125. Šaybānī, *Maḫārij* 72.
126. Id., *Muwaṭṭaʾ* 212.
127. Ibid. 184.

the first example, not the general obligation to undertake it, which, as is well known, is subject to the physical capacity of the pilgrim.

It might also be argued that it is something more than coincidental that both the notion of compensation (*'iwaḍ*) and substitution (*badal*) are used in the *Kitāb* in the same way as by the lawyers. If, for example, the twenty dirhams received in exchange for a dinar are found to contain base or forged coins, the buyer may ask for them to be replaced (استبدل) by genuine coins. This is the substitution of one thing in place of (في مكان) another,[128] which is exactly the same phraseology which we find in the *Kitāb* to explain the grammatical *badal*.[129] It is thus to be distinguished from compensation (*'iwaḍ*), which is essentially a means [131] for making good a defect in an article of gift or sale.[130] The connection between compensation for defects in commerce and the invariable occurrence of *'iwaḍ* in the *Kitāb* in contexts of phonetic defects is too strong to be treated as accidental. By assuming that *badal* and *'iwaḍ* in the *Kitāb* retain the different meanings that they have in law, we can account for the fact that *badal* also occurs in connection with phonologically defective words. The best-known case is that of what are called the *ḥurūf al-badal*, e.g., the *hamza* which consistently replaces the weak third radical in the certain situations. How does the substitute *hamza* in قضاء ,[131] for instance, differ from the *tanwīn* in قاض which is described as compensation (*'iwaḍ*) for the disappearance of the weak third radical?[132] The answer that a lawyer might give would be that in the case of قضاء a defective radical has been replaced by a substitute sound radical, on a basis of complete equivalence, whereas in the second instance a weak radical has been replaced by a compensatory element which is not a radical itself. A sound or a radical may change or be changed into another, which is the kind of *badal* which occurs when Persian words are arabicised,[133] but a defect cannot change into anything: it must be compensated by some alternative sound or radical, which is what happens when the "disliked" form ذُرَيْحِح is abandoned in favour of ذُرَيْرِيح with a *yā'* in the last syllable compensating for the loss of the first *ḥā*.' One last example will show how fruitful this quasi-legal method of approaching [132] *badal* and *'iwaḍ* is. In the same chapter which sets out the compensation of weak third radicals with *tanwīn*, e.g., قاض , Sībawayhi also speaks of the substitution (*badal*) of *kasra* for *wāw* when the latter is preceded by a *ḍamma* as in أدْلٍ from أدلُوٌ*. The *badal* has to be postulated in order to produce a form أدْلِوٌ* which can then be reduced to أدْلٍ in the same way that غَازِوٌ*

128. Id., *Amālī* 17–19.
129. *Kitāb* 1, 186/218.
130. E.g., Šaybānī, *Maḫārij* 13–18.
131. *Kitāb* 2, 340/313.
132. Ibid. 51/56.
133. Ibid. 375/342.

is to غاز, at which point compensation (*'iwaḍ*) takes over. Lastly it is worth noting that the term *badal* is significantly replaced by *qalb* in Šantamarī's commentary.[134]

Other terms, such as *šarṭ*, *naqaḍa* (to contradict), *tamakkana*, *ḥamala* etc. might without much difficulty be shown to be the common property of lawyers, grammarians and ethical writers, but by this stage we would be entering the domain of words that are everybody's common property. Thus we should find ourselves obliged to account for the coincidence (if such it be) that in the context of *manzila* in ethics we also find the ideas of *raf'* and *ḫafḍ*, of which *Kalīla wa-Dimna* provides several examples.[135] Another very interesting parallel which may also be coincidental is the fact that the Aristotolian triads[136]

1. just — 2. lawful, 3. fair

1. unjust — 2. unlawful, 3. unfair

appear to correspond remarkably well with the Arabic

1. مستقيم — 2. جائز، 3. حسن

1. غير مستقيم — 2. غير جائز، 3. قبيح

but this may reflect nothing more than a universal tendency to arrive [133] at the same scheme, or, which would not harm our case at all, it may be an echo of some Aristotelian influence upon primitive Arab ethics.

Such correspondences as these indicate, if anything, that the resources of Arabic in both legal and grammatical subjects were more than adequate: we find that these two sciences are conspicuously free of loan words. Only *qiyās* is positively identified, for *'illa*, the only other claiment, occurs in dubious circumstances in the *Kitāb* in its Syriac-inspired[137] meaning of "cause," and then never frequently enough to qualify as a significant part of Sībawayhi's terminology in any other meaning but "phonological defect."

Ethics is not free from methodological influences, but it, too, seems to have coped with the need for an abstract terminology of human behaviour without resorting to direct borrowing. In particular the words denoting a "way," e.g., سبيل, نحو, طريقة, were fruitfully extended, as we shall see in the next chapter. The conclusion must be that linguistic self-sufficiency is proof of cultural self-sufficiency, an axiom which is more observable in its converse, in that Arabic of all languages is least able to disguise the foreign elements of its vocabulary. This, combined with the acknowledged fact that Arabic grammatical

134. *Kitāb* 2, 51/56.

135. See above pp. [108–9].

136. Aristotle, *Eth. Nic.* 1130b.

137. See Köbert, *Orientalia* (NS) 14, 280.

nomenclature fits no other language but Arabic, must be taken as the strongest possible evidence against J. Fischer's claim of Greek influence. That identical methods have been applied in both cases has, I hope, become clear from considering the number of essential, and indeed indispensible terms that are shared by law and grammar.

[134] In addition to demonstrating the close technical correspondences, I would also like to show that there were opportunities for the grammarians to meet and learn from the lawyers. There is plenty of circumstantial evidence to support the claim that lawyers and grammarians were in frequent and continual contact.

Let us start from the assumption that Sībawayhi did not come to Baṣra to study grammar at all. This is not unreasonable, as we have already seen that the number of genuine grammarians before Sībawayhi is so insignificant as to make it extremely unlikely that grammatical studies were famous enough to attract students to Baṣra. Moreover the story of Sībawayhi's encounter with Ḥammād ibn Salama must, if it is true, be based on the historical fact that Sībawayhi came to study *ḥadīṯ*, *fiqh* and the early history of Islam (*āṯār*)[138] and may either be taken as independent confirmation of this, or as a natural inference from the affair with Ḥammād ibn Salama.

Apart from his role as catalyst in this particular episode, Ḥammād ibn Salama merits our attention on his own account. Though primarily a specialist in *ḥadīṯ*, noted for the purity of his language and his scorn for solecisms,[139] he was also enough of a grammarian to find a place in some of the grammatical biographies in his own right.[140] Ibn Qutayba, while placing hm under the heading of *ḥadīṯ* specialists, describes him as "an expert on grammar and Arabic language,"[141] and Baġdādī writes of [135] him that he and Sībawayhi were better grammarians than Naḍr ibn Šumayl and Aḫfaš.[142] Lastly we may note Yūnus ibn Ḥabīb esteemed him highly enough to take instruction in grammar from him.[143] It will thus be readily appreciated that in Ḥammād's circle grammar and law were studt ied side by side. Indeed there seems to have been a lively interest in grammar on the part of jurists and traditionists, if we are to believe the picture painted by Fück. He lists the following, among others, who were noted for their excellent command of Arabic:[144] Ḫālid ibn al-Ḥāriṯ (*ḥadīṯ*, d.186), Bišr ibn al-Mufaḍḍal (*ḥadīṯ*, d.168.7), ʿAbd al-Wāriṯ ibn Saʿīd (*ḥadīṯ*, d.180), ʿAbdullāh ibn Idrīs al-Awdī (*ḥadīṯ*, d.192), Wahb ibn Jarīr (*ḥadīṯ*, d.206), Sufyān ibn ʿUyayna (*ḥadīṯ*, d.198) and Abū al-Zinād (*fiqh* d.130).

---

138. Baġdādī, *Taʾrīḫ Baġdād* 3, 195, quoted by Zubaydī, *Ṭabaqāt* 66.

139. See Fück, *Arabīya* 41.

140. Zubaydī, *Ṭabaqāt* 47, Anbārī, *Nuzha* 40, Suyūṭī, *Buġya* 1, 548, Sīrāfī, *Aḫbār* 42, Qifṭī, *Inbāh* 1, 329, Abū Ṭayyib, *Marātib* 66.

141. Ibn Qutayba, *Maʿārif* 503.

142. Baġdādī, *Taʾrīḫ Baġdād* 12, 196.

143. Zubaydī, *Ṭabaqāt* 48, Sīrāfī, *Aḫbār* 43.

144. Fück, *Arabīya* ch. 3.

By way of contrast Fück also mentions scholars who were well-known for their inability to speak good Arabic: the most famous is Abū Ḥanīfa, who stands in the curious critical position of being accused, on the one hand, of uttering the grave solecism بأبا قبيس (in other versions بأبو قبيس) while having, on the other hand, the credit for writing a work of grammar. Both stories are forgeries and tend to cancel each other out, though we do have another incident which suggests that Abū Ḥanīfa had but small acquaintance with grammar.[(a)] In a meeting with Abū Zayd, the *soi-disant* anonymously cited informant of Sībawayhi, Abū Ḥanīfa utters a *ḥadīṯ* containing the sentence يدخل الجنّة قوم حفاة عراة منتنين قد أحمشتهم النار which Abū Zayd corrects to منتنون قد محشتهم.[(b)] On being told that Abū Zayd was a Baṣran who claimed [136] (uncharacteristically) the meanest share of knowledge among them, Abū Ḥanīfa exclaims "How fortunate must be a people among whom you are the meanest!"[145]

The grammatical problem, the correction of منتنين to منتنون (perhaps due to colloquial influence), and a mix-up (possibly arising from confusion in writing) of the radicals *ḥ-m-š* and *m-ḥ-š*, probably typifies the kind of grammatical argument which arose in discussion of *ḥadīṯ* material. Such discussions might easily have been caused by the mistakes of others listed by Fück, e.g., Abū Šayba Ibrāhīm ibn ʿUṯmān (*qāḍī*, d. 169), ʿĪsā ibn Yazīd ibn Da'b (*ḥadīṯ*, d. 170), Ibn Šankar al-Sindī (*ḥadīṯ*), Nāfiʿ (*qāri'*, d. 169), Hušaym ibn Bašīr (*ḥadīṯ*, d.189) and Mahdī ibn Muhalhil (*ḥadīṯ*, pupil of Hišām ibn Ḥassān who died 147/8). Though these could make but a negative contribution to the study of grammar, their linguistic deficiencies must have attracted the attention of scholars such as Ḥammād, Ayyūb al-Saḫtiyānī[146] and Aʿmaš,[147] whom Fück singles out for their particular insistence on grammatical correctness. Fück's aim in identifying scholars by their ability in Arabic was to show that the language was on the verge of decay, and that the main purpose of the grammarians was to arrest the decay and fix the language in a deliberately archaic form. That assumes that purism alone is enough to stimulate the growth of grammar, but it can scarcely have been Sībawayhi's motive. In the first place a prescriptive grammar such as [137] would answer Fück's requirements would rely on authority alone (as do the later Arabic grammars such as *Alfiyya* and *Ājurrūmiyya*), and would never need to establish at such length the systematic and theoretical justification for a usage. Secondly the language in which Islām was enshrined (as opposed to the language in which day to day business was conducted) was indeed an archaic language but one which nevertheless had to be stabilised and properly understood for very practical reasons. Thus Fück is only half right to describe the discussion of أنا قاتل غلامك as "hair-splitting" and "not stemming from living speech."[148] The fact is that the grammar of this sentence carries with it two differ-

145. Baġdādī, *Ta'rīḫ Baġdād* 9, 79, Anbārī, *Nuzha* 128.
146. See Fück, *Arabīya* 40.
147. Ibid. 41.
148. Fück, *Arabīya* 49.

ent meanings with correspondingly different legal consequences, أنا قاتلٌ غلامَك meaning "I shall kill your slave." and أنا قاتلُ غلامك "I have killed your slave." The difference is noted by Sībawayhi (1, 74/87 and 179/211) though he does not regard it as an inevitable result of using the constructions. We may compare it with the sentence هنّ حواج بيت الله, which is used by Ibn Fāris to illustrate the advantages of Arabic over other languages in the way different meanings can be expressed simply through different *iʿrāb*, i.e.,

هنّ حواجُ بيتِ الله إذا كنّ قد حججن وحواجٌ بيتَ الله إذا أردن الحج [149]

In Farrā' we find a similar interpretation of Sūra 21, 35, كُلّ نَفْسٍ ذائقةُ المَوْتِ. According to the majority usage of this construction, as in the above examples, this should mean "every soul has tasted death," [138] but Farrā' has to concede that the *tanwīn* is frequently lightened into an *iḍāfa* construction, although he does not appear to be entirely at ease with the topic.[150] To describe the dispute over أنا قاتل غلامك as hair-splitting, then is to overlook the real difference in meaning that was involved, even though it can be admitted that the problem was more apposite to the "dead" language of the religious and legal sciences, than the living speech of the 2nd century A.H. The real danger in Fück's attitude is of neglecting the genuine relevance of that "dead" Arabic to all aspects of the daily life of a people who certainly no longer spoke it themselves, but were still ruled by it in every department of their culture.

For Islām had become, by the time of Sībawayhi, a religion of nostalgia:[(a)] in less emotive terms it could be said that, the impetus of Islām having now waned to the point where it was necessary to ask how Islām should conduct itself, the only source of information lay in the recollection of the way in which it used to exist. From being a matter of inspiration, it had become a matter of record, and, like all religious institutions, found itself faced with the problem of defining itself on the basis of frequently uncertain or conflicting versions of what it used to be.

That is an ethnic generalisation which I submit with a certain reluctance, in the hope that it will be found to apply to the development of grammar simply as one of the many interdependent activities to which Muslims resorted in their search for Islām. It enables me to say what [139] has already been said in a different way,[151] that in this period all Muslim scholars were working towards the same end, looking for the same ideal, responding to the same need. And if the lawyers were effectively striving to produce a linguistic formulation of what had hitherto been a customary law, the traditionists to compile a linguistic account of the foundation and establishment of Islām, and the Qur'ān readers to furnish a linguistically unalterable version of what others had passed

149. Ibn Fāris, in Suyūṭī, *Muzhir* 1, 330. *Kitāb* 1, 46/55 mentions the sentence but does not discuss it[(a)].
150. Farrā', in Maḫzūmī, *Madrasat Kūfa* 281[(b)].
151. E.g., Gibb, *Arabic Lit.* 39.

on in various forms as God's word, then we should realise that none of these aims could ever have been achieve in such an unstable medium as the Arabic depicted by Fück, and therefore that if grammar did not exist already it would have been necessary to invent it.

For this reason we would expect to find the grammarians in contact with scholars in other disciplines. ʿĪsā ibn ʿUmar not only studied under Ḥasan al-Baṣrī, but also took Qur'ān readings from Ibn Kaṯīr (d. 120) and Ibn Muḥaysin (d. 123).[152] He had his own قراءة and is listed among the Readers[153] as well as giving instruction in the Qur'ān.[154] It is even said of him that he attempted to make his readings of the Qur'ān conform to the rules of grammar,[155] which, if it is not a historical slander, confirms what I have said about the unity of purpose which characterises early Muslim scholarship.

ʿĪsā was a teacher of Sībawayhi; indeed, some say ʿĪsā's two lost works, the *Ikmāl* and the *Jāmiʿ*, were absorbed by Sībawayhi into his [140] *Kitāb*.[156] Another of Sībawayhi's sources, though probably not a direct personal contact, was ʿAbdullāh ibn Abī Isḥāq. We cannot, unfortunately, make too much of the fact that de Slane describes him as learned "in law and grammar," for that is not in the Arabic text,[157] but it is significant that he took readings from Yaḥyā ibn Yaʿmar and Naṣr ibn ʿĀṣim. This is interesting because both of these are classed as grammarians[158] in the legendary period of Abū al-Aswad, but both, too, are recorded as Readers and traditionists. Yaḥyā ibn Yaʿmar is, of course, credited with the invention of the vowel pointing of the Qur'ān, which makes his link with the ren ligious sciences particularly strong,[159] and he was also a source of *ḥadīṯ*.[160] Naṣr ibn ʿĀṣim was apparently associated with the Qadariyya,[161] which suggests that his grammatical and Qur'anic studies might have been closely linked. Yaqut describes him as "a *faqīh*, an expert in Arabic among the *fuqahā'*," but connects him with the Ḫawārij.[162] ʿAbdullāh ibn Abī Isḥāq himself, who has been taken by no less a scholar than Pellat to be the first Arab grammarian,[163] was sufficiently interested in the Qur'ān to have an argument about the word بِمَلْكِنَا , in Sūra 20, 87, with the noted Qāḍī of Baṣra, Bilāl ibn Abī Burda.[164] Another

152. Ibn Ḫallikān, *Wafayāt* 2, 420.
153. Ibn Qutayba, *Maʿārif* 531, and cf. Pellat, *Milieu Baṣrien* 79.
154. Ibid. 519.
155. Ibn Ḫallikān, *Wafayāt* 2, 420.
156. Yāfiʿī, *Jinān* 1, 307.
157. Ibn Ḫallikān, *Wafayāt* 4, 288.
158. E.g., Sīrāfī, *Aḫbār* 22.
159. Flügel, *Gram. Schulen* 27, Zubaydī, *Ṭabaqāt* 23.
160. Sīrāfī, *Aḫbār* 22.
161. Ibn Qutayba, *Maʿārif* 625.
162. Yāqūt, *Iršād* 7, 210.
163. Pellat, *Milieu baṣrien* 130, n5.
164. Zajjājī, *Majālis* 241.

Qāḍī of Basra, Muḥammad ibn ʻAbdullāh al-Anṣārī (d. 215) is actually supposed to have disputed with Sībawayhi about the plural of the word جواب.[165]

We may gain some idea of the way different topics were discussed [141] in the same *majlis* from the anecdote about the Medinese *faqīh* Abū Nawfal ibn Abī ʻAqrab:

> Šuʻba said, I used to meet Abū ʻAmr ibn al-ʻAlā' at the place of Abū Nawfal ibn Abī ʻAqrab. I would ask him about *ḥadīṯ* specially, and Abū ʻAmr would ask him specially about poetry and language. And I never wrote down anything of what Abū ʻAmr asked him, and Abū ʻAmr never wrote down anything of what I asked him.[166]

This shows us at one and the same time how legal and linguistic matters could be discussed in the same place and why, perhaps, the two topics are seldom recorded in the same document. Šuʻba, himself a contemporary of Ḥammād ibn Salama and noted tradif tionist, was also an acquaintance of Aṣmaʻī, and was, in fact, described by the latter as an expert in poetry,[167] which suggests that he learnt something from Abū Nawfal even if he did not bother to write it down!

Several other names can be found of people whose work took them across the narrow boundaries often imposed by the specialist biographies.

Abū Muʻāwiya Šaybān ibn ʻAbd al-Raḥmān al-Tamīmī (d. 164–70) was a reliable transa mitter of *ḥadīṯ*, a pupil of Ḥasan al-Baṣrī and, in addition, a grammarian. He was highly praised for the soundness of his *ḥadīṯ* by Aḥmad ibn Ḥanbal on the one hand,[168] while in Ibn Saʻd's list of transmitters he receives the bare title of grammarian against his name.[169]

Al-Ḍaḥḥāk ibn Muzāḥim Abū al-Qāsim al-Balḫī (d. 105–6), as well as being a graml marian, was also known as a transmitter of *ḥadīṯ* and interpreter of the Qur'ān.[170]

[142] Naḍr ibn Šumayl (d. 203) one of the four pupils of Ḫalīl and contemporary with Sībawayhi, rose to high rank in the world of jurisprudence. He is described an an expert in obscure vocabulary, poetry, grammar, tradition, chronicles and jurisprudence.[171] He became Qāḍī of Merv, where he was the first to introduce the *sunna*, and there he administered justice fairly and lived a praiseworthy life.[172] Despite this legal career he does not seem to have written any books on law, though his philological output was considerable.[173] On the other hand he has left some interesting remarks. It was he who said of Abū Ḥanīfa

165. Ibid. 175.
166. Suyūṭī, *Muzhir* 2, 304.
167. Ibid. 308.
168. Anbārī, *Nuzha* 30–31.
169. Ibn Saʻd, *Ṭabaqāt* 7, 2, 67(a).
170. Yāqūt, *Iršād* 4, 272.
171. Zubaydī, *Ṭabaqāt* 60, Ibn Qutayba, *Maʻārif*, 542.
172. Yāqūt, *Iršād* 7, 219.
173. See Ibn al-Nadīm, *Fihrist* 83.

that until he appeared and plunged them all into argument, people were fast asleep as far as *fiqh* was concerned,[174] and to Naḍr ibn Šumayl is also attributed the remark that he had never seen anyone more learned in the *sunna* after Ibn ʿAwn than Ḫalīl ibn Aḥmad.[175] These two observations clearly reveal Naḍr ibn Šumayl's interest in law despite the apparent will of the biographers that he should go down in history primarily as a grammarian.

Ḫalīl himself was a friend of the traditionist Ayyūb al-Saḫtiyānī. This latter, who is described as the "lord of the jurists" (سيّد الفقهاء),[176] has been selected by Fück for his extraordinary concern for grammatical accuracy in *ḥadīṯ*,[177] and was apparently the cause of Ḫalīl's return to orthodoxy after a period of adherence to the Ibāḍite sect.[178] The return [143] must have been complete for, apart from Naḍr ibn Šumayl's tribute, Ḫalīl also attracted the admiration of no less a *faqīh* than Sufyān al-Ṯawrī for his piety.[179] Sufyān himself seems to have cared little for grammar,[180] but it is interesting to note that Ayyūb al-Saḫtiyānī once attended with Yūnus and Sulaymān al-Taymī a *majlis* presided over by the traditionist ʿIkrima. When ʿIkrima broke off teaching to listen to a singing-girl, Ayyūb was the only one who did not abandon the frequenting of ʿIkrima – presumably on the very laudable grounds that his desire for knowledge was greater than his sense of etiquette.[181] It seems that Ayyūb, Sulaymān and Yūnus were familiarly seen together, along with Ibn ʿAwn, for Ibn Qutayba reports a story in which Aṣmaʿī says "of the four Sulaymān was the most devout, Ayyūb was the best in law (أفقههم), Yūnus the strictest with money and Ibn ʿAwn the most controlled of tongue."[182]

We have already met one pupil of Ḫalīl, Naḍr ibn Šumayl, and he is commonly referred to with Sībawayhi and two others, ʿAlī ibn Naṣr and Mu'arrij ibn ʿAmr, to make up a quartet of disciples. ʿAlī ibn Naṣr (d. 187) must be regarded as one of Ḫalīl's failures: he receives his ritual place in the grammatical biographies, but seems to have produced no works or left any pupils by which his title of grammarian could be justified. On the other hand he is also listed as a transmitter of *ḥadīṯ*, one who was considered reliable by Aḥmad ibn Ḥanbal.[183]

Mu'arrij, on the other hand, seems to have been mainly interested in grammar, though there are serious inconsistencies in his biography, [144] which makes him of little

174. Baġdādī, *Ta'rīḫ Baġdād* 13, 345.
175. Suyūṭī, *Muzhir* 1, 64.
176. Ibn Ḥajar, *Tahḏīb* 1, 398
177. Fück, *Arabīya* 40
178. Zubaydī, *Ṭabaqāt* 45
179. Yāqūt, *Iršād* 4, 181
180. Goldziher, *Muh. Stud.* 2, 201
181. Ibn Qutayba, *Maʿārif* 456
182. Ibid. 476
183. Ibn Ḥajar, *Tahḏīb* 7, 390

use as a witness. For example it is stated in one place that he came to Baghdad "with Ma'mūn,"[184] which could scarcely have been the case if it is correct that Mu'arrij died in 195 A.H., since Ma'mūn did not arrive in Baghdad until 198 A.H. It is also perplexing that Mu'arrij came to Baṣra, on his own admission with no knowledge of *qiyās*, and learnt about it from Abū Zayd al-Anṣārī.[185] This is not to be expected in one who is recorded as a pupil of Ḫalīl.

Grammarians, as I have shown, were also interested in the religious sciences – indeed it is perhaps not too banal to point out that the only material they had to work on at all was what the Qur'ān, *ḥadīṯ* and poetry provided, the last being used, of course, as collateral evidence for the language of the Qur'ān and the *ḥadīṯ*.

In the same way lawyers are found to have an interest in grammar. Muḥammad ibn al-Ḥasan al-Šaybānī (d. 189) must have been particularly close to the grammarians, because one of his legal works (a *Kitāb al-aymān*) is said to be "based on the principles of Arabic."[186] He is also praised by Šāfi'ī (himself no mean scholar of grammar)[187] for his eloquence in the following terms:

> If I wanted to say that the Qur'ān had come down in the language of Muḥammad ibn al-Ḥasan I would say so on account of his eloquence ... Whenever Muḥammad ibn al-Ḥasan deals with a legal problem it is as if a Qur'ān came down to him with not a piece misplaced, neither too early nor too late.[188]

[145] Šaybānī is described as "advanced in the science of Arabic, grammar, arithmetic, and having great acumen,"[189] and in one of his collections of traditions (presumably his edition of Mālik's *Muwaṭṭa'*) he inserted "disquisitions on various obscure points, particularly those connected with grammar."[190] In addition he may have been an acquaintance of Kisā'ī, since they both died on the same journey with Rašīd.[191] There is a curious story involving Farrā' which runs as follows:

> Bišr al-Mārisī said to Farrā,' "I want to ask you a question of law." Farrā' answered, "Ask." Al-Mārisī said, "What do you say of a man who is negligent during the two (compensatory) prostrations of negligence?" Farrā' said, "There is nothing against him." Al-Mārisī said, "Why?" Farrā' answered, "I have made an analogy in the way of our grammatical methods, namely, that the diminutive

184. Baġdādī, *Ta'rīḫ Baġdād* 13, 258
185. Yāqūt, *Iršād* 7, 195, Baġdādī, op. cit. 13, 258, Ibn Ḫallikān, *Wafayāt* 3, 459.
186. Ibn Ya'īš, *Šarḥ al-Mufaṣṣal* 1, 14.
187. Yāqūt, *Iršād* 6, 368, and cf. Suyūṭī, *Muzhir* 1, 65.
188. Baġdādī, op. cit. 2, 175–76.
189. Ibn Abī al-Wafā,' *Ṭabaqāt* 44.
190. Ibn Ḫallikān, *Wafayāt* 2, 590.
191. Anbārī, *Nuzha* 84, Sīrāfī, *Aḫbār* 45.

> cannot be made smaller, and likewise no attention is paid to negligence within negligence."[192]

This is a fatuous anecdote in itself, but the interesting point is that Anbārī then goes on to say that, according to another version, it was Šaybānī who posed the question to Farrā'.

Šaybānī himself was a pupil of Abū Yūsuf, and Abū Yūsuf was certainly acquainted with Kisā'ī,[(a)] with whom he seems to have crossed swords more than once. On one occasion Kisā'ī retorted in reply to a slighting remark from Abū Yūsuf,

> [146] I am better than you because I am good at what you are good at (i.e., *fiqh*) and am also good at what you are not good at (i.e., grammar).

Kisā'ī substantiated this boast by (somewhat improbably) defeating Abū Yūsuf in a discussion of a legal problem, whereupon Abū Yūsuf "went away and studied grammar."[193]

On another occasion Rašīd sprang upon Abū Yūsuf the problem of whether a triple divorce is affected through the phrase عزيمة ثلاث or عزيمة ثلاثا in the verse[(a)]

فأنتِ طلاقٌ والطلاقُ عزيمةٌ   ثلاثًا ومَنْ يَخْرُقْ أعقُّ وأظلم

Abū Yūsuf's first reaction is "That is a legal-grammatical question" (هذه مسألة فقهية نحوية) but he finds himself unable to give a satisfactory answer. Kisā'ī is informed and, of course, produces the right answer.[194]

An even earlier encounter between a lawyer and a grammarian took place when Abū Ḥanīfa crossed swords with Abū 'Āṣim al-Ḍaḥḥāk ibn Maḫlad (d. 212). The latter was something of a practical joker and came up to Abū Ḥanīfa saying, "Would you like me to fetch a policeman?" to which Abū Ḥanīfa, who happened to be in difficulties at the time with a crowd of people, replied that he would. Abū 'Āṣim then required him to learn all the *ḥadīṯ*s he had on him, and Abū Ḥanīfa thereupon set to learning them. When he had finished he asked for his policeman, [147] to which Abū 'Āṣim replied, "I only said, 'would you like me to fetch one?' I didn't say I was going to." Abū Ḥanīfa turned to the crowd and said, "Look how I have been putting it over on people for goodness knows how long, and now this lad has just put one over on me."[195]

Abū 'Āṣim was a source for Buḫārī and a student, amongst others, of Awzā'ī, which attests his legal achievement, while his place in the *Ṭabaqāt* of Zubaydī is good evidence of his grammatical accomplishment.

192. Anbārī, op. cit. 101–2.
193. Yāqūt, *Iršād* 5, 187, Zajjājī, *Majālis* 257.
194. Zajjājī, op. cit. 338–39.
195. Suyūṭī, *Buġya* 2, 13[(a)].

Muḥammad ibn Sa'dān al-Ḍarīr (d. 231) was probably too young to have been present at the debates between Sībawayhi and Kisā'ī, as reported by Zubaydi,[196] but he is chiefly noted for the ineptitude with which he applied his defective knowledge of the fundamentals and branches of *qiyās* to the problem of the Qur'anic readings that he took from Ḥamza.[197]

Muḥammad ibn al-Munāḏir (d. 197) is, for some reason, never included among the pupils of Ḫalīl when they are spoken of as a body, but, like Kaysān[198] and Marwān al-Naḥwī,[199] is always overlooked. He seems to have shared Abū 'Āṣim's taste for practical jokes. One day he taunted Yūnus about his humble origins by asking him how the name Jabbūl declined. For this he was called a son of a whore by Yūnus, unfortunately without witnesses, as Yūnus did not like to be reminded of his birthplace. Next day he returned with witnesses but Yūnus, to the dismay of Ibn al-Munāḏir, refused to repeat the abuse.[200] Apart from his personal qualities, however, it is noteworthy that he took *ḥadīṯ* instruction [148] from both Sufyān al-Ṯawrī and Sufyān ibn 'Uyayna, and that the latter even used to ask him about difficult grammatical points.[201] The same Sufyān ibn 'Uyayna also met Kisā'ī, according to Zajjājī, in Baṣra and in the presence of Yūnus.[202]

One last anecdote will serve to show how easily lawyers and grammarians could discuss their specialties in one company. The story is told by Ibn Karāma that

> we were with Wakī' one day and someone said, "Abū Ḥanīfa has made a mistake." And Wakī' said, "How can Abū Ḥanīfa make a mistake when he has such people as Abū Yūsuf and Ẓufar with their *qiyās*, and Yaḥyā ibn Abī Zā'ida and Ḥafṣ ibn Ġiyāṯ and Munḏil with their memory and traditions, and Qāsim ibn Ma'an with his knowledge of dialect and of Arabic, and Dāwūd al-Ṭā'ī and Fāḍil ibn 'Iyād with their asceticism and piety?"[203]

Qāsim ibn Ma'an (d. 175), a *qāḍī* in Kūfa, has been described as a man who

> "surpassed all his contemporaries by the variety of his information."[204]

196. Zubaydī, *Ṭabaqāt* 70, 71.
197. Yāqūt, *Iršād* 7, 12.
198. Abū Ṭayyib, *Marātib* 86.
199. Baġdādī, *Ḫizāna* 1, 447.
200. Yāqūt, *Iršād* 7, 107f. A different version in Ibn Ḫallikān, *Wafayāt* 4, 589.
201. Fück, *Arabīya* 42.
202. Zajjājī, *Majālis* 254.
203. Baġdādī, *Ta'rīḫ Baġdād* 14, 247.
204. Ibn Ḫallikān, *Wafayāt* 3, 26, n. 4.

He was a pupil of Abū Ḥanīfa, yet under him studied no less a philologist than Ibn al-A‘rabī,[205] and he even finds his way, via the *Ṣiḥāḥ* of Jawharī, into Rabin's *Ancient West Arabian*,[206] as well as into grammatical biographies.[207] He also taught *ḥadīṯ* to ‘Alī ibn Naṣr, better known as a pupil of Ḫalīl.[208] Although none of his many works survives, the tributes that are paid to him must rest on some historical truth, the essence of which seems to be that in [149] the first two thirds of the second century A.H. grammar, law and much else besides were all discussed in the same *milieu* and often by the same people. It is thus a reasonable supposition that Sībawayhi was conversant with legal matters and friendly with legal theoreticians.

There are various items in the *Kitāb* itself which strengthen this impression.

Apart from the methodological terminology which I have shown above to be identical, one purely legal term makes an appearance in the *Kitāb*, namely, استثناء. Sībawayhi says of the unusual direct[(a)] form of the verb in

وألحق الحجاز فأستريحا

that it is allowable on the weak grounds that it is equivalent to a hypothetical event depending on the occurrence of the action of the main verb. In this respect, he says, the meaning is like that of the expression أفعل إن شاء الله which asserts something with the reservation (استثناء) that it may not happen.[209] *Istiṯnā'* is a key term in law, with particular reference to the avoidance of perjury either by enunciating the "exceptive" formula إن شاء الله or simply intending it,[210] and Sīrāfī is probably right to say of its occurrence in the *Kitāb* that it has been borrowed from the lawyers.[211]

It may well have been from the same context as *istiṯnā'* that Sībawayhi drew the example يا ذا الجارية الواطئها أبوه,[(b)] for the verb وطئ, with its convenient ambiguity, is found in one of the oaths which must have given great trouble to conscientious husbands until Šaybānī [150] showed how to get round it.[212] Certainly the sentence[213] الوضيعة أيها البائع can come from no other source but the law, for it simply reproduces the words of the *muḍārib* in a contract of *muḍāraba*.

In another place Sībawayhi gives a long string of examples all of which are legal expressions:

205. Ibn al-Nadīm, *Fihrist* 109.
206. Op. cit. 94–95.
207. E.g., Zubaydī, *Ṭabaqāt* 146.
208. Ibn Ḥajar, *Tahḏīb* 7, 390.
209. *Kitāb* 1, 399/448.
210. E.g., Šaybānī, *Maḫārij*, first Chapter .
211. Jahn, *Kitāb* 1, §252, n. 21.
212. Šaybānī, *Maḫārij* 45.
213. *Kitāb* 1, 284/326.

قولك بعت الشاء شاةً ودرهمًا وقامرته درهمًا في الدرهم وبعته داري ذراعًا بدرهم وبعت البرّ قفيزين بدرهم وأخذت زكاة ماله درهمًا لكل أربعين درهمًا وبيّنت له حسابه بابًا بابًا وتصدّقت بمالي درهمًا درهمًا [214]

This serves as a useful reminder that it is not a mere coincidence that "Zayd" and "ʿAmr," the two heroes of the *Kitāb*, should spend so much of their time buying clothes, selling houses, counting dirhams, waiting "until the sun rises," hunting, and pursuing other such pastimes, for all of these activities are found in legal contexts, either because they are acts of commerce or because the *šarīʿa* is concerned with them. Although it might seem obvious that a student of a language should choose examples which reflect the daily life of its speakers, it can also be said with much truth that some of the examples one finds in the works of modern linguists scarcely breathe with any of the life that we find in Sībawayhi's illustrations.

Another expression with a legal ring to it is the proverb قضيّة ولا أبا حسن, meaning "A case, and no Abū Ḥasan [to judge it],"[215] Abū Ḥasan referring to ʿAlī.[a] We might also include here such expressions [151] as له علمٌ علمُ الفقهاء[216] and أمّا جُهْدَ رأيي[217] which are presumably clichés, the latter being redolent of Ḥanafī style.

There is no need to stress that كم منكم شاهدٌ على فلان[218] is a legal expression, and perhaps we may also add إنّ في ألف درهم لَضربٌ[219] "Indeed there will be a minting up to 1000 dirhams."[a] Here, too, belongs the proverbial expression بَيْعَ المَلَطى لا عهدَ ولا عقدَ[220], "a *malaṭā* sale, with no bond and no contract."[b]

On one occasion Sībawayhi uses a legal example in a most interesting way: speaking of the need to start a sentence with something known to the listener, he says that it is no good saying رجلٌ ذاهبٌ , you must add something like رجلٌ من بني فلان سائرٌ . In the same way when you are selling a house you do not simply say حدٌّ كذا وحدٌّ كذا, but you say حدٌّ منها كذا وحدٌّ منها كذا, where منها makes حدٌّ precise enough to be comprehensible.[221] It needs no emphasis that the sale of a house requires a definition of the extent of the property, which is a legal way of making a vague thing specific, so that Sībawayhi's example offers a very real parallel between the grammatical and legal processes.[c]

Other legal examples in the *Kitāb* include أتي الأميرَ لا يقطعُ اللصّ (1, 402/453), حضر القاضيَ امرأةٌ (1, 202/235), عليه شَعرُ كلبين دَيْنًا (1, 257/298), إنّ ألفًا في دراهمك بيضٌ (1, 245/285), and there are many others which attest to the legal and commercial realities of Sībawayhi's time, but

214. *Kitāb* 1, 165/196.
215. Ibid. 310/355.
216. *Kitāb* 1, 151/181.
217. Id. 1, 418/470.
218. Id. 1, 256/297.
219. Id. 1, 99/119.
220. Id. 1. 115/137.
221. Id. 1, 137/165.

[152] I hope the impression of a legal background is now strong enough to be taken as established. I have found several fragments of *ḥadīṯ* in the *Kitāb*, though it has been averred that the *Kitāb* contains no *ḥadīṯ* material,[222] or at the most only one *ḥadīṯ*.[223] There is also reason to suspect that some of Sībawayhi's chapters, particularly §93 (1, 167/197) and those dealing with *laqab*s, *nisba*s, *kunya*s and the *ẓurūf*, may have been constructed with the lawyers in mind.

It occurs to me, in conclusion, that I have made no attempt to prove that, of the two disciplines, law did in fact, pre-date grammar. I have already hinted that it is essential to assume this fact,[224] which I take for granted on the grounds that the converse is absurd and that simultaneity is historically impossible. But I may cite Gibb as one who also presumes that law preceded grammar in Islam,[225] and for good textual proof I would point to the fact that, although the topics of both law[226] and language occur in Ibn al-Muqaffaʿ, the legal material shows the same vocabulary as later usage, whereas what he has to say about language reveals absolutely no knowledge of any grammatical ideas. This, by the way, in spite of the fact that he is supposed to have met Ḫalīl.[227]

It seems probable that Sībawayhi, having met lawyers and traditionists[(a)] and learnt something of their methods, decided to apply them thoroughly and consistently to the problem of Arabic grammar. In doing so he took their analogical method and their notion of permissibility, and added [153] the ethical notions good, bad, right and wrong (which the lawyers did not use to any great extent) to provide both formal and functional criteria for his grammar. The transfer of ethical terms to linguistic contexts is moderately developed in the writings of Ibn al-Muqaffaʿ, and there is every reason to suppose that for Sībawayhi it was a natural and inevitable extension of an innate Arab attitude. The credit must go to Sībawayhi, however, for the conviction which he seems to bring to the rigorous and all-embracing application of these borrowed ideas to Arabic, and the prudence which he shows in attempting to provide rational explanations for a non-rational process. In the ensuing chapters we shall see how the *Kitāb* expounds this ethically-based type of grammar with complete inner consistency and in accordance with principles which were obviously consciously developed to meet the requirements of this new system.

222. Ḥadīṯī, *Abniyat al-ṣarf* 64.
223. Zakī, *Al-Ḥayāt al-adabiyya* 184.
224. Above p. [96].
225. Gibb, *Studies* 15.
226. E.g., *Kalīla* 61 (S. 37, Y. 82), *Al-adab al-Kabīr* 104.
227. Zubaydī, *Ṭabaqāt* 45.

Summary

[326] In the absence of all evidence of a Greek borrowing, the suggestion is made that Arabic grammar derives its principles from those of law.

Sībawayhi was not the first to use legal and ethical terms about language: the ethical writers frequently deal with speech. There follows an examination of the key terms of Islamic ethics, law and Arabic grammar, based mainly on the writings of ʿAbd al-Ḥamīd and Ibn al-Muqaffaʿ in ethics, and Šaybānī and Abū Yūsuf in law.

It emerges that the terms *mawḍiʿ*, *manzila*, *qiyās*, *ḥasan*, *qabīḥ*, *mustaqīm*, *jāʾiz* and *wajh* are all used in each of the three spheres in the same way.

Other terms, such as *sabīl*, *laġw*, *saʿa*, *ittisāʿ*, *badal* and *ʿiwaḍ* show themselves to be used in grammar in meanings which correspond exactly with their legal connotation.

Furthermore all three disciplines are remarkably free from loan words (there are only *qiyās* and *ʿilla* of these), and the conclusion is drawn that the self-sufficiency of vocabulary is proof of self-sufficiency of origin in the matter of grammar.

Historical evidence is then adduced to show that lawyers and grammarians were in frequent contact. Sībawayhi, in fact, came to Baṣra to study not grammar, but law. As depicted by Fück, Arabic was in an unstable state at the time, and this, together with Islam's increasing dependence on the past, especially in law, made grammar an inevitability. But this grammar is not an instrument of purism, for purism alone is insufficient to account for the lengths to which Sībawayhi goes in his arguments.

Several grammarians known to be active in law, and lawyers interested in grammar are listed, and the chapter concludes with examples of sentences of purely legal origin which are to be found in the *Kitāb*.

Addenda to Chapter Three

The contents of this chapter formed the basis of Carter 1972a. Since then the works of Talmon and Versteegh have added much detail (see ch. 1 heading): in particular Versteegh 1993 offers an alternative origin for much of the early grammatical terminology, namely the writings of the Qur'anic exegetes, particularly those of Kūfa.

[94] (a) Zakī gives Suyūṭī's *Iqtirāḥ* as his source, but this could not be traced. The connection between law and grammar is, however, well recognised, and forms the whole topic of the *Ṣāḥibī* of Ibn Fāris. Although the parallel is not complete, we can also mention here the formulation by Suyūṭī, *Muzhir* 2, 312, that the sciences of lexicography (*luġa*) and Ḥadīṯ "are brothers, which flow from the same valley," *aḫawāni yajriyānī min wādin wāḥid*. See also [313] (b).

[97] (a) More unjustifiable sarcasm: Weil's edition of the *Inṣāf* is a treasury of late grammatical thought.

[102] (a) I.e., "magnification" as in "my soul doth magnify the Lord" of the Christian liturgy.

[104] (a) The specimens given here from Sībawayhi are merely for illustration: in Chapter Five, especially [212]–[216] we shall see how Sībawayhi identifies every type of *mawḍiʿ* in which parts of an utterance can occur, listed in [209].

[104] (b) It is all the more annoying that elsewhere Jahn translates *mawḍiʿ*as "syntaktische Stellung" 1, 372/448, i.e., "syntactic position," which is absolutely correct.

[104] (c) The publication history of *Kalīla wa-Dimna* is not helpful, and material is taken from three editions, none of which agrees entirely with the others. The spelling Sheikho is retained (though Cheikho would be more correct) to distinguish between his ed. (S) and that of Cairo (C).

[105] (a) Remarkably the same scene is presented in the *Kitāb* in a purely linguistic context: even a blind man, says Sībawayhi, can use the verb *raʾā* "see" in the sense of "consider, regard" as a sentential verb, and say *raʾaytu zaydan il-ṣāliḥa* "I regarded Zayd as the good man." (*Kitāb* 1, 13/1, 18, cf. Carter 2007, 40). Note that Sībawayhi had no special term for such verbs, which the later grammarians called *afʿāl al-qalb* "verbs of the heart," cf. [293] and Carter 2011, 123.

[107] (a) The most important feature of *manzila* in grammar (and also in its legal antecedents) is that parity of status can only exist between elements of different form classes. The most obvious case is that of the *manzilat ism wāḥid* "the status of a single noun" enjoyed by a number of complex syntactic units, and associated with the theories of Ḫalīl, see above [38]–[45]. See also [256]ff on the different status of the true and pseudo-*iḍāfa* in this regard.

See Baalbaki 1999b on "coalescence," his term for assigning the same status to elements of different kinds.

[108] (a) Note the words *rafīʿ* "high" and *ḫāfiḍ* "low" in some of the quotations, possibly not unrelated to the same terms in the context of case and mood inflections, cf. [298] (a).

[111] (a) Wansborough 1977, 166 presents Ibn al-Muqaffaʿ as "what must be the earliest, or almost the earliest" reference to analogy in Arabic. Be that as it may, it helps to anchor this development in the period immediately preceding Sībawayhi.

[113] (a) 207 times in all its conjugated forms, as we now know from Troupeau 1976! On its origins see below [115] and note (c).

The most important feature of this word in the *Kitāb* is that it is only one of at least six terms used by Sībawayhi to deal with similarities and regularities in language, the others being *ḍāraʿa* and cognates, *šabbaha* and cognates, *naẓīr*, *miṯl*, *ka-* and *jarā majrā/ujriya mujrā* (see Carter 1998b, 5). Versteegh 1980 gives a good account of the history of *qiyās*, though the post-Sībawayhian developments lie outside the scope of this thesis.

One aspect of *qiyās* and its concomitant terms which is not given appropriate emphasis by Versteegh is that for Sībawayhi analogy was not limited to the activities of "grammarians" or observers of the language, but was practised by the speakers themselves. Indeed speakers are always making comparisons between elements even if they were not entirely identical, see examples below in [173]–[175]. Thus when Sībawayhi instructs his reader: *fa-ʿalā hāḏā fa-qis hāḏā l-naḥw* "so on this [model] make an analogy for this way [of speaking]"(quoted below, [159]) he is not talking to grammarians but to those who wish to imitate correctly the regular language. Likewise when he declares *lā yanbaġī laka an taqīsa ʿalā l-šāḏḏi l-munkari fī l-qiyāsi* (1, 351/398, quoted [114]) "you ought not to base analogies on rarities which have no known analogical forms," again he is not talking to grammarians.

A second feature of analogies of all kinds is that they can be circular, or perhaps reciprocal would be more accurate, see [188] (b). A simple example from Carter 1998b, 6f will suffice: the syntactic "resemblance" *muḍāraʿa* of the imperfect verb to the agent noun accounts for the independent and dependent inflections of the verb, while the same resemblance in the other direction accounts for the verbal operation of the agent noun when it keeps its *tanwīn* (as in *ḍāribun zaydan*). Clearly these bi-directional similarities are perceived by the speakers, and have nothing to do with the construction of an ideal theoretical form of the language by grammarians.

[114] (a) See Baalbaki 1989 for a special study of the term *aṣl* "basic [form]" in the *Kitāb*; it also occurs again below in [159], [237] and [296].

[114] (b) Here *al-munkar* follows Būlāq, where Derenbourg has *al-munkasir fī l-qiyās* "where the standard is broken." For *al-šāḏḏ*, here translated "rarities," a more appropriate rendering might be "the abnormal," in keeping with the modern usage of this word.

[115] (a) So for that matter is Wansborough 1977, 167, and they are surely not the only ones.

[115] (b) "Say to my servants they should say that which is best," i.e., in their disputes with the unbelievers. Here the fem. *allatī* is taken to imply *al-kalima* "the [word] which is best."

[115] (c) Schacht's etymology has not been challenged, that *qiyās* reflects the Hebrew *hiqqiš* and cognates, a calque of Greek *sumballein*, lit. "to beat together," referring to an exegetical technique for comparing similar biblical passages (see M. Bernard, *EI²*, art. 'Ḳiyās,' published 1980, citing Schacht 1959, 99, in turn based on Margoliouth 1910).

Versteegh 1980, 14, accepts this etymology without comment but relegates it to a footnote, and it plays no role in his argument. For Sībawayhi, however, its origins are irrelevant: it was part of the inherited vocabulary available to him, and what is important is how he himself used it, see [113] (a) above. It is difficult to see the relevance of the much later loan word *qānūn* (Versteegh, op cit. 20ff) to *qiyās* in general and to Sībawayhi in particular, as there is no sign of this term in the *Kitāb*.

[122] (a) The original text could not be consulted, but the Arabic for "latitude" here is almost certainly *saʿa*, cf. the same concept in Sībawayhi below, [130] and [195]f.

[123] (a) See [218]ff.

[123] (b) "It is not right that you should give the listener information about something he cannot identify, for this does not put him in the same status of knowledge as yours." This is the Būlāq reading: for *fī l-maʿrifa* the Derenbourg text has *wa-huwa l-maʿrifa*,

i.e., "the same status as yours, namely, having knowledge." The point at issue, *istiqāma*, is unaffected by this variation. The quotation appears again below, [219].

As the terminology of definiteness shows, the Arab concept is one of presence or absence of knowledge, see [250] (a) As far as predication is concerned this knowledge is crucial, since there is no existential copula verb (see Carter 1997) and the usual boundary marker in predication is the change from a definite, i.e., known subject to an indefinite, i.e., not yet known predicate.

The parallel between our concepts of the "given" and the "new" in predication theory is clear, and there is a similar parallel in cases where the predicate happens to be more definite than the subject. This is particularly common with locative predicates, e.g., "a man is in the house," see [270] (a), and in some languages a special structure has evolved, typically in English "there is a man in the house," while Arabic, lacking a copula, merely inverts the subject and predicate (*taqdīm wa-ta'ḫīr*), thus *fī l-dāri rajulun* "in the house [is] a man," thereby privileging the Def. - Indef. sequence of the equational sentence and, by the same token, bearing out Sībawayhi's observation above that the speaker must start with something known to the the listener.

The same rule applies when agents are less definite than their objects or complements, and there is an excellent illustration of this kind of inversion in Sūra 112 vs. 4 *lam yakun lahu kufuwan aḥadun* lit. "there has never been to Him, as someone equal, anyone," i.e., "there has never been anyone equal to Him." Curiously Sībawayhi in *Kitāb* 1, 21/27 does not specifically evoke the definiteness principle for this verse, but instead explains that the word order was inspired by the "care" *'ināya* and "concern" *ihtimām* of the speaker (God!) to name the elements in order of importance. What is interesting here is that the sequence "Him," "someone equal" and "anyone [at all]" exactly reflects the hierarchy of definiteness both in Arabic and in general linguistic theory (Carter 2015, 38).

[127] (a) "Yellowed pages" renders *al-ṣaḥīfa l-ṣafrā'* literally, according to some Western image of ancient wisdom on faded pages, but might just as well mean "gold[en] leaves," expressing the value of the contents.

[128] (a) Or "without trying to find some acceptable way out of it." Jahn *ad loc.* is going too far to render *wajh* as "Analogie."

[129] (a) For *sabīl* perhaps "remedy" would be technically closer, i.e., "[legal] way [to deal with the issue]."

[129] (b) "A statement which is null and void, and has no [legal] effect."

[135] (a) The legal school of Abū Ḥanīfa was notorious for its specious and casuistic reasoning, cf. the disparaging remark of a commentator on Ibn Mu'ṭī (d. 628/1231) that his over-schematic argument "followed the Ḥanafī school," (Carter 2003, 180f and n. 28).

[135] (b) As quoted by Abū Ḥanīfa, the Ḥadīṯ reads "there will enter Paradise a people who are barefoot, naked, bad-smelling, having been scorched (?) by the Fire." However, there are problems with the final verb, translated provisionally as "scorched." The Baġdādī source could not be checked, but Ibn al-Anbārī has *aḥšathum* in the printed text, clearly a misprint, as the editor glosses it as *iḥtašama* in the footnote, "the burning of skin

and bone." Furthermore, an online source, quoting , *Aḫbār al-muṣaḥḥifīn* of al-ʿAskarī (d. 382/933, Brockelmann, *GAL*, S 1, 193), reads it as *aḥmašathum*, for which the dictionaries offer no sensible meaning, nor does it appear in the *Nihāya* of Ibn al-Aṯīr. The most likely reading is *qad imtaḥašū bi-l-nāri* "having been burnt by the fire," which we do find in the *Nihāya*, under *maḥaša*, also quoted by the editor of Ibn al-Anbārī. As far as this thesis is concerned the issue is irrelevant, since we are concerned with the incorrect *muntinīn*, but the reading *aḥmašathum* has been adopted in the thesis text precisely because it looks wrong anyway, hence would qualify to be mentioned in the *Aḫbār al-muṣaḥḥifīn*.

[137] (a) Suyūṭī is here quoting from the *Ṣāḥibī* of Ibn Fāris, 191, which should have been picked up in the original thesis.

[138] (a) The phrase is inspired by Wansborough 1978, 141.

[138] (b) Maḫzūmī is here quoting a manuscript version of *Maʿānī* 2, 202.

[141] (a) The reference to Ibn Saʿd could not be checked: Sezgin, *GAS* 9, 44 cites a different edition, VI, 262.

[145] (a) At least as certain as we can be, given that they were contemporaries, and numerous encounters are reported in the *Majālis* literature.

[146] (a) This is the middle of three lines by an unknown poet, see Fischer/Braünlich 1945, 222 (under *ašʾamu*), Yaʿqūb 869 (*aẓlamu*) for citations. It is not found in the *Kitāb*, but its appearance in the *Majālis* is certainly earlier than those listed in the above sources.

[147] (a) Exactly what is meant by *šurṭī* here is not clear, but some kind of "policeman" is the most likely. In spite of being listed as a grammarian in Zubaydī, *Ṭabaqāt* 51, this person was not admitted to the company of grammarians in Sezgin *GAS* 9 but is mentioned several times in *GAS* 1 as a transmitter of Ḥadīṯ.

[149] (a) Here "direct" must seem very obscure for the *manṣūb* verb, or "subjunctive." It is replaced now by "dependent," see further [298].

The hemistich can be translated as "and I will reach the Ḥijāz and then rest" (see Fischer/Braünlich 1945, 54, Yaʿqūb 1992, 162, for this very frequently quoted line.

[149] (b) *Kitāb* 1, 208/243. See also [195] (a) for the "latitude" by which this ambiguous verb enabled the lawyers to wriggle out of promises.

[150] (a) The example has already appeared above, [48].

[151] (a) The translation is that proposed by Jahn. However, Lane, following *Siḥāḥ* and *Tāj al-ʿarūs*, renders it "Verily I have to make a journey for the sake of, or on account of, a thousand dirhems," according to the idiom *ḍaraba fī l-tijāra* "travel on business." To complicate the picture, Sībawayhi invokes, on this same page, another idiomatic use of *maḍrab*, the moment when a she-camel is ready to be mounted by a stallion. We cannot know whether the Arabs charged a fee for this, as is normal in horse-breeding nowadays, but if so, there would be a third possible translation of Sībawayhi's example.

[151] (b) The transliteration *malaṭī* in the original thesis has been corrected to *malaṭā*, following Jahn's reference to this word in *Lisān al-ʿArab*. However, the word itself is unexplained: a connection with the Anatolian town of Malaṭya seems unlikely.

[151] (c) Real life applications of this formula are in Khoury 1993, nos. 55 to 58, regarding the sale of land and various properties, where we find the boundaries expressed as *ḥadd*. Two of the documents are dated to the third/ninth centuries.

[152] (a) The substantive corpus of Ḥadīṯ has not been touched at all in the research for this thesis: we might expect that it would contain many close parallels to the ethical principles and criteria expounded in the early legal texts and the works of Ibn al-Muqaffaʿ and ʿAbd al-Ḥamīd discussed above.

Chapter Four
"Grammar" and "*naḥw*"

In order to understand what grammar was to Sībawayhi it is necessary to understand what he meant by *naḥw*. It has already been pointed out that our word grammar is not a translation of the Arabic, either in significance or in substance, nor is it even strictly accurate to say, as Flügel did, that *naḥw* forms only one part of Arabic grammar, the other being *ṣarf*.[1] Lastly it is also to be remembered that Sībawahi did not mean by *naḥw* what subsequent Arab usage took it to mean.[2] The inevitable result of approaching the *Kitāb* from any of these fallacious standpoints will be to misunderstand Sībawayhi, as I propose to demonstrate for all three misconceptions in turn.

Any grammatical metalanguage is necessarily an abstraction, words about words and nothing more.[(a)] It must, therefore, be of peculiar significance that the metalanguage of Arabic grammar should use the same words as are current in ethical contexts. To use words which normally apply to human behaviour as terms of grammar is tantamount to declaring that language is a form of behaviour.[(b)] This is important because there are other ways of regarding language, e.g., as applied logic, as a system of coded signals, as a game, as an aesthetic monologue and so on, which makes Sībawayhi's choice automatically significant in that it straightway tells us what, in his opinion, language was not.

[155] Language, for Sībawayhi, was behaviour: behaviour is a way of doing things, and *naḥw* means exactly that—a way of speaking. Because of this, the act of speaking is judged by the same standards that Arabic uses to judge other acts, as "good" (*ḥasan*), "bad" (*qabīḥ*), "right" (*mustaqīm*) and "wrong" (*muḥāl*). For the same reason the different processes of speech, e.g., describing, negating, constructing, excepting, calling etc. are all clearly recognised for what they are, which is acts of the speaker, and denoted by verbal nouns, e.g., *waṣf, nafy, binā,' istiṯnā,' nidā,'* respectively. It is only a matter of refinement that the social act of interrupting someone else's speech and the linguistic act of putting

1. Flügel, *Gram. Schulen* 12.
2. See above pp. [61]f.

an adjective where a noun should be both turn out to be ethically bad.[3] They are both behavioural items and therefore susceptible to behavioural criteria.

What is particularly striking about behaviour as a concept in Arabic is that there seems to be no single word for it, but instead, it is denoted by several words all of which have the same literal meaning. This has, of course, long been realised in the field of law: Vesey-Fitzgerald has written of the word *šarīʿa* that it

> originally meant the path or track by which camels were taken to water, and so by transfer the path ordained by God by which men may achieve salvation. This conception of a path or way of life is very common in early Islām. It occurs again in the word *sunna* and in the name of the earliest Māliki law book, the *Muwaṭṭa'* of Mālik himself.[4]

[156] An example from Abū Yūsuf shows that the image was still strong in his time:

اعمل لأجل مفضوض وسبيل مسلوك وطريق مأخوذ وعمل محفوظ ومنهل مورود [5]

and in the space of a few lines Marwān, in advising his son ʿAbdullāh, speaks of "soundness of behaviour" (صحة الطريق), "the path of truth" (منحى الحق), "a way to imprison" (سبيلاً لمحبس) and "a way to punish" (مجاز لعقوبة).

Apart from the الصراط المستقيم of the Qur'ān we have also encountered مسالك, محجّة and مذهب in ʿAbd al-Ḥamīd.[6] To these we can add قصد as in

مشْي القصد من دواعي المودّة [7]

and it is enough to point to the literal meanings of such metaphors as نهج, صواب, بلاغة, دليل, أراد, مجرى, and أدب to show that Arabic has particularly exploited this possibility of its vocabulary. The linear motion that all these words imply is the basis of Arabic ethical terminology in that it supplies the exclusive metaphor in which human behaviour is expressed. There seems to be, for example, no concept in early Arabic of a "body politic" in which society is anatomised into members. Significantly the metaphors of animal behaviour offered by *Kalīla wa Dimna* remain parables even to this day. Only the herd (رعيّة) seems to have achieved metaphorical status in [157] early Arabic sociology, which metaphor is reinforced by its synonym السوقة. Arabic is thus relatively poor in this sphere, though it makes up for it by the number of linear direction-words it employs. True there are "classes" (طبقات) and, rarely, "ranks" (مراتب), but these are never defined in the early

3. Cf. above p. [118].
4. Vesey-Fitzgerald, in Khadduri, *Law in the Middle East* 1, 86.
5. Abū Yūsuf, *Ḫarāj* 3.
6. Above, pp. [112] and [127].
7. Ibn al-Muqaffaʿ, *Al-adab al-Kabīr* 111.

writers, who stick to the simpler division into الخاصّة and العامّة, and there is the expected distinction between "high" and "low" status, but these, too, are not developed beyond the notion that functions increase with status. Islamic ethics at this early stage is thus seen to be based on a very simple framework whose principle concepts may be briefly stated as follows: man's life is a movement along a line (طريقة, سنّة etc.) which may be plotted on a vertical axis of status (منزلة) and a horizontal axis of function (موضع). To waver from the (ideally) straight line (الصراط المستقيم) is wrong (محال) and bad (قبيح) because it brings about an incongruity of status and function, the good man being one whose status and function are in perfect accord. Life, in the Arab view, is in the deepest sense a *sīra*, a journey.

I have not done justice to the Arab ethical writers by thus reducing their speculations to the form of a graph, but I hope that its implications will be found to apply to any particular ethical case. It has the advantage of emphasising the linearity of behaviour as the Arabic metaphor expresses it, and, as I have formulated it, the scheme is also very apt for comparison with the system of Sībawayhi.

The linearity of Sībawayhi's grammatical metaphor is clearly evident in the fact that *naḥw* in the *Kitāb* is often replaced or accompanied by synonyms,[a] [158] of which I give some examples:[a]

1) *wajh* and cognates

1, 161/192	كذلك توجّه سائرَ الحروف من ذا الباب
1, 316/360	هذا وجه الكلام
2, 423/381	الوجه في هذا النحو الواو
2, 257/242	فكذلك هذه الأبواب فعلى نحو ما ذكرت لك فوجّهْها
1, 34/44	هذا ضعيف فالوجه الأكثر والأعرف النصب
1, 126/151	وإن شئت كان على الوجه الآخر

2) *ṭarīqa*[b]

1, 234/237	ليس هذا طريقة الكلام
1, 258/300	فلزم هذا هذه الطريقة في كلامهم كما لزمت إنّ هذه الطريقة في كلامهم
2, 413/373	فعلى هذه الطريقة فأجرِ هذا النحو
2, 272/253	فهو لا يتغيّر كما أنّ فَعَلَ منه على طريقة واحدة
2, 206/199	ليس ذا لهنّ طريقة يَجرين عليها في الكلام

3) *maḏhab* and cognates

1, 176/203	وجعل مِن فيها بمنزلتها في الاسم وهذا مذهب قويّ
2, 315/288	أذهبوها في الوقف كما ذهبت في الوصل
2, 102/104	فهذا أقيس والأول مذهب
2, 391/354	الأولى في منزلة الواو في فردوس وكلا الوجهين صواب ومذهب

4) *sabīl*

2, 241/229	فاعرف هذا النحو فأجرِه على سبيله
2, 298/275	وجعلوا هذا سبيلها ليفرّقوا بينها وبين الألف

[159]

2, 301/277	ولم يكونوا ليفتحوا فيلتبس بالنصب لأنّ سبيل هذا أن يُكسر
2, 91/93	فهذا سبيل ما كان من المنقوص على ثلاثة أحرف

5) *šar‘*

1, 207/242	لم يجعل الآخر حالا وقع فيه الأول لكنّه أثنى عليه وجعلهما شرعًا سواءً وسوّى بينهما في الإجراء

6) *sunna*

1, 62/74	إلا أنّ القراءة لا تخالف لأنّها سنّة

7) *jarā*, *majrā* etc.

1, 60/72	وقد يجري هذا في زيد وعمرو وعلى هذا الحد
1, 177/208	فأُجري الدهرُ هذا المُجرى فأَجرِ الأشياء كما أجروها
1, 291/334	فإن رفعت الواو تركتها على حالها لأنّه حرف أجري على هذا الأصل
2, 157/155	فلمّا كانت كذلك أجريت مُجراها في الوقف

If we compare these with the use of *naḥw* in the *Kitāb*, which is illustrated by the following as well as in the above instances:

1, 207/242	سترى هذا النحو في كلامهم
1, 202/236	هذا النحو كثير في القرآن
1, 268/310	لأنّ الشيء إذا كثر في كلامهم كان له نحو ليس لغيره مما هو مثله
1, 313/357	ومن هذا النحو قول الشاعر ...

2, 167/163	فعلى هذا فقِسْ هذا النحو
2, 280/260	فيشمّ كأنّه ينحو نحو فُعِلَ فكذا نحَوا نحو الياء
2, 230/219	وهما في المعنى نحوٌ من الوجع

[160] we see at once that, although in the *Kitāb naḥw* far outnumbers the other terms in the list, it is still not a specific term for "grammar," but only one of several terms denoting a "way" of speaking. It is never used in the sense of a science of grammar, either as if Sībawayhi regarded *naḥw* as a native description for the discipline he practised, or as if it were meant to correspond to anything like the *téchnè grammatikè*, and on these grounds alone I can confidently dismiss any pretensions that, as technical terms, *naḥw* and *téchnè grammatikè* are linked. When he is not using *naḥw* in the meaning of "like," "sort," or "towards," Sībawayhi simply uses it in the same way as he uses the other direction-words, to indicate a "way" of speaking, exactly as such words occur in the ethical writers to mean a "way" of acting.

The second fallacy falls by the same token: our modern distinction between *naḥw*, syntax, and *ṣarf*, morphology,[(a)] certainly fits the structure of the *Kitāb* but not its terminology. For one thing, *ṣarf* is not used in the *Kitāb* to mean morphology, but only to denote the act of giving a word its full declension, in which sense the term *ṣarf* might profitably be related to its commercial origins and translated as "giving full currency." And for another thing, the term *naḥw*, as well as being devoid of any general technical meaning, as I have shown, is, if anything, more common in the second volume of the *Kitāb* than in the first. The reason is simple: morphology provides infinitely more opportunities for the exercise of analogy than does syntax, and so *naḥw* in the meaning [161] of "like" and "sort" is bound to occur more frequently in morphological contexts, just as we have seen to be the case with the term *qiyās* itself.[8] For Sībawayhi, then, the "way" of speaking comprehended not only the putting together of words but the putting together of parts of words. This is why *ḥarf* is a unit of such indeterminate size in the *Kitāb*: it can denote anything from a sentence to a single sound because all that falls within the scope of *naḥw*. Furthermore, all the methods and criteria which Sībawayhi uses in the first volume—status and function, analogy, good/bad, right/wrong etc.—are applied with equal ease to the morphological problems of the second volume, so that there can be no grounds for maintaining that Sībawayhi divided his studies into two branches.[(a)]

That the later Arabic meaning of *naḥw* is not that which we find in the *Kitāb* should now be clear. To take, for example, Qudāma's phrase[9] صناعة النحو and to try to translate it on the basis of what نحو means in the *Kitāb*, would be an instructive penance for those who simply extrapolate the later meaning of *naḥw* into the *Kitāb*, particularly for those who,

8. Above p. [113].
9. Above p. [62].

having done so, fail to notice that the modern term simply will not fit any of Sībawayhi's meanings.[(b)] One of the most glaring examples of this anachronistic approach in a place where it is least excusable is the recent study by Reuschel. In a chapter dealing with the fundamentals of Arabic grammar Reuschel, ignoring the *Kitāb* almost completely, reproduces the stale generalisations of Weil's introduction to the *Inṣāf*. The unfortunate result is a description of Arabic grammar which quite fails [162] to accord with the principles of the book about which Reuschel is writing and which (presumably) he had closely studied.

The cure for each of the three fallacies is a long and arduous one. Whatever it was that Sībawayhi understood by *naḥw*, and whatever may have been his concept of "grammar," the only way to find out is to read the *Kitāb*. There is a minimum of formal exposition of his principles, and the treatment of each grammatical problem mostly proceeds from axiomatic definitions which would all have to be gathered up to give any overall picture of a Sībawayhian grammar. Nevertheless, the *Kitāb* constitutes the only definition of what Sībawayhi conceived to be grammar, and it is my hope in the remainder of this chapter and in the ensuing chapters to set out and examine the principles of grammar as they are found in the *Kitāb*.

Everything I have so far said about the *Kitāb* points towards a sustained social metaphor as the basis for its grammatical system. Not only are the criteria the same as those of ethics and law, and not only are the parts of speech personified into "sisters," "mothers" and "daughters,"[(a)] but there are also numerous other personifications which, since some of them have already been pointed out by Weiss,[10] I will content myself with merely listing here. Weiss notes that the *Kitāb* uses the terms *ʿamila fī*, meaning "to have an effect on something," that words are said to have a "power" (*quwwa*), an "effect" (*taʾṯir*, but I have not found it in the *Kitāb*)[(b)] and that a word may be "occupied" (*mašġūl*) or even "idle" (*fāriġ*). His investigation goes no further, and so I may add the, perhaps, obvious personifications of "sound" (*ṣaḥīḥ*) and [163] "defective" (*muʿtall*), "dominant" (*ġālib*), "self-sufficient" (*mustaġnī*), "be loyal" (*aḫlaṣa*), "transitive" (*mutaʿaddī*), "going beyond the limit" (*yujāwiz al-ḥadd*), "being well-established" (*tamakkun*), and "full currency" (*taṣarruf*) and even "dead" (*mayyit*) and "alive" (*ḥayy*) as examples of the extent to which the parts of speech themselves are personified and their behaviour expressed in human terms.

We have, as a result, two parallel processes which come under Sībawayhi's consideration: the behaviour of the speaker as he uses his language, and the internal "behaviour" of the words which make up what he says. Both are extensions of the ethical methods that I have shown to be used by Ibn al-Muqaffaʿ, and we may now make a useful distinction between the transference of ethical ideas to the domain of man's linguistic behaviour, which remains a perceptible social act, and the problem of the behaviour of speech itself, to which ethical methods can only apply as pure metaphor. The latter adaptation of ethical ideas, having regard to the thoroughness with which it is carried out in a work

10. Weiss, *ZDMG* 64, 387.

which evidently has no antecedents worth speaking of suggests that Sībawayhi himself may justly claim credit for the invention of what is now Arabic grammar. Although he was certainly not the first to describe speech as "good," "bad," "right" and "wrong," etc., because the external aspects of speech had long been part of the purview of the ethical writers, there are good grounds for believing, as I have already suggested,[11] that the internal aspects of Arabic speech had never been studied before in the way that Sībawayhi studies them.

[164] The novelty of Sībawayhi's method may perhaps be inferred by examining those curious terms *raf'*, *naṣb*, *jarr* and others like them, which have never been satisfactorily accounted for.[(a)] The explanation I am about to propose is based on the assumption that this group of terms represents a more primitive stratum than the criteria and nomenclature of the sort represented by *ḥasan, muḥāl, waṣf, istiṯnā,' nidā'* etc. What distinguishes the two groups most clearly is the fact that what I have taken to be the earlier terms bear no obvious relationship to anything grammatical, while the terms in the newer group are unmistakably descriptive in their meanings. The archaic group comprises the following terms: *raf', naṣb, jarr, ḫafḍ, jazm, binā,' isnād, 'aṭf, imāla, iḍāfa, i'timād, ta'līq, sabab*. Two things deserve to be noticed about these words. In the first place it is curious that, although their technical meanings are so divergent, their literal meanings should have so much in common. Thus *raf'* and *ḫafḍ*, *naṣb* and *imāla*, are orthodox antonyms, *isnād, iḍāfa, imāla, i'timād*, and *'aṭf* are virtually synonyms, *ta'līq* and *sabab* are close in meaning, while the real-life activities represented by *raf', naṣb, jarr* and *jazm* might all be said to belong to the process of building, *binā.'* This last word invites comparison with another famous metaphor in Arabic philology, and it is sufficient to list such terms as *bayt, miṣrā', watad, sabab* and the word *'arūḍ* itself, to realise that our group of enigmatic grammatical terms might allow themselves to be explained in the same way as those of prosody. I will go no further, however, than to suggest that the literal meanings of these grammatical terms make it probable that they were all conceived [165] as one unified metaphor, as were the terms of prosody.

But, secondly, they have another peculiarity which connects them more closely with Ḫalīl, and thus strengthens the belief that they represent an early stage in the history of grammar. *Naṣb* and *imāla* in the *Kitāb* are antonyms in the purely phonological sense, and there we also find in phonetic contexts the terms *raf', i'timād* and *binā.'*[12] That Ḫalīl had a peculiar interest in phonological problems I have already shown,[13] and I would not regard it as implausible that these terms found their way into the general context of Arabic grammar via some adaptation on the part of Ḫalīl. In this connection it is note-

11. Above p. [34].
12. Cf. Fleischer, *Kl. Schr.* 1, 306, 2, 82 on the phonetic origin of the case names
13. Above p. [44]f.

worthy that among his phonological terminology as listed by Ḫwārizmī[14] there should occur such terms as *najr* (wood-carving), *qaʿr* (tree-felling), *nabra* (a raising) and *iḍjāʿ* (a laying down). We might, then be justified in assuming that it was Ḫalīl's evident *penchant* for "building" metaphors which accounts for the occurrence of such terms as *naṣb* and the like in the *Kitāb*.[(a)]

We should still, however, find it difficult to connect even the metaphorical meaning of these building terms with any grammatical situation, but I believe one explanation may furnish a reason. In the context of Arabic writing we find the term *musnad*, referring to the South Arabian inscriptions, (a loan word,[(b)] and probably not related to *isnād* except by folk-etymology). In the same context we also find *mā'il*[15] and *mustaqīm*[16] and even a *ḫaṭṭ manṣūb*,[17] all of which obviously describe the appearance [166] of the script. There is, moreover, a possibility that *jazm* may be connected with the Syriac *gezmē* ("cut roots") referring to the angular nature of the Kūfic script.[18] We shall, perhaps, never know how a word like *jarr* could ever refer to a grammatical case, but it is easier to think of it as referring to some conformation of written letters, even though the actual shape which elicited this curious term, or any of its fellows, may be impossible to determine. It is certainly not difficult to imagine that *binā,' iḍāfa, ʿaṭf, isnād* etc. do give some sort of literal account of the orthographical situation in which two words might find themselves when linked grammatically. This graphic origin of the older terms of grammar may explain, perhaps, their curious meanings.

If this digression has succeeded in its purpose, two points should emerge. First, some plausible concrete basis for an understanding of the terms will have been provided, which should render a small service to those, such as Jahn, who regard them as untranslatable.[(b)] Second, since this whole process can be assumed to have taken place about the time when the terms *iʿrāb* and *iʿjām* came into use (i.e., before Ru'ba,(a) who uses them in a quotation in the *Kitāb*, 1, 382/430), we can conclude that these terms do belong to a more archaic period than the *Kitāb*. In effect, since Ḫalīl uses them but is never credited with the invention of grammar, we are enabled to perform a simple subtraction which leaves Ḫalīl and his primitive phonology on the one hand and Sībawayhi and his new style of [167] grammar on the other, thereby giving a more precise idea than has hitherto been attempted of the exact nature of Sībawayhi's debt to Ḫalīl.

To return to our *mutūn*, we are now in a position to lay down the broad outlines of the grammar devised by Sībawayhi. From the fact that he treats language as behaviour, certain important conclusions follow. Two of these, that the way we speak is in part de-

14. Ḫwārizmī, *Mafātīḥ* 44–6[(c)].
15. Abbott, *North Arabic Script* 23.
16. Id. 22.
17. Id. 33.
18. Abbott, *North Arabic Script* 7.

termined by our listeners, and that the value-criteria of speech are the same as those of any social act, will be dealt with in the next chapter. Three other points remain to be discussed here, and I shall start with the most general.

The similarities between social and linguistic behaviour are too obvious to need emphasis: both are entirely conventional, based on tradition and, in our period, purely synchronic in the sense that no historical development was sought in examining the past, but only guidance for present action. Whatever the term used to denote the course of action thus arrived at, *sunna*, *šarīʿa*, *naḥw*, the very words tell us that they were identical in quality. Sībawayhi, therefore, describes Arabic as a way of speaking just as the lawyers describe Islām as a way of behaving. It is, according to this approach, not even necessary to command or prohibit certain ways of behaving, for it is sufficient to say, as we do in English, "it is not done" or "it is not said," and that is precisely how Sībawayhi describes his hypothetical examples, which he calls *tamṯīl*,(a) and of which he says لا يُتكلم به.[19]

[168] A more extended example of this method of treating language as a process, one might also say an activity, is offered by the following extract:

> Know that not every word after which the verb is expressed has its verb elided. On the contrary, you suppress only after those words and in those places where the Arabs do so, and express what they express, and treat in the way that they do these things, which they lighten as having the same status as those parts of sentences(a) which they elide, and other things in speech. Not every word has something either elided or retained, such as يكُ and يكون and لم أبَل and لم أبال, and that does not bring them to do it with other similar words,(b) nor does it bring them to restore something and say أوْمُرْ for مُرْ or أوخُذْ for خُذْ or أوكُلْ for كُلْ. So as far as these things are concerned, stop where they stop and then go by regular analogy afterwards.[20]

This brings me to the second point, for just as it is clear that Sībawayhi is describing a situation in speech which has no other justification than the fact that it is so, it is also evident from this passage that the final authority on the way to speak is the Arab speakers themselves. Who those Arabs were I do not intend to discuss here, as it has already been surveyed in general terms in the opening chapters of Rabin's *Ancient West-Arabian*. From this work I borrow the conclusion that it was more than likely that no direct contact occurred [169] between Sībawayhi and the Bedouin,(a) but probable that his informants were simply the professional *rāwīs*, which would included Ḫalīl and Yūnus.[21] With a manifest bias towards Eastern dialects (a Ḥiǧāzī usage is on one occasion described as

---

19. E.g., *Kitāb* 1, 28/37, 373/418.
20. *Kitāb* 1, 113/134.
21. Rabin, *Ancient West-Arabian* 23.

"the good old Arabic language, but ... [22]), the *Kitāb* frequently exhorts the reader to speak in the way laid down by the usage of the Arabs:

> Do you not see that if you said طعامًا لك and شرابًا لك and مالاً لك intending the meaning of the independent form which contains the meaning of a prayer, it would not be allowed because this way of speaking is not used as the previous way is used. This will show you and make you realise that you are obliged to make these words behave as the Arabs make them, and to mean what they mean.[23]

> The expression of pity is used for the wretched or afflicted person and the like and not for every adjective or noun; on the contrary, express pity only for those for whom the Arabs express pity.[24]

> If you said هو منّي مجلسَك or متكأ زيد or مربطَ الفرس it would not be allowed. In this respect use what the Arabs use and allow what they allow.[25]

To Sībawayhi's credit, these prescriptions evidently apply to the grammarians as well. We have already seen how the grammarians and the [170] Arabs disagreed, and where Sībawayhi's sympathies lay,[26] and there is plenty of evidence to support the claim that he held the usage of the Arabs to be binding on those who studied their language:

> Know that not everyone who "inclines" the *alif* agrees with other Arabs who also "incline,"[(a)] but each of the two parties might well contradict his partner and make "direct" what his partner "inclines" and *vice versa*. Likewise one whose dialect makes the *alif* "erect" may not agree with another who also makes the *alif* "erect," but his situation with his partner will be the same as in the case of the first two and their *kasra* in "inclining." And if you see an Arab like that, then by no means imagine that he speaks a bastard tongue,[(b)] because this is simply the way they are.[27]

The account of the phenomenon of reduplication, with its emphasis on the economy of effort favoured by the Arabs in pronunciation,[28] provides a lengthy example of the reliance upon the actual speech-habits of the Arabs which Sībawayhi preached (in this case taking his ideas from Ḫalīl). On another occasion he says that we often do not, in fact,

22. *Kitāb* 2, 474/424, and cf. 1, 21/27.
23. Id. 1, 138/166.
24. Id. 1, 216/255.
25. Id. 1, 174/206.
26. Above p. [18].
27. *Kitāb* 2, 284/263.
28. Id. 2, 443/397.

know how a word with a final weak radical is going to behave until we have heard the Arabs use it.[29]

On the other hand Sībawayhi warns, as we have just seen, that the Arabs are frequently inconsistent:

> [171] There are many things in their speech which are compared with similar things without being alike in every respect.[30]

and they even "make one thing like another even when they are both different."[31]

For Sībawayhi to have made such an observation at all not only reveals that he had a preconceived system against which Arab usage was measured, but also demonstrates a critical sense and responsibility which have been much neglected, probably as a result of the other features of the *Kitāb*, such as its complexity and detail. I, therefore, do not feel that it is stating the obvious to bring attention to this element of Sībawayhi's work. He nevertheless keeps an open mind: speaking of the unexplained definite article of some Arab names he says

> Every name which occurs permanently with the *alif-lām* has the status [of the star-names].[(a)] And if it is an Arab name which we know, without knowing from where it is derived, this is only because we are ignorant of something known to others, or because some knowledge which reached the first one so named has not reached the last to bear that name.[32]

It does not need stressing that such an attitude is very unusual in a people who take great delight in providing etymologies where none exist, often going to ridiculous lengths in the process.[33]

[172] Another expression of common sense which deserves to be given more prominence is found in Sībawayhi's conclusion to the chapter on the number of radicals of which Arabic words are made up:

> We have only written down those indeclinable nouns and non-nouns of three or more radicals which are in frequent use and spoken by the majority, because these are hardest to explain. For the obvious is always hardest to explain to anybody, because it is used itself to explain things, so that it is like attempting an explanation of an explanation. Do you not see that if somebody asks what is the meaning of أيّان and you say متى then you have made it clear. But if he then asks what is the meaning of متى [and you say في أيّ زمان], he has asked you about

29. Id. 2, 166/162.
30. *Kitāb* 1, 168/198, cf. 1, 77/93, 341/389. 2, 37/40, 84/87, 103/105.
31. Id. 2, 88/91.
32. Id. 1, 228/268.
33. See Brockelmann, *GAL* Supp. 1, 561, n. 1 on the name Khallikān.

> the obvious and you will find yourself hard put to produce something which will clarify the obvious.[34]

This shows a laudable desire to avoid infinite regression, and is testimony to a merit in Sībawayhi's approach which has never been appreciated.

Of his contact with the actual Bedouin speakers there is, of course, doubt,[a] but it need not be questioned that his purpose was to recover and faithfully reproduce "their way of speaking," كلامهم.

> Concerning the use of the direct form[b] when the verb is supressed and its expression has been abandoned because of self-sufficiency. I hope to give you examples of this with the supressed verb restored in order that you may know what the [173] Arabs wanted to say.[35]

> Likewise their proverbial expression اللهمّ ضبعًا وذئبًا, if you asked them what they meant by it they would say اللهمّ اجمعْ أو اجعلْ فيها ضبعًا أو ذئبًا.[36]

> Know that they do not use عسى فعلُك, as they dispense with it through أن تفعل just as most of the Arabs dispense with saying عسيا and عسوا through عسى, and dispense with لو ذهابُه through لو أنّه ذاهبٌ. Know furthermore that they do not use the verbal noun in this context just as they do not use the noun replaced by يفعل after عسى and كاد. This is abandoned because it is in their way of speaking to dispense with one thing through another.[37]

From this obvious submission to Arab usage and the accompanying fact that this was a deliberate choice on Sībawayhi's part it follows, and this is the third point I wish to deal with, that the process of analogy is not something carried out by the grammarians, but an action of the speakers of the language themselves. The Arabs "make one thing like another even if it is not the same in every respect, and you will see much of that in their way of speaking."[38] This idea is repeated or given a particular application on numerous occasions in the *Kitāb*:

> They make the apodosis like the predicate to an initial term[a] even though it does not resemble it in every respect.[39]

34. *Kitāb* 2, 349/312. The bracketed clause probably interpolated, see Jahn, n. 69 to §508.
35. *Kitāb* 1, 116/138.
36. Id. 1, 108/128.
37. Id. 1, 426/477.
38. Id. 1, 77/93 and above, p. [171].
39. Id. 1, 110/130.

> [174] They do not elide what they have made it resemble or that whose status they have given it.[40]
>
> As for the Ḥijāzīs, they have made ما like ليس since their meanings are the same just as in some places they make لات like ليس.[41]

One must distinguish, however, between this intuitive process of making analogies, which is invariably denoted in the *Kitāb* by the verb *šabbaha* and the artificial making of analogies, usually called *qiyās*. The latter, of course, opens the door for interminable disputes of the kind which took place between the "Kūfans" and "Baṣrans," but even the former kind of analogy is vulnerable to objection, in that it is always possible to deny that an analogy exists just because a grammarian claims to have detected it. Some of the weakest parts of the *Kitāb* involve such an element of misapprehension[(a)] as, for example, when Sībawayhi claims that the *lām* of initiality (لام الابتداء)[(b)] and the *lām* of *iḍāfa* have different vowels "because they want to distinguish between them,"[42] or, this time from Ḫalīl, that إنّ and its sisters have two effects like كان and its sisters but, because إنّ etc. are not full verbs "they distinguish between them as they distinguish between ما and ليس."[43] These explanations are manifestly pure guess-work, and the only thing to be said in their favour is that they are at least an attempt to explain linguistic phenomena from the point of view of the speakers of the language.

[175] More typical of Sībawayhi in this respect is, as we might expect from the quotations already given, the way in which he insists that grammarians' *qiyās* should not go beyond the limits of the natural analogy of the Arabs:

> Whoever says هُوَيْنِر ought not to base analogies upon it just as he would not base an analogy upon the speech of anyone who said أُبَيْنُون or أُنَيْسِيان unless you hear something from the Arabs and confirm it and produce parallels for such irregularities.[44]

Perhaps because Sībawayhi does not take the trouble to repeat such sentiments as these on every other page, he has been wrongly accused of an excessive rigidity in his methods. Perhaps, too, if he had composed a preface to the *Kitāb*, incorporating the ideas I have presented in the last few pages, the good features of his method would not have been obscured by that fatiguing thoroughness of his. It is ironical that the very success with which Sībawayhi achieved his purpose, namely to account for all the phenomena of Arabic, has resulted in the apparent fossilisation of the language. But this is a mistaken

40. *Kitāb* 1, 295/339.
41. Id. 1, 21/28.
42. Id. 1, 289/341.
43. Id. 1, 241/280.
44. *Kitāb* 2, 126/125.

impression, for it ought to be obvious that once there is nothing left to explain the science of grammar must lose its dynamism and degenerate[(a)] into a mere procedural bickering. I would go further than Fleisch and say that this stagnation and loss of initiative began with the very completion of the *Kitāb*, and that, to borrow Fleisch's words, Arabic [176] grammar from that time has been nothing but the "exploitation de l'héritage grammatical."[45]

A feature of Sībawayhi's grammar, which might be a result of legal influences, is the apparent restriction to two members of all the grammatical units. This has long been observed in the case of the largest units such as the sentence itself, *mubtada' - ḫabar*, and the adjectival unit of *mawṣūf - ṣifa*. In the section on form and function classes I shall have more to say about these "binary units," as it is convenient to call them, but at present some general remarks may serve as a background to this element of Sībawayhi's grammar. It has already been suggested that Arabic grammar resembles Roman law to the extent that neither admits a third party in a contract,[46] and the same might be said of Islamic law which, though it admits, for example, that *širka* may be contracted between two or more parties, seems in theory to restrict this and every other kind of contract to the ideal limit of two partners. The opening words of the *Kitāb*, which lay down two well-defined categories of word and a third whose only definition is that it is not one of the other two, seem to embody this same principle, or at least to reflect an attitude identical to that which is discerned in Islamic law.

We shall also have occasion to discuss the fact that Sībawayhi relies heavily on the existence of a listener for every utterance, so that it would not be an extravagance to maintain that, for Sībawayhi, the use of language was a binary act in itself. There is, with one exception,[47] no [177] suggestion in the *Kitāb* that anything, even a poem, can be uttered in a vacuum or that Arabic can be spoken for its own sake without the need to convey anything to anybody. Far from amusing himself with what might be said if no-one were listening, Sībawayhi actually appears to seek out for special mention those cases where the presence of a listener enables the speaker to omit parts of what he would have said if they were not already obvious to the listener. Furthermore, like the lawyers and their convention of reducing even multiple *širka* contracts to two parties for the purposes of discussion, Sībawayhi thinks of poetry as being addressed to only one listener, for one suffices to account for the grammatical state of the poem.[48] The only exception to this seems to be one case where a Qur'anic construction depends on a plurality of listene

45. In Loucel, *Arabica* 11, 64.
46. Above, p. [65].
47. *Kitāb* 1, 114/136[(a)].
48. *Kitāb* 1, 25/33, 98/118.

ers, *muḫāṭabūn*,[49] but that is hardly very significant against the innumerable times that speech is treated as though it were addressed to only one listener.

The system of binary units on the grammatical level may reflect the essentially binary nature of communication on the personal level as just set out, or the same conclusion may have been reached simply by isolating pairs of words and deciding that third items did not naturally combine with the binary units thus established. At all events Arabic grammar seems to have developed a morphology which almost imposes this interpretation of the facts: while it is relatively easy to account for the binary units which share the same "case," e.g., *mubtada' - ḫabar*, [178] *mawṣūf - ṣifa*, and those in which the second element is oblique in form e.g., *muḍāf – muḍāf ilayhi* and all the pairs beginning with a *ḥarf jarr*, it is not so easy to account for all the words which appear in direct form, such as the five "objects," the *ḥāl* and so on. The later grammarians came to the conclusion that these words were an extraneous element (*faḍla*) in the sentence,[50] and by so doing articulated what must also have been Sībawayhi's attitude in his handling of the binary units, although, strangely enough, he does not expressly say so. It is easy, however, to infer from the way Sībawayhi deals in binary units, that, for example, the verb and its agent consistute a unit, with all the various objects considered as mere extras. I specifically mention this example because Reuschel, who rightly recognised the binary structure of Arabic grammar, gives as one of his examples the verb and the *maf'ūl bihi*,[51] which only goes to show what a difference there is between recognising a thing and understanding it. The whole purpose of the notion of *ta'addī* as developed by Sībawayhi is to show that "objects" of the verb are inherently external items to which the action of the verb can only extend by "going beyond" its agent, as Reuschel should have observed. What is truly perplexing about this notion is not that Praetorius should have completely overlooked the equation of *muta'addī* and the Latin "*transitivum*,"[52] but that these ideas should be so close when the historical likelihood of their being connected is so remote.[(a)]

[179] Binary units offer unlimited possibilities of analysis: the Arabic equivalent of a syllable may perhaps be regarded as a vocalised consonant, i.e., the binary unit of a consonant and vowel, and every successively larger combination of constituents seems to fall naturally into binary units.[(a)] This prompts me to make a slight digression in which it will be seen that Sībawayhi's way of working bears an impressive resemblance to a very modern style of analysis called Immediate Constituent Analysis (I.C.A.). I would preface this exercise in comparative "linguistics" across the ages by this remark of R. H. Robins, in which the emphasis is mine:

49. Id. 1, 160/191.
50. Cf. *Alfiyya* vs. 277 and commentators.
51. Reuschel, *Ḫalīl* 15.
52. See above, p. [78].

> It will be observed that the processes of immediate constituent analysis illustrated here, by which the longest and most complex sentence can be reduced by analysis to successive expansions of one of a few basic sentence structures, bear some resemblance to the traditional processes of 'parsing and analysis' of school grammars. As has been emphasised throughout, however, and this is one of the main features of modern linguistic analysis, no attention has been paid to the individual meanings, discoverable or assumed, of the words or word groups in the sentences under examination, but only to their synactic relations with one another as members of grammatical constructions.[53]

It is remarkable that virtually every instance of the word "meaning" (*maʿnā*) in the *Kitāb* relates to what is now known as grammatical meaning, [180] and that lexical meaning plays, to all intents and purposes, no role at all in Sībawayhi's system. So it might well be fruitful to examine the *Kitāb* to see whether it uses any of the ideas of I.C.A.

One is struck at once by the fact that many binary units in Arabic are designated by terms which, by their etymological relation, reveal the syntactic unity of the constructions they describe, e.g., *iḍāfa* (*muḍāf, muḍāf ilayhi*), *waṣf* (*ṣifa, mawṣūf*), *nafy* (*ḥarf nafy, manfī*) and so on. Any pair of words to which these terms apply would automatically form a basic pattern of I.C.A. and be bracketed together. That the "nominal sentence" itself forms one of these "favorite sentence types," as the resultant patterns are called, is made obvious in a fourfold manner in the *Kitāb*, firstly through the terms *musnad, musnad ilayhi*, secondly through the terms *mubtada', ḫabar*, thirdly through the notion of *binā'* in which the second element is *mabnī* upon the first, and fourthly through the device of the mutual "need" (*iḥtiyāj*) of one constituent for the other. The verb, which is always analysed into the binary unit *fiʿl, fāʿil*, naturally provides the other of the two "favourite sentence types" which exhaust the potential of Arabic sentences. On grounds of simple terminological fact, then, we would expect a Sībawayhian analysis to correspond exactly to a modern I.C.A. One example will suffice to demonstrate this:

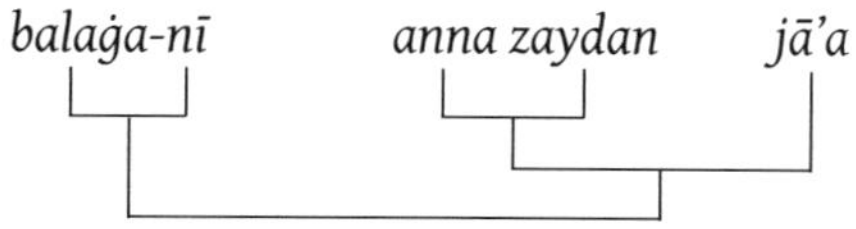

[181] We can see at a glance that the right-hand stemma embraces all the words أن زيدًا جاء thus making them into one half of a binary unit, or, in Sībawayhi's own words,

> Do you not see that you say بلغني أنّ زيدًا جاء and أنّ زيدًا جاء, all of it, is one word?[54]

53. Robins, *General Linguistics* 240.
54. *Kitāb* 1, 364/410.

When he says "one word"[(a)] Sībawayhi is actually refering to مجيء زيد , the paraphrase for أنّ زيدًا جاء , but we already know that the parts of any *jarr* construction are, by definition, "as though they are one word,"[55] so that the process described by Robins, the reduction to "successive expansions of one of a few basic sentence structures," can genuinely be seen working in this example from the *Kitāb*. In fact, Sībawayhi makes a point of stating wherever possible that a compound (binary unit) is equivalent to a single word,[(b)] e.g., the noun and its adjective (1, 178/210), أيّ and its various attachments (1, 350/397), أنّ and its noun and أنْ and its verb (1, 410/461, and cf. 372/418), الذي and its synonyms ,ما مَن , أيّهم , etc. with their attachments (1, 390/438, and cf. 364/410), من and verbs attached to it (1,352/399 and cf. 2, 41/45), the vocative noun and its adjectives (1, 265/306) and لا and the noun it denies (1, 300/345). It goes without saying that any of these combinations would have to be treated in I.C.A. terms as binary units, so that in broad outline Sībawayhi has prefigured the I.C.A. method to a degree which would certainly astonish R. H. Robins and numerous other linguists who cannot see further back than de Saussure.[(c)]

[182] There is at least one case where I.C.A. can actually clarify one of Sībawayhi's arguments.[56] The verbal analysis of the two types لا غلامَ ظريفًا لك and لا غلامَ ظريفَ لك , in which the form of the adjective hinges on the different ways of making binary units out of the first three words, is at once made easy to grasp by comparing the I.C.A. of the two sentences, which shows us exactly where the binary units are:[(a)]

1.
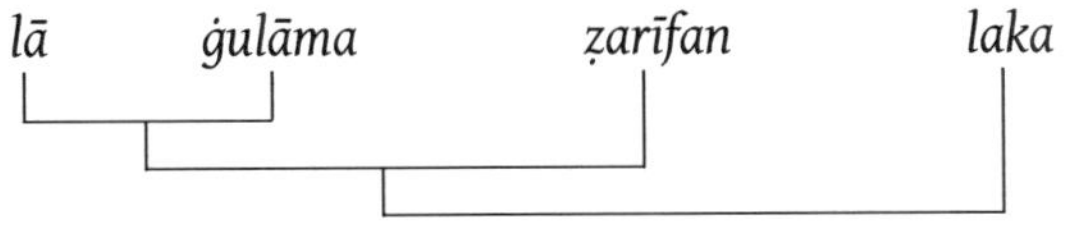

2.
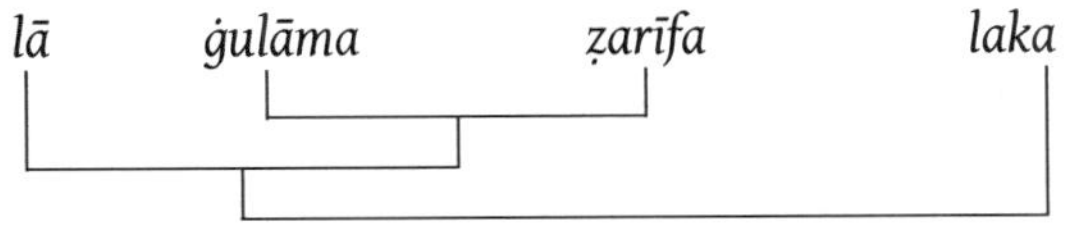

The problem is then raised, how do additional adjectives behave and this prompts Sībawayhi to the remark, most interesting for our purposes, that "three separate things do not have the status of one noun."[57] The second adjective must, therefore, take the *tanwīn* which shows that it is not construed as part of the لا غلامَ unit, although the first adjective still retains its option of taking or omitting *tanwīn*, so that the I.C.A. would yield the following alternatives :

1.
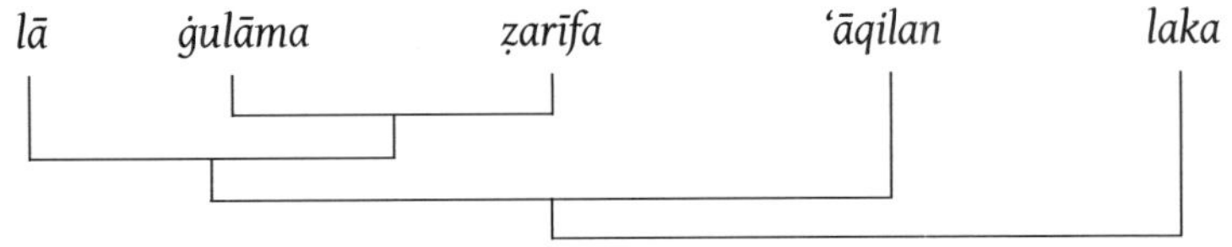

55. Id. 1, 254/295.
56. *Kitāb* 1, 306/351.
57. Ibid.

2. *lā* *ġulāma* *ẓarīfan* *ʿāqilan* *laka*

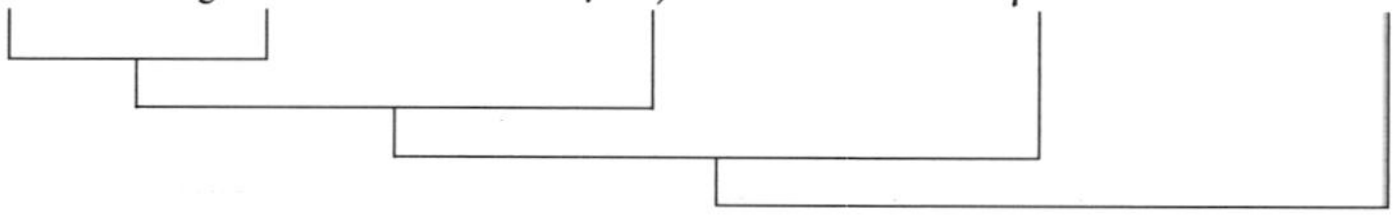

[183] The first analysis demands that, after غلامَ ظريفَ have been combined into a binary unit, لا should take priority over عاقلاً in forming the second binary unit with the now single term غلامَ ظريفَ, for عاقلاً only qualifies لا غلامَ not غلامَ alone. It is also to be noted that عاقلاً is in the direct and undefined form,[a] which is a coincidence that Sībawayhi somewhat unfairly takes for granted when he compares the sentence under analysis with another, to wit لا غلامَ فيها ظريفًا. By introducing فيها, which is structurally ambivalent in that it may be taken either as a predicative phrase or a neutralised term, Sībawayhi implies that ظريفًا here is comparable with قائمًا and other extraneous terms in sentences of the type فيها رجلٌ قائمًا, where the extraneous term assumes the direct and undefined form as a non-essential part of the sentence.[58] That فيها has been deliberately introduced by Sībawayhi to allow him to invoke its ambiguity is proved by the subsequent argument in which the adjective is required always to be direct and undefined in form.[59] The proof rests superficially on the fact that in لا رجلَ فيها عاقلاً the natural binary unit رجلَ عاقلاً has been split by the intervention of فيها, but from the examples, particularly لا ضاربًا زيدًا لك, which are adduced to support his case it is clear that the real explanation for the phenomenon is based on the behaviour of the *tanwīn-naṣb* construction which I shall deal with in Chapter Six. Here it is enough to say that the chief peculiarity of this construction is that it represents a paraphrase of the so-called [184] improper *iḍāfa*, and it is therefore a binary unit which, by the looseness of its combination, forms a kind of antithesis to the indivisible true *iḍāfa*.[a] Sībawayhi uses this principle, though only with respect to the alleged indivisibility of *ṣifa* and *mawṣūf*, when he says that فيها prevents the form عاقلٌ from occuring in لا رجلَ فيها عاقلاً, for the principle of such constructions requires that the second element of an improper *iḍāfa* takes the direct and undefined form when *tanwīn* on the first element intervenes to prevent *iḍāfa*, i.e., ضاربُ زيدٍ must become ضاربٌ زيدًا. Significantly لا حسنًا وجهَ الأخِ فيها is one of Sībawayhi's examples in the very cases we are discussing.

We may have wandered from the idea of immediate constituent analysis, but the sentences just discussed do bring out in an interesting way yet another similarity between I.C.A. and Sībawayhi's methods. They both find it difficult to cope with units which are not directly linked with a neighbouring word, when it becomes necessary to deform the orderly series of branches by allowing the lines to cross, as Robins' Latin example shows:[60]

58. *Kitāb* 1, 222/261.
59. Id. 1, 306/351.
60. Robins, *General Linguistics* 240.

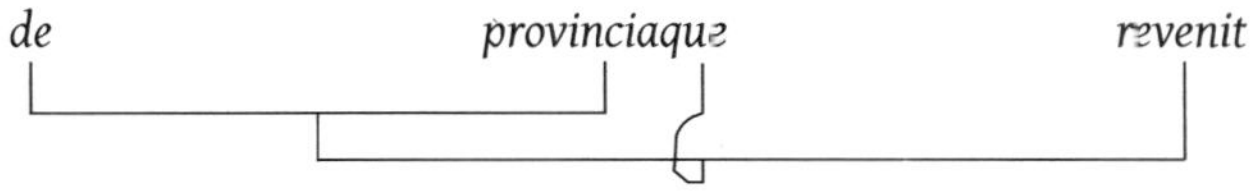

Robins concludes that such "cross-cutting of word boundaries" is generally rare, for it would tend to make such words "less useful as a basic unit of grammar." That is a strange statement for a linguist to [185] make, since usefulness is presumably not meant in any technical sense here. But it does reveal an unexpected similarity of attitude between Robins and Sībawayhi which is all the more remarkable because it concerns the same difficulty in Arabic as we have just met in Latin. A large number of Arabic words and phrases which are collectively known as *ẓurūf*, are characteristically ambivalent in their grammatical relationship with the rest of the sentence, as we have seen in the case of لا رجلَ فيها عاقلاً. Whether they are treated as predicates or are neutralised, they appear to disrupt the unit of noun and adjective, thus throwing other adjectives to the end of the sentence as extraneous elments. We find, for instance that the I.C.A. for the predicative use of فيها turns out to be almost the same as the Latin one above.

while the only difference in the case of the neutralised

is that by definition it has no connection with the rest of the sentence.[(a)] It is *laġw*, and this seems to me to correspond exactly to what Robins vaguely calls being "less useful as a basic unit of grammar," for it is a feature of the *ẓurūf* that they are "neutralised until it is as if the speaker did not mention them in that place." [61]Sībawayhi thus makes explicitly part of his system what Robins only surmises, but both are [186] identical responses to the same problem, which brings I.C.A. and the system of the *Kitāb* even closer together in spirit. What unites them more than anything is the utter linearity of both kinds of analysis, which itself causes the "neutralised" words to be the problem that they are. They both share, too, in the limitation that they cannot distinguish (in Sībawayhi's case because he did not wish to) between structurally homologous sentences. Thus I.C.A. cannot show in what way these two sentences differ:[62]

61. *Kitāb* 1, 207/243.
62. Robins, *General Linguistics* 244.

The war was started by Germany

The war was started by 1939

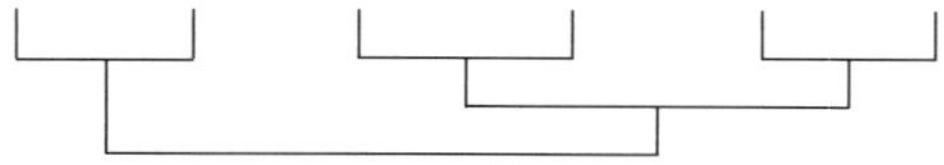

and it does not require a specially sharp eye to perceive the structural identity of such sentences as

ضرب زيدٌ عمرًا
كان زيدٌ عاقلًا
ذهب زيدٌ ذهابًا
كُسِي زيدٌ ثوبًا

Although these sentences are analysed by Sībawayhi into parts with different names according to the different functions they perform, his linear method (*naḥw!*) cannot account for the semantic differences which underlie the structurally identical patterns. On the other hand the linear method offers peculiar advantages in determining the nature of a sentence, to which I shall turn in the next chapter, so that the [187] inadequacies of the approach are offset by its usefulness in other ways. To that extent, as I hope to show, Sībawayhi has made more out of his proto-I.C.A. than modern writing would suggest can be done with the present system, which has been largely superseded by Transformational Grammar. At any rate I feel that Sībawayhi, if he did not have the jargon of modern linguistics, certainly reached a level of analysis which is equal to any of the achievements in I.C.A.[(a)]

The formalism which both I.C.A. and and Sībawayhian *naḥw* require is, perhaps, the outstanding feature of the *Kitāb*. There is no reason to suppose that the restriction, almost totally, to the purely formal aspects of Arabic was anything but a deliberate choice on Sībawayhi's part. Nor need we ask whether this choice was due to any difficulties of semantics or vocabulary deficiencies under which Sībawayhi might have laboured: only a few Arabs in any century would know all the words listed in the second volume, and still less could they be sure of correctly conjugating the verbs or forming the plurals of the thousands of examples which make up this part of the *Kitāb*.

The choice of formalism, deliberate though it was, was probably conditioned by Sībawayhi's background, in which law and ethics played a part, and which are, as we have seen, very much concerned with the formalities of human behaviour and its appearance as beautiful (*ḥasan*) or ugly (*qabīḥ*). A further influence in the direction of formalism would undoubtedly be the adoption (in the virtual absence of any other alternative), of the linear metaphor expressed by *naḥw*. This yielded in speech terms what Martinet calls the "chaîne parlée," a string of words [188] which could only be analysed in the sequence in which they were uttered, and a situation in which the effect of a word upon the one immediately following becomes peculiarly important to the analyst.[(a)]

We may gain some impression of the lengths to which Sībawayhi carried his formal approach by looking at the various occasions on which he uses the word ضارع.[(b)] Normally the *muḍāri'* is taken to refer exclusively to the verb form يفعل etc., in which connection it is indeed used in the *Kitāb*, (1, 2/3). But the same term is also used to indicate the resemblance between the adjective and the end of a single word (because the noun and adjective together equal a single word) (1, 34/45), between indeclinable and declinable nouns (1, 3/4), between interrogative and conditional particles (1, 40/51), between the word فُلوس and the singular pattern فعول (2, 16/16 and other examples nearby), between defined words with *alif-lām* and those which are defined without it (1, 348/395), between adjectives and nouns (1, 96/117), between the conditional particles and the second term in an improper *iḍāfa* (1, 406/457), between الآن and أين (2, 48/51), between the adjectival أفعل pattern and the verbal form (2, 1/2), between one letter and another (2, 459/410, 461/412), between the adjective عَدُوّ and the nouns whose form it has (2, 201/195) and between the form أفعل of surprise and the other verb forms (2, 268/251). It will be seen from this selection of examples that the formal resemblance between the nouns and imperfect tense of the verb, from which the latter gets its name of *muḍāri'*, is only one of many such resemblances which were covered by the same term. It is doubtful [189] whether Sībawayhi would have recognised *muḍāri'* as referring exclusively to a verb form. The one case in Reckendorf where *muḍāri'* is cited not referring to a verb form[63] scarcely gives any real hint of the breadth of the term as it is used in the *Kitāb*.

The usefulness of the formal approach to Arabic lies in Arabic's relatively small range of grammatical forms: all the verbs, for example from first to fifteenth forms,[(a)] fit into two basic paradigms containing only thirteen items (1st, 2nd, 3rd singular, dual and plural). Whatever the difficulties offered by the broken plurals, they are certainly compensated by the simplicity of the nominal case system, just as the constant use of the oblique case after prepositions strikes the Indo-European eye as enviably simple. It follows that the three "form-classes" of Arabic (i.e., noun, verb, and everything else outside those two easily identifiable classes) have to perform a great many functions, which is why Sībawayhi gives only the broadest description of the functions of noun, verb and particle, in the first chapter of the *Kitāb*. It is, in fact, the paucity of form-classes which accounts for the frequency of the verb ضارع in the *Kitāb*, for resemblances become inevitable in a language like Arabic. In Chapter Five I shall describe the "function-classes" identified by Sībawayhi and into which the "form-classes" were distributed. In the meantime it is important to bear in mind that for Sībawayhi there was no role in grammar for absolute meaning, whether based on lexical [190] or semantic distinctions, nor is it a part of Sībawayhi's method that such considerations should be relevant to grammati-

63. Reckendorf, *Arab. Syntax* 111, referring to *mūqidan* in *yā mūqidan nāran*, said to "resemble" the *muḍāf*, scil. *yā mūqida nārin*. Cf. also de Sacy, *Alfiyya*, notes on vs. 199.

cal analysis, even in determining such a fundamental issue as the nature of the sentence itself. Some exceptions, mostly trivial, might serve to prove this rule.

Given the system of derived verbs which Arabic and the other Semitic languages deploy, it would be surprising if Sībawayhi did not pay some attention to meaning when discussing them. He provides paraphrases to explain, how, for example, أفرح relates to فرح and so on,[64] but does not discuss the principle behind such changes of meaning, preferring to proliferate examples. Jahn's translation at this point, which leaves out the examples,[(a)] consequently acquires a very truncated appearance.[65] The extent to which semantic issues were discussed is best illustrated by these thoughts of Ḫalīl's on the subject:

> Ḫalīl maintained that when you say فَتَنْتُهُ or حَزَنْتُهُ you do not want to say جعلته حزينًا or جعلته فاتنًا as is the case when you say أدخلته meaning جعلته داخلاً. Instead what you want to say is جعلت فيه حُزْنًا or جعلت فيه فتْنَةً just as you say كحلتُه, i.e., جعلت فيه كُحْلاً and دهنته, i.e., جعلت فيه دُهْنًا. You say فعَلْته on its own without wanting فعَلْتُه here to mean anything different from حَزِنَ or فتَنَ. If you do want that you say أحْزَنْتُه or أفْتَنْتُه.[66]

[191] It is worth noting here that the principle agent of semantics in Sībawayhi's grammar is the will of the speaker, as Ḫalīl's words show, and that the purpose of the *Kitāb* is to show the Arabic speaker how to put into words what he wants to say in the way that will ensure that it is understood as he meant it to be. The explanations of the derived verbs, then, are more often expressed as "what people say" rather than attempting to use any abstract criterion of absolute meaning.[67]

There is one area, however, in which a semantic idea seems to have been applied with some thoroughness, and we may attribute this to an excessive tendency to find analogies in the language. The belief seems to be that words of similar meaning will have similar form, and as well as being applied to the verbs (derived forms yield corresponding derived meanings, intransitive verbs have intransitive form), it is also somewhat sweepingly applied to the nouns. Thus, as is well-known, nouns denoting trades or professions, places, instruments etc. have a characteristic form. But the principle is taken even further, on the grounds that the Arabs have a natural tendency to use similar forms for words of similar meaning.[68] Although there is certainly some truth in this belief, I doubt whether there is enough to substantiate such arguments[(a)] as

> They say سَخِطَه سَخَطًا because it is compared with غَضِبَ in that both the form and the meaning are one. The forms ساخِطٌ and سَخِطْتُه prove that it goes into the

64. *Kitāb* 2, 247/233ff.
65. Esp. §444.
66. Id. 2, 248/234[(b)].
67. E.g., *Kitāb* 2, 249/236.
68. Id. 2, 222/213 to 239/226 *passim* and cf. 2, 167/163.

> category of actions that are seen and heard because this is one which is made to occur in someone else.[69]

[192] On the other hand the stricture that elatives cannot be formed from adjectives denoting "colours or characteristics" is not really semantic, but, as the full sentence makes clear, simply a formal objection to words "which have the pattern أفعل" being made into elatives.[70]

Sometimes it is necessary to cede to usage, and a semantic reason is then sought for it. Hence the explanation that it is possible for inanimate objects (جُثث) to be subjects of sentences in which the predicate is a temporal clause, e.g., الحَرُّ حين تأتيني, but persons may not become subjects in such sentences.[71] By contrast the assertion that nouns of place are closer to proper nouns, while nouns of time are closer to verbs,[72] seems an uneasy simplification, though perhaps not so whimsical as the claim that words denoting nearness are more able to decline fully (أشدّ تمكّنًا) than words denoting remoteness.[73] These, like the idea that the verb is "heavier" than the noun[74] and that nouns are prior to verbs,[75] are of dubious value in Sībawayhi's system, though it is much to be deplored that such aspects of the *Kitāb* seem to be regarded as typical of the whole work.[(a)]

It will be noticed, however, that the examples given in the preceding paragraph do not so much involve lexical meaning as grammatical meaning, which is to say that when Sībawayhi discusses meaning he is properly concerned with the function of the words in question as parts of sentences, not as entries in a dictionary. We have already seen how reluctant he was to commit himself to defining the absolute meaning of [193] any word,[76] and it is significant that he never bothers to supply equivalents for the difficult words in poetry. In one case where he does provide synonyms, when dealing with animal names of the *kunya* pattern, e.g., أبو الحارث for أسد etc.,[77] it is precisely because the "meaning" of such words is not a lexical matter, but a choice of the speaker. Other cases where meaning is at issue discover themselves to be concerned with purely grammatical meaning, such as the discussion of conjunctions و ,فـ ، ثم, أو,[78] or the interminable treatment of the various possibilities in لا تأتني فأحدّثك,[79] not forgetting the complications inherent in the use of حتى

69. Id. 2, 225/215.
70. *Kitāb* 2, 268/250.
71. Id. 1, 57/69.
72. Id. 1, 12/16.
73. Id. 1, 245/284.
74. Id. 1, 5/6.
75. Ibid.
76. See above, p. [172].
77. *Kitāb* 1, 224/263.
78. Id. 1, 185/218.
79. Id. 1, 372/418 [(b)].

as a conjunction.[80] But all these arguments ultimately rest on the foundation that what sentences mean is a matter of convention, the convention being none other than the "way" Arabs speak. Lawyers have made much of this in their *ḥiyal*-literature, where the conventions are manipulated shamelessly to the advantage of the party concerned,[(a)] and under the general heading of معاريض الكلام this has always been a feature of Arabic culture. Many anecdotes are related in which a dangerous situation is averted or a humorous one created by verbal tricks which are simply exploitations of the possibilities which convention allows.[81] Sībawayhi was certainly aware of this potential, for he writes

> It is not allowed for غير to have the status of the noun which, when after إلا, constitutes an initial term (e.g., as in ما مررت بأحد إلا زيدٌ خيرٌ منه). That is because they have not [194] given غير the meaning of إلا as an initial term, but have only given غير the meaning of exception in every place where it has the status of مثل and it stands for exception. Do you not see that if you said أتاني غير عمرو you would have stated that he did not come even though it would be right (قد يستقيم) [for it to mean] that he had actually come, and so in certain cases of exception غير is sufficient.[82]

The first part of this quotation simply concludes the argument by which the form of غير is determined by taking it as equal in status to the noun which follows إلا, and need not concern us. What is interesting is that Sībawayhi has explicitly recognised that أتاني غير عمرو is only taken to mean "People came to me except 'Amr" because that is convention, even though the sentence could also mean "People came to me other than 'Amr (who also came)." This is well observed on Sībawayhi's part, and should go a long way towards refuting Fleisch's charge[(a)] that the *Kitāb* is superficial work, especially as this is not the only time when Sībawayhi displays a fine appreciation of the conventions upon which meaning is founded:-

> You say أتاني رجلٌ meaning one man, not two, and you say ما أتاك رجلٌ meaning more than one man [came], and you say أتاك رجلٌ meaning a man and not a woman, and you say ما أتاك رجلٌ meaning not a man but a woman came, and one says أتاني اليوم رجلٌ meaning someone with all his strength and might, and you say ما أتاك رجلٌ meaning only weaklings came. And if you say ما أتاك أحدٌ it [195] becomes a general negation for all of these and that is how it behaves in speech.[83]

Other examples of the same order immediately following this most interesting passage oblige us to conclude that Sībawayhi was very much aware that the meaning of a sen-

---

80. Id. 1, 367/413[(c)].
81. E.g., Šarīšī, *Šarḥ maqāmāt al-Ḥarīrī* 3, 150, Šaybānī, *Maḫārij* 4–6, Suyūṭī, *Muzhir* 1, 572f.
82. *Kitāb* 1, 327/374.
83. *Kitāb* 1, 20/27.

tence often goes beyond its grammatically distinguishing features. The point is reached where the meaning intended is the one chosen by the speaker, even though his words may be identical in form with those expressing other meanings. Against the will of the speaker, however, is set the restraining factor of the listener, whose expectations, as we shall see in the next chapter, govern the choice of the speaker by imposing upon him the obligation to make himself understood.

Both speaker and listener are responsible for what Sībawayhi calls "latitude of speech" سعة الكلام, the conventional broadening of the strict rules of speech,(a) which is proof enough that the rules themselves are also a matter of convention. English practises the same latitude, and we may fruitfully compare "playgoer" (nobody "goes a play") with Sībawayhi's example

يا سارقَ الليلِ أهلَ الدار[84]

for nobody steals the night, though "night-thief" would immediately be understood by an English reader.(b) Other examples will show how sensitive Sībawayhi was to this aspect of Arabic usage:

> Similarly in their speech is the expression بنو فلان يطؤهم الطريق which simply means يطؤهم أهل الطريق. They also say [196] صدْنا قنويْن meaning '[we hunted] in Qanawān' or '[we hunted] the wild animals of Qanawān,' because Qanawān is the name of a place. Of similar latitude are أنت أكرم عليّ من أن أضربك and أنت أنكد من أن تتركه, which mean only أنت أكرم عليّ من صاحب الضرب and أنكد من صاحب تركه.[85]

He says of the line(a)

تَرْتَعُ مَا رَتَعَتْ حَتّى إذَا ادكرَتْ فَإنّمَا هِيَ إقْبَالٌ وإدْبَارٌ

> They have made (the camels) into going backwards and forwards, which is allowed in latitude of speech, as in نهارك صئم وليلك قائم.[86]

and for a final example:

> They have made (the camels), as in نهارك. As for له صوتٌ صوتُ حمار, you know very well that the voice of the donkey is not the same as the first voice, but it is only allowed to be independent by latitude of speech.[87]

84. Id. 1, 75/89.
85. *Kitāb* 1, 89/109.
86. Id. 1, 141/169.
87. Id. 1, 152/182.

> What we learn from this willingness to accept the fact that the strict rules of speech are not always observed is that Sībawayhi had a far humbler attitude towards his data than many of his critics have shown towards him. We may take it that the rules which he formulated represent the minimum rather than the maximum amount of prescriptive grammar, if such it can be called, and we ought to recognise that only a descriptive grammarian could ever admit in writing that the principles he sets down are not universally valid. On these grounds alone Sībawayhi hardly qualifies for inclusion under the general slander that Baṣran grammar is "Procrustean," which is an image to which Westerners all too readily resort [197] in this context.[88]

His "grammar," as I have so far depicted it, is evidently much better conceived than has hitherto been granted. He shows himself to have no illusions as to the reliability or correctness of Arab speech, which is an attitude he surely acquired from his masters Ḫalīl and Yūnus, and he reveals enough confidence in his own theories to disagree, occasionally rather violently, with them. This has almost no bearing on the "character" of Sībawayhi, which Hadīṯī and Mubārak have somewhat vainly tried to estimate on virtua ally no evidence,[89] but it is valuable as an indication of the responsibility Sībawayhi felt and reveals for the system propounded in the *Kitāb*. We can, on the strength of this, claim that nothing in the *Kitāb* is fortuitous or meaningless, and that the work deserves, even demands to be given a respectful examination. Only by taking him seriously can we appreciate the virtues of Sībawayhi's approach, as this thesis is designed to show. The concept of the binary unit on the grammatical level, exhaustively exploited by Sībawayhi, remains to this day an essential ingredient of Arabic grammar. Likewise the use of the idea of human behaviour as the model for grammatical behaviour, and the assumption that language is based on similarities which the speakers consciously use, are features which, because of the way Sībawayhi applies them, raise the *Kitāb* above its numerous heirs. It is time to see that in detail, as in general, the work of Sībawayhi is far more thorough and systematic than is sometimes admitted.

Summary

[326] The word "*naḥw*" in the *Kitāb* does not mean "grammar." *Naḥw* is only one of various synonymous terms used in Arabic to denote behaviour, and it is obvious that Sībawayhi regarded language as a form of behaviour. The term *naḥw* itself has several synonyms in

88. E.g., Glazer, *JAOS* 62, 106, Rescher, *ZA* 23, 43.
89. Ḥadīṯī, *Kitāb Sībawayhi* 27f, Mubārak, *Rummānī* 126f.

the *Kitāb* and is not equivalent to *téchnè grammatikè*, nor does it represent syntax to the exclusion of morphology (*ṣarf*).

[327] In the *Kitāb* we find that the terminology is based on a sustained social metaphor. This is contrasted with a group of older terms which have in common a connection, in their literal meanings, with building. They are probably related to the terminology of prosody and may represent a personal contribution by Ḫalīl to Arabic phonology which was adapted and expanded by Sībawayhi in grammar.

The broad outlines of Sībawayhi's grammar are then depicted: language is a process and a social act, in which the Arabs provide the authoritative source material, though they are themselves inconsistent and unreliable. Sībawayhi avoids infinite regression in matters of meaning, and regards analogy as a process practiced by speakers of Arabic as well as grammarians.

Language, being social, is a binary act for Sībawayhi, who thus shares the lawyer's views on the binary nature of contracts. Arabic is, therefore, divided into binary units. There follows an extended comparison with the modern method of Immediate Constituent Analysis, which throws light on Sībawayhi's method. In particular the formalism of the *Kitāb* and of I.C.A. is shown to have useful consequences in his linear type of analysis.

Semantic meaning plays only a minor role in the *Kitāb*, for it is recognised as a matter of convention. We must assume, from the evidence of Sībawayhi's competence given in this chapter, that he is to be taken seriously.

Addenda to Chapter Four

The contents of this chapter formed the basis of Carter 1983 (grammar as an ethical discipline) and 1991 (the ethical origins of grammatical terminology), also sections of Carter 1972a (the linear nature of language) and Carter 1973a (grammatical functions as binary units).

[154] (a) Metalanguage has attracted some interest. As Guillaume 1986, 61 has pointed out (see [51] (a) above) Sībawayhi had virtually no metalanguage at his disposal, hence it is difficult sometimes to distinguish between object language and metalanguage (cf. also Mosel 1975, 1, 4, 9–11). There is even a slight hint of resentment in the secondary literature that Sībawayhi did not follow the conventions of our linguistics, but to make such a distinction at all is unnecessary: it is up to the reader to recognise that the terminology of the *Kitāb* is a continuum which switches unannounced between object language and metalanguage, see examples below in [215] (a), [271] (b), [314] (a).

However, there is no doubt that Sībawayhi and his master Ḫalīl were always perfectly aware of the difference: they often played a game in which Sībawayhi would ask Ḫalīl about the morphological properties of a word after being arbitrarily converted into a personal name, see [88] (a), [181] (a).

Later, of course, once *naḥw* had established itself as an autonomous science, it joined all the other Islamic sciences in distinguishing between its own technical vocabulary (*ism ṣināʿī*) and ordinary lexical meaning (*ism luġawī*), see [161] (a). For a thorough treatment of metalanguage in the later grammarians (effectively Astarābāḏī), see Larcher 2014.

[154] (b) An additional feature of Sībawayhi's metalanguage is that the same term can be used on different linguistic levels. This clearly results from his concept of language as behaviour: thus the criteria *ḥasan/qabīḥ* and *mustaqīm* are used in syntax, morphology and phonology, see [161] (a), which was pointed out by Mosel 1975, 1, 9ff, Abboud 1979, 63. This feature was also noted by Troupeau 1976, who systematically divides the lemmata into technical and non-technical categories: thus *ʿamal* "operation" has three applications, see [78] (a).

One consequence of this is that terms often apply equally to the actions of the speaker and of speech elements within an utterance, to the extent that it is not always clear whether the term has a linguistic or extralinguistic reference, e.g., does *fiʿl* denote "an act" or "a word expressing an act," i.e., "a verb"? There is no doubt that this continuum is an intentional feature of Sībawayhi's analysis, to cover all acts of speech as acts of the speaker. A simple example is the speaker's choice to put a word in the independent or dependent form in exclamations (*Kitāb* 1, 139/166), see also Carter 1973a, 151, n. 46, and below [210] (a).

[157] (a) All the synonyms below are listed in Troupeau 1976, but (and it is the only weakness of the work) for words which are very frequent, viz. *wajh*, *jarā*, Troupeau does not itemise every occurrence. It is worth looking up further examples, however, as those below are only a selection.

[158] (a) The data are not presented in order of appearance in the *Kitāb*; the sequence in fact appears to be random, and if there was any rhetorical purpose behind it, that is no longer discernible. However, it should be noted that this is only a selection of a much larger pool of examples.

[158] (b) An excellent example can be added here from Ḫalīl: *hāḏihi ṭarīqatu kulli ḥarfin kāna mutaḥarrikan*, *Kitāb* 2, 62/52–53. As a rule this thesis makes no attempt to distinguish whether the terms originate from Ḫalīl, but see [164].

[160] (a) This thesis pays little attention to Sībawayhi's morphological interests, though the topic occupies about a half of the *Kitāb*. By way of justification it can be claimed that he applies exactly the same principles and criteria to morphology as he does to syntax (see [161]), and this is evident in some of the examples offered.

It remains an open question how much of this aspect of the *Kitāb* is owed to his master Ḫalīl. In one case we can be sure of Ḫalīl's contribution, namely in the theory that some morphological events result from frequency of usage, *kaṯrat al-istiʿmāl*, which term is explicitly attributed to Ḫalīl a number of times by Sībawayhi (e.g., 1, 120/143); see Dayyeh 2012 on the relationship between frequency and elision (*ḥaḏf*). We may link this with another notion of Ḫalīl's, namely ease of articulation, e.g., such expressions as *laqītuhu amsi* "I met him yesterday," reduced from *laqītuhu bi-l-amsi* "to make it easier on the tongue" *taḫfīfan ʿalā l-lisān* (1, 253/294), and cf. [168] (a) on affective language.

In one lengthy interaction which spreads over many chapters Sībawayhi asks Ḫalīl what would be the form of a word if it became a personal name, see further [181] (a); in another morphological context Baalbaki 1999a examines the uncertainly over whether the place name Hajar is fully (*hajarun*) or semi-declinable (*hajaru*), and Carter 1990 looks at the pausal form of *qāḍī* with a view to showing that when Sībawayhi said that it is formed by removing the last consonant and leaving unchanged what comes before that consonant, he meant the short vowel *i*, so that *qāḍī* (= *qāḍiy*) becomes *qāḍi*, not *qāḍ* as it is most often interpreted.

A short study of Stem II verbs by Leemhuis 1973 concludes that this Stem was not exclusively intensive for Sībawayhi but also factitive/resultative. For this reader it is a pity that the article does not take account of another perception of Sībawayhi, in 2, 361/331, that prosodically Stems II and III are identical, that is, II *fa"al-* and III *fā'al-* both have the structure CVCCVC-. This is of great significance for our understanding of syllable structure in general and the poetical metres in particular.

[161] (a) The most impressive evidence of the continuity of Sībawayhi's terminology over both areas of syntax and morphology (cf. [154] (b) above) is the application of the criterion of *istiqāma* to a morphophonological process: it is not right *lā yastaqīm* to pronounce the final radical of the imperative and apocopated doubled verbs without a vowel (**rudd, *yarudd*), presumably meaning that this prevents the listener from interpreting the intended meaning: the Ḥijāzī solution, *urdud, yardud*, shows how morphology can override phonology, given that two closely adjacent consonants are normally assimilated (see *Kitāb* 2, 163/159).

This *istiqāma* is not a formal feature: if it were structurally incorrect it would be called "bad Arabic" *qabīḥ*, or *lā yaḥsun*, as in §566 on *iddiġām*, where Sībawayhi states that he has listed all the consonants in order to show those combinations which it is "good" or "not good" to assimilate.

As the examples show (though not exhaustively illustrated here) all the words for "way" occur throughout both volumes of the *Kitāb*, just as frequently in phonological and morphological contexts as in syntax.

[161] (b) Cf. Carter 1985b.

[162] (a) Sara 2007 contains some regrettable mistakes of Arabic, but none more bizarre than the translation of *banāt al-yā'* as "structures with the *yā'*," and *banāt al wāw* as "structures with the *wāw*"as if *banāt* "daughters" were derived from *banā* "to build," e.g., p. 15f and *passim*.

[162] (b) It is a relief to be able to report that Troupeau 1976 did not find it either. The notion emerges in later grammar to refer to the "effect" *ta'ṯīr* of verbs upon their direct objects, cf. [178] (a).

[164] (a) Two sets of terms are involved, one denoting cases and moods, the other the short vowels. Versteegh 1993, 28–32, still favours (cf. 1977) a Syriac inspiration for both sets, borrowed in "the early stages of Syriac grammar, in which the system was based on Greek grammar without any traces of Arabic influence" such as we see, as Versteegh

points out, in later Syriac and Hebrew grammar. He links this with the introduction of diacriticals inspired by Syriac orthography, which has long been accepted.

No position need be taken on this here, as the story is finished by the time the *Kitāb* was composed, when we are confronted with two closely similar systems, one attributed to Ḫalīl, the other to Sībawayhi. Since Ḫalīl's terminology is only preserved in later sources (principally the *Mafātīḥ al-ʿulūm* of Ḫwārizmī, see [56]), the relationship between the two is not certain. Danecki 1978, for example, argues that Sībawayhi's phonological system is both more complex and of an earlier date than Ḫalīl's.

We must be grateful to Versteegh 1993 125–30 for a valuable insight, that the use of the two historically discrete sets of terms, one morphological, the other phonological, became confused, with terms from one set being used in the other context. This is excellent evidence of a transitional stage, with no particular bearing on the remote origins of the terms, and it was later schematicised into differences between the "Baṣran" and "Kūfan" schools. This is only to be expected, but for us it has high relevance for certain irregularities in Sībawayhi's terminology which can hardly be connected with "schools" at such an early stage, see [301] (a).

But there is still no satisfactory account for the syntactic meaning of the terms *rafʿ*, *naṣb*, *jarr/ḫafḍ*, *jazm*. They do not relate to the phonetic properties of the case endings, even less to their meaning (unlike the Graeco-Latin terms). It is impossible to eliminate the common underlying metaphor of building which we see in so much grammatical terminology, but the inspiration which chose these terms for the nominal and verbal inflections is now unrecoverable, with only *jazm* "cutting off" implying any obvious correlation between the phonetic and the morphological events.

[165] (a) To this we should certainly add Ḫalīl's special term *sanad* for the subject of a sentence, see [70] (a). Anecdotally Ḫalīl is connected with building and language by Zajjājī, *Īḍāḥ*, in Versteegh 1995, when he compares the structure of language with that of an elegantly erected house whose principles of construction can be inferred by the wise observer. Versteegh 94 attaches this trope to Classical Latin sources, but its presence in Zajjājī has no implications for such contacts with Ḫalīl.

[165] (b) The term *musnad* was used by the Arabs to refer to inscriptions in Old South Arabian script, and is derived from the OSA word *msnd* meaning "affixed to a wall" as a kind of votary tablet and then to any inscription on rock, see Beeston, *EI*², art. Musnad. A connection with the syntactical notion of *musnad* in the context of predication (see previous note) seems most unlikely but it could, of course, relate to the common meaning of both terms, "something fixed."

[165] (c) The set of terms preserved by Ḫwārizmī partially overlaps those used by Sībawayhi, but their separate existence is unaccounted for. W. Fischer 1985 concludes that they represent an earlier stage of development which was discarded by Sībawayhi.

[166] (a) Ru'ba died about 145/762, see above [14]

[166] (b) On translatability see [298] and comments thereon in the Addenda.

[167] (a) See now Ayoub 1990, also [273].

[168] (a) Here, as elsewhere, cf. [244] (b), the term "sentence" has intruded into the translation, though there is no exact equivalent in Sībawayhi's text.

[168] (b) Sībawayhi is referring to the non-productive anomalies he has discussed in *Kitāb* §5. As part of his attempt to provide an exhaustive description of every observed linguistic usage he also accounts for the many deviations which arise in affective speech, see Carter 2015.

[169] (a) In the light of Levin 1994 (see [172] (a) below), this assertion should now be withdrawn or at least toned down. It remains true that we do not know what class of Bedouin the grammarians consulted, that is, whether they spoke Classical Arabic all the time as their everyday tongue, or were specially proficient in a Classical variety of the language that they did not use among themselves informally, rather like Latin today.

[170] (a) "Incline" here renders the concept of *imāla*, more familiarly termed *a*-raising or palatalisation; see Levin 1992 (where also references to his earlier treatments), Levin 2000a, 262 for additional bibliography. Sara 2007 presents an annotated translation of the relevant chapters on *imāla* in the *Kitāb*, but see above, [162] (a).

[170] (b) "Bastard tongue" is unnecessarily picturesque for the simple original *ḫallaṭa fī luġatihi*, literally "has mixed up his [dialect] pronunciation." But *luġa*, as well as denoting "language" in general and "dialect" in particular, can also refer to the individual features of a dialect, and since the issue here is the polarisation of those dialects which do raise the *a* and those which do not (i.e., as isoglosses), there is something illegitimate about randomly combining both processes. In fact, as we see, Sībawayhi goes on to say that such confusion is normal in language and nothing to worry about.

[171] (a) E.g., *al-ṯurayyā* "the Pleiades," never seen without the article, unlike such personal names as al-Ḥasan/Ḥasan, where the distribution is not systematic (see an example in [48] above). For the Pleiades we also find *al-najm*, lit. "the Star" taken to refer *sui generis* to the Pleiades, which is the context in which this issue is being treated. See Marogy 2012 on the arbitrary definiteness of personal names.

[172] (a) Since this was written there has been more support for the view that Sībawayhi had substantial contact with Bedouin both directly and indirectly: Levin 1994 (1998) documents Sībawayhi's use of Bedouin informants in great detail. Interestingly they are always referred to in the *Kitāb* by tribal name or region, or generically as "Arabs," never as "Bedouin."

Certainly we cannot question the fact that Sībawayhi was observing actual speech: some situations he describes can only occur in the spoken language, such the *badal al-ġalaṭ* "substitution of error," e.g., *ra'aytu zaydan ʿamran* "I saw Zayd [correct that, I mean] 'Amr" (*Kitāb* 1, 64/75), various exclamations, and hedging and stalling in order not to lose one's place in a conversation, see [209] (a).

To this extent (though it is not strictly relevant to Sībawayhi's grammatical theories), the *Kitāb* provides good evidence that the Classical language was in full use in his time, apparently in all registers. This has some bearing on the theories for the origins of the dialects, which we will not explore here. Levin op. cit. 236f gives a brief outline, and we should add to his biography Vollers 1906, whose case for the underlying colloquial nature of the Qur'anic text has stirred up much controversy, and is still part of the debate.

[172] (b) For "direct," i.e., *manṣūb*, we now prefer "dependent," see further [298] (a).

[173] (a) "Initial term" more or less literally renders *mubtada' [bihi]* "what is started [with]," more familiarly, but less accurately, translated as "subject" or "topic" see further discussion at [71] (a).

[174] (a) In spite of the advice given in [290], the present writer (who is not alone in this) has not shrunk from accusing Sībawayhi of weaknesses in his argument, e.g., [191], [222], [259], [268], [276]. This at least demonstrates that my deplorable arrogance is not aimed solely at my European fellow scholars. By way of reparation, [268] (a) discusses a feature of Sībawayhi's reasoning which confirms beyond doubt the superiority of his intellect.

Note also that Sībawayhi did not escape criticism from his successors, particularly Mubarrad, see Bernards 1997. One such criticism appears in Šantamarī's commentary on the *šawāhid*, in *Kitāb* 1, 121/145, where "Sībawayhi is wrong (*ġaliṭa*) to permit the independent form of *yadāha* in *tuwāhiqu rijlāhā yadāhā* 'the two back legs [of the wild ass] race against its two front legs.'" The construction would scan anyway as *yadayhā*, which raises deeper issues about an older invariable dual form, cf. Rabin 1951, 67f for an early treatment, but it might simply be that the underlying reciprocal meaning of *wāhaqa* here has interfered with the rules for agent and object inflection.

[174] (b) The ponderous literal translation of the "*la-* for starting [nominal sentences]" is meant to focus on the nature of the linguistic event without recourse to such Latinisms as Wright's "inchoative or inceptive *la.*"

[175] (a) This degeneration is a leitmotiv of Baalbaki 2008, e.g., 62, 236, 250. See also below [289] (b) on the fate of the *Kitāb*.

[176] (a) Unlike the Qur'anic example in [177] below, which is simply an exegetical problem as to how many people are addressed, the issue here is soliloquy, which Sībawayhi defines as the case where "it is as if the speaker and the listener are the same," *kunta fīhi ka-l-muḫāṭab*. It stands to reason that soliloquy nevertheless has to abide by the same rules as communication between two people.

[178] (a) In spite of the obvious parallelism between *muta'addī* and *transitivum* (to which we should add Greek *metabatikós*), all meaning the same thing, there is no way to document the connection: the most we can do, if so inclined, is to "suppose that the Arabic terms are calques of the Greek." See Versteegh 1977, 83, cf. id. 1993, 25, where the assumed provenance remains unrevised, though at 202 Versteegh admits that the exact pathway of transmission is unknowable.

What we do know is that Sībawayhi made coherent use of the concept in a nexus of syntactic principles unique to Arabic, as described by Levin 1979a (1998), accounting for the grammatical relationship between verbs and their objects, independently of their semantic relationship. See also Taha in *EI*[2], art. Ta'addī. This allowed Sībawayhi to offer a unified syntax for types of verbs not normally regarded as transitive, such as *kāna*, see

Levin 1979a (1998), and for sentential verbs which behave as transitive towards mental objects, even though they have no physical effect (*ta'ṯīr*) on them, cf. Carter 2011, 122–4 (note that Sībawayhi does not himself invoke the term *ta'ṯīr*, see [162]).

Saad 1979 offers a brief but useful survey of transitivity in Sībawayhi with a glance at the relationship between transitivity and passivisation. Bobzin 1981 (1983) examines transitivity in terms of the number of arguments a verb can take, concluding that for Sībawayhi transitivity is associated wholly with case-assignment: in this framework indirect transitivity by means of a preposition was analysed as operating differently from the way directly transitive verbs operate upon their objects.

One most important product of Sībawayhi's analysis is that he identified the correlation between dependent forms (i.e., objects of one kind or another) and structural redundancy, real or potential, cf. [265] (a). For the *maf'ūl [bihi]* Kasher 2012 shows that, since it is applied by Sībawayhi to several different syntactical categories (direct object, agent of passive verb, object in annexation to a verbal noun, the *ẓurūf* under certain conditions) it cannot be considered as a simple equivalent of our "direct object," as Mosel has pointed out. He further notes (19) that Sībawayhi uses *maf'ūl* is a sense more akin to "the meaning of the passive participle of the verb at stake" than to a purely grammatical category, and concludes that the term has both semantic and syntactic properties.

It is too late for the present writer to give up using "object" and move to "patient" as Kasher recommends (though we still favour the pair "agent/patient noun" on the morphological level). However, there is no doubt that Sībawayhi is entirely consistent in his recognition of the dual relationship, syntactical and semantic, between all verbs and their dependent elements. As for Kasher's suggestion (22f) that the *bihi* in both *maf'ūl bihi* and *mubtada' bihi* is illusory, this is a most plausible suggestion as regards Sībawayhi, but one wonders whether the subsequent grammatical tradition may not have canonised those expressions in the urge for terminological consistency.

[179] (a) Arabic orthography is binary, *ḥaraka/sukūn*, representing the very restricted syllabic structure of Classical Arabic as CV or CVC, the latter also including long vowels, which are accounted for by Ḫalīl as combinations of short vowels and homorganic semivowels, see [56] (a). Since a comparable binary structure was also perceived at the morphological level (root consonants + patterns/augments) there is a natural binarism at all levels.

It may be noted in passing that this thesis pays almost no attention to questions of phonology or morphology, due to a merely personal preference, itself slightly reinforced by the sequence of topics in the *Kitāb*, but see [37] (a). However, we would not accept the claim of Danecki 1985, 130 n. 22, that the phonological sections of the *Kitāb* are a mere appendix added while Sībawayhi was in Baghdad.

[181] (a) As already mentioned, this notion of equivalence to a single word has its origins in Ḫalīl's morphophonological approach, which Sībawayhi adapted for syntax, see [37]–[45], esp. [44]f. What might be considered a transitional example is Ḫalīl's own paraphrase of *'alimtu annaka munṭaliqun* "I know that you are departing" as *'alimtu nṭilāqaka* "I

know about your departure" where, as he explains, *anna* (meaning the whole clause) is "like a single noun" *ka-l-ismi* (*Kitāb* 2, 30/32).

Note that the context of Ḫalīl's remark is a linguistic game in which Sībawayhi asks him what would happen to a word if made into a personal name, the point being to establish the boundaries and morphology of the resulting artificially created noun, cf. Carter 1981 (1983).

[181] (b) We can add additional locations for some of these reference, e.g 1,34/45 for the notion that the adjective is the "completion"of the noun, and 1,362/407, 2,336/309 for the examples of *allaḏī* and *an* with their clauses as having "the status of a single noun."

[181] (c) De Saussure would have had at his disposal the translation of Jahn, and the question was asked by J. Fück in 1955 as to whether he actually had read it, see Carter 1987/88, 211, n. 20. The answer, however, is not known.

[182] (a) The sample sentence is the negative of *laka ġulāmun ẓarīfun*, where the obligatory inversion with indefinite subjects/topics (see [123] (b) above) has two side-effects, (i) the ambiguity of *laka* is removed (as predicate it cannot be a structurally redundant locative phrase) and (ii) the unity of *ġulāmun ẓarīfun* is evident in its full agreement of case and definiteness. The issue of redundancy is best illustrated by an example not used here: Sībawayhi contrasts *fīhā 'abdullāhi qā'imun/qā'iman*, where *fīhā* is a *ẓarf* and may be neutralised, with *fīka 'abdullāhi rāġibun*, where *fīka* is part of the phrasal verb *raġiba fī*, and cannot become the predicate, hence there is no option of *rāġiban* (*Kitāb* 1, 223/262). See also [270] (a) on locative predicates.

[183] (a) For these terms "dependent" and "indefinite" are now preferred, see [250] (a) and [298] (a) respectively.

[184] (a) Details in [256]–[261].

[185] (a) The source is *Kitāb* 1, 307/351, where Sībawayhi is concerned to show that the third element *'āqilan* has to preserve its *tanwīn* to avoid creating an illegal unit of three elements, either by being marked as an extraneous element after the complete utterance *lā rajula fīhā*, or by forming the unit *rajula 'āqilan* with *fīhā* neutralised. In both cases the result is the same, and the incorrect sequence *rajula fīhā 'āqila* is avoided.

[187] (a) Precursorism is not the goal, and the wording in Carter 1973, 157 is unfortunately easy to misunderstand as a claim that Sībawayhi in some way founded this approach.

[188] (a) Not to mention to the listener, who can only decode the elements in the string in the order in which they are received.

[188] (b) See Carter 1997. The relationship of *muḍāra'a* is bidirectional, indeed circular, or even spiral, cf. [113] (a) and Carter op. cit. 6f.

[189] (a) Ullmann 1966, 137–40 has identified four higher derived stems with infixes *ran*, *lan*, *'an* and *ḥan*, which he numbers XVI, XVII, XVIII and XIX respectively.

[190] (a) Ḫalīl seems to regard Stem IV as a simple causative, without identifying (here at least) its declarative sense. Ibn Jinnī, *Ḫaṣā'iṣ* 3,253, in a chapter on how a knowledge of grammar insures against heresy, takes the Stem IV in *man aġfalnā qalbahu* in Sūra

18, 28 as declarative, "him whose heart we have found to be neglectful" and not the causative "whose heart we have made neglectful." As a Muʿtazilī Ibn Jinnī could not accept that God caused sin, and he proves his point with the next sentence *wa-ttabaʿa hawāhu* "and who follows his own desires," which, he says, cannot be the result of God's making him forgetful, because this requires *fa-* to indicate causality (or we might say, has to be subordinated ("and therefore follows....") and not coordinated to the previous sentence ("and also follows"). Of this insight Ibn Jinnī remarks, "If someone spent sixty years in the service of this science (i.e., grammar, *naḥw*), and was never blessed [with success] in any topic but this one, he would not have wasted his time or be any the less fortunate or happy for doing so."

[190] (b) This criticism is unfair, since Jahn has merely moved all the examples to the notes, where they receive due comment and interpretation.

[191] (a) It is always risky to find fault with Sībawayhi, see [174] (a). With this present topic he is by no means as vulnerable as represented here: the power of analogy cannot be overestimated.

[192] (a) See Baalbaki 1979. These hierarchies may be usefully compared with the *a priori* facts of Aristotelian science. They are not incompatible with the linearity of *naḥw*: the higher the status (*manzila*) of an element the more syntactic positions (*mawāḍiʿ*) it can occupy, and correspondingly the more elements it has the power (*quwwa*) to operate on (*ʿamal*). However, the role of these hierarchies in the *Kitāb* is relatively minor: most of them are disposed of early in the work, in the *Risāla* section, cf. [293]. The term *rutba* "rank," which is not rare in later grammar, does not occur anywhere in the *Kitāb*, nor indeed do any of its cognates.

The hierarchical term *daraja* "degree" does appear in the *Kitāb*, but only once. Curiously it involves a demotion in rank: in *Kitāb* 2, 48/53, Ḫalīl is reported as saying that *ʿamrawayhi* is regarded as a foreign name, but is invariable, unlike the partially inflected *ismāʿīlu/ismāʿīla*, because the speakers "have downgraded it" *ḥaṭṭūhu darajatan*, i.e., set it lower in the inflectional hierarchy. Troupeau 1976, with some justification, does not list *ḥaṭṭa* as a technical term, though he does label this sole instance of *daraja* in the *Kitāb* as a methodological term.

[193] (a) Cf. above p. [129] in discussing the legal terminology *sabīl* and *ittisāʿ*. The example in [149] (c) uses the ambiguity of *waṭiʾa*, either "to step on" or "to have sexual intercourse," to enable a person to promise not to do one of these two while meaning the other, and thus evade his promise.

[193] (b) These have all been rounded up and made sense of by Baalbaki 2008, 209–215, as a specimen of the way Sībawayhi starts with a simple model sentence and gradually introduces complex syntactical variations, which he explains as he goes along.

[193] (c) See Talmon 1993a.

[194] (a) See above, [82].

[195] (a) See Versteegh 1990a, Dayyeh 2015.

[195] (b) "O thief of the night [stealing from] the people of the house," an anonymous fragment of Rajaz poetry (see Yaʻqūb 1992, 1151). A clearer example of this latitude in English is "shoplifter." Unlike a "weightlifter," who lifts weights, a shoplifter does not lift shops but only "lifts" (i.e steals) *in* shops. As it happens, "people of the house" is itself an example of such latitude, they being stolen *from*, rather than simply stolen.

[196] (a) The plural translation here is an error: "[The camel] grazes for as long as she grazes until, when she calls to mind [her calf], all she does is [run anxiously] back and forth."

Chapter Five
The Principles and Criteria of the *Kitāb*

We have already seen that Sībawayhi based his analysis of Arabic upon certain well-defined general assumptions, the most important being that the structure of Arabic can be expressed as a range of binary units. If he had started the *Kitāb* by treating phonetics first, which is a fashion currently enjoying the status of a dogma, it would have been easy for him to prove that his binary units were composed of progressively larger constituents, from the consonant-vowel unit up to the initial term and predicate unit, i.e., by doubling finite quantities. Instead he starts with something he does not define and proceeds to halve it until he reaches the level of phonetics, which is a choice that, if nothing else, demonstrates that Sībawayhi was a grammarian first and a phonetician last.[(a)] By adopting the method of dividing up a unit of indeterminate length Sībawayhi confirms the inherent similarity of his approach with the system of Immediate Constituent Analysis. At the same time he avoids the insuperable difficulty of defining a sentence in terms of its parts, and this, in turn, reveals the soundness of his intuition, for it is universally true that we do not actually speak in sentences, even though we may write in sentences. The unit of language in the *Kitāb* is thus not the sentence, the *jumla* of the latter grammarians,[(b)] but "what you say," your *kalām*. I do not believe that the refinements of the later grammarians, with their categorisation of sentences into *jumla ismiyya*, *fi'liyya* and *ẓarfiyya*, reflect any primitiveness in Sībawayhi, for these categories are already implicit in the *Kitāb*. The absence of the later terms may be taken as evidence that the ideas they denote were not important enough [199] to Sībawayhi to merit being explicitly named. In the case of *jumla* it is also obvious that there was no need for the term, because Sībawayhi defined his largest unit of speech, the *kalām*, from an entirely different point of view. The word *jumla* was certainly available for Sībawayhi to use if he had wanted to—it occurs at least seven times in the *Kitāb* in meanings ranging from "in short" to "a total,"[1] and this must confirm that

1. *Kitāb* 1, 91/111, 410/461, 2, 7/8, 229/219, 263/247, 285/263, 298/275.

he was not interested in establishing an independent concept of the sentence. He was right in the long run: Ibn Hišām records that "every *kalām* is a *jumla* but the converse is not true,"[2] which is tantamount to an admission that *jumla* is a useless concept as long as it still remains necessary to define *kalām* before you can tell whether you have a *jumla* or not! How far apart Ibn Hišām and Sībawayhi were can be appreciated by translating Ibn Hišām's words as follows: "Everything you say is a sentence, but not every sentence is a complete utterance," and noting that Sībawayhi was only interested in what people actually say, i.e., the "complete utterances" of which all normal speech consists.

There are other reasons why it is not advisable to father upon Sībawayhi the notion of "sentence" and thus to translate كلام when it appears to mean that in the text. The fact that it has other meanings is not Sībawayhi's fault but ours, and it is misleading to obscure these different meanings by adopting an inappropriate rendering such as "sentence."

Kalām, for example, is frequently used as the antithesis of *ši'r*, poetry:[(a)] [200]

1, 33/43	ولكنّه قد يجوز في الشعر وهو ضعيف في الكلام
1, 237/277	وهذا كلامٌ أكثره يكون في الشعر وأقلّ ما يكون في الكلام
1, 335/382	هذا باب ما يجوز في الشعر من إيّا ولا يجوز في الكلام

in which connection it is interesting to note that, although *naṯr* is never used in the *Kitāb* to mean "prose," which is always termed *kalām*, yet the phrase نثرتُ كلامًا is used once to illustrate the two meanings of نَثَرَ , the other being نثرتُ ولدًا.[3] Since Sībawayhi is obviously familiar with the basic terminology of prosody, and uses, amongst others إقواء , غناء , قافية , ردف , كسر البيت , رويّ, it can be inferred that he wrote before the Greek-based ideas of rhetoric had penetrated Islām.

Kalām is also used to denote specifically the way the Arabs speak, كلامهم, which is clearly also the basic meaning when Sībawayhi used كلام without qualification. Examples of the former:

1, 127/153	وهو قليل في كلام العرب
1, 20/26	وسترى . . . من هذا النحو لكثرته في كلامهم
1, 291/334	واعلم أنّ ما يُجعل بمنزلة اسم ليست فيه هاء أقلّ في كلام العرب
1, 92/116	ربّما جرت الصفة في كلامهم مجرى الاسم

When used without qualification, *kalām* may either refer elliptically to the speech of the Arabs, e.g.,

---

2. De Sacy, *Anthol. gram.* 73.
3. *Kitāb* 2, 250/236[(a)].

1, 148/177	وهذا تمثيل وإن كان لا يستعمل في الكلام
2, 239/226	وليس في الكلام فعُلتُهُ متعدّيًا
1, 240/279	فما حذف في الكلام لكثرة استعمالهم كثير

or it may be used in a more technical sense which corresponds approximately to our "proper sentence," e.g., [201]

1, 45/55	فلو قلت أزيدًا ضربت عمرًا ضربت أخاه لم يكن كلامًا
1, 195/228	إنما الكلام أن تقول هذا خاتم حديد . . . وخاتم من حديد
	لم يجد بدًّا من أن يقول أنا إن تأتني آتك لأنّ أنا لا يكون كلامًا
1, 395/444	حتى بني عليه شيء

Here it is not difficult to perceive that by *kalām* Sībawayhi still understands the "speech of the Arabs," for that is what the *Kitāb* sets out to describe, and it follows that when he says that something is "not speech" without qualification, he nevertheless means that it is not the correct speech of the Arabs. A further use of *kalām*, however, seems to abandon the idea of the speech of the Arabs and to refer instead to speech itself, particularly to parts of what people say:

1, 53/64	فما بعد المبتدأ في هذا الكلام في موضع خبره
1, 49/61	وكلما طال الكلام ضعف التأخير
1, 301/345	فالكلام بمنزلة اسم مرفوع مبتدأ
	وانتصب الرجل لأنه ليس من الكلام الأول وعمل فيه الكلام
1, 258/299	الأول فصارت الهاء بمنزلة التنوين

But the usage of *kalām* illustrated in the last two groups of examples does not justify the rendering "sentence" for every occurrence of the term *kalām* in the *Kitāb*. We would find it difficult to cope with the following, for example:

	ولم يكن مثل إيّاك لو أفردته لأنّه لم يكثر في كلامهم كثرة إيّاك
(1, 117/138)	فشبّهت بإيّاك حيث طال الكلام وكان كثيرًا في الكلام

Jahn gets round this by only translating the second instance of *kalām* as "Satz" and ignoring the others. He also introduces the word "Phrase" into his translation, thereby considerably confusing the issue, for no such term is found in the *Kitāb* or even in Arabic grammar generally.[4] [202] An accurate rendering can be achieved simply by reproducing *kalām* as "speech," viz.

4. Jahn, *Kitāb* 1, 175[(a)].

> And it (رأسَك والحائطَ) is not like إيّاك , when you put it on its own, because it is not as frequent in their speech as إيّاك , and is likened to إيّاك only because the speech is lengthy and it is common in speech.[(a)]

The lesson that this passage teaches is that Sībawayhi might have had a very good reason for preferring to retain what seems to be a very vague expression instead of coining a specific technical term. Jahn's translation, as so often, precludes this view by making it impossible to recognise the original Sībawayhi, but we will find that there are indeed great advantages in not delimiting the unit of speech at this level.

By far the greatest advantage in this connection is the fact that the absence of a fixed concept of the sentence makes it impossible to object to any item which, though used in speech, does not appear to contain the required number of constituents to form a sentence. As soon as the *jumla*[(b)] concept came into being, the practice of *taqdīr*[(c)] arose solely to fill up what the new method decided were gaps in the sentence, or, to characterise it in the spirit of the later grammarians as they appear to us, the facts were forced to submit to theory. Sībawayhi, on the other hand, did not concern himself with what sentences ought to be, but concentrated on what they actually were. He recognised that a *kalām* can be of any length, and so he laid down criteria for determining only the beginning and the end of a speech.

Likewise he appreciated, perhaps intuitively, that [203] the meaning of a sentence is not discovered by adding up the meanings of its parts, as if a sentence of ten words were twice as meaningful as one with five.[(a)] Instead he took the view that a sentence is constructed and used to say only one thing, and that the construction (grammar) and use (intelligibility) of the sentence are the only aspects of it which can be usefully analysed by the grammarian. And underlying all this was his belief in the act of communication as something which requires both a speaker and a listener, the latter being a restraining factor on the form of speech as well as providing (which is not as obvious as it ought to be) the only reason for the speaker to open his mouth at all. Under these circumstances a sentence is not what a grammarian says it should be, but what he perceives to be the act of communication by means of speech.

By the same token, what is left out of the speech is not something which the grammarian can restore by *taqdīr*, but something which the situation, the tacit consent of the listener or simply the habit of centuries makes it unnecessary to utter. I am not suggesting that Sībawayhi made no attempt to restore the missing parts of speeches as an aid to understanding: but that is not the *taqdīr* described by Weil, with understandable repugnance, as "the forced application of *qiyās* to a recalcitrant expression whose forms cannot be explained by analogy; it is the other side of the medal of *qiyās*."[5] Sībawayhi justifies his restoration of elision on the grounds that his sentence-criteria themselves are

5. In Anbārī, *Inṣāf*, intro. 26.

fulfilled by the sentences with elision as much as by sentences with no elision. This will emerge particularly clearly when we examine the [204] role of the listener in Sībawayhi's grammar.

For the speaker, if I may resort to a truism, there is no doubt about the length of a *kalām*: it is bounded by silence and, in the words of a far greater linguist than myself,[a] you "begin at the beginning, and go on till you come to the end." Both the beginning and the end of the *kalām* as Sībawayhi understands it are marked by formal features which are all the more distinctive in that they can only occur at the beginning and end of Arabic speech.

The beginning of every Arabic *kalām* is, theoretically, a vocative expression (*nidā'*), whose formal qualities need no emphasis here. What is so ingenious about Sībawayhi's approach is that he accounts for the almost complete absence of vocatives at the beginning of Arabic speech (excepting, naturally, those whose purpose is specifically to call someone), by pointing out that since we always talk to someone, we can dispense with an explicit vocative:

> The first part of every speech is always a vocative, unless you leave it out because you can dispense with it by the fact that the listener is standing before you. But it is the first part of every speech and through it you attract the attention of the person you are speaking to.[6]

The end of a speech receives its formal sign in Arabic by being pronounced with *waqf*, which is nowhere explicitly stated in the *Kitāb*, but which may be inferred from §§490–502 (2, 302–320/277–293) on the [205] problems of *waqf*.[a]

For Sībawayhi, then, a given stretch of speech bears its own signs of starting and finishing, the vocative (explicitly or implicitly) and the lack of final inflection.[b] These two features are, moreover, not found anywhere else in speech: even today Arabic writing seems to reflect this situation through the convention by which books are written as though the entire work, or at least its individual chapters, consist of a single sentence, and every new paragraph is introduced by a conjunction which links up eventually with the initial *bismillāh*[c] of the first page. And instead of full stops, Arabic uses *waqf*, so that every sentence is read as a separate speech addressed to a reader whose attention, once attracted by the *bismillāh*, is maintained by the conjunctions which bind every sentence. In passing it is also significant that Arabic, even more than English, preserves the convention of using قال to refer to what people "say" in their books.

Another advantage which *kalām* possesses over *jumla*, and therein lies the superiority of the one system over the other, is that *kalām* denotes an act of the speaker, while *jumla* denotes nothing more than a figment of the grammarian's imagination. As an act

6. *Kitāb* 1, 274/316.

of the speaker, a *kalām* is inherently suitable for judgement by ethical criteria, which we shall see later to be the basis of the grammatical use of *ḥusn* and *qubḥ*, and, as an act, it suggests a convenient method for analysing its components, namely into parts of speech which themselves act in whatever way their status and function require. There is thus a smooth and natural transition (or, in other words, Sībawayhi preferred not to make any distinction) between what the speaker does and what his words do within the sentence. I shall [206] now examine this element of Sībawayhi's system.

It is striking that nearly all the grammatical categories in the *Kitāb* are, like *kalām* itself, expressed in the form of verbal nouns, and that the names of the items belonging to these categories are invariably from the same root, e.g., *waṣf*: *ṣifa*, *mawṣūf*. It seems that, apart from setting up a tripartite division into noun, verb and particle,[(a)] Sībawayhi established a much larger range of "parts of speech" according to their function. This creates a slight problem, however, as the original three "parts of speech" find themselves shared out among over sixty[(b)] different functions, in which case we ought to ask ourselves what was the point of identifying three "parts of speech" when they are not used in isolation to denote individual functions. By this I mean that the term *ism* without qualification does not refer to any grammatical function: we must first be told that it is a *mubtada*,' a *mubdal* or *ism kāna* etc. before we know what its function is. I believe that the purpose of Sībawayhi's first chapter may best be understood by adapting his own anthropomorphic metaphor and supposing, for a moment, that the three "parts of speech" correspond to something like the concepts of "male," "female" and "neuter" in the human context. This is not, of course, to say that nouns are male, verbs female, and so on, but it may give some idea of the quality of the distinctions made so early in the *Kitāb* and so soon abandoned in favour of functional distinctions. The three "parts of speech" are, in effect, the three types of word (identifiable by their form and approximate range of meanings) which are available to be used in the dozens of different functions specified by Sībawayhi.[(c)]

To that extent the three [207] "parts of speech" are much less important to Sībawayhi than might on the face of it be expected. Granted that there are occasions when one "part of speech" can function as another, or (much less commonly) has the form of another,[(a)] the only useful byproduct of this primitive classification is that it determines the morphology of words once they are recognised as nouns or verbs, and it is obvious that the first chapter of the *Kitāb*, which is brutally short, is intended merely as a guide to this last-mentioned problem. We must conclude that the chapter is short because the subject does not really interest Sībawayhi. The second chapter, on the other hand, deals with purely grammatical behaviour, and its length, as well as the many comparisons between nominal and verbal behaviour, testify to the proper area of Sībawayhi's interest. It is only when we ask what we can learn from the first chapter of the *Kitāb* in relation to what the rest of the book is about, that we begin to understand how little Sībawayhi could have owed to Greek grammar and how dangerous it is to take any of his words in isolation. The topics of the first chapter are, in fact, of scarcely any consequence for Sībawayhi's main preoccupation, as may most easily be gathered from the fact that if he had started with Chapter Two, the contents of Chapter One would have been taken for granted by anyone who could already tell the difference between a noun and a verb. Compare this with the law, which discusses in great detail the behaviour of men and women, yet there can be few books of law which do not take for granted the difference between the male and the female, and this is exactly the kind of distinction which Sībawayhi is making in his opening chapter.

[208] It is, therefore, misleading to think of the *ism*, *fi'l* and *ḥarf* as "parts of speech," and it would be closer to the purposes of the *Kitāb* to refer to them as "kinds of word," without attempting to connect them with any specifically grammatical analysis.[(a)] If we examine the *Kitāb* as a whole it is quite clear that Sībawayhi did have a unified grammatical system in mind, but it does not base itself on three, still less on eight "parts of speech." Instead the *Kitāb* appears to concentrate on the functions performed by words in sentences, and the status which enables words to carry out their prescribed range of functions. The interplay of status and function, in short, is the whole subject-matter of the *Kitāb*, just as it is of works in which the status and function appertain to human beings, for it is only to be expected that, if the terminology of these disciplines is identical, their methods should also prove to be the same.

The index of any work of *fiqh* will show that it deals almost exclusively with human actions: a list of the functions discussed by Sībawayhi leads to the conclusion that his concern was with acts of language. *Kalām* itself means nothing more or less than the act of speaking, and all the functions which make up *kalām* are likewise denoted by verbal nouns in the *Kitāb*, e.g., *waṣf*, *ibtidā'*, *iḍāfa*, *nidā',* *nafy*, *istiṯnā'* and so on. Furthermore the index of the work of *fiqh* should, ideally, provide a definition of all the different ways in which a Muslim may or may not behave, and, by the same token, a list of all the functions described by Sībawayhi enumerates all the different ways in which it is possible to speak. The comparison can be extended even further, for both [209] law and grammar are interested only in acts which are legally or grammatically identifiable (i.e., by their form and effect), while neither is concerned with acts that are neutral. Thus the law ignores the acts of minors because they have no legal consequences, and grammar ignores such linguistic acts as lying, joking, shouting and the like because they have no characteristic grammatical consequences.

A tentative list of the functions mentioned by Sībawayhi will, perhaps, give some idea of the scope of his interest and, more significantly, the nature of the analysis which he also applied to Arabic:

> *waṣf, waṣl, iḍāfa, binā', ibtidā,' isnād, nidā', nafy, nudba, istiġāṯa, qasam, istiṯnā', 'aṭf, istifhām, badal, faṣl, iḍmār, išāra, ibhām, i'rāb, i'jām, raf', naṣb jarr, jazm, waqf, ḥaḏf, takrīr, qaṭ', ġalaṭ, ta'kīd, ḥikāya, ḥašw, taḥḏīr, taḫṣīṣ, qiṣṣa, kināya, iltibās, madḥ, ta'ẓīm, taṣġīr, taḥqīr, ta'ajjub, mubālaġa, šatm, taraḥḥum, muḫāṭaba, jam', taṯniya, ījāb, taṯbīt, ta'wiḍ, ilġā', tanbīh, tab'īḍ, ta'rīf, tanwīn, mujāzāh, amr, nahy, ta'ḫīr, taqdīm, imāla, išmām, iddiġām.*

Even this list, with over sixty items, may not be complete,[a] but I hope it will show that, if we are to think at all in terms of "parts of speech" then there must at least be as many parts as there are functions: In fact it emerges from the *Kitāb* that each function is normally expressed in two parts, and is none other than the "binary unit" I have already mentioned.[7] This can be shown in diagrammatic form, where the relation [210] between the binary unit and the function which unites its two parts emerges in striking clarity, e.g.,

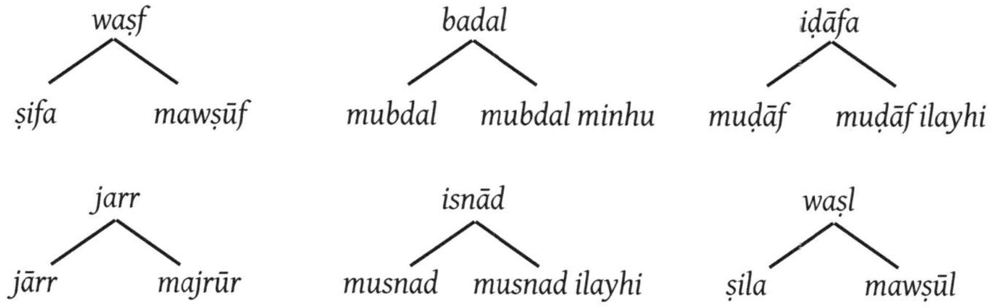

Every function is thus seen to consist of two parts, whose names could be used to provide an albeit unwieldy inventory of "parts of speech." But such an exercise would not be very rewarding, both because the list of functions may not be complete, and, more important, because the triadic system which I have used to throw light on Sībawayhi's system cannot be applied to every function with the same results. The function of elision (*ḥaḏf*) for example, would yield a ludicrous triad consisting of nothing (*al-maḥḏūf*) on one side and nothing (what is left after elision) on the other![a] In addition I have to admit that the function triad is unable to cope with the *ḥāl* and *sabab* constructions,[t] and that to devise a triad for any of the verbal objects and *manṣūbāt* would be mere graphic casuistry.

Nevertheless the triads illuminate very well what must have been the germ of Sībawayhi's system, and can also be used to provide in diagrammatic form a definition of the *ḥarf* which should dispense with the need for any further speculation on that vexed topic:

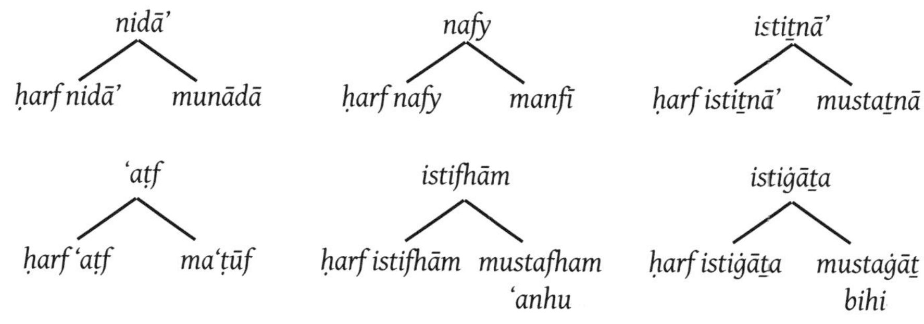

7. Above, p. [176].

[211] It is no longer possible to equate *ḥarf* with *súndesmos* or *árthron*. To what in modern jargon might be called a functional moneme Sībawayhi deliberately refrained from giving a specific name, because it was easier for him to call it a mere "bit" of speech and only then to define it by adding the name of the function it performed.

As for the pregnant phrase جاء لمعنى which has produced so many critically stillborn attempts to define the *ḥarf*, it should be obvious that its interpretation must depend on what Sībawayhi means by معنى not what others think he ought to mean.[(a)] Those Arab definitions which explain *ḥarf* as "a word which indicates a meaning outside itself only"[8] have falsely assumed that by معنى Sībawayhi meant the intrinsic, lexical meaning of a noun or verb, or at least the meaning of "noun-ness" and "verb-ness," which is misguided and misleading. When Sībayhi uses the word معنى he invariably uses it in conjunction with one of the function terms, e.g. *maʿnā al-naṣb* (1, 37/48); *maʿnā al-tanbīh wa-l-taʿrīf* (1, 222/260); *maʿnā al-taḫṣīṣ* (1, 40/51); *maʿnā al-taʿajjub* (1, 37/165); *maʿnā al-qasam* (2, 149/146); *maʿnā al-amr wa-l-nahy* (1, 401/452); *maʿnā al-istiṯnāʾ* (1, 327/374); *maʿnā al-taraḥḥum* (1, 255/217); *maʿnā al-tanwīn* (1, 179/211).

These examples show that *maʿnā* for Sībawayhi chiefly referred to grammatical meaning, hence the later term معاني النحو which we find, for example, in the works of Jurjānī[9] which merely formalises what Sībawayhi left informal. It is quite in keeping with *maʿnā al-kalām* (1, 375/420) or *maʿnā al-ḥadīṯ* (1, 39/50) [212], for a *kalām* only has one meaning, which is not the sum of the lexical meanings it may contain, but the single purpose for which it, as a single act of communication, was uttered.[(a)] We have here a most valuable clue to Sībawayhi's functional view of language, which is confirmed time and again by the use of the listener as the point of reference by which the speech is judged.[10] The *ḥarf*, against this use of *maʿnā*, now appears for what it is, i.e., a simple instrument for indicating a given function, and the problem of its intrinsic meaning does not arise. Indeed, because whatever technical meaning *ḥarf* may have comes exclusively from the function term which qualifies it, it can be claimed that it is scarcely a technical term at all.[(b)] Sībawayhi, as Weiss showed[11], certainly used it in too many senses for it to have any technical precision, and what are we to make of such expressions as هذه الحروف التي هي أسماء للفعل which we find in the *Kitāb*?[12] One thing we cannot do is translate them in the way Fischer would seem to favour.[(c)] By abolishing lexical meaning, and particularly by ignoring the meaning of the classes of noun and verb, Sībawayhi avoided a great many problems of grammar which have since, unfortunately, been reintroduced into *Kitāb* studies by those who did not recognise Sībawayhi's functionalism.

8. E.g., Fākihī, *Ḥudūd* 3, and cf. Sīrāfī on *Kitāb* 1, 1/2 in Jahn's notes.
9. Jurjānī, *Dalāʾil* 254, 255, 266ff [(b)].
10. Cf. below p. [241].
11. See above p. [65].
12. *Kitāb* 1, 102/123, 105/125.

An unmistakable indication of Sībawayhi's interest in function is his use of the term *mawḍiʿ*.(d) We have seen that position and function are virtually synonymous in linguistic parlance.[13] Perhaps, then, it is not surprising that Reuschel, for example, should translate *mawḍiʿ* variously into [213] "Platz" (39), "Stelle" (23, 55), "Position" (23) and "Funktion" (35, 47). Against these, Jahn's "Gebrauchsweise"[14] looks irresponsibly vague, but Reuschel himself does nothing to bring us to an understanding of the *Kitāb* by using so many different renderings without justifying any of them.

Since the subject of the *Kitāb* is كلام العرب, it is inevitable that موضع should stand chiefly for موضع في الكلام, for just as "place" in the ethical sense means "place in society" (a phrase which was evidently taken for granted by the early writers who use موضع without qualification),[15] so a "place" in the grammarian's field of study must be a "place in speech." Hence the function of كلّ is described in the following terms:

موضعه في الكلام أن يعمّ به غيره من الاسماء بعد ما يذكر [16]

and of the conjunctions و and فـ he says:

الواو لا يكون موضعها في الكلام موضع الفاء [17]

On another occasion the same idea, in slightly different words, is used to describe the functions of رويد and حيهلّ:

مجراهنّ واحد ومِوضعهنّ من الكلام الأمر والنهي [18]

It should be clear from these examples that there is, to all intents and purposes, no difference between the ethical use of موضع and the grammatical use, which will receive its final proof when we turn to the criteria of *ḥusn* and *qubḥ*. It also emerges that موضع clearly means [214] function in the most modern technical sense. A "place" in speech may refer to something as small as the pronoun suffix:

ولا يقع "أنا" في موضع التاء التي في فعلتُ [19]

as large as a whole sentence:

---

13. Above p. [104].
14. Above, p. [104].
15. But cf. *manzilatun fi al-dunyā* above, p, [106] .
16. *Kitāb* 1, 234/274.
17. Id. 1, 379/425.
18. Id. 1, 105/126.
19. *Kitāb* 1, 330/377.

وذلك لأنه حمل الفعل على موضع الكلام بأنّ هذا الكلام في موضع يكون جوابًا [20]

or to the "cases,"

حمل الآخر على موضع الكلام وموضعه نصب كما كان موضع ذلك موضع جزم [21]

Its most common use, however, is to refer to the function of individual words, as, for example, the various functions of imperfect verbs in independent form (*muḍāri'*, *marfū'*):[(a)]

> اعلم أنّها إذا كانت في موضع اسم مبتدأ أو اسم بُني على مبتدأ أو في موضع اسم مرفوع غير مبتدأ ولا مبني على مبتدأ أو في موضع اسم مرفوع غير مبتدأ ولا مبني على مبتدأ أو في موضع اسم مجرور أو منصوب فإنها مرتفعة وكينونتها في هذه المواضع ألزمتها الرفعَ [22]

or to other functions themselves:

> من does occasionally occur in a place (موضع) where even if it did not occur the speech would be right (مستقيم), and it is an emphasis in the status of ما, except that it makes oblique because it is a particle of *iḍāfa*. Thus when you say ما أتاني من رجل, or ما رأيت من أحد, if you left out من the speech would still be good Arabic (حسن) but you emphasise with من because this is a place (موضع) for the partitive function (تبعيض).[23]

Here *mawḍi'* is very clearly shown in close connection both with *ḥasan* and [215] *mustaqīm*, and we have a very good idea of the ethical import of the term. It is to be expected that one of its uses will be to describe the timing of an actual utterance or linguistic act from the point of view of its social context:

إنما يريد في هذا الموضع أن يَذكرَ المخاطبَ برجل قد عرفه قبل ذلك [24]

and it is reasonable to claim that every occurrence of *mawḍi'* is, therefore, equivalent to the full phrase "place in speech." It is thus a true technical term in that it covers, amongst other things, everything that is implied by the word "function." But *mawḍi'* straddles the two types of linguistic behaviour that I have previously mentioned,[25] for it covers the linguistic act both externally and internally, so that a one-word translation into "function" may turn out to be too precise for every occurrence of the term while "place" is too vague.[(a)] Both words can be used as the occasion demands, however, as they

20. Id. 1, 398/448.
21. Ibid.
22. Id. 1, 363/409.
23. Id. 2, 334/307.
24. Id. 1, 221/260.
25. Above, p. [163].

both represent legitimate shades of meaning in *mawḍiʿ*. But the only way to appreciate the technical use of this term in the *Kitāb* is to restore to it its full ethical flavour, whereupon the wide range of its applications, in which it resembles two other key terms in the *Kitāb*, *naḥw* itself and *kalām*, will be narrowed down by the unified ethical approach which underlies them. The "places" where acts of speech occur are the inseparable concomitants of the "acts" that occur there, i.e., the functions which I have listed [216] above, and we shall now examine the criteria by which these linguistic acts are judged.

Any discussion of this problem must begin by looking at the only chapter in the *Kitāb* where the criteria are set out deliberately and formally. The chapter in question was relegated to a footnote by Reuschel,[26] which, in view of certain observations he subsequently makes,[27] is testimony to an alarming superficiality of approach. For ease of reference I reproduce here the relevant chapter, which falls naturally and without rearrangement into numbered sections:[28]

هذا باب الاستقامة في الكلام والإحالة . فمنه مستقيم حسن ومحال ومستقيم كذب ومستقيم قبيح وما هو محال كذب.

1. فأما المستقيم الحسن فقولك أتيتك أمس وسآتيك غدًا
2. وأما المحال فأن تنقض أول كلامك بآخره فتقول أتيتك غدًا وسآتيك أمس
3. وأما المستقيم الكذب فقولك حملتُ الجبل وشربتُ ماء البحر ونحوه
4. وأما المستقيم القبيح فأن تضع اللفظ في غير موضعه نحو قولك قد زيدًا رأيت وكي زيدٌ يأتيك وأشباه هذا
5. وأما المحال الكذب فأن تقول سوف أشرب ماء البحر أمس

What now follows is an attempt to justify the translation of this chapter with which I shall be concluding this section of the thesis. To start with the most trivial point of all, it is unfortunately necessary to point out that, try as I might, I cannot achieve the feat of interpretation of Hartmann and discover not five but six categories of correctness in [217] this chapter.[29] For all his subtlety, however, Hartmann was long ago surpassed by the native wit of Sīrāfī and Aḫfaš, who, between them, added no fewer than three extra categories, which I shall mention in their place.

The first pair of terms, *mustaqīm* and *ḥasan*, lay down two different kinds of correctness which it is supremely important to keep apart. Jahn's translation of these two terms, which he had to defend with some vigour, turns out to be the opposite of the meanings which he admits are found "in countless places" elsewhere in the *Kitāb*,[30] which is depressing evidence of the lengths he would go to in support of his belief that Sībawayhi

26. Reuschel, *Ḫalīl* 15.
27. See below, 237.
28. *Kitāb* 1, 7/8.
29. See above, p. [86].
30. Jahn, *Zum Verständnis* 8.

did not know what he was talking about. So, for *ḥasan* he gives us "(dem Sinne nach) angemessen," and for *mustaqīm* "(grammatisch) richtig,"(b) and the only redeeming feature of this blunder is that he does not use these "translations" uniformly throughout the rest of the *Kitāb*. His error springs from his decision to favour Sīrāfī's interpretation whenever it appeared more congenial than what Sībawayhi was trying to say. For example, to help the puzzled reader through this difficult chapter, Sīrāfī offers this commentary on *mustaqim kaḏib*:[31]

كل كلام لم يكن في لفظه خلل من جهة اللغة والإعراب فهو كلام مستقيم وقد تبيّن في مثل هذا أنّ
قائله كاذب فيما قال فنحكم على كلامه أنّه كذب غير مستقيم من حيث كان كذبًا إلا أنّه مستقيم اللفظ

[218] and it is obvious at once that Sīrāfī has taken *mustaqīm* to refer to grammatical correctness in spite of the fact that Sībawayhi, as can be seen in paragraph 4 of this chapter, clearly intends *ḥusn* and *qubḥ* to cover that aspect of correctness. Sīrāfī himself is only following Aḫfaš, whose remark containing the spurious category *mustaqīm al-lafẓ* is printed as note two in Jahn's notes to Chapter Six. Apart from the fact that this is a serious misinterpretation of Sībawayhi's meaning, there is also the objection (not foreseen by Jahn) that if *mustaqīm* is to mean "grammatically correct" then *ḥasan* cannot mean anything at all. Alternatively, if *mustaqīm* had two meanings (as Aḫfaš and Sīrāfī appear to believe) we are forced to ask why Sībawayhi makes no mention of them, as well as noting that for *mustaqīm* to have two meanings would leave *ḥasan* even worse off than before. Some idea of the critical chaos into which the Arab commentators could lead the credulous Westerner may be gained from Jahn's translation of the fourth paragraph of this chapter: "was (grammatisch) richtig aber (der Wortstellung nach) incorrect ist."(a) That correct grammar already includes correct word order seems to me to be a most elementary fact.

Fortunately Sībawayhi was at all times a better grammarian than Jahn, and the use of the terms *mustaqīm* and *ḥasan* in the *Kitāb* as a whole is a much safer guide than the uninspired guessing of the commentators.

Mustaqīm means "straight" and "right" in the ethical sense,(b) and it is worth asking how such a term came to form part of Sībawayhi's grammar. The answer lies in the importance he placed on the role of the listener in determining correctness of speech, which is, in turn, a reflection of [219] the social nature of speech as Sībawayhi saw it and its resultant susceptibility to ethical criteria. He is, therefore, enjoining the speakers of Arabic to speak in a way that is socially "right." The practical applications of this in grammar are very succinctly expressed in the statement:

31. in Jahn, *Zum Verständnis* 8.

لا يستقيم أن تخبر المخاطب عن المنكور وليس هذا بالذي ينزل به المخاطب منزلتك في المعرفة [32]

This makes it quite clear that the element which is *mustaqīm* is that which relates to the listener's comprehension of what is said.[(a)] To this extent *mustaqīm* carries some of the sense of our word "intelligible," and it is certainly true that many of the expressions that are dismissed as not *mustaqīm* have in common the property that their meaning is not clear. Thus the sentence زيد أخو عبد الله مجنون به, which some might consider to be ambiguous enough already, ceases to be *mustaqīm* if the adjectival phrase أخو عبد الله is inverted to read زيد مجنون به أخو عبد الله. The sentence is chosen to illustrate Sībawayhi's claim that adjectives are not freely invertible, for the first version means, "Zayd, the brother of 'Abdullāh, is in love with him ('Abdullāh)," while the second could only mean "The brother of 'Abdullāh is in love with Zayd."[33] The point is not that the inversion of the adjectival phrase changes the meaning, but that it produces nonsense, for Zayd in the second example is alleged to be in love with himself.

[220] On another occasion Sībawayhi says that it is not *mustaqīm* to invert after ما in the following fashion: ما زيدًا عبدُالله ضاربًا and ما زيدًا أنا قاتلاً.[34] The root of this problem is that ما, like ليس, is sometimes used to negate a whole proposition, (as كان is used to affirm one) e.g., لَيسَ كُلَّ النَّوى تُبْقِي المَسَاكِينُ. Here the inversion which occurs within the negated proposition must not be allowed to suggest that any part of it (e.g., المساكين) is the subject of ليس, for the only permitted subject would be كلّ, in independent form. What marks the normal use of كان and ليس off from this other use (nowadays dealt with under the heading of ضمير الشأن) is that the negation or affirmation of a whole proposition precludes the concordance of كان and ليس with any part of it, which is why Sībawayhi abruptly disallows كانت زيدًا الحُمَّى تأخُذُ, in which inversion is not allowed because الحمّى is already the correct subject[(a)] of كانت. It follows, *a fortiori*, that after ما no inversion of any kind is allowed, because it has not the power and currency of ليس,[35] and, therefore, its use is restricted. The only way to retain the inversion after ما is to treat it as a Tamīmī ما, structurally equivalent to أمّا, "as though you said أمّا زيدًا فأنا ضاربٌ and then as if you had not said أمّا at all, i.e., زيدًا أنا ضاربٌ," which can then correctly be negated by ما because, unlike the Ḥijāzī ما, the Tamīmī ما does not imply any connection between itself and any part of the sentence.

[221] The point of this tortuous and forbidding argument may, in fact, derive from nothing more than the desire of the Eastern grammarian to show up the limitations of a Western Arabic construction, for Sībawayhi confesses at the end of the chapter that the problem hardly arises anywhere in poetry and counts for very little in their speech![36]

32. *Kitāb* 1, 17/22, taking the Būlāq reading in preference to Derenbourg's [(b)].
33. Id. 1, 207/243.
34. *Kitāb* 1, 27/36.
35. Cf. *Kitāb* 1, 22/28.
36. *Kitāb* 1, 28/37.

For our purposes, however, it is an interesting discussion of *istiqāma*, for it appears from the way Sībawayhi treats this situation that the particular objection to ما زيدًا عبد الله ضاربًا is that it would obscure the relationship between ما and the rest of the sentence. Thus the confusion is not one of grammar, though that, too, is violated by this construction, but of meaning, for what you want to say is "it is not so that Zayd is being beaten by 'Abdullāh," and what you imply is, in fact, "It is not Zayd that 'Abdullāh is beating."(a) The lack of *istiqāma* results, then, in the failure to communicate the intended meaning, as can be seen even more clearly from Sībawayhi's second example, ما زيدًا أنا قاتلاً: "It is not so that I am going to kill Zayd," is what you want to say, but what you imply is "It is not Zayd that I am going to kill (but someone else)."

The same problem of communication underlies Sībawayhi's treatment of the type الناس مجزيّون بأعمالهم إن خيرًا فخيرٌ وإن شرًا فشرٌ, which allows various combinations in its grammar.[37] To say إن خيرًا فخيرٌ الخ is allowed by Sībawayhi on the grounds that the part introduced by ف, which is an apodosis to the first clause, is like a nominal sentence. [222] But the use of the direct form in both clauses is explained on the (not very plausible) grounds that since this is a conditional relationship, both verbs in the clauses would be apocopated, and because one part of the conditional sentence would be unintelligible (لا يستقيم)(a) without the other. Here the weakness of the explanation(b) must not be allowed to obscure the point of the argument, which hinges on the fact that both parts of a conditional sentence are necessary in order for either of them to make sense. Sībawayhi may well be right to ascribe the use of the same case in both clauses (which is less common, he says, than the use of the direct form in the protasis and the independent form in the apodosis) to this feeling that the two halves of a conditional sentence are indispensible to each other. At any rate the rightness (*istiqāma*) of this attraction of cases is not grammatical, but derives from the necessary completion of the sense which the two parts of a conditional sentence mutually supply, hence the resemblance between this situation and that of the nominal sentence,(c) to which Sībawayhi alludes in this context, where the *istiqāma* is seen to depend on the completion of the sense rather than on any grammatical features.

As well as covering the intelligibility of speech, i.e., the effectiveness of the communication from the point of view of the listener, *mustaqīm* appears to relate to the way in which the speaker succeeds in saying what he wants to say. This has already been suggested in the case of the Ḥijāzī negative, above, but other examples make it even clearer.

A conditional sentence beginning with an oath may not be expressed [223] in the form of apocopated verbs: you must say والله إن أتيتَني لا أفعلُ because the apodosis is, in fact, syntactically dependent (معتمد) on the oath. The only way to avoid this is to neutralise the oath by moving it to the interior of the sentence, i.e., أنا والله إن تأتني لا آتك whereupon the

37. Id. 1, 109/130.

rest of the sentence becomes constructed upon أنا.[38] With an oath it is permissible to leave out the لا which negates the apodosis: it is no surprise, therefore, to find Sībawayhi saying

> You can say والله إن أتيتني آتيك meaning لا آتيك . If you mean the coming will occur, it is not allowed, but if you deny the coming and want it to mean لا آتيك, that is right (*mustaqīm*).[39]

The rightness of the speech is obviously a result of the speaker's choice of the exact words which will convey his exact meaning. In this particular case his choice of words yields only one meaning in the listener's mind, and it is the speaker who would be wrong to mean anything else by what he said. We may compare this with the meaning of غير as an exceptive particle, where Sībawayhi clearly states that, although غير is customarily used as an equivalent to إلا , it can rightly (*mustaqīm*) be used in its normal sense to mean "other than," although it is doubtful whether Sībawayhi intended this ambiguity to be exploited in actual speech.[40]

[224] There is, then, more to *istiqāma* than intelligibility. It is not *mustaqīm* to point to someone and say to him "this is you,"[41] because there is no need to bring the listener's attention to himself: in other words language is being put to a use for which it was not devised.[(a)] Similarly it is not *mustaqīm* to say أيّهما عندك عندك in the meaning "Which of the two that are with you is with you?" though it can be right if عندك is merely repeated for emphasis,[42] nor is it *mustaqīm*, as we have seen already in another example, to say such things as رجلٌ خيرٌ منك as if they were sufficient to make sense.[43] All these occurences of *mustaqīm* involve a failure to communicate, generally through a failure to observe the conventions of speech as they govern not the grammar of words but the choice of which words to use. There is a striking resemblance in this attitude to correctness and Bloomfield's observation on speech-communities:

> Obviously, the value of language depends on people's using it in the same way. Every member of the social group must upon suitable occasion utter the proper speech-sounds and, when he hears another utter these speech-sounds, must make the proper response. He must speak intelligibly and must understand what others say.[44]

38. *Kitāb* 1, 395/444.
39. Id. 1, 395/445.
40. See above, p. [193].
41. *Kitāb* 1, 59/79.
42. Id. 1, 433/484.
43. Id. 1, 350/397.
44. Bloomfield, *Language* 29.

"Value," "proper," "suitable" are scarcely what would now be accepted as scientific terminology, but they aptly express the attitude which was deliberately and thoroughly developed by Sībawayhi into the notion of *istiqāma*. It seems, therefore, that the best translation for this idea, [225] the one which comes closest to Sībawayhi's purpose, is simply "right," for it is used in the *Kitāb* to denote the social obligation of the speaker to speak in the way society demands, the penalty for not doing so being, of course, that he fails to make himself understood and thereby casts himself out from society.[(a)] If Sībawayhi had used the phrase النحو المستقيم, I for one would not have been surprised: his grammar is only a particular application of the very same principle which is embodied in the Quranic phrase الصراط المستقيم.

The other criterion of correctness, *ḥasan*, also shows itself to be firmly based on ethical considerations.[(b)] We have seen that for the ethical writers one of man's most important tasks was to "put things in their right place,"[45] for to do so is *ḥasan*, while not to do so is *qabīḥ*. We may fruitfully compare this with Sībawayhi's own definition of *qubḥ*, in the fourth paragraph of the chapter under discussion: "putting things in the wrong place," whence it appears beyond doubt that *ḥusn* and *qubḥ*, in grammar as in ethics, are always associated with *mawḍiʿ*. We find these ideas used in the *Kitāb* in conjunction through the whole range of meanings contained in *mawḍiʿ*:

1, 246/286	فقبح عندهم أن يدخلوا الواجب في موضع التمنّى
1, 45/54	ولإذا موضع آخر يحسن فيه ابتداء الأسماء بعدها
1, 122/147	لو قلت أخذته بصاعدٍ كان قبيحًا لأنه صفة ولا يكون في موضع الاسم
1, 336/384	ألا ترى أن القياس قد قبح إذا وضعت "ـني" في غير موضعها
1, 400/451	وليس كل موضع يدخل فيه الفاء يحسن فيه الجزاء

[226] Since the "cases" are also included among the *mawāḍiʿ* we can expect to find that their use is judged by the same standards of *ḥusn* and *qubḥ* as every other function:

1, 195/228	وذلك قولك مررت برجلٍ فضةٌ حليةُ سيفِه وإنما كان الرفع في هذا أحسن من قبل أنه ليس بصفةٍ ولو قلت له خاتمٌ حديدٌ وهذا خاتمٌ طينٌ كان قبيحًا
1, 400/451	وإذا قلت لا تدنُ من الأسد يأكلْك فهو قبيح إن جزمت
1, 94/115	ومما لا يحسن فيه إلا النصب قولهم سير عليه سحرًا

Thus *ḥusn* and *qubḥ*, as well as serving to distinguish between what is grammatically correct and incorrect, are also applied to the formal correctness of every use of the language. Even *iddiġām* is subect to this:

45. Above, pp. [101]f.

وإنما وصفتُ لك حروف المعجم بهذه الصفات لتعرف ما يحسن فيه
2, 455/406 الادّغام وما يجوز فيه وما لا يحسن فيه ولا يجوز

and so it is, perhaps, too narrow a rendering to speak of "grammatically correct" for *ḥasan* and "grammatically incorrect" for *qabīḥ*. I suggest that for these terms the natural English equivalents would be "good Arabic" and "bad Arabic," since these English expressions retain the ethical flavour of the original. No loss of precision results, as we have Sībawayhi's definition of *qubḥ* to guide us, and in any case it is our own concept of grammar which is too narrow. Sībawayhi analysed the "way" the Arabs spoke in terms of a great number of functions, so that "good Arabic" is effectively the Arabic which makes correct use of all these functions. A further advantage of such a translation is that it perfectly accommodates the expression أحسن, which it is nonsensical to translate as "more [227] correct," but "better Arabic" conveys it exactly. We know from the disagreements in the *Kitāb* that *ḥusn* is not an absolute criterion, but a subjective one which often had to be buttressed by casuistic arguments. It is, therefore, a sign of Sībawayhi's scrupulousness that he leaves the concept of what is good and bad Arabic vague enough to accommodate at least those cases where some Arabic usages are, apparently, better than others.[(a)] We have seen this in the case of the dissimilation of reduplicated verbs—a Ḥijāzī usage which is "good old Arabic" but where the reader is left in no doubt that Sībawayhi favours the assimilated Tamīmī form.[46] Another example concerns the sentence رأيت زيدًا وعمرًا كلّمته, where the fact that the first noun is constructed upon the verb makes it "better Arabic" that the second should be likewise.[47] Moreover in this case it is "better Arabic in their opinion" (أحسن عندهم), i.e., in the opinion of the Arabs, which reminds us of the conventional basis of "good" and "bad" Arabic. It is as though Sībawayhi's main purpose in using *ḥusn* and *qubḥ* was to show the reader of the *Kitāb* how to regulate his linguistic behaviour (*kalām*) by making sure that every different way he talked (i.e., in any of the sixty-odd *mawāḍi'*)[(b)] was morally good (*ḥasan*). The same sort of idea has already been expressed in another context:

> The will of God is that men should pursue *ḥusn* (beauty) and avoid *qubḥ* (ugliness) of life and character.[48]

This is a lawyer's outlook, but from what we have seen of Sībawayhi's use of the same notions it is quite clear that his purpose and theirs were one [228] and the same.

Between them *ḥasan* and *mustaqīm* cover all the aspects of correctness which Sībawayhi considered relevant. They occur together not infrequently:

---

46. Above, p. [169].
47. *Kitāb* 1, 35/46.
48. Vesey-Fitzgerald, in Khaddury, *Law in the Middle East* 1, 97.

1, 127/152	ولو قلت ما صنعت وما زيدٌ لم يحسن ولم يستقم
1, 58/67	وقد يحسن ويستقيم أن تقول عبدَالله فاضربْه
	ولو قلت هذا رجلٌ خيرٌ وهذا رجلٌ أفضلُ وهذا رجلٌ أبٌ
1, 192/229	لم يستقم ولم يكن حسناً
	ألا ترى أنّك لو قلت فيها عبدالله حسن السكوت وكان
1, 222/261	كلامًا مستقيمًا كما حسن واستغنى قولك هذا عبدالله

This last example suggests a further application of the ideas of *ḥusn* and *istiqāma* which points, in turn, to a more systematic approach than Sībawayhi is usually given credit for. What he implies is that these criteria of *ḥusn* and *istiqāma* are each made recognisable by certain features in the words actually expressed. On the structural level Sībawayhi requires that the sentence should be complete enough for silence to follow without any apparent deficiency in the utterance. In only a few cases, notably the *iḍāfa* construction and the conditional sentence, are both parts formally required in every such utterance,[(a)] and even they can be dispensed with if the situation justifies it, so what Sībawayhi is saying is not that there is a prescribed minimum content in a given sentence, but that there is a point where the sentence contains enough constituents to be formally complete, after which it is good Arabic to stop speaking. Once again I stress that Sībawayhi is not thinking in terms of the *jumla* but of the *kalām*, for the definition of a *jumla* requires that all the [229] possible reasons for elision would have to be specified in advance,[49] while the *kalām* can always be taken as it comes, and reasons for any structural elisions found as and when they are needed. We may link this concept of the fitness for silence with that of *waqf*, already dealt with above,[(a)] which together provide an excellent means for determining the end of a *kalām*.

The other criterion is self-sufficiency, *istiġnā,'* and it will readily be appreciated from its occurrence in the last quotation above, that it is inherently linked with *istiqāma*. Further proof of this is the fact that both *istiqāma* and *istiġnā'* are themselves intimately bound up with the listener, e.g.,

1, 328/376	فكل ذلك خذف تخفيفًا واستغناءً بعلم المخاطب بما يعني
1, 166/196	وتركوا ذكر الكرّ استغناءً بما في صدورهم من علمه وبعلم المخاطب

and we may conclude that the element of self-sufficiency is that aspect of the sentence which makes it intelligible as a whole to the listener. It follows that if, in an elision, the structural completeness of the sentence remains unaltered (because the elided word still retains its grammatical effect), the only criterion for elision is the self-sufficiency of the utterance, and its consequent *istiqāma*. This is not at first sight obvious, until we take into account this fact that elided words still count towards the structural completeness of the sentence. The listener will always recognise what kind of word has been elided but since

49. This is a permanent defect of Transformational Grammar.

he may not know the meaning of that word, it becomes clear that it is the latter which determines the rightness of the elision. A perfect example of this [230] is the verse (Sūra 33, 35) وَالحافظينَ فُرُوجَهُم وَالحافظات والذّاكرين اللهَ كثيرًا والذّاكِرات, in which the listener well knows what words have been left out after الذاكرات and الحافظات, and so the elision is *mustaqīm* although, from the purely structural point of view, any direct object would have been grammatically correct.[50] This is evidence of an acuity in Sībawayhi which is not always found in students of language in any period, and is therefore all the more to be prized.

After *ḥasan/qabīḥ* and *mustaqīm*, only *muḥāl* remains to be examined. It shares with *qubḥ* the distinction of being the only term which Sībawayhi explicitly defines in the chapter under discussion, and is explained there as "when you contradict the beginning of your speech by the end of it." This is no logical contradiction, any more than *istiqāma* is logical correctness. The contradiction, as Sībawayhi's examples show beyond a shadow of a doubt, is a purely grammatical one: you do not start off an utterance with a word which, from its form, has the function of indicating the past and then follow it with a word which indicates the future. Nor do you start off with a form whose function is unequivocally future in meaning only to conclude with one that is exclusively past in sense. By stressing the grammatical contradiction of *iḥāla* and ignoring whatever contradictions of lexical meaning may be entailed it is easier to understand the use of *muḥāl* in the *Kitāb* as a whole. It is helpful in this connection to bear in mind the importance Sībawayhi attaches to [231] the expectations of the listener,[51] for the essence of *iḥāla* is that it disappoints those expectations by a sudden and meaningless change of grammar. Thus it is *muḥāl* to say هذه ناقة وفصيلها الراتعان because the implications of الراتعان cannot be reconciled with ناقة وفصيلها, for one of the words allegedly qualified by الراتعان is undefined,[(a)] and the listener simply does not know what الراتعان has to do with the rest of the sentence.[52] Similarly it is *muḥāl* to say عبدالله هو فيها when the هو referred to is not 'Abdullāh, just as it is *muḥāl* to say عبدالله نعم الرجل when الرجل does not refer to 'Abdullāh.[53] Clearly the *iḥāla* in these two cases does not lie in the form of the words but in the meaning that the speaker gives them.[(b)] Both the *alīf-lām* and the pronouns have in common the fact that they refer to something already known, so that for the speaker to intend something other than what the listener will assume him to intend is an abuse of the language and is rightly called *muḥāl*. A last example will confirm this, though the argument itself is based on very shaky claims: the particles لـ and حتى before verbs assume an elided أنْ before the verb. If this أنْ were not assumed then the speech would be *muḥāl* because لـ and حتى do not combine with verbs, but only with nouns.[54] The premiss may be false, but if granted, it certainly follows that un-

50. *Kitāb* 1, 29/37.
51. See below, p. [249].
52. *Kitāb* 1, 211/247.
53. Id. 1, 259/300.
54. Id. 1, 362/407.

less أنْ is assumed to intervene between لـ or حتى and their verbs, the listener who expects a noun to follow these particles will be disappointed.

[232] In translating *muḥāl* I have considered both "improper" and "wrong" as possibilities. "Improper" has to commend it the fact that it is the antithesis of "proper," which is still used to describe normally correct sentences,[55] while conveying at the same time the ethical connotation of the Arabic. But it is too weak for what is, after all, the complete destruction of communication and denial of the purpose of speech. The word "wrong" has in it all that is in "improper" as well as being familiarly coupled with "right," and this coupling of *mustaqīm* and *muḥāl* seems to be best reproduced in English by adopting the words "right" and "wrong." This also allows us to render لا يستقيم by "it is not right" without implying that it is actually "wrong," for these terms are by no means antonyms in English or Arabic.[(a)]

Chapter Six of the *Kitāb* is now translatable as follows:

> What is right and wrong in speech. This comprises: right and good Arabic, wrong, right and false, right and bad Arabic, and wrong and false.
>
> 1) Right and good Arabic is when you say أتيتك أمس or سآتيك غدًا.
>
> 2) Wrong is when you contradict the beginning of your speech with the end of it, e.g أتيتك غدًا or سآتيك أمس.
>
> 3) Right and false is when you say حملتُ الجبل or شربتُ ماء البحر.
>
> 4) Right and bad Arabic is when you put what you say in the wrong place, e.g قد زيدًا رأيتُ or كي زيدٌ يأتيك and the like.
>
> 5) Wrong and false is when you say سوف أشرب ماء البحر أمس .

[233] Certain observations are prompted by this chapter. In the first place paragraphs three and five are obviously there to preclude any possibility of truth and falsehood being mistakenly associated with grammar.[(a)] In fact, unless this is so, the fifth paragraph becomes redundant, as no wrong utterance is accepted as part of the language, true or false.

Secondly it is interesting that Sībawayhi, in paragraph four, appears to allow what is right but bad Arabic. In practice this is soon abandoned, as it is not in a grammarian's interest to recommend that people should speak badly. The idea does occur on one other occasion, precisely in the chapter on poetic licence:

> ويحتملون قبح الكلام حتى يضعوه في غير موضعه لأنه مستقيم ليس فيه نقص [56]

55. E.g., Robins, *General Linguistics* 233.

56. *Kitāb* 1, 9/12. Better *naqḍ*, following ʿAbd al-Salām Hārūn 1, 31[(b)].

but it is obviously not designed to encourage the spread of bad Arabic. It simply illustrates the care and skill with which Sībawayhi worked, for he recognised that bad grammar alone was not sufficient to disqualify sentences, and that those sentences which were readily comprehensible in spite of their bad grammar could still be accepted in the language, though only as poetic licence.

Thirdly, as we have seen from the examples, there is no doubt as to what Sībawayhi meant by his criteria, except what is created by the misinterpretations of his commentators. *Mustaqīm* is seen, by comparing paragraphs one, three and four, to be independent of structural correctness, so that the interpretation مستقيم اللفظ which was read into this chapter by Aḫfaš,[57] is utterly without foundation. Another sub-classification of *mustaqīm* which plumbs new depths of crassitude is Aḫfaš's [234] identification of a type *mustaqīm ḫaṭa'*,[58] which is explained as "that which is unintentional, such as ضربني زيدٌ when you mean ضربتُ زيدًا. It scarcely needs stressing here that the one thing Sībawayhi is not interested in is mistakes of that kind, where the simple negligence of the speaker results in an all-correct sentence but one which is not what he intended to say. Only once does Sībawayhi turn his attention to this type of error, and that is probably for the sake of illustrating the difference between what is "right" and "wrong." It concerns the *badal al-ġalaṭ*, a construction which has been solemnly incorporated ever since into virtually ever grammar as though it could be expected to appear in a literary text at any moment. Sībawayhi distinguishes between two uses of مررتُ برجل حمار, one of which is "wrong" and the other "good Arabic." The "wrong" use is that which asserts that the man and the ass are identical, and this furnishes a good example of what Sībawayhi meant by "when you contradict the beginning of your speech by the end of it." The "good Arabic" is merely the replacement (*badal*) of the correct word for one uttered by mistake.[59] Of *ḫaṭa'* there are traces in the *Kitāb*,[60] but scarcely enough to justify the interpretation offered by Aḫfaš. *Mustaqīm al-lafẓ* lingers on—it is found in the *Fihrist*, for example,[61] but it remains a gratuitous and misleading distortion of Sībawayhi's term.

Of even less use for the *Kitāb* is Sīrāfī's observation that the simple *muḥāl* is distinct from the *muḥāl kaḏib* by virtue of the fact that the former is unverifiable – "you cannot say that it is true or false."[62] [235] He seems to have mistaken Sībawayhi's purpose here, which was clearly to show that truth and falsehood have nothing to do with grammar. As is often the case, Sībawayhi's over-emphasis has confused his critic, for Sīrāfī finds himself in the position of defining *muḥāl* as that which is meaningless and unverifiable

57. Above, pp. [217]f.
58. In Jahn, note 2 to §6(a).
59. *Kitāb* 1, 186/218.
60. E.g., *Kitāb* 1, 344/392, 409/461.
61. Ibn al-Nadīm, op. cit. 39.
62. In Jahn, note 1 to §6.

and then, blindly following Sībawayhi, he ventures in to the realm of the *muḥāl* himself by implying that there is, notwithstanding, a category of meaninglessness which can be called a lie. Sībawayhi did not worry about the meaning of his *muḥāl* examples, for their very form makes them nonsensical whether the meaning and veracity are taken into account or not.

Fourthly there are some remarks I would like to make about the criteria of *ḥusn* and *qubḥ*. Reuschel has claimed that the terms *ḥasan* and *qabīḥ*, together with *jāʾiz*, "were probably used mainly for stylistic distinctions,"[63] and that "*jayyid* refers to grammatical correctness while *qabīḥ* expresses a stylistic judgement."[64] The error is elaborated by Beeston as follows:

> For Ḫalīl, a locution is *qabīḥ* 'vicious' when the application to it of the general principles of Arabic syntax leads to it yielding either (a) a sense different from the one intended, or (b) a logically absurd or non-meaningful utterance."[65]

For type (a), it should now no longer be necessary to point out, Sībawayhi used negative forms of *mustaqīm*, while type (b) is exactly what *muḥāl* was devised to represent. Whether Ḫalīl himself used the same [236] criteria is not certain, but since Sībawayhi evidently deserves most of the credit for the purely grammatical side of the *Kitāb*, it can be argued that it is also irrelevant.[(a)]

As for Reuschel, he is right only in claiming that *jayyid* has a grammatical force: it is one of several synonyms of *ḥasan* which are found in the *Kitāb*, e.g.,

jayyid

1, 31/41	فإذا قدّمت الاسم فهو عربيّ جيّد
1, 56/68	ولا تريد به أضربُ زيدًا فيكونَ على أول الكلام رفعتَ عنده فجيّد
1, 96/116	والنصب عربي كثير جيّد
1, 248/288	ولو ابتدأ فرفع كان جيّدًا
2, 452/404	وهذه الحروف التي تمّمتها اثنين وأربعين جيّدُها ورديئُها

jamīl

1, 58/69	ومما يدلّك على حسن الفاء ههنا أنك لو قلت هذا زيد فحسن جميل
1, 222/261	ولو قلت مررت بهذا الرجل كان حسنًا جميلاً
1, 202/235	إذا طال الكلام كان الحذف أجمل
2, 419/378	كلا القولين حسن جميل

63. Reuschel, *Ḫalīl* 16.
64. Ibid., 30, n. 2.
65. Beeston, *BSOAS* 25, 343.

ṣaḥīḥ

فهذا ان جعلته استفهامًا فإعرابه الرفع فهو كلام صحيح	1, 353/400

To this list we might add certain instances of *qawī* which seem to refer to grammatical correctness, e.g.,

كأنه قال هذا رجل مضروب وهذا رجل مكرم ورجل مهان فإن حذفت	
الهاء جاز وكان أقوى مما يكون خبرًا	1, 45/34
وترك ذلك في أظنّ إذا كان لغوًا أقوى منه إذا وقع على المصدر	1, 64/52
فإن قلت سير عليه طويل من الدهر وشديد من السير فأطلت الكلام	
ووصفت كان أحسن وأقوى وجاز	1, 96/117

[237] The list can be increased by giving examples of the synonyms of the complementary term *qabīḥ*, viz.

ḫabīṯ

هذا كلام خبيث موضوع في غير موضعه	1, 233/273
وتقول إنّ أحدًا لا يقول ذلك وهو ضعيف خبيث لأنّ أحدًا	
لا يستعمل في الواجب	1, 318/363
وأما كُراع فالوجه فيه ترك الصرف ومن العرب من يصرفه يشبهه	
بذراع لأنه من أسماء المذكر وذلك أخبث الوجهين	2, 19/19
ولو قلت مررت بزيد أول من أمس وأمس عمرو كان قبيحًا خبيثًا	2, 149/146

radī'

وقد جاء في الشعر حسنة وجهها شبهوه بحسنة الوجه وذلك رديء	1, 83/102
فيقول مررت بعبدالله خيرًا منه أبوه وهو لغة رديئة	1, 200/233
فهذه الأشياء فيما يجزم أردأ وأقبح منها في نظيرها من الأسماء	1, 406/457
فقد تكلّم ببعضه العرب وهو رديء	2, 458/410

There is also the occurrence of the term *ḍa'īf* in grammatical contexts, corresponding to the use of *qawī*:

فأصل الابتداء للمعرفة فلما أدخلت فيه الألف واللام وكان خبرًا حسن	
الابتداء وضعف الابتداء بالنكرة إلا أن يكون فيه معنى المنصوب	1, 137/165
وتقول سير عليه طوران طور كذا وطور كذا والنصب ضعيف	1, 97/117
واعلم أنّ كفى بنا فضلاً من غيرنا أجود وفيه ضعف إلا أن يكون	
فيه هو لأنّ هو من بعض الصلة وهو نحو مررت بأيّهم أفضل	1, 231/270

Not only, then, does Sībawayhi describe Arabic as "good" (*ḥasan*) and "bad"(*qabīḥ*), he also calls it "fine" (*jamīl*), "excellent" (*jayyid*) and "strong" (*qawī*) when it is correct, and "abominable" (*ḫabīṯ*), "vile" (*radī'*) and "feeble" (*ḍā'īf*) when it is incorrect.[(a)] There is no reason to suppose that these terms are anything but alternatives to *ḥasan* and [238] *qabīḥ*, or to assume that they have anything to do with style, and Jahn, for example, is quite wrong to render *qabīḥ* as "stilistisch incorrect."[66] Their ethical tone is unmistakable and confirms the ethical basis of the two principal terms, *ḥasan* and *qabīḥ*. It is impossible to connect *qabīḥ* in particular with any stylistic notions in the light of Sībawayhi's definition of the term in his sixth chapter. And it is even less likely that, to follow Reuschel's reasoning to its logical conclusion, a work of grammar should use the allegedly stylistic criteria of *ḥusn* and *qubḥ* immeasurably more frequently than the relatively uncommon term *jayyid* which is supposed to indicate grammatical correctness. But Reuschel himself seems to have no confidence in his own theories, since he translates *qabīḥ* as "inkorrect" on the very page following the suggestion that *qabīḥ* denotes a stylistic value-judgement.[67]

The translation I have proposed for Chapter Six may, at first sight, appear to have precious little to do with grammar, but I do not doubt that its ethical tone will strike the reader forcibly. This will not be the effect of any bias of interpretation on my part, but the natural and illuminating result of a literal translation. The chapter itself is an expository one, and so we must assume that where Sībawayhi does not supplement the terminology with special and technical explanations, the terms are, indeed, meant to be taken in as near a literal sense as is [239] appropriate to the subject. In other words, he chose *ḥasan* not because it means "grammatically correct" but because it means "good," and that, furthermore, he chose to regard grammatical correctness, amongst other features of language, as "good" in the purely ethical sense. We are obliged to conclude that for the author of the *Kitāb* at least, it was in itself "good" and "right" to speak in language that was "good" and "right."

As if to drive home the ethical basis of the system, Sībawayhi frequently calls upon the listener (*muḫāṭab*) to provide a justification or excuse for a linguistic situation. The role of the *muḫāṭab* in the *Kitāb* points to a far more thorough approach to language by Sībawayhi than has, to my knowledge, ever been appreciated. It is one thing to take a corpus of utterances and devise a grammatical system which will account for all the phenomena in the given material, but it is quite another to analyse Arabic on the principle that its use and forms are dependant just as much on the presence of a listener as on the existence of a speaker. For Sībawayhi, nothing is said in isolation, everything is addressed to a listener: "la parole est moitié à celuy qui parle, moitié à celuy qui le escoute," as it was put many centuries later by Montaigne.[(a)] The effect of this approach is to place upon the speaker nothing less than a responsibility to make himself understood. In that light

66. Jahn, translating *qabuḥa fī l-kalām*, *Kitāb* 2,387 line 18 in Derenbourg (Būlāq 1,436).
67. Reuschel, *Ḫalīl* 31.

the prescriptive element of the *Kitāb* can be seen to be fully justified, for adherence to the rules of linguistic behaviour as expounded by Sībawayhi is not slavish obedience to a grammarian's whim but the only way to make certain that what one says will be understood. [240] The social rejection which is the punishment for speaking incomprehensibly is the only pressure which Sībawayhi brings to bear: both the ideas of "right" (*mustaqīm*) and "good" (*ḥasan*) Arabic represent the judgement of society upon linguistic usage, and the grammarian, like the lawyer, does no more than articulate and execute the verdicts imposed by society.[(a)]

The responsibility of the speaker towards his listener is developed by Sībawayhi in two ways. The obvious dependence of all language upon the prior knowledge which alone gives our words meaning is applied in the *Kitāb* to the question of those elisions and deviations from the normal speech-pattern which can only be explained by assuming that the listener knows enough to supply the missing elements. Secondly, this prior knowledge is made the basis of an approach which even today appears remarkably sophisticated, namely, that the listener, from his knowledge of the language, will anticipate and expect the speaker to finish his speech in a particular way according to the manner in which he started. Both the responsibilities of the speaker and the expectations of the listener are, therefore, important factors in determining the linguistic form of a speech, for the listener's prior knowledge and the need to fulfil his expectations between them account for the obligation upon the speaker to make himself understood.

Thus the Qur'anic construction exemplified in this quotation from Sūra 6, 27:[(b)]

وَلَوْ تَرَى إِذْ وُقِفُوا عَلَى النَّارِ

is explained in the following terms:

[241] The Arabs leave out the apodosis in this kind of statement (خبر) in their speech because the person addressed knows for what purpose this way of speaking was devised.[68]

Similarly the direct form of أخاها in the following lines of verse:

لقد حَمَلَتْ قَيْسُ بنُ عَيْلانَ حَرْبَها عَلى مُسْتَقِلٍّ للنوائبِ والحَرْبِ
أخاها إذا كانت غِضابًا سَمالَها عَلى كلِّ حالٍ من ذَلولٍ ومن صَعْبِ

is explained in this way:

> The direct form is here due to the fact that you do not wish to tell the people, or the one you are talking to, about something they do not know. They already know as much as you do about it, so you make it into a term of praise and mag-

68. *Kitāb* 1, 403/453.

> nification; its direct form is due to a verb, as if you had said اذكرْ أهلَ ذاك or اذكر المقيمين [(b)] but it is a verb which it is not usual to express.[69]

As it happens أخاها could also have been written as أخوها and أخيها without straining the grammar in any way,[70] so that it is the choice of the direct form which has to be explained. The formal reason, an elided verb, is less convincing than the other half of the explanation, which shows very well how the interaction of speaker and listener brings about a specific grammatical situation. Both of the examples just given are actually ascribed directly to Ḫalīl, which suggests that he was the first to apply this interesting technique. It is, however, frequently used without acknowledgement by Sībawayhi, who may, therefore, be credited with the decision to follow through the implications of the *muḫāṭab* [242] concept more thoroughly than Ḫalīl might spontaneously have done. This is a problem which frequently arises in the study of the *Kitāb*, and the precise degree of innovation attributable to Sībawayhi is impossible to ascertain. In the case of the *muḫāṭab* there is little doubt that Ḫalīl must have introduced the idea to his pupil. But Sībawayhi, rather than Ḫalīl, makes full use of the concept of *istiqāma* (which we know to be intimately bound up with the *muḫāṭab*), and this leads me to believe that it was by Sībawayhi's choice, and on his own initiative, that this particular type of analysis was developed to the extent that we see in the *Kitāb*

At all events the listener is frequently called upon to account for a linguistic situation. This is particularly common with elision: phrases such as حينئذ الآن , لا عليك , كاليوم رجلاً are possible because "the listener knows what you mean" (1, 94/114), and in the case of لا عليك it is even possible to use the full form لا بأس عليك "by way of emphasis even though the listener knows what you mean" (1, 303/347). The full form of expression in giving dates of the month is seldom used, but instead ليال is missed out of the phrase, e.g., لخمس بقين, furthermore, the "days" which should be counted along with the "nights" are subsumed under the feminine word ليال, but the listener still knows that "the days are included in the nights" (2, 180/174). Even when no specific word can be reinstated in an elision, the listener's knowledge is sufficient to account for it, as in إنا معشرَ قريش نفعل, where معشر is explained thus:

> [243] "It is as if one said أعني, but this is a verb which does not appear and is not actually used, as is also the case with the vocative, because they can do without it through the knowledge of the listener." (1, 284/327)

69. Id. 1, 213/250.
70. See Šantamarī's comment on this verse in the margin of *Kitāb* 1, 250 (Būlāq).

In matters of trade an interesting situation exists. On the one hand it is sufficient to sell wheat without mentioning the quantity, i.e., “the wheat is sixty dirhams” for the listener will know that this means sixty dirhams for a *kurr* (six ass-loads). On the other hand

> You are not allowed to say بعت داري ذراعًا meaning ‘I sold my house at a dirham per cubit’ because the listener will think that the whole house is only one cubit large. (1, 166/196)

Perhaps the importance of the listener emerges in the clearest possible way in the case of definition,[a] pronouns and demonstratives. Of definition, Sībawayhi says:

> When you say مررت برجل you are only stating that you have passed by one of those to whom this name applies, and you do not mean any particular man known by the listener. But if you introduce the *alif-lām* you are bringing his attention to a man he already knows. (1, 187/220)

Of the pronouns Sībawayhi says:

> “The pronoun cannot be qualified by an adjective because you only use pronouns when you think that the person you are talking to already knows whom you mean.” (1, 190/223 and 188/220)

[244] The situation with the demonstratives is very interesting because they, too, should only be used to refer to something or somebody already known to the listener, despite the fact that they are called “the particles of making vague.” Thus it frequently arises that the speaker is not certain that the listener knows whom he intends, and so further qualification has to be added. In the case of vocatives

> You say يا هذا الرجل and the demonstrative and the noun after it have the status of one noun. So it is not in the same status as when you say يا زيد الطويل where you first say يا زيد with the intention of stopping there, then, fearing that he will not be known, you describe him as الطويل. When, on the other hand, you say يا هذا الرجل you have no intention of stopping at هذا, and would only add a qualification after you thought that he would not be known. (1, 265/306)[a]

This quotation shows how even يا هذا الرجل might prove to be too vague to the listener, and require further qualification, as well as revealing the importance of speaking within the range of the listener’s knowledge in the ordinary vocative يا زيد. This emerges even more clearly in the problem of the sentence-type هذا عبدالله منطلقًا, and Sibawayh’s discussion of this case offers a fine example of the kind of “parsing” we find in the *Kitāb*:

> هذا is a noun and initial term on which what follows is to be constructed, i.e., عبدالله, and it alone will not be a sentence[b] until something is constructed on it or it is constructed on something before it. The initial term is the *musnad* and what is constructed on it is the *musnad ilayhi*. The effect of هذا on what follows [245] it is like the effect of an oblique particle or a verb on what follows

> it. The meaning is that you wish to bring [the listener's] attention to the fact that 'Abdullāh is going away, not that you wish to make 'Abdullāh known to him because you suspect that he does not know him .... [similarly] when you say هو زيد معروفاً , the word معروفاً becomes a *ḥāl*, because you mention to the listener a person whom he does not know, or you suspect he does not know, and it is as if you said "Look how well-known he is" or "cleave to him, well-known that he is." (1, 218/256)

What we learn from this, apart from the interesting description of sentence-structure, is how much the form of an Arabic speech is linked with the listener's state of knowledge.[71] There are times, indeed, when the speaker appears to be in mental conversation with the listener to such an extent that he adapts the construction of his sentence:

> You say مررت برجل عبدالله as though you had been asked 'by whom did you pass?' or you thought that you had been asked that and substituted something better-known in the place of رجل. (1, 192/224)

> You can say مررت بقومك الكرامَ if you are putting the listener in the position of one who already knows them, just as you say مررت برجل زيدٌ, putting the listener in the status of someone who asks 'Who is he?' even if he does not actually say so. (1, 215/252)

> [246] If it were good Arabic to say فيها قائمٌ it would be permissible to say فيها قائمٌ رجلٌ without it being an adjective, but as if someone had said فيها قائمٌ and then someone else had said 'Who is that?' or 'What is that?' and the reply was رجلٌ or عبدالله. This is certainly allowed even though it is feeble. (1, 237/276) [(a)]

> If you like you can put صوت in the direct form [and say مررت به فإذا به صوتٌ صوتَ الحمار] in the way we have explained without its being a *ḥāl*. It is as if it were an answer to the question 'In what situation?' or 'How?' and the like, as if the listener said 'How did it happen?' as if you made the listener have the status of someone who said that and you wanted to make the situation clear. (1, 151/181)

> You also say مررت برجليْن مسلم وكافر where you make the noun collective and seperate the adjectives. If you like you can make the مسلم and the كافر into substitutes [for رجلين] as though in answer to someone who asked 'By what sort of man did you pass?' Or if you like you can use the independent form as though in answer to the question 'What sort were they?' This is how we speak, even if the listener does not ask out loud, because what you say follows the extent of the questions he might pose if he were to ask you. (1, 182/214)

71. See below, p. [247].

The text of this last passage is marred by apparently gratuitous changes of pronoun which have misled Jahn into translating the final sentence as though it referred to the way the listener speaks, which is absurd.

[247] We can now see that, in the literal sense of the word, the speaker is 'responsible' to the listener, in that much of what is said is dictated by the questions it may be designed to answer. There remains a further extension of this principle which Sībawayhi uses in the *Kitāb*, namely the expectations of the listener.[(a)] This is particularly important for the nominal sentence, which employs a minimum of grammatical apparatus, and which, therefore, is more strictly controlled than such well-marked constructions as the *manṣūbāt*. One is not allowed, for example, to start a nominal sentence with an idea too vague for the listener to understand.[72] The grammatical reason for this is that, by definition, the initial term is the foundation of the sentence, the predicate being literally "built upon it" and "propped up against it," so that for the sentence as a whole to mean anything at all it must first be based upon something within the listener's knowledge. If Jahn and others had taken Sībawayhi's point here there would probably not have been nearly as much nonsense written about the alleged confusion over "*musnad*" and "*musnad ilayhi*," which, as far as Sībawayhi is concerned, can only mean "subject" and "predicate" respectively.[(b)] That is the meaning demanded by Sībawayhi's theory of the nominal sentence, and it is quite misleading of Jahn to remark that these terms are used in the *Kitāb* "in a meaning which diverges from the normal usage."[73]

But it is not enough to start a nominal sentence, i.e., utter an initial term (*mubtada'*); the moment this is done the listener's expectations will have been aroused, and both rightness and good Arabic [248] require that these expectations should be fulfilled by the utterance of a predicate. Though this is certainly true of the nominal sentence in general, it is best illustrated from cases where the sentence itself is part of some larger unit, e.g., as an object of ظنّ or in connection with كان, and it is worth noting that in any case كان-sentences are explicitly included in the discussion of nominal sentences in Chapter Three of the *Kitāb* (1, 6/7). Of such sentences Sībawayhi says:

> If you said كان زيد you would have started with something as well-known to the listener as to yourself and he would then expect a predicate, so that if you said حليمًا you would have made him know what you knew. And if you [just] said كان حليمًا he would expect you to let him know who this adjective belonged to, for this person is the initial term within the verb even if it might be expressed only later. (I, 22/17)
>
> If you say كان رجل ذاهبٌ, there is nothing in this which you make known to him that he did not know before. And if you were to say كان رجل من آل فلان فارسًا it

72. Above, p. [219].
73. Jahn, note 6 to *Kitāb* §117.

would be good Arabic because the listener needs to be told that that man is from such and such a family, which he did not know before. And if you were to say كان رجل في قوم فارسًا it would not be good Arabic because no-one would deny that there is a rider somewhere in the world and that he belongs to a certain people. In this way (*naḥw!*) it is either good or bad Arabic. (1, 20/26).

This is allowed [i.e., the use of separative particles] with those verbs whose following nouns are in the status of initiality[(a)] in order to make known that the speaker has separated the noun, [249] and that it is, as far as the person spoken to expects and anticipates, one of those cases where the speaker has no choice but to mention a predicate to the listener, because if you start with a noun you have only done so for the sake of what follows, and if you make an initial term you are obliged[(a)] to mention something after the initial term, otherwise what you say will be corrupt and not allowed. (1, 346f/394)[(b)]

Doubtless these and other similar passages contain the seeds of the *ifāda* principle which was to supersede the idea of *istiqāma* in grammar, but they also illustrate just how emphatically Sībawayhi charges the speaker with responsibilities towards the listener, and how much the listener anticipates what is to come when he hears the beginning of a nominal sentence.[(b)] That is precisely why it is not "right," for example, to say زيدٌ فاضربْه, where your first word has the appearance of an initial term and is actually nothing of the sort.[74] Such a usage would clearly cause confusion to a listener expecting a predicate.

The same principle is applied to the sentence إنّ ألفًا في دراهمك بيضٌ, which behaves like the undefined subjects of كان and ليس because the listener needs you to make this known to him as he needs you to do in the case of ما كان أحد فيها خيرٌ منك. (1, 245/285)

and we find a similar approach in the explanation of several constructions where the grammar alone is not enough to account for the fixed meaning of a given way of speaking, e.g.,

[250] You say أنت الرجل كلّ الرجل but هذا عبد الـه كل الرجل and هذا أخوك كل الرجل are not such good Arabic as the example with the *alif-lām* because by saying this you only mean 'This man who excels in perfection.' You do not mean to make كل الرجل into something by which you make what precedes it better known and brings the listener's attention to it, as you do when you say هذا زيد and then, fearing that he will not be recognised, you add الطويل. But in the case of كل الرجل you construct your speech upon something which you are certain is known [to the listener] and then you add the information that he is perfect in his qualities." (1, 190/233)

74. *Kitāb* 1, 58/69.

It also emerges from this and preceding examples that our own concepts of "definition" and "indefinition"[(a)] may be too closely connected with the speaker to correspond accurately to *maʿrifa* and *nakira*, for it seems very likely that by these terms Sībawayhi is mainly referring to the state of the listener's knowledge. It is, after all, always possible for the speaker to use an "undefined" word while yet knowing perfectly well to what specific entity it refers; a "defined" word, on the other hand, is only defined by virtue of being known to the listener.[75]

Still more dependent on the knowledge of the listener are such expressions as السعادة أحبّ إليك أم الشقاء؟, where the speaker "knows very well that bliss is dearer to [the listener] than wretchedness and that the person asked will answer 'Bliss,' but he [251] wants to make his companion realise something and to tell him something." (1, 434/484)

This explanation may well have been induced by the examples of Qur'anic sarcasm which precede it, but it is also generally valid for rhetorical questions.

In those cases where the situation makes parts of the speech superfluous, e.g., when you suddenly catch sight of someone (1, 240/279) or see someone obviously setting out on pilgrimage (1, 109/129), we still have to assume the presence of a *muḫāṭab*, and in these two examples just given there is no doubt that it is the person whose presence causes the elision who is also the one addressed. The social nature of speech is thus made unmistakably clear, and survives even in the later grammarians in their respect for the "context of the situation" as an influence on grammar.[(a)]

But only Sībawayhi, it seems, took the concept of the *muḫāṭab* so far. For him the act of speech was always directed towards a listener whose role, far from being passive, was often active enough to cause the speaker to modify his words in mid-sentence. On a far wider scale the *muḫāṭab* provides the only justification for a prescriptive grammar, providing that it is accepted that the purpose of speech is communication, and not, as so often seems to be the case, that to speak correctly is an end in itself. That could never be said of Sībawayhi. The pains he took to establish the actual circumstances of communication are well illustrated by this final example from the *Kitāb*, concerning the "wrong" sentence هو زيدٌ منطلقًا:

> [252] You do not say أنا or هو until you have dispensed with naming the person, because أنا and هو are two signs of the suppressed noun, and people only suppress when they know that you know who they mean. The exception is when a man is behind a wall or somewhere where you cannot know who he is, and you say to him 'Who are you?' and he replies 'I am Zayd, going about your business.' Then it is good Arabic. (1, 219/257)

It is, after all, only the context which makes this use "good Arabic" when elsewhere it would be "wrong." That is the essence of ethics, too, for many actions are only good or

75. Cf. above, p. [245].

bad by virtue of their timing. The constant appearance of the *muḫāṭab* in the *Kitāb* seems to me to confirm the ethical basis of Sībawayhi's system, in that the final judgement of right and wrong, good and bad, in language as in life, rests with the person at whom actions are directed and the circumstances in which they occur.[(a)]

Summary

[327] From the arrangement of the *Kitāb* we know that Sībawayhi put grammar before phonology. He does not, however, use the idea of the *jumla* in his treatment of the sentence, but speaks only of *kalām*. A *kalām* is bounded by silence, starts with a vocative and concludes with *waqf*. There is no need to specify the contents of a sentence when these criteria are used, and so we find no role for *taqdīr* in the *Kitāb*.

Kalām is an act which is divided up into the grammatical "functions," of which over seventy are mentioned in the *Kitāb*. The contrast with the three "parts of speech" shows that "functions" were Sībawayhi's main interest. Each function consists ideally of two members, and these form the binary units into which Arabic is analysed. *Ḥarf* simply means a word which performs a certain function within such a binary unit.

Mawḍiʿ is a true technical term in the *Kitāb*, since it is invariably short for "a place in speech," hence "function" and "place" are the only correct translations. It is subject to ethical criteria and used in grammar in the same way as in ethical contexts.

The sixth chapter of the *Kitāb* explicitly lays down the criteria of correctness, which are discussed prior to offering a translation of this chapter.

Mustaqīm means morally right, hence intelligible, and may be translated in grammar as "right," since its use in the *Kitāb* relates to the listener's comprehension of speech, and it thus has a true social import.

[328] *Ḥasan* and *qabīḥ* describe the form (i.e., structure) of Arabic and can be translated as "good Arabic" and "bad Arabic." They often occur together with *mustaqīm* in assessing the correctness of utterances.

Muḥāl means "wrong," and refers to a perversion of the language which results in failure to communicate.

The other important element in Sībawayhi's grammar is the listener, who, by his presence and expectations, affects the form of speech. He provides the justification for the prescriptive element in the *Kitāb*.

Addenda to Chapter Five

Part of this chapter formed the basis of Carter 1973a (the criteria of correct speech and the function triads).

[198] (a) As we have seen ([38]) Jahn found this order unnatural. Although the same criteria and system are applied to phonology as to the other branches, it is not explored in this thesis in any depth. However, a number of works have appeared in recent decades

which give a good idea of the range of topics covered in the final sections of the *Kitāb* (in chronological order): Vollers 1893, Schaade 1911 (this item in the original bibliography at [324]), Semaan 1968, 1976, Bakalla 1979, 1980, 1982, Al-Nassir 1993, Sara 2007.

Some of these are partial treatments or go beyond the *Kitāb*, but Bakalla 1979 can be recommended for its technical comprehensiveness and bibliography. Al-Nassir 1993 also has a useful bibliography, though he seems unaware that Bakalla's 1970 thesis had been reworked as Bakalla 1982.

One issue which has attracted much attention, but will not be touched upon here, is the disputed meaning of the terms *majhūra* and *mahmūsa*. The articles 'Ḥurūf al-Hidjā'' by Fleisch in *EI*[2] and 'Majhūra/Mahmūsa' by Danecki in *EALL* cover the ground generally, and the monographs above also have their points of view, though the topic remains without a definitive solution.

[198] (b) The word *jumla* does not occur in this sense anywhere in the *Kitāb*, see [202] (b).

[199] (a) See now Iványi 1991, especially 211ff.

[200] (a) The literal meaning of *naṯara* is "scatter seed" exactly like English "broadcast," and Sībawayhi's example *naṯartu kalāman* actually has the sense of "I spoke too much." He gives another example before this one, *naṯartu waladan* "I had abundant children," suggesting that scattering seed is the primary sense of this verb.

[201] (a) Since Sībawayhi has no specific term for "sentence," nor for "clause," nor "phrase," but calls them all *kalām* or *qawl*, he cannot be fairly represented by imposing those categories upon him.

Curiously the present thesis makes no mention of *qawl* as a technical term apart from its meaning of "verdict, opinion, statement," in [15]f, [28], but it is, of course, the principle indicator of an item of data in the *Kitāb*, along with its verb *qāla*.

This is not a trivial matter: Sībawayhi devotes some pages to *qāla*, showing that this verb is unique in that its direct object is always a passage of reported speech *ḥikāya*, and thus identical with its own *mafʿūl muṭlaq* (i.e., *qawl*, cf. Guillaume 1985). The implications for the epistemological and legal status of a *qawl* were well recognised, see Carter 2011.

[202] (a) The thesis does not make it clear that the text translated here has just been quoted above (*Kitāb* 1, 117/138). What is meant by "because the speech is lengthy" *ḥayṯu ṭāla l-kalāmu* is not clear, but it seems to indicate that the utterance is not yet finished, rather than that it goes on for a long time, and so might better be translated as "when/because the speech is prolonged," i.e., continues beyond the first word. It is probably connected with Ḫalīl's use of the concept, e.g., in *Kitāb* 1, 262/303, where he explains the dependent form *yā ʿabdallāhi* in the vocative as due to the "prolonging of the utterance" *ḥīna ṭāla l-kalāmu*, meaning that it is not complete at *ʿabd-*, contrasting with the *yā zaydu*, which is *mufrad*, i.e., a single term, exactly as *iyyāka* (single term) contrasts with the compound *ra'saka wa-l-ḥā'iṭa*.

[202] (b) Since the term *jumla* is lacking in the *Kitāb* in the meaning of "sentence" there should be little need to discuss it here. Inevitably, however, it appears in Western

works on sentence structure, usually contrasting it with *kalām*. Talmon 1988 covers all the issues thoroughly, other treatments in Goldberg 1988 (2007), 53–61 (includes later developments).

One feature of the word which deserves more emphasis is that as a technical term *jumla* is an entirely internal neologism: even if there is any influence from parallel expressions such as Latin *summa,* no point of contact can be determined, cf. Carter 2006, 463ff.

[202] (c) See [296]f on *taqdīr*.

[203] (a) It is implicit in Sībawayhi's concept of a meaningful utterance that the meaning is the product, not the sum, of its parts. Since each part is a unit, the product, 1 x 1 x 1 etc., will always be one (= "sentence meaning") and, as a consequence, if there is any meaningless element in the series, 1 x 1 x 0 etc., the product will be zero, that is, a meaningless utterance. See further [212] (a) and *muḥāl* below, [230] *et seq.*

[204] (a) Such allusions can no longer be taken for granted: the great linguist is Lewis Carroll.

[205] (a) In fact *waqf* can occur <u>within</u> a *kalām* at any chosen breath unit, see below, [244], where pause is optional and the speaker's choice affects the inflection or parsing. Internal *waqf* is also a prominent feature of Qurʾān recitation, and such pauses are clearly marked in the text, and not always unanimously accepted: there is an example in Sūra 4, v. 10, see [10] (a), where a pause has to be inserted to prevent a misinterpretation. In a completely different context pause can actually be prevented by hedging and stalling to keep one's place in a conversation, see [209] (a).

[205] (b) More precisely the lack of final short vowels, which are mostly inflectional. With compound inflections such as masc. plur. -*ūna* only part of the inflection, the -*a*, is lost, to give -*ūn*.

[205] (c) The form *bismillāh* is retained here as a *verbatim* quotation; it is mostly referred to as the Basmala, the verbal noun of the delocutive quadriliteral verb *basmala*, "to say *bi-smi llāhi l-raḥmāni l-raḥīm.*"

[206] (a) This is carelessly formulated: we can assume that Sībawayhi inherited a considerable corpus of technical terms and categories, probably including the tripartite division, see further [164]f, also Carter 1972, 80f.

[206] (b) This number is now known to be too low, see further [209] (a).

[206] (c) Another approach, found in the late grammarians, is to treat the three qualitatively as three different kinds of word, rather than quantitatively as three members of a set or parts of a whole. In the qualitative system nouns can be both subjects and predicates, verbs can only be predicates, and particles can be neither.

[207] (a) For example *muḍāriʿ* verbs which behave like nouns in their inflection, and the verbal pattern *afʿal* appearing in elative nouns and adjectives denoting colours and defects. The *afʿal* pattern in the exclamatory verb (*fiʿl al-taʿajjub*) is a point where the system breaks down, and it became a well-known controversy whether it was in fact a noun or a verb (see Carter 2015, 39 and reference there to H. Fleisch).

[208] (a) As with *ḥarf* above, see [65] (a), the tripartite division has been another challenge to Western preconceptions, and remains so to this day.

The position stated in the thesis is unaltered, that the functions are more important than the formal categories. Mosel 1980, 30ff (with references to Mosel 1975) briefly enumerates the parts from the perspective of contemporary Western linguistics. The scholarly, historical and exegetical issues canvassed by Diem 1974 (2007), Guillaume 1988 (2007) and Suleiman 1990 belong more to the period after Sībawayhi, valuable as they are in themselves. Diem certainly makes us think harder about the nexus of noun, substantive and adjective, and the many categories labelled simply as nouns which we would call pronouns. Guillaume rejects out of hand an Aristotelian origin for the division; he remains close to the the short passage in which Sībawayhi sets out the three parts, and is more concerned to follow up the subequent theoretical innovations by grammarians who clearly were subject to Greek influence. Suleiman's main focus is on the history of Sībawayhi's categories in the later grammarians, to which we can add Versteegh 1995, Chapter One, on al-Zajjājī's interpretation of the problem.

On pronouns, it is worth noting that the Arabic terminology draws on a completely different imagery: instead of pronouns simply being replacements for nouns (which concept is seen in Syriac grammar as *ḫlāf šmā*, literally "deputy noun" as a calque from Greek, appearing also as *ḫawālif* "deputisers" as a calque in Fārābī, Versteegh 1977, 50f and 1993, 25 respectively). Instead the pronominalisation in general is expressed as *iḍmār* "keeping hidden in the mind," one of whose derivatives, *ḍamīr*, stands generally for our "pronoun," but also extends to translate the notion of "conscience" in modern Arabic. What marks this concept off even further from the Western system is that *iḍmār* also covers what we would call the suppression of any element, such as particles and verbs: we can hardly speak of "pronominalising" a particle or a verb, yet Ḫalīl and Sībawayhi regularly speak of elements being *muḍmar*, e.g., prepositions in [38], verbs in [168], the conjunction *an* in [231] (there carelessly *muḍmar* is rendered "elided"). The difference is even more striking when we consider that pronouns are a surface feature in Western languages, while Arabic has many suppressions for which no surface realisation is possible.

[209] (a) The list is certainly not complete, and a figure of seventy is easily surpassed by adding (largely from Carter 1973a, 150f), *taḏkīr/ta'nīṯ* "making masculine/feminine," *tarḫīm* "truncating [in the vocative]," *iẓhār* "manifesting" as antonym of *iḍmār*, *qalb* "inversion," *tafḍīl* "expressing a preference" (i.e., with the elative pattern), *tankīr* "making indefinite," *mubālaġa* "exaggeration, hyperbole," *isti'nāf* "making a fresh start (syntactically)," *itbā'* "making an element agree with a previous element," *taḥḍīḍ* "inciting," *inkār* "expressing incredulity," all of which have specific linguistic manifestations (see Carter 2015, 46f on this last). Perhaps also the cases of self-abasement and boasting mentioned in [22] might be added, as they do have formal linguistic implications.

On the other hand, hedging and stalling, although they are recognised and described by Sībawayhi, do not appear to have received a special name: only later do we find *taḏakkur* "thinking of what to say" and *ta'āyī* "being at a loss for words," (Carter id. 47).

Whether *naʿt* "describing [adjectivally]" qualifies as a function is still obscure, see further [301] (b), and it may serve little purpose to treat *taqdīr* as a function. It remains to establish, through an exhaustive search in Troupeau 1976, exactly how many such functions and triads Sībawayhi had at his disposal.

Note that in some cases above a verbal noun has been listed although only the verb and/or participle is found in the *Kitāb*, and not the complete triad. This would still leave us with a number of verbal nouns which Sībawayhi himself did not use, e.g., *tamyīz, ifāda*, see [293].

The abstract (but not the original thesis text) has been amended to "seventy" at this point to reflect the additions mentioned here.

[210] (a) This is not well thought out, and overlooks a property of the triads which was not fully recognised at the time of writing, namely that in some triads the speaker is himself an operator *ʿāmil*, see Carter 1973a, 151 and n. 46, also [154] (b) Thus in the set above, those where both arms of the triad are passive (*mubdal/mubdal minhu* etc.) have the speaker as their operator. In the case of elision *ḥadf*, therefore, the "elider" would be the speaker, and the first arm would contain what he had in mind to elide *al-maḥdūf*, the second arm being empty after the elision: this would match the *badal* structure perfectly, in that the speaker simply replaces the first element by another, zero in the case of *ḥadf*. (This replaces the less developed reference to *ḥadf* in Carter 1973a, 152, where the two arms of the triad are occupied by the elider **al-ḥādif* and what he elides *al-maḥdūf* respectively).

[210] (b) It can be argued that these structures lie inherently outside the binary scheme anyway. For the *ḥāl* the default dependent case is itself a redundancy marker in later grammar, though Sībawayhi does not term it *faḍla*, see [265] (a). For *sabab* we could probably draw a triad in which one arm was itself another triad, but such an exercise does not seem worth while: the issue with *sabab* is cohesion between units, see [285]–[287] and Carter 1985a.

[211] (a) The examples on this page should make visible the definition of the *ḥarf* as an element which only appears as the left hand member of a triad. In other words it is an instrument, not an agent or operator, for the latter is always the speaker: when "negating," for example, it is not the *ḥarf nafy* which negates, but the speaker who uses the *ḥarf nafy* for that purpose, or as Sībawayhi puts it in a chapter heading (§175), *al-nafy bi-lā*, indicating that *lā* is the instrument of negation.

In practice this is largely ignored, and the *ḥurūf* are freely said to operate, as *lā* is said to operate on the *manfī* here, but this is only a convenience: true agency remains with the speaker, just as when a knife is said to cut it is the wielder of the knife who is the agent, and the knife merely an instrument.

[211] (b) A curious parallel for this concept occurs in mediaeval Western grammar, *modi signficandi* "ways of signifying." It can be seen at once that the two main concepts "way" and "meaning" are inverted in the European scheme, and it is hardly likely that

the two are historically connected. Nevertheless, the goals of their enquiries are similar, to account for the "way" words and speech have "meanings."

[212] (a) The idea has been used above in its negative form, that an utterance becomes meaningless when any of its constituents are meaningless, see [203] (a).

[212] (b) In its vagueness *ḥarf* is the equivalent of the suffix -eme used in Western linguistics, the difference being that in the latter we meet grapheme, phoneme, morpheme, syntagmeme, lexeme etc. at different levels of analysis, while the Arab grammarians were content with unmarked *ḥarf* wherever the context made it clear, only adding the function name when necessary.

For the "parts of speech" in general see [208] (a).

[212] (c) This is J. Fischer: it would clearly be nonsense to equate *ḥarf* with *súndesmos* in the example just given "these elements (*ḥurūf*) which are the names of actions." Sometimes Sībawayhi's use of *ḥarf* seems almost perverse: speaking of the oblique operators in annexation, he refers to what we call "prepositions" such as *bi-*, *li-* as "that which is neither noun nor *ẓarf*," although to our mind they are *ḥurūf*, but this term he here applies instead to the *ẓarf*: "as for the *ḥurūf* which are *ẓurūf* such as *ḫalfa*, *amāma* etc." (*Kitāb* 1, 177/209. On another occasion he calls the active participles *ḥurūf* (id. 1, 79/92), and in an interesting echo of the very first definition of the *ḥarf* in §1, he ascribes the restricted behaviour of the quasi-participial adjective (*ṣifa mušabbaha*) to the fact that "it is neither a verb nor a noun with verbal meaning" (id. 1, 82/100, and cf. [254] et seq.). In 2, 361/331 Sībawayhi refers to the verb stem *fāʿala* as a *ḥarf*, and in 1, 345/393 the free pronouns are called *ḥurūf*.

Ḫalīl also uses *ḥarf* for non-specific units, such as *tanwīn* and the *alif-lām* (id. 2, 58–9/63), which fit, of course, the standard definition, since they do indeed "come for a meaning," viz. *tankīr* and *taʿrīf*, two of the functions recognised by Sībawayhi.

See Levin 2000b, 25f for an inventory of the different usages of *ḥarf* and 26f for some of the "meanings" denoted by the *ḥarf jāʾa li-maʿnan*.

[212] (d) A closely related term which has not been mentioned at all in this thesis is *mawqiʿ*, lit. "place of occurrence." Although it looks like a synonym of *mawḍiʿ* it is not used in the same way in the *Kitāb*: *mawqiʿ* and its verb are purely distributional, referring to the simple fact of the occurrence of an element in a certain place, without regard to what it is doing there. A couple of examples will make this clear: *al-ṣifa lā taqaʿu mawāqiʿa l-asmāʾi* (1, 96/116) "adjectives do not occur in the same places as nouns," *lam lā yaqaʿu baʿdahā faʿala* "[the verb form] *faʿala* does not occur after [the word] *lam*," (1, 407/457); note here the easy movement in and out of the metalanguage, cf. [154] (a). Moreover the notions of *mawqiʿ* and *mawḍiʿ* occur contrastively, e.g., *iʿlam anna kulla mawḍiʿin taqaʿu fīhi anna taqaʿu fīhi annamā* (1, 414/465) "know that in every *mawḍiʿ* (i.e., function) where *anna* occurs *annamā* also occurs." This contrast is obscured by Baalbaki 2008, 182–3, who translates both *mawḍiʿ* and *mawqiʿ* by "position."

Versteegh 1978 gives more examples of *mawqiʿ* and related terms, and (274) comes to a similar conclusion about the difference between *mawqiʿ* and *mawḍiʿ*. One feature he does not stress is that *mawḍiʿ* is subject to the criteria of *ḥusn/qubḥ*, in other words is a structural term, while *mawqiʿ* remains distributional and is therefore subject only to quantification ("occurs frequently" *kaṯīran*, "does not occur [at all]" *lā yaqaʿu*, "occurs now and then" *qad yaqaʿu*, and so on). There is also the possibility that the later grammarians he quotes in the article have modified Sībawayhi's concepts.

The idea of Owens 1990 (see index) that the root *waqaʿa* denotes "governance" (his term) is not convincing. In that context *waqaʿa* means simply that the verb "happens" in real life to the direct object (or "is made to happen" *awqaʿa*), in which sense the later grammarians applied it to transitive verbs (*wāqiʿ*), contrasting with *lāzim* "intransitive."

[214] (a) The original text of the thesis was here in serious error and the correct contents have been inserted.

[215] (a) The formulation is obscure here. The issue is one of metalanguage, or when does a word become a technical term: cf. [154] (a). Other examples in [271] (b), 314 (a).

[217] (a) In [233]–[235].

[217] (b)."appropriate (for the sense)" and "(grammatically) correct" respectively.

[218] (a) "That which is (grammatically) correct but (in word order) incorrect." By *grammatisch* Jahn probably means here morphologically rather than syntactically, but since correctness of both morphology and syntax (and indeed phonology) are covered by *ḥasan/qabīḥ* in the *Kitāb*, this distinction is invalid.

[218] (b) *Mustaqīm* occurs as a calque of Greek *orthos* as a grammatical case in Fārābī, see Versteegh 1977, index s.v. *mustaqīm*, corresponding to the Latin *casus rectus*, but this is clearly unrelated to Sībawayhi's term. Versteegh 1993, 34 does not mention the Fārābī connection (nor in 25, 27) but leaves the Greek origin unmodified even for Sībawayhi, albeit now with the general qualification that it is not a direct import in the *Kitāb*, unlike Fārābī's usage.

[219] (a) See above, [123] on the obligation upon the speaker to convey information, whose success will be judged by the listener.

[219] (b) see above, [123] (a).

[220] (a) "Subject" is acceptable here in the special case of *kāna* since this class of verb does not have "agents." see [71] (a): instead of *fāʿil* the term used is *ism kāna* "the [subject] noun of *kāna*," and likewise the formal direct object of *kāna* is termed its *ḫabar* "predicate" and not *mafʿūl bihi*, even though this verb is regarded as formally "transitive."

[221] (a) Sībawayhi seems to be making a distinction between two kinds of negation, that which negates the contents of a statement, and that which negates that a statement is being made at all: see Larcher 2014, Chapter XVIII, for a thorough review of this phenomenon from the perspective of the pragmatism of the late grammarians, especially Astarābāḏī.

[222] (a) "Unintelligible" here is a careless choice, as it scarcely differentiates *lā yastaqīm* from *muḥāl* "absurd." A better rendering is simply to say it is "not right," for which reason it cannot be understood correctly.

[222] (b) Once again we are venturing to criticise Sībawayhi—a risky enterprise in the light of [290], and cf. [174] (a).

[222] (c) Sībawayhi is invoking the principle that once a subject has been uttered, the speaker is obliged to follow it up with a predicate, see [247]–[249], quoting *Kitāb* 1, 346/394.

[224] (a) Theoretically this should eliminate phatic utterances, but Sībawayhi is well aware that such utterances can succeed in certain contexts. For example the sudden appearance of a person whom the speaker recognises by his deportment (*āya*, cf. our notion of body language), can be greeted with the exclamation "'Abdullāh! Good Lord!" (*Kitāb* 1, 240/279, quoted below [251] and see also Carter 2007, 29f), which is clearly phatic at the level of sentence meaning, but perfectly adequate at the level of utterance meaning. For context of situation see [251] (a).

[225] (a) The ability to speak correct Arabic eventually became part of the definition of a Muslim, see Carter 1983, and note that Sīrāfī demolishes his Christian opponent by accusing him of incompetence in Arabic, see [51].

[225] (b) Studies of Sībawayhi's grammatical terminology, perhaps understandably, do not give a great deal of weight to the ethical and aesthetic underpinning of the criteria of *ḥusn* and *qubḥ*, even though English linguistics is familiar with the concept of the "well-formed"and the "ill-formed," these presumably inherited from Western theories of aesthetics equating [perfect] beauty, goodness and truth. Mosel 1975 does not discuss the criteria of correctness at all, beyond a passing reference (17, n. 1) to *ḥasan* in the meaning of "grammatically correct" and *mustaqīm* as "meaningful and comprehensible," following Jahn 1894. For *muḥāl* see below, [231] (b).

Abboud 1979, 61–63 on the other hand renders *qabīḥ* as "bad, incorrect," which preserves the ethical tone; he also uses ethical terminology such as "deviant" or "aberrant" for incorrect forms generically, likewise Guillaume 1993, 143f accepts the ethical basis of Sībawayhi's criteria.

[227] (a) There is even an elative of *jā'iz*, i.e., *ajwaz* "more permissible," occurring twice in the *Kitāb*, 1, 431/482; 2, 74/77. See Baalbaki 1979, 7, 22, for other examples of graded criteria.

[227] (b) The number sixty is now out of date, see [209] (a).

[228] (a) To these should be added the equational sentence, where the utterance of a topic raises in the listener the expectation of a predicate, see [247]ff.

[229] (a) "Fitness for silence" renders *ḥusn al-sukūt*, at which point the pausal form is permitted. See [204]f and [205] (a). Of course there are silences and silences, and the listener will determine whether the utterance is self-sufficient. Interruption is only possible at breath groups, and here the speaker can preempt interruption by saying "um" and "er," by which device the speaker indicates that it would be "bad" *qabīḥ* for the listener to take over the conversation, see [209] (a). We may compare this with the remark of Sībawayhi's older contemporary, Ibn al-Muqaffa', quoted above in [118], that a person who interrupts "has not spoken well" *lam yuḥsin al-kalām*.

[231] (a) For "undefined" read now "indefinite," see [250] (a).

[231] (b) This formulation is somewhat loose and may lead to confusion with the *ġayr mustaqīm* catgegory. The essential difference is that *mustaqīm* always means something but not necessarily what was intended, while *muḥāl* can never mean anything to anyone.

Noy 2012 has examined in detail the background and meaning of the term *muḥāl* and its 45 occurrences in the *Kitāb* to argue that Sībawayhi uses it to denote "ungrammatical sentences," by which Noy understands sentences with a syntactical inconsistency. Whether Sībawayhi was interested in the pedagogical opportunities is questionable, but we can certainly agree that the artificial construction of *muḥāl* sentences for the purpose of testing a syntactic hypothesis fits very well with Sībawayhi's descriptive goals, that is, to find systematic justifications for his verdicts on the inadmissibility of utterances. After all, it is easy to describe what you <u>can</u> and <u>do</u> say but much harder to state why a certain structure <u>cannot</u> ever be used. Common sense also tells us that there will be very few naturally occurring *muḥāl* utterances: there is only one prose example in the *Kitāb* (Noy 39f), and there are none at all in the Qur'ān or poetry.

[232] (a) Put more coherently, "wrong" *muḥāl* is in no way synonymous with "not right" *lā yastaqīm*, *pace* Noy 2012, 31. It is unfortunate that Noy's translation of the terms opposes *mustaqīm* and *muḥāl* as simple antonyms, "grammatical" and "ungrammatical" respectively.

[233] (a) As Sībawayhi makes clear (cf. also [217]), lying has no distinctive linguistic features, and so plays no part in his criteria of correctness. Abboud 1979, 61, may be taking this aspect of the *Kitāb* a little too seriously by listing *kaḏib* as a criterion: the operating ethical principle is the same one which regulates legal discourse, namely that the purpose of instruction is to teach people to behave well, not badly: if they want to behave badly, and lie, that is a moral, not a linguistic matter. By default Muslims are assumed to speak truthfully to each other.

[233] (b) This reading is preferred because an utterance can still make sense (*mustaqīm*) even though defective (*fīhi naqṣ*) whereas an utterance containing a contradiction (*naqḍ*) can never be *mustaqīm* in any way, only *muḥāl*.

In both cases the comprehension of the whole utterance as a unity—either imperfectly or not at all—is the issue, and it is very important to note that this pair of terms is not gradable, unlike the *ḥasan/qabīḥ* set, where there is no absolute standard of formal correctness, see [226]f, [227] (a).

[234] (a) The error persisted, and is reproduced by Tawḥīdī (d. 411/1023) in his discussion of the debate between Sīrāfī and Abū Bišr, above in [51], see Endress 1986, 265f.

[236] (a) It still needs to be determined whether Ḫalīl had any identifiable role in bringing these ethical criteria into circulation or to Sībawayhi's attention. His name is associated with *muḥāl*, see Noy 2012, 39f.

[237] (a) We can add to this list *bāliġ* in the statement (*Kitāb* 1, 110/131) that the dependent case in a certain construction is *jayyid bāliġ* "excellent and effective," and *jayyid bāliġ* is used again in 1, 329/377; for an exceptive construction. If it is indeed a true tech-

nical term, it might correlate better with *mustaqīm* than with the structural set. Another term which has slipped through the net is the root *k-r-h* "be disliked, dispproved of," see Troupeau 1976.

[239] (a) *Essais*, Book 3, Chapter13, De l'expérience (p. 339 in the Classiques Garnier ed.).

[240] (a) Buburuzan 1993 has reviewed Sībawayhi's analysis of speech acts in the *Kitāb* as exhibiting strong parallels with Pragmatism in the modern sense, that is, of "doing things with words" *à la* Grice and Austin. Many utterances are analysed by Sībawayhi as part of an interaction between speaker and listener in a real-life context, as will appear in some of the examples in the following pages of the thesis. The idea was taken up in Carter 2007, in support of the theory that there was an intrinsic similarity between Sībawayhi's approach to language and that of the lawyers: both treat language as a contractual process, used between speakers/actors who are of sound mind and capable of forming intentions.

This view also accounts for the conventionality of linguistic features, cf. Marogy 2012b on the "Politeness Principle" (itself seemingly an offshoot from Pragmatism) which governs the making of statements, and the related notion of "identifiability" which comes close to the underlying sense of the term *ma'rifa* for "definite," especially for unmarked items (cf. [250].

[240] (b) Lit. "Were you to see lo and behold they have been stood over the Fire (of Hell)."

[241] (a) "Qays ibn 'Aylān have waged their war against one who withstands alone the vicissitudes of battle, [we praise him] as a brother to those challenges, when they are fierce he will ride against them on the back of any steed, docile or fractious." The poet is Ḏū l-Rumma, see Fischer/Braünlich 1945, 26 (*min ṣa'bi*), Ya'qūb 1992, 120 (*min ṣa'bi*).

[241] (b) The imperative verb *uḏkur* is printed with a final *sukūn* in Derenbourg, a rare lapse, where Būlāq correctly has a *kasra*; the Hārūn edition opts for 1st person verbs here, *aḏkuru* for both, without giving any reason.

[243] (a) Here as elsewhere "definition" should be replaced by "definiteness," see [250] (a) and [298] (a).

[244] (a) The option of "stopping" (*waqf*, see [204]) here is very significant, as it implies that the binary unit (in this case noun + adjective) does not extend over the pausal boundary in *yā zaydu | al-ṭawīlu*, whereas in *yā haḏā l-rajulu* the noun phrase *hāḏā l-rajulu* is a binary unit with the "status of a single noun" (see [181] (a) on this). This is somewhat obscured by the convention in this thesis of transliterating in full junctural form: the first utterance should be *yā zayd* [potential pause] *al-ṭawīl*, the second *yā hāḏā l-rajul* with no internal pause.

[244] (b) Here the word "sentence" has intruded into the translation, in spite of the reservations about this concept above, [83]. Where Sībawayhi simply says *kalām* in this context it should be understood as "a [right and good] utterance" *kalām [mustaqīm ḥasan]*.

Admittedly this full formulation has not been confirmed in the *Kitāb*, but it is implicit in the chapter which sets out the criteria of correct speech as *mustaqīm ḥāsan*, see [232].

NB In the corresponding section of the abstract [328] "sentences" is now replaced by "utterances"

[246] (a) "even though it is feeble" renders *'alā ḍa'fihi*, see [237] for this synonym of *qubḥ/qabīḥ*.

[247] (a) We can add here a notion, *tawahhum*, described by Baalbaki 1982, 234–8, as "comprehension," meaning the process by which a listener works out the formal and syntactical categories within the utterance. It is therefore subjective, and may vary among speech communities. Sībawayhi also uses the term to denote the restoration of elisions and the drawing of analogies. This is a most valuable insight into a term completely neglected in this thesis. All the more fascinating is the fact that the root notion of *wahm* is strongly associated with wrong opinions and baseless fantasies, and one wonders just how critical Sībawayhi is being. On the whole the results of *tawahhum* are not stigmatised as incorrect, but on two occasions the term occurs in association with *ġalaṭ*, but never with *ḫaṭa'*, suggesting there is a progression of error upwards from *ḫaṭa'* to *ġalaṭ* to what may be just on the other side of the border of correctness, *tawahhum*. The acid test would be to establish whether the *tawahhum* forms were normative: they appear not to be.

[247] (b) See [70] (a), and [305]f.

[248] (a) "status of initiality" is a very unhelpful translation of *bi-manzilatihā fī l-ibtidā'*; Sībawayhi is simply asserting that agent nouns have the same syntactic status as the subjects/topics of nominal sentences, in that both require completion by a predicate. A better translation would be "status of words used to begin equational sentences," avoiding the Latinate abstraction of "initiality," a class of terminology which is entirely absent from the *Kitāb*, see below, [293]. In general the Latinate translations are intrinsically unsuitable for the functions, which are all named as verbal nouns by Sībawayhi (see [208]ff), so, for example, "predicating" ought always to be preferred to "predication," but sometimes this cannot be avoided.

[249] (a) "You are obliged" renders *wajaba 'alayka*. This particular passage is followed by the comment "this is the explanation of Ḫalīl" *hāḏā tafsīr al-Ḫalīl*, which reminds us that the notion of the obligation on a speaker to take the listener's expectations into account is linked with Ḫalīl elsewhere in the *Kitāb*, see [242] etc.

For *wājib* in the sense of "assertive" utterance see 58 (c).

[249] (b) The combination of the listener's expectations and the requirement of definiteness in the subject together compensate for the absence of a copula verb in Arabic, see [123] (b).

[250] (a) These terms are to be replaced throughout by definiteness and indefiniteness. In our own terminology these refer to the ability to state the dimensions of an object, its place, time and qualities, while the corresponding Arabic *ma'rifa* and *nakira* respectively denote literally that the object is "known" or "unknown" in the social sense,

perhaps more delicately "recognised" or "unrecognised," and this conditions the way information is conveyed, as we have seen in [123] and elsewhere.

As in many languages, definiteness may be marked (def. article) or unmarked (personal and proper names). In the latter case the recognition by both speaker and listener is extralinguistic. Sībawayhi also covers the case where a personal name might belong to somebody the listener does not know or needs more information about, as in the examples above, [244]f.

[251] (a) Known as *lisān al-ḥāl* in later grammar. Since Sībawayhi treats the listener as part of the context of every utterance anyway, he had no need for such a term. Some of his examples clearly imply body language as part of the context, see [224] (a).

[252] (a) The *muḫāṭab*/listener is even required in soliloquy, except that he is the same person as the *mutakallim*/speaker, see [176] (a).

Chapter Six
Twenty Dirhams

One construction which displays at once the concision and the versatility of Arabic is the *iḍafa*, which encompasses "une infinité de rapports différens"[1] within the framework of a single grammatical bond. Reckendorf reduces this infinity to a mystical fourteen, and there is much to be learnt from the wasted diligence with which he attempts to categorise the innumerable uses of the *iḍāfa* into some scheme of his own devising. With an insight which is beyond my grasp he distinguishes, for example, between a class of "Genitiv des in einem Bereich Befindlichen,"[2] illustrated by حوران الجنود and a "Genitiv des Besitztums,"[3] illustrated by شاهبور الجنود and on another occasion he identifies a class of "Genitiv der Form"[4] merely on the basis of the occurrence of the phrase فضّة الدراهم.[(a)] Such labours serve only to exaggerate the flexibility of the *iḍāfa* and the futility of trying to distribute it into semantic categories.[(b)] What is worse, such attempts as this have probably caused the neglect of an interesting and equally important problem of Arabic grammar: if *iḍāfa* covers all non-verbal subordination, what is the explanation for the common occurrence of the direct form (*naṣb*) after a non-verbal operans, such as الحسن وجهًا , عشرون درهمًا , كم رجلاً , إنّ زيدًا and so on? The conventional explanation, that the first words in these pairs have a verbal force, is only a faint reflection of a long and important argument which Sībawayhi spreads over five chapters of the *Kitāb*, and which I now propose to examine and set in its place in the *Kitāb* as a whole.

[254] It is well-known that the participle (*ism al-fā'il*)[(a)] forms a kind of *iḍāfa* with its direct object, e.g. ضاربُ زيدٍ. It is assumed, probably correctly, that this construction is simply an alternative to the primary form ضاربٌ زيدًا and in this assumption lies the key to the argument of Sībawayhi. It enables him to prove that the occurrence of direct forms after

1. De Sacy, *Gram. arabe* 2, 48 (my emphasis).
2. Reckendorf, *Arab. Synt.* 142.
3. Id. 144.
4. Id. 141.

certain words is, at least theoretically, due to the power (*quwwa*) of that word, by analogy with the "power" of the verb. But, much more important, it also allows him to establish, for present and future purposes, an entirely different type of grammatical bond from the *iḍāfa*. Possibly due to the excessive attention paid by later grammarians to the "proper" and "improper" *iḍāfa*s, this other construction, which in many ways is complementary to the *iḍāfa*, has never been given a name. I shall call it, for reasons which will become obvious, the *tanwīn-naṣb* construction.

The existence of verbal power in the participles need not be questioned, though their occurrence in *iḍāfa* constructions shows that they have temporarily abandoned their verbal effect in favour of of the nominal effect which they acquire in *iḍāfa*. This grammatical (functional) ambiguity is best shown in the form of a diagram:

ism al-fāʿil —— verbal effect: ضاربٌ زيدًا
ism al-fāʿil — — — nominal effect: ضاربُ زيدٍ

The continuous line shows the assumed norm, and the broken line indicates the result of analogical extension. The *ṣifa mušabbaha*, which I shall call the quasi-participial adjective, produces the following diagram:

ṣifa mušabbaha — — — verbal effect: عشرون درهمًا
ṣifa mušabbaha —— nominal effect: حسنُ الوجهِ

[255] Analogical extension is seen to have occurred in both directions: the quasi-participial adjective comes to exert verbal effect and the true participle nominal effect. It is clear from the nomenclature (*mušabbaha*) that the primary analogy is felt to have extended from the participle to the "adjective which resembles the participle,"[a] and, as a result, that the nominal effect of the true participle is only secondary. The first part of Sībawayhi's argument in the relevant five chapters deals with the purely formal analogies which exist between the participial and quasi-participial constructions, and it is more economical to reduce them to the form of a comparative table (the page references are all to volume 1):

	Participle		Quasi-participle
1.	(70/82) يضربُ زيدًا	1.	(82/101) حسنٌ وجهُه
2.	(70/82) ضاربٌ زيدًا	2.	(82/101) عشرون درهمًا
3.	(82/76) ضاربُ زيدٍ	3.	(82/100) حسنُ الوجهِ
4.	(77/93) الضاربُ زيدًا	4.	(83/103) الحسنُ وجهًا
5.	(77/93) الضاربُ الرجلَ	5.	(84/103) الحسنُ الوجهَ

6.	الضاربُ الرجلِ	(77/93)	6.	الحسنُ الوجهِ	(83/103)
7.	الضاربون الرجلَ	(78/94)	7.	الطيبون الأخبارَ	(84/103)
8.	الضاربو زيدٍ	(78/94)	8.	الطيبو أخبارٍ	(84/104)

It will be seen from the page numbers that, with the notable exception of عشرون درهمًا, the examples are all dealt with in approximately the same sequence; since there is no quasi-participial expression حسنٌ وجهًا to correspond to ضاربٌ زيدًا, Sībawayhi has to leave عشرون درهمًا until the next phase of the argument. So far we have only a large-scale exercise in *qiyās*, though the reasoning is occasionally circular. [256] Thus الضاربُ الرجل is explained on page 77/93 as as being formed by analogy with الحسنُ الوجه, but on page 83/103 he merely states that الحسنُ الوجه is to be compared with الضاربُ الرجل! The only excuse for this is that the two constructions no doubt influenced each other in the ordinary course of Arabic speech, and so the circularity is inherent.[a]

From the table above certain general conclusions can be drawn. Obviously the "improper" *iḍāfa*, which I shall henceforth call the pseudo-*iḍāfa*, is equivalent to, and a paraphrase of the *tanwīn-naṣb* construction. It also emerges that the definition[b] of the *muḍāf* in the pseudo-*iḍāfa* is independent of the state of the *muḍāf ilayhi*, and, perhaps less well-known, but more important for this particular argument, that in the pseudo-*iḍāfa* the contrast between definition and indefinition has been neutralised, so that الحسنُ الوجهَ and الحسنُ وجهًا both mean the same thing. Lastly we note that the presence of *tanwīn* in the *muḍāf* evidently makes both types of *iḍāfa* impossible. All of these formal deductions are later put to use by Sībawayhi.

Before turning to the next stage of the argument, however, we must consider some very interesting remarks which Sībawayhi makes about the relationship between the parts of a pseudo-*idāfa*. Since he never explicitly defines the semantic relationship between the parts of a true *iḍāfa*, his observations on the pseudo-*iḍāfa* are our only guide to the nature of the true *iḍāfa*.

He first declares that the pseudo-*iḍāfa* is quite distinct from the true *iḍāfa*:

> [257] Know that the Arabs regard the participle lightly and so they elide the *nūn* of *tanwīn*, but no change of meaning occurs. The object[a] is then put into the oblique form because of the removal of the *tanwīn* from the particle, which results in its having the effect[b] of making the object oblique. This occurs with the participle as an alternative[c] to the *tanwīn*, and behaves exactly like غلامُ عبد الله in form, because it is a noun, even though it is not like it in meaning or effect. The removal of the *tanwīn* for the sake of lightness does not change the meaning at all and does not make the word defined. (1, 71/83)

This line of argument assumes a knowledge of two features of the true *iḍāfa*, which we only find mentioned separately through the *Kitāb*, viz. that the true *iḍāfa* defines its *muḍāf* by the definition of its own *muḍāf ilayhi* (cf. 1, 160/190), and that the relationship between its parts can be expressed by the preposition ل (cf. 1, 301/345). This tells us very little, however, about the meaning of the true *iḍāfa*, and it is clear from this and other discussions that Sībawayhi prefers to take its meaning for granted and concentrate on its grammatical behaviour. We should also note in the above argument the suggestion that the pseudo-*iḍāfa* and *tanwīn-naṣb* constructions are mutually exclusive, but freely interchangeable constructions in which the meaning (i.e. the relationship between the parts) is the same in both cases.

What marks off the pseudo-*iḍāfa* from the true *iḍāfa* is the fact that the pseudo-*iḍāfa* is linked intrinsically with some other part of the sentence, while the true *iḍāfa* is a self-contained unit. This structural unity of [258] the true *iḍāfa* (cf. 1, 254/295) will later be contrasted with the essential separateness of the two terms in a *tanwīn-naṣb*, but for the moment we must concern ourselves with the other aspect of the constructions. Clearly the true *iḍāfa*, being equivalent to a single noun, can function as an initial term (*mubtada'*), predicate or in any of the places where a noun can occur, while it is immediately apparent that the pseudo-*iḍāfa* is simply a complex adjective which cannot occur alone. As it is not a "possessive" *iḍāfa* there must be some other link between its parts and this link is called *sabab* by Sībawayhi, and described in the following terms:

> When you say هذا حسنُ الوجه and هذه حسنةُ الوجه the adjective applies to the first noun and then you join it to the وجه and to everything else connected with it (مِن سببه) as I have mentioned, in the same way that you say هذا ضاربُ الرجل and هذه ضاربةُ الرجل except that in meaning the حسن belongs to the وجه while the ضرب belongs to the person striking. (1, 82/100)[a]

The *sabab*, then, is what connects the *muḍāf* to the *muḍāf ilayhi* in a pseudo-*iḍāfa*, whether the two terms are in the relationship of verb to object,[5] verb to subject, or merely linked in some way which the sense demands but which is clearly not the same as the indissoluble bond of true *iḍāfa*.

The adjective in a pseudo-*iḍāfa* is now seen to have a double reference: backwards to the noun it qualifies, and forwards to whatever is connected to it by a *sabab*.[6] It matters not that this *sabab* is impossible to specify [259] in semantic terms, though it will be found in practice that it invariably consists of enlarging upon the meaning contained in the first word, as حسنُ الوجه shows. What matters is that Sībawayhi has identified the purely grammatical features of a syntactical bond which accounts for all the non-verbal subordination not already covered by *iḍāfa*. For we must remember that he has already implied that the pseudo-*iḍāfa* is equivalent to the *tanwīn-naṣb* construction, and it is this latter construction, exemplified in عشرون درهمًا, that Sībawayhi uses in more than a score

5. Cf. below, p. [286].
6. Cf. above, pp. [20]–[21].

of cases to explain the occurrence of a direct form in the absence of any effective verbal operans.

It remains for him to prove that عشرون درهمًا is, in fact, equivalent to a pseudo-*iḍāfa*. Since there is no construction of the type حسنٌ وجهًا in Arabic, a formal *qiyās* between it and ضاربٌ زيدًا is out of the question, and so the argument is based on a skillful application of principles already established in the preliminary discussion.

By way of introduction he begins with the behaviour of the elatives, in those cases where the permanent separation of the operans and what it affects (*ma'mūl*) precludes any sort of *iḍāfa* and imposes a *tanwīn-naṣb* construction, e.g. هو خيرٌ منك أبًا and هو أحسنُ منك وجهًا.[7] From this it follows (though Sībawayhi evidently regards it as too obvious to point out) that عشرون cannot occur in an *iḍāfa*, because it has already been shown that *tanwīn* prevents *iḍāfa*, and it must, therefore be followed by a direct form.

The next point requires rather more ingenuity, and it cannot be said this part of the argument rises much above the level of casuistry.[(a)] It is [260] best to turn a blind eye to the deficiencies of the pleading and to look forward to the cause in which it was undertaken. Sībawayhi has to prove that in any *tanwīn-naṣb* construction the second element, as well as being direct in form, must also be both singular and undefined. The groundwork has already been done: by comparing الضاربُ الرجلِ , الضاربُ زيدًا and الحسنُ الوجه , الحسنُ وجهًا. Sībawayhi has concluded that the *muḍāf ilayhi* in all these is undefined because the *alif-lām* on the *muḍāf* has prevented *iḍāfa*, and so must have "the status of *tanwīn*"[8] or be a substitute (*badal*) for it.[9]

Further support is gained from the fact that words like خير and أحسن "do not have the power (*quwwa*)[(a)] of the quasi-participle,[10] which explains both their restricted morphology (in predicative use they have only the one form, with no variations for number or gender) and the fact that words "connected with them" (من سببه) are undefined. It is a statement of linguistic fact, rather than the satisfactory product of cogent reasoning, when Sībawayhi says that these words "are fixed into one mode" (ألزم فيه وفيما يعمل فيه وجهًا واحدًا).[(b)]

The next stage is to compare أول الرجال with أول رجل, where it is clear that the meaning in either case is effectively "the first man," about which Sībawayhi claims, perhaps with justification, that

> as they lighten it by eliding the *alif-lām* they also lighten it by forsaking the plural form. (1, 85/104)

7. *Kitāb* 1, 84/104.
8. *Kitāb* 1, 77/93.
9. Id. 1, 83/103.
10. Id. 1, 84/104.

It is now possible for Sībawayhi to declare that عشرون درهمًا is precisely such an instance where, in the word it affects, both the *alif-lām* and the [261] plural form have been dispensed with as unnecessary, q.e.d. He thus reaches the point where he can offer some sort of explanation, founded step by step on the preceding argument, for the combination of a non-verbal undefined word with an undefined singular word in the direct form. The original verbal power of the participles, however, has been successively diluted as he deals with the adjectives of pseudo-*iḍāfa*, with elatives, and, eventually, the numerals. From the way in which the argument continues until it finally embraces the unique phrase لدن غدوةً, it seems that the original notion of verbal power was regarded all along as insufficient in itself to account, as عشرون درهمًا will soon be called upon to do, for such phenomena as كم رجلاً and the like. Subsequent uses of عشرون درهمًا often invoke a rather different idea, namely, the effect of one part of a sentence[(a)] upon another, and other general princples emerge, involving such factors as the function of the *tanwīn* and the relationship (*sabab*) between the parts of a *tanwīn-naṣb*, which, though embodied in عشرون درهمًا, take us much further than the implications of the quasi-participial pseudo-*iḍāfa* to which عشرون درهمًا was originally likened. By extending the chapter to include لدن غدوة، عشرون درهمًا، and the behaviour of numerals and elatives, Sībawayhi makes it plain that his real purpose was to provide the proof for a *locus probans* that he could use later to account for all direct forms in the absence of any verbal operans. This is, therefore, a convenient moment to turn to the other grammatical principle illustrated by عشرون درهمًا, i.e. the separative function of the *tanwīn*.

As far as I know this function has not been recognised by any subsequent grammarian: the usual accounts of the *tanwīn* state that there are up to six [262] kinds in Arabic,[(a)] signifying full inflection (*tamakkun*),[(b)] indefinition (*nakira*), compensation (*ʿiwaḍ*), correspondence (*muqābala*), nasalisation (*tarannum*) and exaggeration in rhyme (*al-ġālī*).[11] Apart from the last one these are all to be found in the *Kitāb*; the *tanwīn* of exaggeration is probably a later invention, since the verse in which it is said to occur is quoted in the *Kitāb* but without the feature for which it has been singled out.[12] None of these functions, however, adequately reproduces the separative function which Sībawayhi identified and used, in the form of عشرون درهمًا, to explain various grammatical phenomena.

The ultimate source of the notion of a separative function is undoubtedly Ḫalīl's idea of the completed word and the role of the *tanwīn* in marking this completion. We have already seen that, for Ḫalīl, such elements as the feminine ending, the *nisba* ending, the *muḍāf ilayhi*, the object of the verb in يا ضاربًا رجلاً,[(c)] the second half of compound words and of the compound numerals were all equivalent to a *tanwīn*.[13] Two points emerge from this idea, and both are applied by Sībawayhi to problems involving عشرون درهمًا.

11. E.g. Fākihī, *Ḥudūd* 12.
12. *Kitāb* 2, 328/301.
13. above, pp. [39]ff.

The first is that the morphologically complete word which Ḫalīl described in terms of *tanwīn* will also reveal itself to be grammatically complete and able to stand alone. Although in doing so I anticipate the examples of عشرون درهمًا which will be given below, I must here give in full the part of the *Kitāb* which sets down عشرون درهمًا as a symbol not only of the completed word, but also of the completed sentence, which is [263] Sībawayhi's exe tension into syntax of Ḫalīl's morphological idea of *tanwīn* at the level of the single word:

> As for their expression داري خلفَ دارك فرسخًا , the word فرسخًا is made direct because خلف is a predicate to داري and so this is a speech in which one part has already had its proper effect on the other and is thus self-sufficient. But by saying داري خلف دارك it remains vague and it is not known how far behind, so the speaker adds فرسخًا or ذراعًا or ميلاً, wanting to make this clear. The effect of this speech on these terms of distance is to make them direct, just as عشرون does in عشرون درهمًا . It is as if this speech were something with *tanwīn* (شيء منوّن) having an effect on something that is not part of the same term or identical with it, similar in status to أفضلهم رجلاً . (1, 176/207)

It is clear from this passage that عشرون epitomises the completed sentence,[(a)] and that it can only be followed by words in direct form, such as the "Temjîz," which Jahn invariably interpolates into his translation, though nowhere in the *Kitāb* does Sībawayhi ever use such a term.[(b)]

In the case of له عسلٌ ملءُ/ملءَ جرّةٍ we have an interesting situation, where ملء ought to be independent because it describes the honey, but

> the direct form is allowed like the direct form in عليه مائةٌ بيضًا after the sentence is finished (بعد التمام) (1, 262/303).

By بعد التمام Sībawayhi obviously means after the *tanwīn* of مائةٌ at which point the sentence is syntactically complete and self-sufficient, which Jahn somewhat ponderously brings out by rendering these two short [264] Arabic words as "dass alle sur Bildung des Satzes nothwendigen Bestandtheile als vorher vorhanden gedacht werden."[(a)]

This sentence-final *tanwīn* will also account for such specimens as هو نارٌ حمرةً (1,198/231), about which Jahn is thoroughly confused. He assumes first that when حمرة is called a *ḫabar* the term *ḫabar* "as elsewhere in Sībawayhi, also includes Ḥâl and Temjîz," which is dubious,[(b)] and then claims that نار "must be considered as in the meaning of a verb, otherwise there could be no Temjîz,"[14] To be sure he is only paraphrasing the errors of Sīrāfī, but it can hardly fail to strike the reader of the *Kitāb* that the whole purpose of the عشرون درهمًا argument is to eliminate the need to posit any verb at all in the situations covered by عشرون درهمًا. The verbal effect, which in the participles derives from their verbal origins, becomes, in the case of عشرون درهمًا, the effect of the completed sentence upon

14. Jahn §110, n. 8.

subsequent additions to it, and هو نارٌ حمرة is just such a case, even if Sībawayhi does not actually say so.

The same is true of another construction of similar form:

> Know that things are described by what is identical with them or part of the same term as in the expression هذا زيد الطويلُ. When the describing word is identical but not part of the same term, e.g. هذا زيد ذاهبًا or is neither identical nor part of the same term, e.g. هذا درهم وزنًا, it can only be in the direct form. (1, 237/276)

Leaving aside the interesting remarks on the differences between true adjectives and the *ḥāl* and "*tamyīz*," it is clear that these sentences fall [265] into the same category as داري خلف دارك فرسخًا (above, p. [263]) which is analysed in exactly the same terms, but which includes عشرون درهمًا as confirmation. Since this latest example is dealt with some twenty pages after Sībawayhi has accounted for هذا عبد الله منطلقًا,[15] we must assume that it is an alternative, structural analysis of what is usually explained on semantic grounds as an explanatory *ḥāl*, but which must now also be regarded in structural terms as a supplementary component of an already complete sentence taking, as a result, the direct form. The implications of this for the *manṣūbāt* in general are interesting: we might claim that Sībawayhi's method of analysis implies that all the *manṣūbāt* are, in theory, additions to already complete sentences, which is another way of substantiating the assertion of the later grammarians that the *manṣūbāt* are all extraneous (*faḍla*).[(a)] This tendency is seen at its clearest in the case of ويحَه رجلًا, of which Sībawayhi says رجلًا

> is made direct because it is not part of the first speech, but the first speech has an effect on it and the ـه of ويحه acquires the status of *tanwīn*. (1, 258/299)

This brings us to the second point which emerges from the separative function of the *tanwīn*.

It has already been shown that the pseudo-*iḍāfa* is the result of leaving off the *tanwīn* of the participial adjective, and that the converse is also true, i.e. that forms such as خير , عشرون etc., where the *tanwīn* is permanent, will not be able to form *iḍāfas*.[16] The *tanwīn*, in the same way that it marks the end of a completed sentence, prevents any further [266] dependence (which in non-verbal cases can only be shown through *iḍāfa* and oblique forms) even between parts of the same sentence. This is probably an idea of Ḫalīl's, if we are to believe that the following quotation faithfully transmits his actual argument:

> He said that if you separate كم from its noun by something which is self-sufficient for silence or is not, then you must treat it in the way of those who give it the status of something with *tanwīn*, because it is bad Arabic to separate the *jārr*

15. See above, p. [244].
16. Above, p. [259].

> from the *majrūr* as the oblique word is part of the word that makes it oblique and they acquire, as it were, the status of one word. But the word with *tanwīn* is separated from the word it affects as when you say هذا ضاربٌ بك زيدًا, and you do not say هذا ضاربُ بك زيدٍ. (1, 254/295)

Strictly speaking the intervening بك in the last example is phonetic, since separation is already effected by the presence of the *tanwīn* of ضاربٌ, but the argument requires that, even without *tanwīn* on ضارب, *iḍāfa* should be prevented. This passage makes it plain that, irrespective of the structural completeness of a sentence, the *tanwīn* marks the limit of a word's power to make a following word oblique (*majrūr*).

The same argument is applied in reverse to the type لا يدَيْن بها لك:

> The retention of the (dual) *nūn* is better Arabic, and that is the proper style (وجه).[(a)] When you say لا يديْ لك and لا أبا لك the noun has the status of a word which has nothing between it and the *muḍāf ilayhi*, like لا مثل زيد. But just as it is bad Arabic to say لا مثل بها زيد and separate the parts, it is bad Arabic to say لا يديْ بها لك. (1, 302/347)

[267] Here we see the connection between *tanwīn* and separation very clearly, for the phrase لك is felt to be equivalent to a *muḍāf ilayhi* when it immediately follows لا أبا or لا يديْ, but as a predicate when it is separated from them.

It appears, then, that the *tanwīn-naṣb* is the only alternative construction to the *iḍāfa* and that to explain it when it occurs in عشرون درهمًا is to lay the foundations for an explanation of all cases where a direct form occurs after a non-verbal operans. It will also be seen from examples already given and from those to come, that, while the true *iḍāfa* and the *ṣifa* and *mawṣūf* have in common the fact that their parts are either included in, or identical with each other, the *tanwīn naṣb* is characterised by the formal non-identity of its parts.[17] The identity or inclusion which marks the true *iḍāfa* and the *ṣifa-mawṣūf* combination is replaced, in the pseudo-*iḍāfa* and the *tanwīn-naṣb*, by the *sabab* which links the meaning of the two parts of the construction in the same way that any direct term is linked with the verb which affects it, and generally standing in the same specifying relationship to the operans as the various *maf'ūls* to their verbs.[(a)] There is a symmetry between verbal effect and the *tanwīn-naṣb*, indeed it is the foundation of the case built up in support of عشرون درهمًا , but I think that it is a mistake to infer from the argument of the chapters in which عشرون درهمًا is established, that for every occurrence of an undefined direct word there must be a concealed verbal operans. It is, for example, absurd to look for one in هو نارٌ حمرةً or even in هذا عبد الله منطلقًا. For Sībawayhi it was undoubtedly the formal resemblance between these constructions and ضاربٌ زيدً [268] which stimulated the development of the theory that a sentence as such could exert an effect on words added

17. Cf. above, p. [264], and below *passim*.

after its completion, and from the way he argues for عشرون درهمًا and the use he later makes of it, it appears that he was not inclined to believe that a hidden verb lay beneath every *tanwīn-naṣb* construction.

I shall now list all the grammatical problems in which عشرون درهمًا is invoked as a *locus probans*.

1. 1, 16/20. Typically, عشرون درهمًا occurs as evidence long before its admissibiity has been established.[a] It is used to buttress a somewhat forced argument concerning the *ḥāl*. Sībawayhi alleges that the *ḥāl* is to be distinguished from the second direct object of the doubly transitive verbs by the fact that the subjects and objects of the verb "intervene between the verb and the *ḥāl*" (حال بينه وبين الفعل)[b] and prevent the *ḥāl* from having the status of a *maf'ūl* or a *fā'il*,

> just as the oblique words intervene between what makes them oblique and what follows them when you say لي مثله رجلاً and لي ملؤه عسلاً, likewise ويحه فارسًا. In the same way the *nūn* in عشرون prevents what follows from being oblique when you say عشرون درهمًا.

With the word-play on *ḥāl* and حال بين, and the tenuous connection between the interference of the *nūn* in عشرون درهمًا and that of the verbal complements in the case of the *ḥāl*, this must surely rank as one of the weakest passages in the *Kitāb*.[c]

2. 1, 36,38/47,49. Amongst the numerous byproducts of discussing the conjunction of two inverted verbal sentences, e.g. عمرٌو لقيته وزيدٌ كلّمته are problems involving إنّ , e.g. إنّ فيها زيدًا وعمرٌو أدخلته [269] and the like. If the second noun is taken to be dependent on إنّ it must nevertheless have independent form because إنّ is not a verb,

> but is only in the status of a verb, just as عشرون درهمًا and ثلاثون رجلاً are in the status of ضاربٌ عبد الله even though they are neither verbs nor particles. (1,38/49)

It is, of course, possible to say إنّ فيها زيدًا وعمرًا أدخلته if you are one of those who always makes inverted direct obects direct in form. Once again عشرون درهمًا is used before it has been proved, in this case to demonstrate that even words which are not verbs can have verbal effect. This is not to say that they presupose an elided verb: what Sībawayhi says seem to be designed to forestall precisely that assumption, though his efforts have met with no success.

3. 1, 85/104. Only now is عشرون درهمًا proved to be a *locus probans* for the *tanwīn-naṣb* construction, details of which I have given in the above analysis of Sībawayhi's argument.[a] Note that عشرون درهمًا will be used to account for several types of grammatical situation, e.g. separative *tanwīn*, extraneous terms added to already completed sentences, qualification of a word by one that is neither included in it nor identical with it etc., all of which are different aspects of the same construction.

4. 1, 154/184. What is nowadays called the *maf'ūl lahu* is explained by Sībawayhi in the following terms:

> it is in direct form because it denotes that for which the event occurred and because it is an explanation of what precedes it and why it is so. It is not an adjective to what precedes it nor included in it, and takes direct form as does درهمًا in عشرون درهمًا.

[270] Jahn, by adding "(wie der Temjîz, z. B.)" misleadingly implies that عشرون درهمًا is a symbol only of that construction, to which, in any case, Sībawayhi never refers directly. We have seen that عشرون درهمًا has a far wider application than the "Temjîz," in this instance being used to explain the need for direct forms when the terms of qualification are neither identical with nor included in the terms they qualify. The explanation is so brief that the reference to عشرون درهمًا would be meaningless if it were not intended to recall the whole argument of the chapters in which عشرون درهمًا itself was established and justified.

5. 1, 170/201. In accounting for the direct forms in what the later grammarians call the *maf'ūl fīhi*, Sībawaihi invokes the idea of the effect (*'amal*) of one part of a sentence upon another:

> these words are direct in form because they denote where the event occurred and what it was in. The preceding words affect them as علمًا is affected by what precedes when you say أنت الرجل علمًا, or as درهمًا is affected by عشرون when you say عشرون درهمًا. In the same way these words are affected by what follows and what precedes them.

This time the non-identity principle which characterises the two parts of a *tanwīn-naṣb* is passed over in favour of the effect of sentence-parts which is also embodied in this construction. Clearly Sībawayhi does not wish to suggest that the *ẓurūf* are direct in form because of any verbal effect. The choice of the nominal sentence أنت الرجل علمًا proves this. It also emerges in the rest of the *Kitāb* that Sībawayhi is principally interested in the behaviour of the *ẓurūf* in nominal rather than verbal sentences.[18] [271] For this reason he treats them, and the type أنت الرجل علمًا, as examples of sentence-effect,[19] hence the occurrence of عشرون درهمًا in this context.

6. 1, 171/202. In the same problem the *locus probans* is used as part of a general enunciation of principle which is worth translating in full:

> All these *ẓurūf* take direct form by virtue of what is said to be in them and at the same time is different from them, and which then acquires the status of the word with *tanwīn* which affects what follows it, such as عشرون[(a)] and هو خيرٌ منك عملاً. And هو خلفك and زيدٌ خلفك also acquire that status. The operans which affects خلف is that it denotes a place for someone to be in and that it functions as a

18. Cf. Jahn, §120, n. 7[(a)].
19. Cf. *Kitāb* 1, 161/192.

> predicate for him,[b] as though you had said عبد الله أخوك, where the second part is made independent by the first and has an effect on it whereby the speech becomes self-sufficient even though one part is separate from the other.

The reasoning of this passage is easier than the reader of Jahn might suppose, though Jahn makes it more difficult by unaccountably translating منفصل in the last line as "nicht getrennt."[c] What Sībawayhi is saying is that the parts of a nominal sentence have an observable effect on each other, i.e. the *mubtada'* makes the *ḫabar* independent in form, and the resulting combination of two inseparable parts produces a self-sufficient speech. In the same way the type of sentence which has a *ẓarf* [272] as its predicate, though it exists to state a different kind of relationship between its parts (namely that the initial term is "in" the predicate, not, as in nominal sentences, that the initial term "is" the predicate), nevertheless forms a complete sentence of mutually affecting, separate parts. It only remains to account for the direct form of the *ẓarf* predicate, which is done by making a simple analogy between the effect of an initial term upon a predicate and the effect of a word with *tanwīn* upon what follows it. Unless we are to take "word with *tanwīn*" to include verbs (which is a possible extension of the *tanwīn-naṣb* theory that Sībawayhi did not undertake) it is wrong to claim, as Sīrāfī and others do, that the *ẓarf* is always directly affected by a verb, implicit or explicit. Sībawayhi makes it plain that the direct form of the *ẓarf* is due to entirely different causes.

7. 1, 176/207. This passage has already been translated (above, p.[263]). It expresses with great clarity the principle of non-identity which distinguishes the *tanwīn-naṣb* from the true *iḍāfa*. This contrast suggests that the true *iḍāfa* denotes an inclusive relationship between its parts which, in syntax if not in meaning, is certainly confirmed by the indivisibility of the *iḍāfa* and its status as one word, while the pseudo-*iḍāfa* and its paraphrase, the *tanwīn-naṣb*, denote an exclusive relationship, syntactically confirmed by the separability of the parts in the case of *tanwīn-naṣb*. This is to some extent supported by the fact that true *iḍāfa* is a structurally independent part of the sentence, whereas pseudo-*iḍāfa* is always connected to some other word in the sentence.

[273] The alternative construction proposed by Abū 'Amr,[20] viz. داري من خلف دارك فرسخان only confirms the essential non-identity of terms in a proper *tanwīn-naṣb* construction, for in these circumstances فرسخان cannot be a *badal* of من خلف. In effect, all that has happened is that the specifying role of فرسخين has been transferred to خلف, so that Abū 'Amr's sentence really means "My house is two parasangs in respect of its behindness of your house," and Sībawayhi can call it a "strong practice" (مذهب قويّ) wthout violating any of the principles he himself works on.

8. 1, 180f/212f. Sībawayhi wishes to prove that مثل in *iḍāfa* forms an undefined unit, which he does in two ways. First he says that it can occur after رُبَّ, as in the verse[a]

---

20. *Kitāb* 1, 176/208.

يا رُبَّ مِثْلِكِ في النساءِ غَرِيرَةٍ بَيْضاءَ قد مَتَّعْتُها بطَلاقِ

and for his second proof he calls upon عشرون درهمًا:

> cf. the Arabs' expression لي عشرون مثله and لي مائةٌ مثلُه, in which they treat مثله as having the status of درهمًا in عشرون درهمًا or مائة درهم. The word مثل and its sisters have, as it were, their *tanwīn* elided, as if you had said مثلٌ زيدًا or قيدٌ الأوابدَ, which are only hypothetical examples.[(b)] But they are like عشرون and مائة in that they are fixed in one pattern, which is the *iḍāfa*, although you really want it to have the meaning of *tanwīn*.

This seems to conflate two arguments: the combination مثله is regarded as occurring as the second part of a *tanwīn-naṣb*, in which case it is undefined, but then مثل itself is compared with the first part of a *tanwīn-naṣb* [274] as though the (pseudo-)*iḍāfa* of مثل was equivalent to the *tanwīn-naṣb* construction in that the first term is always undefined. The "meaning" of the *tanwīn* in this case is purely that of signifying indefinition, but the grammatical consequences are, of course, the same as if the *tanwīn* were simply an integral part of the word, as it is in عشرون.

9. 1, 222/260 According to intention, the sentence هذا الرجل منطلقٌ can also be said as هذا الرجل منطلقًا if منطلقًا is intended to indicate the state (*ḥāl*) of the man when the sentence is uttered. This is a preliminary to a discussion of such types as فيها عبدالله قائمًا and the like, and the origin of the direct form is probably its displacement from the function of predicate into the superfluous function of *ḥāl*.

> When you say فيها زيد it is as though you had said استقرّ فيها زيد even if no verb is mentioned, and [the rest of the speech] takes direct form by virtue of what is said to be in it,[(a)] just as درهمًا takes direct form after عشرون because it is not an adjective to it, nor correlated with the same thing.

Here, as in number 5 above, it is the behaviour of the direct forms in nominal sentences which interests Sībawayhi. There is no doubt that the introduction of the verbal idea through استقرّ was intended only to account for the meaning of the *ẓarf*-sentence and not its form. The latter is already easy to explain in terms of sentence-effect and the principle of non-identity, both of which are covered by عشرون درهمًا.

10. 1, 232/272. The elative expression هو أول فارس مقبلاً poses a problem. There are those who claim that أول فارس is defined because it is equivalent to أول الفارس, but this is dismissed as impossible by Sībawayhi, who states that it is equivalent to الأول من الفرسان. We are thus immediately reminded of the paraphrase of [275] عشرون من الدراهم which Sībawayhi has previously used to prove that عشرون درهمًا is undefined; and in this case too, عشرون درهمًا is adduced to prove that أول فارس is undefined.

The point of similarity between the elative *iḍāfa* and the phrase عشرون درهمًا is not formally explained by Sībawayhi, but it may be inferred from his argument in proof of عشرون درهمًا itself. There we learn that one feature of the elatives is that they are separated from the term "connected" with them, hence the undefined direct terms which follow them (as *tamyīz* in modern terms) e.g. هو أحسن منك وجهًا. We know from other remarks in the *Kitāb*, i.e. that الله أكبر means أكبر من كل شيء,[21] and that هذا رجلٌ أفضلُ is "not right,"[22] that for Sībawayhi every elative presupposes an implicit "منك" or some such term of comparison. There is, therefore, no possibility that such *iḍāfa*s as أول فارس and أفضل رجل etc. were felt to be true *iḍāfa*s by Sībawayhi. The elative, whether it forms a partitive or explanatory *iḍāfa*,[23] is always a pseudo-*iḍāfa* in that the component terms are separated by the comparative idea in "منك" and the like. The *muḍāf ilayhi* in either case remains something "connected" with the *muḍāf* by the *sabab* relationship, hence the *tanwīn-naṣb* which often replaces elative *iḍāfa*, e.g. خير رجل في الناس becomes خير الناس رجلاً. It is the *sabab* relationship which unites the elatives and عشرونَ درهمًا.

[276] 11. 1, 235/274f. The title and opening lines of the chapter are best left to speak for themselves:

> Chapter concerning that which takes direct form because it is not included in the preceding word nor identical with it.
>
> That is when you say هو ابن عمّي دِنْيًا and هو جاري بيتَ بيتَ. These are states in each of which something has occurred. They take direct form because the speech has had an effect on them as الرجل does[(a)] on علم when you say أنت الرجل علمًا, where علمًا is direct in form according to the explanation I have already given,[24] and it has been affected by what precedes it in the same way that عشرون affects درهمًا when you say عشرون درهمًا, because درهمًا is not part of عشرون nor identical with it.

12. 1,241/279. The problem of the direct forms which occur after the "five particles," viz. إنّ ، أنّ ، لكنّ ، ليت ، لعلّ provokes a lengthy explanation, mostly about عشرون درهمًا, which may reflect a certain diffidence on Sībawayhi's part as to whether this is really a satisfactory interpretation of the five particles. After summarising the arguments by which he established عشرون درهمًا he concludes with the, by now, familiar remarks on the non-identity of the parts in the *tanwīn-naṣb* construction, adding ضاربٌ زيدًا by way of extra illustration. The relationship between the direct word and its preceding *munawwan* word is given somewhat more attention in this passage—it is not an epithet (*na't*) or *muḍāf ilayhi* to what precedes it, and it is singular because "it is one thing by which the number is made clear."[(b)] (There may be an echo of this in a curious phrase of Ḫalaf al-Aḥmar, الواحد الخارج من الجماعة which [277] he uses to describe precisely the nouns in direct form which follow numbers like عشرون.)[25] Only the fact that these considerations are basically irrelevant to the problem of إنّ diminishes their interest, and the value of this attempted

---

21. *Kitāb* 1, 199/233.
22. Id. 1, 192/229.
23. Cf. Wehr, *Elativ* 578f.
24. Cf. *Kitāb* 1, 161/192 and above, p. [270].
25. Ḫalaf, *Muqaddima* 53, 58[(b)].

explanation probably lies in its adherence to the purely formal resemblances between عشرون درهمًا, إنّ زيدًا and ضاربٌ زيدًا which obviously inspired Sībawayhi to seek, without much conviction or success, for some deeper connection between them.

13. 1,250/291. Sībawayhi makes better use of عشرون درهمًا in explaining the interrogative function of كم:

> As for interrogative كم, when it is made to affect what follows it, it has the status of a word with full currency (يتصرّف)[a] in speech which has *tanwīn*, which has affected what follows it because it is not an adjective to it nor correlated with what it is correlated with: such a word is عشرون and the like, e.g. ثلاثون and أربعون. If someone says كم لك he will have asked about a number, because كم is only used to ask about a number here. The person who answers must say "20" or whatever number he likes. And if someone says كم لك درهمًا or كم درهمًا لك he has explained what he is asking about, and you would answer عشرون درهمًا. So كم affects درهمًا in the same way that عشرون does, with لك as a predicate constructed on كم. And know that كم affects everything which it is good Arabic for عشرون to affect, and if it is bad Arabic for عشرون to affect it then it is bad Arabic for كم to do so, for عشرون is a number with *tanwīn*.

It would be superfluous to add anything to this excellent specimen of Sībawayh's reasoning.

[278] 14. 1, 255/296. The other, predicative function of كم is also explained by using عشرون درهمًا, though the connection is not so complete as in the case of interrogative كم:

> You say كم عبد لك لا عبدٌ ولا عبدان and كم قد أتاني لا رجلٌ ولا رجلان, where the nouns are correlated with what كم is correlated with and not with what كم affects, as if you said لا عبدٌ لك ولا عبدان and لا رجلٌ أتاني ولا رجلان. This is because كم explains the number of what it bears upon by means of a singular undefined word just like عشرون درهمًا or like the plural undefined word in ثلاثة أبواب. This is allowed in the كم which occurs predicatively, but as for the one which occurs in the interrogative only what is allowed for عشرون is allowed for it.

Here the only point of similarity between the behaviour of كم and عشرون is that both are followed by undefined words, with the implication that those words are, in effect, singular because of their specifying relationship with the words they follow.[a] It is noteworthy that the predicative كم, along with رُبّ, the numerals 3–10, and the لام الاستغاثة, are the only *jārr-majrūr* combinations which are not called *iḍāfa* in the *Kitāb*.[b]

15. 1, 257/298. The explanation of the direct form which occurs in expressions of degree or quantity, e.g. ليس مثلُه عبدًا or ما في السماء موضعُ كفٍّ سحابًا and the like makes use of two aspects of the *tanwīn-naṣb* construction. The first is that these undefined singular forms are simply lightened versions of the partitive form with من and the defined plural, i.e. من العبيد "just as they have elided the plural after عشرون when they say عشرون درهمًا," and the second point of comparison is that [279] the direct words are neither adjectives to what precedes them nor included in them. The purpose of these direct words, as explained by

Ḫalīl, is to make clear what "sort" (he uses نوع ، ضرب and جنس in this discussion apparently indiscriminately!) is meant by the vague words which precede them. The idea that the *muḍāf ilayhi* is equivalent to (*badal*) a *tanwīn* emerges very clearly from the argument that مثله must be followed by a direct word

> because مثل is in the status of عشرون and the oblique word is in the status of *tanwīn* because it prevents *iḍāfa* just as *tanwīn* prevents it.[26]

16. 1, 261/303. This time عشرون درهمًا is used to emphasise a basic dissimilarity between the specifying term in direct form and the emphatic terms أحد ، كراب ، أرم ،كتع, and عريب which occur only after negatives, and so

> they do not serve to bring out one sort (نوع) from another, which might enable them to be affected by what precedes them in the same way that عشرون affects درهمًا when you say عشرون درهمًا. Instead they occur in negative sentences either as subjects or constructed upon something else, hence people say ما في الناس مثله أحدٌ.

Not only, then, do these terms not stand in the specifying relationship of درهمًا to عشرون, but they are also syntactically different from the kind of dependence embodied in that construction.

[280] 17. 1, 266/307. An interesting by-product of the specifying relationship in the pseudo-*iḍāfa* is that, unlike a true *iḍāfa,* it cannot adjectivally qualify demonstratives in vocative structures.[(a)] The reason for this is that demonstratives can only be qualified in this way by definite elements, and in يا ذا الحسنُ الوجه the phrase الحسنُ الوجه is not adjectival but appositional (thus retaining independent case here, unlike the obligatory dependent case in true annexation, e.g. يا عبدَ الله):

> and when you say الحسن you have generalised, and when you say الوجه you have particularised some part of it ... just as you make clear through درهمًا what عشرون consists of when you say عشرون درهمًا.

18. 1,306/350. This time the *tanwīn-naṣb* appears in a slightly different role from its usual one of indicating separation, for in this passage it is argued that it denotes the lack of completion in a word. The reason for this is that certain combinations of words, e.g. حسنٌ وجهه , خيرٌ منه, and ضاربٌ زيدًا are regarded as incomplete unless both constituents are present, due to the *sabab* which unites the two halves. In such cases the presence of *tanwīn* on the first word is a signal that another is to follow, and so fixed is this convention that

---

26. Following Jahn's correction, §143, n. 7.

> it is as though the *tanwīn* becames an addition (زيادة) to the word before its end, like the *wāw* in مضروب or the *alif* in مضارب, and you put *tanwīn* everywhere [in the negative] where you would also put in the vocative, wherever the end of the word lies in what follows it but is not of it.[t]

This is very probably one of Ḫalīl's own arguments, since it accords well with his known preference for phonological matters. The reference to the vocative shows how close the negative and vocative were felt to be, which [281] is why they are treated in consecutive chapters in the *Kitāb*. The *tanwīn* as a sign of incompleteness has already been set out in the section on vocatives as follows:

> The direct form is retained throughout, e.g. يا ضاربًا رجلاً when the speech is lengthy.[a] And Ḫalīl said that يا ضاربًا رجلاً was defined just as يا ضاربُ but the *tanwīn* remains because it is in the middle of the word and رجلاً marks the completion of the word, so that the *tanwīn* becomes a sort of particle (*ḥarf*!) before the end of the word. (1, 282/324).

Thus the negative expressions لا خيرًا منه لك etc. correspond, as Sībawayhi says, to لا عشرون درهمًا لك. Complications arise when prepositional phrases are introduced, since their grammatical ambiguity allows them to be treated either as qualifiers or as predicative expressions. When they occur as close qualifiers of the previous word they will follow the pattern of عشرون درهماً, e.g. , لا مغيرًا على الأعداء لك, لا داعيًا إلى الله لك in which the prepositional phrase "is connected with the first word just as منه with أفعل." But the parts can also be separated, as in لا مغيرَ على الأعداء لك and لا داعيَ إلى الله لك, where the first prepositional phrase is a predicate and the second, as in سقيًا لك, simply shows to whom the sentence is directed. Finally لا آمرَ في الدار يومَ الجمعة in يوم الجمعة can be neutralised to give لا آمرَ يومَ الجمعة فيها in which the predicate, فيها, is delayed and the neutralised term brought forward, thereby preventing *tanwīn* on لا آمرَ. According to whether the "connection" (اتّصال) is regarded as present or absent, certain differences of meaning can be obtained from the use or omission of the *tanwīn*: [282] لا آمرًا يومَ الجمعة would mean those who only gave orders on Fridays, while لا آمرَ يومَ الجمعة would mean all those who gave orders, subsequently restricted by mention of the time. Likewise لا ضاربًا يومَ الجمعة means those who only beat on Fridays, or whatever day it may be.

All this is designed to show the effect of *tanwīn* in cases where two words are in close connection with each other, the connection being, as the use of عشرون درهمًا proves, the *sabab* which unites the two terms of a *tanwīn-naṣb*, although it is called اتّصال in this passage. The difficulties arise when the qualifying phrase (which is by definition equivalent to the *tanwīn*, i.e. to the direct term in a *tanwīn-naṣb* construction) is such that it is not inherently connected with the word before it, and so may either be treated as the second part of a *tanwīn-naṣb* or as a predicate to a different sort of unit, the combination of لا and *manfī*. The problem here may be compared with a similar one treated above,[27] where it was found that Immediate Constituent Analysis was very helpful in clarifying the different kinds of binary unit which operate in these circumstances.

19. 1, 315/360. After إلا the noun may either be in direct form or retain the form it would have had before إلا was inserted. In the first type

> the noun after إلا is outside what the preceding word is in, and affected by the speech that precedes it just as عشرون affects what follows when you say عشرون درهمًا.

[283] In the absence of any other plausible reason, Sībawayhi assumes that sentence-effect comes into play here. He does not investigate the quality of difference which is shared by the *mustaṯnā* and the direct word in a *tanwīn-naṣb* construction, though this may have been in the back of his mind when he chose عشرون درهمًا to illustrate the cause of the direct form after إلا. But at least he does not seek for any verbal operans concealed in إلا.

20. 1,318/363. According to Yūnus and ʿĪsā, certain reliable Arabs say such things as ما مررت بأحد إلا زيدًا , in which زيدًا is clearly not a substitute (*badal*) for the oblique term which precedes it. This kind of exception is called "disjunctive" (*munqaṭiʿ*) by Sībawayhi, since it cuts off the excepted term from the effect of the previous operans,

> and the proof of that is that it comes to mean ولكنّ زيدًا or لا أعني زيدًا, but is affected by what precedes it in the same way that عشرون affects درهمًا when you say عشرون درهمًا.

21. 1, 319/363.[a] The same explanation is offered for the Ḥijāzī usage which is dealt with in the chapter immediately following, illustrated by ما فيها أحدٌ إلا حمارًا:

> They do not like to make the last word a substitute for the first, by which they would apparently become of the same kind (نوع), and so it is correlated with the meaning of لكنّ and affected by what precedes it as عشرون affects درهمًا.

It is possible that Sībawayhi did not use نوع in the meaning of "logical category," as implied by Rabin,[28] and, moreover, that by *istiṯnā' munqaṭiʿ* Sībawayhi was not, as Rabin suggests, referring to the semantic relationship [284] between "major" and "minor" terms, but simply meant the interruption of the verbal effect and its transfer to sentence-effect of the type found in عشرون درهمًا. In any case Sībawayhi does not use the terms *muttaṣil* and *mufarraġ* in the context of exception, and *munqaṭiʿ* occurs only in this one instance, where he is careful to say that it is "*munqaṭiʿ* from what affects the first word," i.e. in the

27. See p. [182]f.
28. Rabin, *Ancient West-Arabian* 181.

purely grammatical sense, contrasted with, for example ما لا يكون العمل فيه من الظروف إلا متّصلاً in another context (1, 90/110).

22. 1, 322/369.[(a)] In another explanation of the direct form after إلا which is attributed to Ḫalīl, Sībawayhi says that

> it is excluded from what the other is included in, and is affected by what precedes it as عشرون affects درهمًا when you say عشرون درهمًا ... the operans is whatever speech precedes [the excepted word] just as درهمًا is neither an adjective to عشرون nor correlated with what it is correlated with or what affects it.

This introduces the idea of difference into the grammatical behaviour of the exceptive particples (cf. no. 19 above), and thus completes the similarity between exception and the *tanwīn-naṣb* construction.

I have not included in this list occurrences such as عشرون رجلاً (1, 261/302, 271/313) or of درهمًا alone (1, 256/297), although they clearly represent the same principle of *tanwīn-naṣb* that is contained in عشرون درهمًا.[(a)] A structurally similar phrase, لدنْ غدوةً, occurs several times in the *Kitāb* (1, 19/24, 22/28, 38/49, 68/79, 87/107, 341/389, 409/461, and 2, 147/145), occasionally in conjunction with عشرون درهمًا. It is taken from a line of poetry which is not quoted in the [285] *Kitāb* but which occurs without attribution in the *Mufaṣṣal,*[29] and in Ibn Yaʿīš, where its provenance is said to be unknown,[30] and it is used to justify unique or otherwise inexplicable constructions, being itself a *hapax legomenon.*[(a)] It forms part of the original argument by which عشرون درهمًا was established and was clearly intended to cover those cases which could not adequately be explained by reference to عشرون درهمًا.

The overall impression produced by Sībawayhi's use of عشرون درهمًا in the *Kitāb* is that he specifically set up the *tanwīn-naṣb* construction as a counterpart of, and sometimes alternative to the true and pseudo-*iḍāfa*. The true *iḍāfa* is a unit of arbitrary but invariable form in which two words can be united in any number of relationships which cannot be more precisely described than by calling them "inclusive." This is a grammatical, rather than a semantic inclusion, in that the resulting unit constitutes an indivisible syntactical whole. In contrast the *tanwīn-naṣb*, which is in theory (but scarcely in practice) separable, denotes what can best be called an "exclusive" relationship in which the second of the two terms provides additional information about some aspect of the first term. The *muḍāf ilayhi* in true *iḍāfa* actually restricts the *muḍāf*, which is why the latter becomes grammatically defined, while the direct word in a *tanwīn-naṣb* effectively amplifies the meaning of the *munawwan* word, and so can never be defined. What links *muḍāf* to *muḍāf ilayhi* in true *iḍāfa* is that the former is either contained in or identical with the latter, in which the *iḍāfa* and *waṣf* share a common quality. But the word with *tanwīn* is only linked

29. Zamaḫšarī, *Mufaṣṣal* 68 (= §205).
30. Ibn Yaʿīš, *Šarḥ al-Mufaṣṣal* 4, 100 (on §205).

to the direct word by a *sabab*, and this "connection" is evidently [286] the same as that which binds the verb to its objects, cf.

> and if a poet is forced to invert (after an interrogatove or negative) when the verb has already been made upon something connected with it (من سببه), the strict form of inflection is nothing but the direct form. (1, 39/50)(a)

Sībawayhi appears to use *sabab* to mean a connection of meaning in the most general way, as, for example in:

> You say ما أبو زينب ذاهبًا ولا مقيمةٌ أمّها with مقيمة in independent form because if you were to say ما أبو زينب مقيمةً أمّها , it would not be allowed because she has no connection with him, (ليس من سببه), for ما only affects أبو زينب and not أمّها.
> (1, 24/31)

The sense here seems to demand that ذاهبًا ولا be restored in the second example.(b) The fact that Zaynab's mother is said to have no "connection" with Zaynab's father shows that by *sabab* Sībawayhi meant exclusively grammatical connections.

Another instance of *sabab* gives us a very clear idea of what is meant to Sībawayhi:

> When you say زيدٌ لقيت أخاه you can, if you wish, make "Zayd" direct in form because when something happens to something connected with another it is as though it happened to that other. (1, 32/43)

This obviously has nothing to with Fleischer's rendering of "Vermittlung,"[31] which was an attempt to explain the extension of concordance (e.g. مررت برجل ضارب أبوه رجلاً) which forms only a minor part of what Sībawayhi understood by *sabab*, and still less does it correspond to de Sacy's "cause." As is [287] often the case, it is safer to take Sībawayhi literally when there is doubt, and by doing so here we discover an admittedly vague but nonetheless grammatically identifiable link between words. It is, as I have shown, an intrinsic part of the *tanwīn-naṣb* construction, and corresponds to the identity or inclusion which is an intrinsic feature of the true *iḍāfa*.

The way عشرون درهمًا is proved is a model example of Sībawayhi's method, both in its formalism and in its concern to find a deeper distinction between *iḍāfa* and *tanwīn-naṣb*. It is, too, typical of him to use عشرون درهما twice before he has proved its validity, which may confirm that the *Kitāb* was written for people who were already familiar with Sībawayhi's ideas.

---

31. Fleischer, *Kl. Schr.* 1, 782(c).

Although Ḫalīl is specifically credited with arguments involving عشرون درهمًا on more than one occasion,[32] it is surely significant that, in the crucial chapters where this *locus probans* is established, he is only quoted twice, and then on very minor points.[33] This seems to suggest that, even if the original idea was Ḫalīl's, Sībawayhi must take the credit for giving it such a wide application in the *Kitāb*. There is no reason to suppose from Ḫalīl's remarks that he regarded the *tanwīn-naṣb* with the same awareness of its potential as did Sībawayhi: the adoption of this *locus probans* and the construction of a theory by which direct forms could be explained without presupposing a verbal operans, must surely be part of Sībawayhi's own contribution to Arabic grammar. Likewise the analysis of the *tanwīn*, of whose separative function Ḫalīl was certainly aware,[34] bears the marks of Sībawayhi's particular interest in grammatical functions. The phrase عشرون درهمًا is, [288] in fact, worth far more than its face value as an illustration of several fundamental and interdependent aspects of Arabic grammar. It cannot be claimed that Sībawayhi took all possible pains to bring عشرون درهمًا to our notice, as it is a feature of the *Kitāb* to take for granted what others might not regard as obvious,[a] but it can with justice be claimed that to overlook the score of occasions on which عشرون درهمًا is used is to miss the essence of the *Kitāb*. Although it is only one of several strands of theory which run through the work, I hope that by repairing the neglect of centuries in this way I shall have restored to the 20 dirhams something of their original, freshly minted lustre, and demonstrated that the *Kitāb* is both more coherent and more systematic than its critics are accustomed to allow.

Summary

[328] The *iḍāfa* is a construction which typifies the economical but versatile nature of Arabic syntax. But another common construction in Arabic, the direct form after an undefined noun or non-verbal word, has not had so much attention paid to it. This construction, which I call the *tanwīn-naṣb*, is symbolised in the *Kitāb* by the phrase عشرون درهمًا. Over several chapters Sībawayhi establishes this phrase as the *locus probans* for the *tanwīn-naṣb* construction, and his arguments are set out in brief.

We learn from these arguments that Arabic distinguishes between a true, inclusive and inseparable *iḍāfa*, and a pseudo-*iḍāfa* which is exclusive in meaning and separable. This pseudo-*iḍāfa* is equivalent to a *tanwīn-naṣb* construction. In the latter the *tanwīn* is seen to exercise a hitherto unidentified function of separation.

There follows an account of the 22 occasions on which عشرون درهمًا is invoked in grammatical argument in the *Kitāb*. Some further, related examples are listed, but not discussed.

---

32. E.g. nos. 15 and 22 above.
33. *Kitāb* 1, 71.84 and 81/99.
34. See above, p. [266].

The characteristic of the pseudo-*iḍāfa* and *tanwīn-naṣb* is that their components are joined in meaning by a link which Sībawayhi calls a *sabab*.

The use of عشرون درهمًا so frequently and so consistently is incontrovertible proof of Sībawayhi's competence and of his highly systematic approach, and criticisms that the *Kitāb* is an inadequate work no longer stand.

Addenda to Chapter Six

The contents of this chapter formed the basis of Carter 1972b and 1985a. The idea was taken up by Owens 1990, 107–110, and rebaptised as SNIP "separation and non-identity principle" (read *locus probans* for *modus probens* in p. 107). Kasher 2009 re-examines the notion with a view to showing that in one case there is no separative element involved, see [263] (a).

[253] (a) To be fair to Reckendorf, we should note that de Sacy, loc. cit., also attempts to classify all the relationships in this way.

[253] (b) By way of comparison, the Arab grammarians reduced all the *iḍāfa* types to three, according to whether they could be paraphrased by *li-* "for," i.e. broadly possessive, *min* "from," i.e. broadly partitive, or *fī* "in," broadly locative, this last a somewhat marginal category.

[254] (a) More accurately here and everywhere else this should be called the "active participle" or, closer to the original Arabic, the "agent noun."

[255] (a) *Al-ṣifa l-mušabbaha bi-smi l-fā'il*, indicating that the adjective has been [syntactically] assimilated to the agent noun. As a by-product, this generalises to the universal statement that all adjectives, of whatever form, are participles in the Arabic theory, and can in principle always be paraphrased by verbs, cf. [71] (a).

There is no sign in the literature of a passive equivalent of this item, **al-ṣifa l-mušabbaha bi-smi l-maf'ūl*, nor would it be expected, since the adjectives concerned are always agents of stative verbs. The corresponding adjectival structure with passive participles is covered, however, by a higher category, the *na't sababī* which embraces all qualifiers, e.g. the *ṣifa mušabbaha* in *al-rajulu l-ḥasanu abūhu*, the *ism al-fā'il* in *al-rajulu l-qā'imu abūhu* and the *ism al-maf'ūl* in *al-rajulu l-muqaddamu ḏikruhu*.

[256] (a) See [113] (a)

[256] (b) Here and in the ensuing pages "definiteness" would certainly be less ambiguous than "definition," see also [250] (a).

[257] (a) That is, the direct object, *maf'ūl bihi*.

[257] (b) By "effect" is meant "grammatical effect" *'amal*.

[257] (c) For *mu'āqiban* "alternative" a more precise rendering would be "in complementary distribution," as that is what Sībawayhi intends here, namely that *tanwīn* and annexation are mutually exclusive.

[258] (a) Characteristically Sībawayhi shifts his focus during his explanation by talking about the action of striking rather than the striker, so in *hāḏā ḍāribu l-rajuli* the strik-

ing (*ḍarb*) belongs to *hāḏā* (my original translation did not adequately render this, and has been amended to "belongs to the person striking") while in *hāḏā ḥasanu l-wajhi* the beauty (*ḥusn*) belongs to *wajh*.

[259] (a) Another facile criticism of Sībawayhi's intellectual achievement: see p. [174] (a).

[260] (a) See [192] (a) on the hierarchical implication of *quwwa*.

[260] (b) *Wajh* was translated as "style" in the original thesis, but given the critical remarks about confusing structural correctness with style (see [235], [238]) it has been emended here to "mode."

[261] (a) That is, a *kalām* or speech act, not a "sentence" as we understand it. cf. [199]f.

[262] (a) The number six has been increased to ten by later grammarians, but the extra four are not unique to nouns; nor are they are part of Sībawayhi's categories so they will not be listed here.

The *ḍāribun zaydan* construction forms the topic of *Kitāb* §37, including also the annexation variant *ḍāribu zaydin* with the same meaning, both patterns being found in the Qur'ān and poetry. The canonical alternation is symbolised in the contrast between *qātilun ġulāmaka* with *tanwīn* and future meaning "going to kill your slave-boy" and the annexation *qātilu ġulāmika* with past meaning "the one who has killed your slave-boy" discussed by the lawyers (see above [137]). The structure is evoked again in *Kitāb* 2, 138/136, where we learn that diminutives are not made from nouns which "have the status of a verb" *bi-manzilat al-fi'l*, i.e. participles: so *ḍuwayribun zaydan* and *ḍuwayribu zaydin* are both "bad" *qabīḥ* if the *tanwīn* (future) meaning is intended, whereas *ḍuwayribu zaydin*, with a past (adjectival) meaning *mā maḍā*, is good (*jayyid*). From this we deduce that *ḍāribu zaydin* in itself may denote either, so it is the intended meaning which determines the correctness of the diminutive (probably the "verbal" sense is disallowed because verbs cannot be made diminutive (Jahn, n. 18 to §386, from Sīrāfī)).

[262] (b) *Tamakkun* "being firmly established," is also labelled *ṣarf* "being fully current" (see [27] (a) on this concept). While Western grammars generally treat *tanwīn* as primarily an indefiniteness marker, the mediaeval position was that its primary function is to mark *tamakkun/ṣarf*.

[262] (c) There is a risk here of appearing contradictory in this example, which might be taken to illustrate a non-separative *tanwīn* on *ḍāriban*. But it is restricted to the vocative, which in this case requires a direct object to make sense, so *rajulan* acts as the completing element of a compound phrase, like *'išrūna dirhaman*. The first element here (*ḍāriban*, *'išrūna*) bears the inflection required by the function of the whole phrase.

A feature of the *'išrūna dirhaman* structure which this thesis did not highlight is particulary important in the context of *yā ḍāriban rajulan*, namely that if a *tanwīn* is heard on *yā ḍāriban*, that is itself a signal that the phrase is not yet complete, for otherwise it would be *yā ḍāribā*. This aspect would always have been at the back of Ḫalīl's mind in treating these utterances as compound units: since the *tanwīn* is compulsory here (because the word is not in a pausal position) the rules for *ʿišrūna dirhaman* apply as stated in no. 18 in [280] for example, where *tanwīn* indicates that the word is not yet complete.

[263] (a) Kasher 2009 argues that in the particular case of the type *huwa ḫalfaka* "he is behind you" there is no separative element intervening between the subject *huwa* and the predicate *ḫalfaka*, because this is not an instance of separation and non-identity but of non-identity alone. This interpretation is entirely plausible and certainly not one which would inevitably inspire any form of refutation. The *distinctio* which Kasher makes between *ʿišrūna* representing a compound utterance (i.e. a complete sentence such as *dārī ḫalfa dārika farsaḫan* "my house is behind yours by a parasang," a typical *ʿišrūna dirhaman* case) and *ʿišrūna* representing only a complete word (also compound, but only part of a sentence, such as *huwa* in *huwa ḫalfaka* "he [is] behind you"), does not seem to have been made explictly by Sībawayhi. He does indeed imply something like this in the key passage in *Kitāb* 1, 171/202 (quoted in Kasher p. 48f) where we are given a sequence of structures on the *ʿišrūna dirhaman* pattern: (1) *huwa ḫayrun minka ʿamalan*, (2) *huwa ḫalfaka* and (3) *zaydun ḫalfaka*, in all three of which the the non-identity principle is clearly stated to apply. What Sībawayhi does not say, however, is that in nos (2) and (3) the *tanwīn*/separation principle also applies: to be sure *huwa* in (2) lacks a *tanwīn* but it is still a "complete noun" like *ʿišrūna*, being a pronominalisation of (3) *zaydun*, to which it is declared identical in terms of its operation on the predicate. We might say, then, that *huwa* is included in *zaydun*, and we should find, for example, that it has similar restrictions, e.g. it cannot be annexed to the next word, which Sībawayhi, in his usual manner, simply does not bother to tell us.

[263] (b) The anachronism is one of several which interfere with our understanding of Sībawayhi (Temjîz again in [264], [270]). Troupeau made a decision to treat the three occasions on which Sībawayhi uses *tamyīz* or *mayyaza* as "methodological" terms, i.e. technical term of syntax, though none is used for what we now call *tamyīz*—instead they refer merely to distinguishing between two different constructions or forms, and we might ask whether they are any more technical than Sībawayhi's use of the same verb literally in *mayyazta matāʿaka baʿḍahu min baʿḍin* "you distinguished some of your merchandise from the other" (*Kitāb* 1, 65/76), which is not listed by Troupeau for obvious reasons.

[264] (a) Jahn's rendering of *baʿd al-tamām*: "that all the necessary components for the construction of the sentence are conceived as present beforehand." By "beforehand" Jahn presumably means that during the utterance the speaker will know when the point of self-sufficiency has been reached, after which the dependent forms must be used for structurally extraneous additions, cf. above on *waqf*, [205] (a).

[264] (b) The error is mine: *ḫabar* is a key concept in Sībawayhi's analysis of the *ḥāl* throughout the chapters on this topic (§§117–126 and elsewhere, for example in [299] below). As for *tamyīz*, apart from the fact that Sībawayhi does not use this term (see above [263]), it may be that Jahn has slightly misstated the situation: in §§127–9 the dependent case arises because the specifying element cannot function as an attributive adjective

(*ṣifa, waṣf*), i.e. agree in case and definiteness: under these conditions the indefinite dependent form is the default, on the pattern of *'išrūna dirhaman*. In both *ḥāl* and "*tamyīz*." Nevertheless, these dependent elements are a kind of *ḫabar*, in that they do predicate something of their antecedent. The paraphase of the *tamyīz* in the verbal sentence *ṭāba zaydun nafsan* as *ṭāba nafsu zaydin* strongly reinforces Sībawayhi's recognition of the predicative quality of these dependent forms.

Clearly *ḫabar* here cannot be directly equated with the "predicate" of a "subject" (*mubtada'*): a parallel with the *ḫabar kāna* suggests itself, but the issue does not seem to have attracted attention.

[265] (a) It must be stressed that the term *faḍla* is not used in the *Kitāb*, even though the concept of syntactical redundancy is recognised in the structure of *'išrūna dirhaman*, in that *dirhaman* occurs only after a syntactically complete segment, see [262]–[265].

[266] (a) Again (see [260]) "style" is an inappropriate rendering of *wajh*, where "[proper] way" or "mode" is all that is needed.

[267] (a) The claim made here that direct objects of verbs are linked to the verb by a *sabab* certainly needs further investigation, as it may well be erroneous or, at best, only true under conditions which have yet to be identified. See further [286] (a).

[268] (a) One of the features of the *Kitāb* which places a great burden on the reader is that it does not deal exhaustively with any topic in one place. Instead the topic will be picked up again from a different perspective, thus the *ḥāl* is dealt with in several places according to which of its eight linguistic features Sībawayhi is concerned with, see Carter 2002. In the same way the phrase *'išrūna dirhaman* is introduced long before Sībawayhi actually establishes its properties as a *locus probans* (Carter 1972b).

This non-linearity has also been pointed out by Mosel 1975, 1, 3, which tends to undermine a claim of a different kind made by Bezirgan 1979, 80, that Sībawayhi's thinking could "easily be translated into simple syllogisms." As it happens the legal type of analogical reasoning used by Sībawayhi can be restated in syllogistic form, but that is not what Bezirgan meant.

The verdict of Mosel 1980, 28 may represent the best approach: speaking of the perceived inadequacies of the *Kitāb*, she states that "in spite of these terminological deficiencies, Sībawayhi never fails to make himself understood, because he always illustrates his statements with examples, most of which are artificially constructed sentences."

[268] (b) The translation reverses the order of *ḥāl* and the verb for clarity. It is altogether probable that *ḥāl* was not at this time a true technical term but an *ad hoc* descriptor for the meaning of the *ḥāl* structure. Mubarrad mentions that it is a term of the *naḥwiyyūn* (*Muqtaḍab* 4, 166, see Carter 2002, 43), implying that it was not universally current in that sense before.

[268] (c) Another unwarranted criticism of Sībawayhi, see [174] (a).

[269] (a) [256] *et seq.*

[270] (a) Jahn's note remarks that Sībawayhi treats *ẓarf* sentences as nominal sentences, as if there were something slightly objectionable about this. As we have seen,

Jahn also found it difficult to believe that the *tamyīz* could occur in verbless sentences such as *huwa nārun ḥumratan*, see [264]. In both cases Jahn is a victim of later theory which wrongly interpreted Sībawayhi's rather casual paraphrase of both the *ḥāl* and the *ẓurūf* as *mustaqarr* "a place to be in" or *istaqarra* "be in a place" (e.g. *Kitāb* 1, 222f/261, in [274]) as implying that there must be a verbal operator for every *ẓarf*. But this is exactly what the *ʻišrūna dirhaman* construction is meant to cover: the dependent form arises from the operation of the preceding complete utterance, as in case no. 6 in [271] below. Moreover, in the example no. 9 in [274] it is explicitly stated that no verbal operator is needed.

Locative predicates have their own problems, all the more so in a language with no copula verb. This is the theme of Kouloughli 2002, and although it extends the discussion to a general theoretical level, it relies greatly on Sībawayhi's analysis, arguing that Sībawayhi recognised the special nature of locatives and their tendency to move into topic position when the logical subject is indefinite. Marogy 2004 takes issue with this interpretation, and (in Marogy 2010) develops the notion further, arguing that the inversion does not change the predicate status of the locative element. See also Kasher 2009, in [263] (a).

Levin 2007 approaches the *ẓarf* from a different perspective, that a *ẓarf* may function as an operator, i.e. in *fīhā ʻabdullāhi qā'iman* the dependent form of *qā'iman* arises from the operation of *fīhā*. Peled 2007 takes a much longer view, but his sections on the type *fī l-dāri zaydun* (158–164) and the "*istaqarra/mustaqirrun* hypothesis" give a thorough account of Sībawayhi's views. We can add here Hnid 2012, a semantic examination of *fī* designed to show how Sībawayhi was able to identify the semantic core of the word, expressed as *wiʻā'* "container" on three different levels, actual, analogical and metaphorical.

[271] (a) Here *ʻišrūna dirhaman* is not cited in full, because the issue is only the feature that the *tanwīn* of *ʻišrūna* is permanent and so no annexation can occur, hence the dependent form is the default in the following word. But in any case *ʻišrūna dirhaman* is quoted in full in the preamble to the chapter, in the previous page.

[271] (b) Here is a splendid example of the nature of Sībawayhi's terminology, which glides seamlessly between the technical and the non-technical, cf. [154] (a): the word *mawḍiʻ* occurs twice in the same line, first literally as the "place" denoted by a *ẓarf*, then as the "function" of the *ẓarf* in the utterance.

[271] (c) The German says "<u>not</u> separated" (my emphasis); Jahn §98 n. 11 may have misinterpreted Sīrāfī's account that the operation of the utterance on the dependent qualifier is possible because they are both connected by the same "copula" (*ribāṭ*), i.e. a pronoun linking the one to the other. But it seems more likely that by *wa-huwa munfaṣil* here Sībawayhi means "even though they are separate," i.e. are not in the same syntagm, which is the whole point of the *ʻišrūna dirhaman* structure.

[273] (a) "How many like you among women, seductive and fair [of face], have I pleasured by divorcing them." The verse is quoted by grammarians (see Fischer/Braünlich 1945, 165, Yaʻqūb 1992, 604) as evidence that *miṯliki*, lit."the like of you," although an-

nexed, must be grammatically indefinite because only indefinite (and singular) nouns may follow *rubba*. In one secondary source *bayḍāʾ* "fair" is rendered as "simple."

[273] (b) "hypothetical examples" renders *tamṯīl*, the term used by Sībawayhi to indicate made up data, see above [167].

[274] (a) The *ḥāl* and the *ẓarf* are both discussed together in this passage, where also the *ḥāl* is termed *mafʿūl fīhi* because, like the *ẓarf*, it indicates "what something is done in," either a circumstance (*ḥāl*) or a place/time (*ẓarf*): in both cases the dependent element is said to be made dependent by the person who is in that state or place/time, *intaṣaba bi-llaḏī huwa fīhi*.

[276] (a) To be strictly consistent Sībawayhi ought to say "just as *anta l-rajulu* does," since it is the whole utterance which operates on the following dependent elements, not simply *al-rajulu* as here. The text seems to be correct, so perhaps Sībawayhi is simply referring to the last element in the chain which affects the following one in the linear spirit of *naḥw*.

[276] (b) This translation is not very clear in itself, and Jahn's German is easier to understand. What it means is that some numbers are followed by singular nouns to express what is being counted.

[277] (a) See [31] (a) on this notion.

[277] (b) There is no guarantee that this is an ancient formulation, as the authenticity of the *Muqaddima* is under a cloud, see [2]–[4].

[278] (a) The reasoning here is difficult: it seems that Sībawayhi is drawing analogies between the two structures of *kam* and the two of the numerals, either oblique or dependent. The plural of the counted nouns after numbers 3–10 is evidently regarded as irrelevant: what is important is that those nouns have the same oblique form as they would have after predicative *kam*.

[278] (b) This assertion has not been checked, but it must have seemed true at the time. In this connection we can add that *iḍāfa* itself is used in two other senses by Sībawayhi, one to refer to the *nisba* formation, see [85], the other to denote the attachment of a verb to its indirect object by means of a preposition, see *Kitāb* 1, 32/42, 393/443, though this is really an extension of the nominal *iḍāfa*, since it is the annexation of the preposition which allows the resulting phrase to be the object of the verb.

[280] (a) The original wording of this paragraph has been adjusted, as it was thoroughly misleading. The discussion centres on two grammatical issues, (i) the second element in a demonstrative construction, e.g. *hāḏā l-rajulu* "this man" is an adjectival qualifier (*waṣf, naʿt*) of the demonstrative noun, "this one, the man," and so agrees with the head word in case and definiteness (contrast *hāḏā rajulun* "this [is] a man"). Thus the poetic example *yā ḏā l-ḍāmiru l-ʿansi* lit. "O this one, the emaciated of the camel" (i.e. "O this one whose camel is emaciated") follows the pattern of *yā hāḏā l-rajulu* "O this man." (ii) The demonstrative *ḏā* is a homonym: in addition to its invariable demonstrative function as "this, that," *ḏā* is also the dependent form of the pronoun *ḏū* "possessor of," as in the

phrase *yā hāḏā ḏā l-jummati* "O this one, the possessor of much hair" where *ḏā l-jummati* follows the rule for annexed vocatives, and takes dependent form.

The problem with *al-ḥasanu l-wajhi* is that it is formally but not intrinsically definite, and so it cannot occur as an adjectival qualifier in full agreement with a demonstrative: in *yā hāḏā l-ḥasan-u l-wajhi* "O this one, [the] handsome of face" it agrees with the indep. case of *hāḏā* but not in its true definiteness, and so must be parsed as a coordinated (*ʿaṭf*) or substituted element (*badal*) where definiteness is neutralised (e.g. *marartu bi-rajulin muḥammadin*). Hence the comparison with *ʿišrūna dirhaman*, where the second element is indefinite. It does not make things easier that Sībawayhi's second example also appears in the form *yā ḏā ḏā l-jummati* with both kinds of *ḏā*, perhaps a scholarly joke. To add to the mix, *ḥasan al-wajh* can appear in the vocative as *yā ḥasana l-wajhi*, obeying the rules for annexed vocatives, or as *ayyuhā l-ḥasanu l-wajhi* in independent form obeying the rules for qualifying the demonstratives, as in *yā ḏā l-ḍāmiru l-ʿansi.*

For the poetic line containing the example *yā ḏā l-ḍāmiru l-ʿansi* (rhyme *wa-l-ḥilsi*), see Fischer/Bräunlich 1945, 127, Yaʿqūb 1992, 472. The other example, *yā hāḏā ḏā l-jummati,* is probably not a poetic fragment.

[280] (b) The translation has been improved here.

[281] (a) See [202] (a) on this notion.

[283] (a) A new section, no. 21 has been created here

[284] (a) Formerly no. 21, see previous note.

[284] (b) We can add here the phrase *lahu ʿasalun milʾu/milʾa jarratin*, where the dependent option for *milʾa* is accounted for on the basis that it follows a completed utterance, see [263]f, and cf. no. 16 in [279].

In *Kitāb* §127 (1,129f/275f) the principle of non-identity is expounded in the context of specifying terms (the "*tamyīz*" of later grammar) without invoking *ʿišrūna dirhaman*, though oddly enough *dirhamun waznan* is cited as an example.

In 1, 254/295 the general principle of separability is invoked in the context of *kam* and contrasted with the inseparability of the true *iḍāfa* without directly citing *ʿišrūna dirhaman*, though this of course has been used to explain the behaviour of *kam* in the surrounding discussion see nos. 13, 14 in [277], [278].

[285] (a) However, there is no reason to assume, as here, that the phrase was taken from the anonymous verse quoted in the *Mufaṣṣal*, which is the only source given in Fischer/Braünlich 1945, 129, Yaʿqūb 1992, 480, rhyme *qāliṣi*, apart from Ibn Yaʿīš's commentary on the *Mufaṣṣal*: a couple of other verses appear in the *Lisān al-ʿarab* under *ladun*. The phrase *min ladun* occurs several times in the Qurʾān, but not in the same format as the unique *min ladun ġudwatan.*

Sībawayhi cites *ladun ġudwatan* eight times as an anomalous structure (including in no. 2 in [268], from 1, 38/49, in the context of *ʿišrūna dirhaman*), and in 1,19/24 he lists it along with other expressions labelled as being "in the status of a proverb" *bi-manzilat al-maṯal*, i.e non-productive, cf. Carter 2015, 37, 59.

[286] (a) To claim here and in [267] that all verbs are linked to their direct objects by a *sabab* now seems an unwarranted over-interpretation. There is indeed a *sabab* in the prose example *lam zaydan aḍribhu*, which follows Sībawayhi's statement here, but it is between *zaydan* and *-hu*, which is why *zaydan* can be given the form of a direct object because the verb is operating on "something connected with it," *min sababihi*.

In Carter 1985a, 53 it is argued that *sabab*, along with *iltibās* (an indirect mode of connection) are cohesive devices, so that *sabab* may be rendered "semantic link," this being an extension of the original sense of "rope, cord" to denote any tie or relationship. There is another extension, in a different direction, to the meaning of "cause, reason," but Sībawayhi's use of the phrase *min sababihi* rules that interpretation out; moreover its collocation with *iltibās* also confirms that the causal sense is not intended.

[286] (b) This statement is incorrect: all Sībawayhi is saying that it is not permissible to say "the father of Zaynab [Topic] her mother is not staying [Comment]," because there is no syntactical connection (*sabab*) between "Zaynab's father" in the topic and "her mother," i.e. Zaynab's, in the comment.

[286] (c) Fleischer's Vermittlung can be rendered "agency" or "intermediary," which is not so far from the truth, but still not what Sībawayhi meant, on which see n. (a) above. Fleischer devotes several pages to the subject, but relies on Zamaḫšarī and Ibn Yaʿīš, so the terms of the discussion are foreign to the *Kitāb*, namely *musabbab/musabbab bihi* (see [293]). Ironically Fleischer comes closer with his literal rendering of *min sababihi* as etwas, das zu dem mit ihm Verbundenen gehört "something which belongs to what is connected with it." The reference to de Sacy is *Gram. arabe* 527, §984, where he translates *sabab* literally as "cause."

[288] (a) See [268] (a).

Chapter Seven
In Conclusion

Some impression should now be emerging of the difference between what the *Kitāb* is and what it has been said to be. I hope there are now grounds to claim that it is certainly not the normative, overdescriptive, superficial, excessively rationalistic, unsystematic, rigid, vague, and ultra-purist work that the various critics—contradicting each other as well as the *Kitāb* – have called it. None of these judgements makes it any easier to solve the greatest problem of the *Kitāb*, why it was written at all.[(a)]

It is clearly not an elementary text-book, nor is it a partisan manifesto of any particular school of grammatical thought. Purism alone would not justify the lengthy explanations by which grammatical prescriptions are supported, nor is the compass of the work wide enough, or precise enough, for it to be an acceptable treatise on the Arabic dialects.[1] It does not deal with many of the trickiest grammatical problems of the Qur'ān,[2] and the thousand lines of verse it quotes also involve only a fraction of the difficulties of Arabic poetic usage. It stands in no tradition of grammatical writing and, worst of all, it never tells us who is supposed to speak in the language it describes, and when.

Eppur si muove. The *Kitāb* to this day is the acknowledged masterpiece of Arabic grammatical achievement, although respect for it does not go so far as to make it well-read. Perhaps if we compare it with another grammatical work of even larger dimensions we may gain some useful insights into the nature of the *Kitāb* and reason for its unpopularity.[(b)] The commentary on Zamaḫšarī [290] by Ibn Ya'īš is at least twice the length of the *Kitāb*, yet it is much more widely consulted than Sībawayhi. It follows that it cannot be the length or the thoroughness of the *Kitāb* which is responsible for its being so neglected. Nor can this be due to any unsoundness or error of grammatical judgement on the part of the author of the *Kitāb*, for Sībawayhi has become, like Saint Augustine, someone with whom it is unwise to disagree.[(a)] Nor is it likely that, because Ibn Ya'īš's terminol-

1. Cf. Rabin, *Ancient West-Arabian* 7.
2. E.g., Sūra 12, 18, 83: صبرٌ جميل .

ogy is more "up-to-date" and sympathetic to modern readers both Arab and European, his work is more popular than the *Kitāb*. What distinguishes the two works is that in the *Kitāb* Sībawayhi is making out a case, while in his *Commentary* Ibn Ya'īš has nothing to say except to retail orthodox grammatical opinions which for centuries have been devoid of originality. The polemical tone of the *Kitāb* may not be its most striking feature, but it is unique in Arabic grammar in the conscious novelty of its approach. Only the *Ḫaṣā'iṣ* of Ibn Jinnī shares this experimental quality with the *Kitāb*, but the independence of Ibn Jinnī's spirit is almost completely overcome by the dead weight of the tradition and material to which he applied himself.[(b)] Sībawayhi had no such tradition to shackle his imagination: instead he had the opposition of his contemporaries and their unwillingness to accept his ideas, against which the *Kitāb* is evidence of a continuous struggle.

The *Kitāb* is, therefore, an apologetic work, a literary defence of ideas not yet conceded by the people for whom the work has written. As far as I know the possibility that the *Kitāb* is an attempt to vindicate the grammatical views of one man against the criticism of his contemporaries has never been put forward as a reason for the composition of the *Kitāb*. In the light of what the *Kitāb* is so obviously not, this may well be the only satisfactory explanation which remains.

[291] If my supposition is correct, the *Kitāb* does not not represent a reaction against the decay of Arabic which resulted from the assimilation of non-Arabs to the Empire, a view which is often advanced to account for the beginnings of Arabic grammar.[3] The *Kitāb*, it is true, refers with respectful nostalgia to the "good old Arabic" of the Ḥijāzīs,[(a)] and relies heavily on the usage of reliable Bedouin informants, but primarily as a source of data, not as a source of authority for what really interested Sībawayhi, namely the way Arabic works. The dominant characteristic of the *Kitāb* is its tenacious search for reasons for linguistic behaviour, and the element of purism and preservation for its own sake is conspicuously lacking. Every quotation, every recorded anomaly, every dialectical difference is used to support and illustrate what is surely the principal component of the *Kitāb*, the numerous pattern-sentences with Zayd, 'Amr and 'Abdullāh which symbolise all the "ways" in which Arabic can be spoken. The dependence on ancient sources, I have already mentioned,[(b)] is due to the fact that no others were available, and it is, perhaps, healthy to remember that pre-Islamic poetry was probably not felt to be as remote from the second century of the Hijra as it seems to us today. Sībawayhi is no more antiquarian for quoting the ancient poets than was Samuel Johnson for using Shakespeare to illustrate the meanings of words in his dictionary.[(c)]

Apart from the numerous statements of principle scattered throughout the *Kitāb*, the only direct evidence we have of Sībawayhi's purpose is the arrangement of the first chapters of the book. The *Kitāb* lacks a preface and all introductory formulae, but instead it is opened by seven chapters which [292] deal with basic problems in the most general

3. E.g., Ibn Ḫaldūn, *Muqaddima* 544, Fück, *'Arabīya* 6[(d)].

way, and, most significantly of all, where not one mention is made of Ḫalīl or of any other grammarian. Reuschel has noted all this, but failed to make any deductions from it.[4] It has long been observed that these opening chapters probably constitute what is known as the *Risāla* of Sībawayhi, but which has never been traced as an independent work.[5] Further confirmation of the existence of a *Risāla* is found in Zajjājī's *Īḍāḥ*, where he refers to his exegesis (*tafsīr*) of the *Risālat Kitāb Sībawayhi* to which he has devoted a separate work.[6] Now the *Īḍāḥ* of Zajjājī is itself a commentary on the topics raised by the first six chapters of the *Kitāb* (the seventh deals with poetic licence) and it seems more than probable that the *Īḍāḥ* is, therefore, one of two commentaries by Zajjājī on the *Risāla* of Sībawayhi, this latter being without doubt the seven introductory chapters of the *Kitāb*.[(a)] These conclusions are the same as those reached before me by Mubārak,[7] but I feel that by positively identifying the *Īḍāḥ* as a commentary on the *Risāla* the problem is thus finally solved, and the prefatory nature of these seven chapters is definitively assured. It is, therefore, of particular importance for the rest of the *Kitāb* that the *Risāla* should make no reference to other grammarians. The amount of information it contains precludes, it seems to me, the possibility that it is a mere summary of contemporary grammatical knowledge, a trite formality to be got over before starting on the meat of the book. If this were so it is hardly likely that the very first chapter of all would have caused so much confusion in the minds of the later grammarians who attempted to understand it! On the contrary, I take it that [293] the *Risāla* is Sībawayhi's decaration of independence, the definitive statement of his position, after which all the knowledge of his masters and predecessors will be pressed into service according to the needs of the system expounded in the *Kitāb* as a whole. The *Risāla* expresses the competence, right and determination of Sībawayhi to disagree, as he often does, with Ḫalīl, Yūnus and others, and though the general principles it sets out are not as interesting sometimes as the particular arguments which flow from them, I do not feel that a mere footnote adequately expresses the relation of the *Risāla* to the "theoretical-linguistic basic principles of the Arabian grammarians," as Reuschel seems to think. The *Risāla* sets out many "basic principles," such as the priority of nouns over verbs, of undefined over defined, of singular over plural, of masculine over feminine, and of "nominal" sentences over others, which Reuschel simply does not mention, although they seem to me to qualify for inclusion in his chapter.[(a)]

The *Risāla* confirms the independence of Sībawayhi as much as his frequent disagrees ment with his masters and forebears: though we lack almost all the essential details of biography about Sībawayhi the man, the character of the *Kitāb* itself stands out clearly enough. There is much to be learnt from contemplating the list of terms usually thought

4. Reuschel, *Ḫalīl* 15, n. 1.
5. De Sacy, *Anthol. gram.* 382, 384, Derenbourg, *Kitāb* 1, intro. vii, n. 4.
6. Zajjājī, *Īḍāḥ* 45 and cf. 102.
7. Mubārak, *Rummānī* 113.

to be indispensible to Arabic grammar but which are not found in the technical vocabulary of the *Kitāb* at all. *Jumla*, *tamyīz*, *fā'ida* and *qānūn* have already been mentioned, and to these can be added *ḥukm*, *lā li-nafy al-jins*, all the abstract nouns of the type *fi'liyya*, *ismiyya*, *ẓarfiyya* etc.,[(b)] *'ibāra*, *al-majhūl*, *mā al-daymūmiyya*, *fā' al-sabab*, *af'āl al-qalb*, *al-nā'ib 'an al-fā'il*, *al-wāw al-ma'iyya*, *murakkab*, *maf'ūl muṭlaq*, *iḍāfa ḥaqīqiyya*, (*istiṯnā'*) *mufarraġ*, *ḍamīr 'ā'id*, *ḏāt al-wajhayn*, *musabbab/musabbab bihi*, and *badal al-ištimāl* etc.[(c)]

[294] This is not to say that Sībawayhi did not recognise the linguistic phenomena denoted by these terms, it simply means that he saw no need to give them specific names, since this would not further his main preoccupation with the way Arabic works. Nowhere is this more apparent than in the case of three terms which appear like warts in virtually every post-Sībawayhian work of grammar, viz. *sabab*, *'illa* and *taqdīr*. I list the occurrences of these three terms in the *Kitāb* so that their relative unimportance for Sībawayhi may speak for itself:

Sabab (meaning "cause") occurs nine[(a)] times in the *Kitāb*, twice in company with *'illa*:

	وهي سبب دخول الرفع فيها, وعلته أنّ ما عمل في الأسماء
1, 363/409	لم يعمل في هذه الأفعال
1, 383/430	ولكنّه أخبر بعلة الدعم وسببه

The other seven occurences are as follows:

1, 371/417	فيصير هذا كقولك سرت حتى تطلعَ الشمس لأنّ سيرك لا يكون
	سببًا لطلوع الشمس ولا يؤدّيه
	ولم يجعل الأول سببًا للآخر ولكنّه جعله ينطق على كل حال وقال
1, 376/422	عزّ وجلّ فَلا تَكْفُرْ فَيَتَعَلّمُونَ فارتفعت لأنه لم يخبر عن الملكين
1, 377/423	أنهما قالا لا تَكْفُرْ فَيَتَعَلّمُونَ ليجعلا كفره سببًا لتعليم غيره
	وإن قلت لا تدن من الأسد بأكلك فهو قبيح إن جزمت وليس وجه
1, 400/451	كلام الناس لأنك لا تريد أن تجعل تباعده من الأسد سببًا لأكله
	وتقول قم يدعوك لأنك لم ترد أن تجعل دعاء بعد قيامه يكون القيام
1, 401/451	سببًا له
1, 403/453	فإذا أدخل الفاء فإنما يجعل الإتيان سبب ذلك
	وكذلك لو ما ولو لا فهما لابتداء وجواب فالأول سبب ما وقع وما
2, 339/312	لم يقع

What is striking about these is that only one (1, 363/409) actually [295] contains *sabab* in the meaning of "grammatical cause." It is, perhaps, the only weakness in Weiss's article that he over-generalises this single instance of a grammatical cause: "the grammatical *'āmil* counts as the cause (سبب) of the inflectional behaviour of a word."[8] For on the

8. Weiss, *ZDMG* 1910, 385 [(c)].

strength of these nine occurrences of the word سبب it must surely appear that Sībawayhi had little, if any interest in abstracting the concept of grammatical causation.[(a)]

This is confirmed by the even less frequent appearance of the term *'illa* in the meaning of "reason" in the *Kitāb*, though it is found in innumerable places in its other meaning of "phonological defect." Apart from the two examples already given with *sabab* above, *'illa* occurs only twice elsewhere:[(b)]

1, 123/147	وأما يا زيد فله علة ستراه في باب النداء إن شاء الله
2, 210/202	وإنما تسمع ذا الضرب ثم تأتي بـلعلة والنظائر

In the first of these two it could be argued that علة does not mean here "grammatical reason" but rather some intermediate idea between "defect" and "reason," such as "excuse" or "loophole," where the defect itself provides a reason for grammatical behaviour. It might thus be compared with *'illa* in commerce, where a defect in merchandise is at the same time the reason for its not being salable. As for the second example of *'illa*, it smacks of a later mode of thought and could easily be an interpolation. In passing, it is worth noting that the *Kitāb* gives evidence of a long-standing connection between علة and نظائر in purely phonological contexts, as can be seen from the occurrence of such phrases as نظائر من غير المعتل and the like.[9] It is also interesting to see علة used in a [296] somewhat ambiguous way, where it is not immediately clear whether it means "reason" or"defect," e.g.,

2, 69/74	إذا ذهبت العلة صارتا إلى الأصل
2, 77/80	إذا أضفت قلت سنوي وهنوي و لعلة ههنا هي العلة في أب وأخ ونحوهما
2, 104/105	واعلم أنّ كل اسم آخره ياء . . حذفت منه الياء التي هي آخره ولا تحرّكها لعلة سنبيّن إن شاء الله
2, 130/128	وكذلك فعائل لأنّ علته كعلة قائل وهي همزة ليست بمنتهى الاسم
2, 266/249	وذلك من قبل أنّ فَعَلَ من هذا الباب لا يجيء إلا على يَفْعِلُ ولا يصرف عنه إلى يَفْعُلُ لعلة قد ذكرناها

In every such case, however, *'illa* is used in the context of the weak radicals, and it would seem that Jahn's "Grund" is not entirely an accurate translation for this particular usage. To be sure the phonological situation arises out of the defective nature of the radicals concerned, but there is nothing to imply that Sībawayhi had any notion of ultimate causality or that he looked any further than the immediate consequences of phonological

9. *Kitāb* 2, 193/187, 194/187, 273/254.

defects in word-formation. Apparently Jahn tried on one occasion to have his cake and eat it too, when he translated من علة as "aus Grund seiner Schwäche."[10]

Taqdīr as the term is used by the later grammarians plays virtually no part at all in the *Kitāb*.[(a)] It is, indeed, used to denote the treatment of *hamza* as equivalent to *'ayn*, no doubt as a way of emphasising the full consonantal status of that sound,[11] but this is in no way like the more [297] familiar use of the term in subsequent Arabic grammars. There are three instances, however, in the first volume where *taqdīr* is used in a syntactic context, viz.

1, 247/287	وصار كقولك ضرب عبد الله زيدًا قائمًا فهو مثله في التقدير وليس مثله في المعنى
1, 259/300	فالهاء إضمار الحديث الذي ذكرتَ بعد الهاء كأنّه في التقدير وإن كان لا يتكلّم به
1, 260/301	ولكنّه منفصل منه كانفصال الأخ منه إذا قلت ذهب أخوه فهذا تقديره

Jahn takes these occurences of *taqdīr* to mean "grammatisch zu erklären," "der Satz so herzustellen" and "die Construction beider Sätze ist dieselbe" respectively,[(a)] which makes their rarity in a work of this kind all the more difficult to understand, and we must ascribe this rarity of the term *taqdīr* to a radical difference in attitude between Sībawayhi and the later grammarians.

Much of this difference is due to the abandonment by the later grammarians of the principles which inspired the first grammarian. We have seen that there is a core of terminology based on the idea of building, which is itself a sort of foundation for Sībawayhi's grammar. The idea of the word as a construction may be Ḫalīl's, but I believe it was principally Sībawayhi who developed the notion of the sentence as a construction. Such terms as *i'timād*, *naṣb*, *binā,' raf'*, and *jarr* certainly have phonological applications, but they also come to apply to purely syntactical relationships between words. For Sībawayhi the structure of the sentence, the "building" or "propping" of one part upon another was far more important than that interloper from Greek logic, the notion that a sentence is that which can [298] be said to be true or false. As early as Mubarrad we find this later idea fully established as the only criterion in the definition of a sentence,[12] which eloquently testifies to the change in purpose which affected Arabic grammar soon after the *Kitāb* was completed. My translation of the terminology of the *Kitāb* is an attempt to restore some of the literal meaning to Sībawayhi's words.[(a)] "Direct" for *manṣūb* is already familiar from French studies of Arabic grammar, and "oblique" for *majrūr* is also a term already current in grammatical contexts. "Independent" for *marfū'* may not always be

10. *Kitāb* 2, 411/371, Jahn 2, 1, 786 (§541).[(b)]
11. Cf. Jahn, §315, n. 41.
12. Mubarrad, *Muqtaḍab* 3, 89.

immediately recognisable, but it would certainly be less so if a more literal translation were attempted. Moreover "independent" does, in any case, have to recommend it the fact that it reflects the freedom from an operans which the later grammarians called *taʿarrī* or *tajrīd*, although Sībawayhi does not formally develop this idea in the *Kitāb*. As for "operans" itself, for the important term *ʿāmil*, I have borrowed it from Erpenius, who so rendered it in his translation of Jurjānī's *Kitāb al-ʿawāmil al-miʾa*.[13] For the verb and other parts of *ʿamila fī* I prefer variations of the theme of "effect" and "affect," following Weiss's direction that this verb is to be taken literally in the *Kitāb* and has nothing whatoever to do with regime. I hope I may be excused for attempting no translation of *ḥāl*, *ẓarf* and *iḍāfa*: to the Arabist these are virtually English loan-words by now and to translate them would only add obscurity to obscurity.[(b)]

These last three terms apart, however, the literal translation of the *Kitāb* should make it easier to appreciate its author's true motives and achievements. The terms themselves are both numerous and diverse in their [299] origins, yet they display an unmistakable unity of application in the *Kitāb*, and to understand this unity is to grasp Sībawayhi's purpose. He certainly drew upon a short and primitive tradition of grammatical studies – perhaps the early works entitled *Kitāb al-waqf wa-l-ibtidāʾ* listed in the *Fihrist*[14] reflect crude phonological ideas arising out of Qurʾān recitation, and are to be connected with Sībawayhi's use of the term *mubtadaʾ* to denote an initial *hamza*[15], but he left them far behind in the way he developed his own idea of the nature of the Arabic language.

This has already been suggested on the basis of the contents of the *Risāla*, which sets out grammatical axioms which are, presumably, of Sībawayhi's own devising. Allowing for the fact that they may have been derived from the current climate of grammatical opinion in which he worked, the originality lies in selecting them and basing so much upon them. Other axioms emerge as the *Kitāb* progresses: the عشرون درهمًا problem involves one very important set of ideas relating to the identity of parts in adjectival and *iḍāfa* constructions against the explicit non-identity expressed by the *tanwīn-naṣb* construction. Another axiom which derives from a similar principle of linguistic behaviour is enunciated by Sībawayhi as follows:

> Know that whatever can behave as an epithet to an undefined word will be, to a defined word, in direct form because that which is an epithet to an undefined word becomes a statement (خبر) to a defined word, as it is not part of that noun.[16]

This axiom obviously accounts for the treatment of the *ḥāl* in particular in the *Kitāb*,[(a)] but it also reveals that Sībawayhi has detected an important [300] principle of Arabic speech,

---

13. See Troupeau, *Arabica* 10, 225–36.
14. Ibn al-Nadīm, *Fihrist* 60.[(b)]
15. *Kitāb* 2, 170/165, 459/410, 475/425.
16. Id. 1, 200/233.

viz. that non-identity produces non-concordance. The opposite of this (the adjectival relationship) is, in fact, stated rather ponderously in the sentence immediately preceding the one I have just quoted:

> Know that as far as the independent and direct forms are concerned, nouns and epithets of what is connected with them or the epithets of what is implicated with them or is implicated with something that is connected with them, behave in the same way as they do in the oblique form.[17]

This is not only a very long-winded way of saying that attributive adjectives stand in complete concordance with the nouns they qualify, it also defines the type of relationship which can exist between adjectives and nouns. The connection (*sabab*) or implication (*iltibās*)[(a)] between noun and adjective here is the same as that between the two terms of a *tanwīn-naṣb*, with the important difference that the adjectival relationship is also one of identity or inclusion which is reflected in the complete concordance of noun and adjective.

Other axioms, such as the "need" of two parts of a nominal sentence for each other and the necessity for the initial term to be defined, have already been mentioned, as also the axiom which states the definition the first part of an *iḍāfa*.[(b)] It is also obvious that Sībawayhi regarded it as axiomatic that pronouns could not precede the nouns they stood for or be adjectives of them, and, on the phonological side, there are the well-known axioms that two quiescent consonants cannot occur consecutively, and that [301] *tanwīn* is the sign of *tamakkun*, full inflectability. Others could be inferred from the *Kitāb* but for our purposes it is enough to have shown that the work is, indeed, based on general assumptions about Arabic which are sometimes formally expressed and always systematically applied. Indeed the homogeneity of the *Kitāb* is astonishing in view of its length and novelty, and it would be a very prejudiced eye indeed that could not discern in it a remarkably consistent and single-minded genius for linguistic analysis.

There is only one major inconsistency in the whole work,[(a)] involving the terms for "adjective." Both *na't* and *ṣifa* are used, the former much less frequently, but without any apparent difference in meaning or technical value.[(b)] I have reflected this inconsistency by translating *na't* as "epithet" and *ṣifa* as "adjective." Jahn, while tartly observing that "this is yet another example of Sībawayhi's still unsettled terminology,"[18] scarcely improves matters by haphazardly translating *na't* either as "Sifa" (!) or "Adjectiv."[19] Still more puzzling is Sībawayhi's apparent failure to distinguish between *ṣifa* and *waṣf*, for the latter is not infrequently used where the former would be expected. I can only surmise that for Sībawayhi it was not important to separate the speaker's act of describs

---

17. *Kitāb* 1, 200/233.
18. Jahn, §35, n. 17.
19. E.g. Jahn, op. cit. 1, 251, 280, 289, 291, 296, 298 and *passim*.

ing (*waṣf*) from the word's function as describer (*ṣifa*), though why this ambivalence is confined to this one function I cannot say. As far as other alleged inconsistencies are concerned, I hope the body of this thesis is enough to show that Sībawayhi was far from faltering in his choice of technical vocabulary.

[302] The fate of the *Kitāb* is parallel with that of Sībawayhi himself: he died an obscure death at a time no-one can specify, and seems to have founded no school. Ibn Jinnī remarks[(a)] that it is rare for Sībawayhi to be quoted as an authority (قلما تُسند إليه) for any anecdote (*riwāya*),[20] and the following lines from Ibn al-Mu'tazz[21]

وإن أشأ فكزيد في فرائضه	أو مثل نعمان لما ضاقت الحيل
أو الخليل عروضيًا أخا فطن	أو الكسائي نحويًا له علل

show how thoroughly the name of Sībawayhi fell into eclipse.[(b)] If he had pupils, they acknowledge no influence: Quṭrub mentions Yūnus and Abū 'Amr ibn al-'Alā' in his *Kitāb al-aḍdād*,[22] but never Sībawayhi. The middle Aḫfaš, who is held to have transmitted the *Kitāb* to posterity,[(c)] does not seem to have been as active a grammarian as many of his contemporaries, though it has to be admitted that his memory was burdened more than most. A certain Nāši' is said to have been a pupil of Sībawayhi, but nothing is known about him,[23] and the same applies to another who was probably a pupil (not noted by Ḥadīṯī), one 'Utbī, who is mentioned as one of the companions (أصحاب) of Sībawayhi.[24] These trifling and very possibly spurious biographical details scarcely measure up to the respect in which the *Kitāb* is supposed to be held, though they may betray the real indifference to that work which lies beneath the lip-service.

Grammar after Sībawayhi has a quite different quality from that which we find in the *Kitāb*. It becomes a game, as, for example, when the middle Aḫfaš himself remarks of a difficult grammatical point in a poem:

[303] Some say that this poem was devised in a mistaken form so that the person who asked about it could find out how much the person he asked understood.[25]

Likewise Mubarrad introduces a truly grotesque sentence into his *Muqtaḍab*,[(a)] one which, he says, is often set to pupils for parsing practice:[26]

الضاربَ الشاتمَ المُكرمَ المعطيَه درهمًا في داره أخوك سوطًا أكْرَمَ الآكلُ طعامَه غلامُه زيدٌ عمرًا خالدٍ بكرًا عبدَ الله أخوك

20. Ibn Jinnī, *Ḫaṣā'iṣ* 3, 312.
21. Ibn al-Mu'tazz, *Rasā'il* 128.
22. Published by H. Kofler in *Islamica* 5.
23. Ḥadīṯī, *Kitāb Sībawayhi* 44.
24. Zubaydī, *Ṭabaqāt* 44, Iṣfahānī, *Aġānī* 17, 16.
25. Baġdādī, *Ḫizāna* 2, 300.
26. Mubarrad, *Muqtaḍab* 1, 22.

In this connection it is also worth pointing out that what distinguishes Sībawayhi's discussion of grammatical points from that which we find in the *Inṣāf* of Anbārī is without doubt the fact that the discussions of Anbārī are in themselves futile and empty, since they lack altogether that interest in the way Arabic works which is such an attractive feature of the *Kitāb*.(b)

How soon the spirit of the *Kitāb* was abandoned in favour of the painstaking pedantry which is now regarded as typical of Arabic grammar it is not easy to say. Certainly as early as the middle Aḫfaš, who is probably responsible for inventing the category of *mustaqīm ḫaṭa'* and *mustaqīm al-lafẓ*[27] it is clear that the *Kitāb* has become a misunderstood work, but against this is the fact that Farrā,' the other great grammarian(c) who was a late contemporary of Sībawayhi (though he may well never have had anything to do with him personally),[28] seems to employ a grammatical method which is substantially the same as Sībawayhi's in terminology, as far as can be ascertained from his *Ma'ānī al-Qur'ān*,[29] and allowing for such well-known "Kūfan" specialities as *'imād* for the separative pronoun, *ḫafḍ* for *jarr* and so on.(d) To be sure Farrā' is reputed to have "introduced philosophical [304] terms into his discourse"[30] but this is scarcely reflected in his surviving works, and I suspect that "philosophical" is a standard term of abuse in Arabic for anything which is in the least degree speculative and abstruse. The ultimate degradation of the *Kitāb* and the triumph of Arab inertia came when Ibn Ḫaldūn suggested that Ibn Hišām was "more of a grammarian" (أنحى) than Sībawayhi, a proposition which was first noted in Europe by de Sacy[31] and which also forms the basis of an uninspiring article by Ṣāliḥ al-Ašṭar[32] who elaborates the idea without in any way adding to it.

We do know that the *Kitāb* was very soon regarded as a work of peculiar difficulty even by prominent Arab grammarians, but Mubarrad's question to the would-be reader of the *Kitāb*, "Have you ever ridden on the sea?"[33] would surely be more appropriate, if mere length were the objection, to the works of Ibn Ya'īš or Ṣabbān. It is not surprising to learn that Ibn Kaysān (died between 299 and 320)[34] found that

> the terms of the *Kitāb* need to be properly expressed and clarified, because it is a book which was composed in a time when people were familiar with such terms, and it confines itself to their ways of thinking.[35]

27. See above, pp. [220], [235].
28. Beck, *Orientalia* (NS) 15, 438.
29. E.g. *Ma'ānī* 1, 51, 52, 89, 389 *et passim*.
30. Ibn Ḫallikān, *Wafayāt* 4, 67.
31. De Sacy, *Anthol. gram.* 222.
32. Ṣāliḥ al-Aštar, *RAAD* 40, 295ff.
33. Sīrāfī, *Aḫbār* 50.(a)
34. Suyūṭī, *Buġya* 1, 19; Sezgin, *GAS* 9, 158–60.
35. Baġdādī, *Ḫizāna* 1, 179.

and it is obvious that the respect which raised the *Kitāb* to the status of a "Qur'ān of grammar"[36] was firmly based on a reluctance to understand it. Much of the work of the later grammarians consists of making explicit what Sībawayhi left implicit, which accounts for the differences in terminology [305] between the *Kitāb* and its successors, but much harm was done, too, by introducing the concept of *fā'ida* into grammar. It is not only unnecessary but it is also misleading to apply what is basically a structural/functional grammar to a problem which properly belongs to semantics. This confusion of methods went unnoticed by Goshen-Gottstein who, while evincing a welcome respect for the success of the traditional grammatical analysis of the Arab grammarians, wrongly accepted (through not observing that it was wrongly conceived) the idea that *isnād* refers to the logical predicability of one noun to another.[37] This is clearly a misapprehension based on the later, logical use of the term *isnād*,[(a)] though it must be admitted that the bare words of Zamaḫšarī's discussion of *isnād* (on which Goshen-Gottstein bases his remarks) do not imply anything more than a "two-ended" (طرفين) construction which may be either structural or semantic in nature.[38] As a matter of fact the concept of *isnād* is only mentioned four times in the *Kitāb*, and I now list these occurrences:

1, 6/7	هذا باب المسند والمسند إليه
1, 218/256	فالمبتدأ مسند والمبني عليه مسند إليه
1, 239/278[39]	فالمبتدأ الأول والمبني عليه ما بعده فهو مسند ومسند إليه
	وضاربٌ ومِنْكَ بمنزلة شيء من الاسم في أنّه لم يُسند إلى مسند
2, 61/66	وصار كمال الاسم كما أنّ المضاف إليه منتهى الاسم

The first example is somewhat perplexing, as it is the title of a chapter which deals exclusively with sentence structure, but in which the idea of *isnād* itself is not invoked. Conversely, in the second and third examples [306] *musnad* and *musnad ilayhi* are obviously glosses on the more familiar notions of *ibtidā'* and *binā.'* The last example is clearly a specimen of Ḫalīl's reasoning, and this instance of *isnād* may well have a purely phonological application.[(a)] Apart from the obvious conclusion that *isnād* counts for almost nothing in the *Kitāb*, its meagre presence is difficult to account for. Perhaps Sībawayhi adapted it from the meaning given to it by Ḫalīl, and used it as a chapter heading as a way of introducing it into his grammatical system. Its occurrence as a gloss in the other two cases might then be due to Sībawayhi's wish to remind us of this novel term. This leaves unexplained the fact that he makes so little use of the innovation, though my suggestion

36. Abū Ṭayyib, *Marātib* 65.[(b)]
37. Goshen-Gottstein, *Preprints* 370, n. 9.
38. Zamaḫšarī, *Mufaṣṣal* §25.
39. Both Būlāq and Derenbourg editions read والمبني ما بعده عليه.[(b)]

is, perhaps, preferable to the supposition that at least the first three occurences are interpolations from a later date.

A similar failure to appreciate the intrinsic merits of the Arab approach through an insistence on applying alien logical methods is seen in Rabin's treatment of a chapter of the *Kitāb* of which he says

> His exposition is far from clear and operates with logical categories which seem to have little bearing on the syntactical distinctions.[40]

This is a serious criticism, an elegant way of saying that Sībawayhi does not know what he is talking about. But Rabin, in his presentation of Sībawayhi's argument, omits certain points of Sībawayhi's case through which everything immediately becomes clear.

The problem concerns the alternation and contamination of two constructions, أما علمًا فعالمٌ, with a direct[(b)] form of the *maṣdar* علمًا and [307] أما العبيدُ فذو عبيد with an independent form of the non-*maṣdar* العبيدُ. Mixed forms, such as أما العلمَ فعالمٌ are found, but need not concern us here (they have briefly been treated above, p. [19]). What seems to puzzle Rabin is why there should be two possible "cases" after أما and what are the grounds for distinguishing them. Sībawayhi makes it quite plain that the presence of the direct form is formally due to the fact that it has been "affected by what precedes and follows it,"[41] more explicitly, "those things in this category which take direct form are what is affected by the speech which precedes or follows it, just as حذر is affected in أكرمته حَذَرَ أن أعبَ."[42] This makes it as clear as possible that the direct form belongs to the category of extraneous elements exemplified by عشرون درهمًا, and we shall find that the similarity extends even further. For Sībawayhi also invokes the familiar principle of non-identity to account for the direct form:

> The direct form is when you do not make the second علم (in the expression أما العلمَ فعالمٌ بالعلم) the same as the first previously expressed, and it is as though you said أما العلمَ فعالمٌ بالأشياء.[43]

This is then contrasted with the independent forms such as أما العلمُ فعالمٌ به, where the referential pronun makes it obvious that the second علم (in به) is the same as the first.

By applying the principles of identity and nonidentity which Rabin seems to have overlooked completely, it becomes easy to see that a *ḥāl*, or even an adjective or noun treated as a *ḥāl*,[44] is by definition not identical [308] with the word to which it alludes, and so must take direct form. Conversely, as Sībawayhi's examples أما العبيدُ فذو عبيد and أمّا

40. Rabin, *Ancient West-Arabian* 183.
41. *Kitāb* 1, 161/192.
42. Id. 1, 163/194.
43. Id. 1, 162/192.
44. Rabin, *Ancient West-Arabian* 184.

ابنُ مزنية فأنا ابنُ مزنية [(a)] are meant to demonstrate, when "you make the first the same as the last," the independent form must be used, a principle which is apparent, incidentally, in the discussion of له صوتٌ صوتَ حمار, see above, p. [196]. Perhaps Rabin would have taken Sībawayhi's point if the *Kitāb* had not been subjected for so long to critical distortion. At any rate it is plain that, although Sībawayhi does not use formal "logical categories," he does refer to and rely on inductive principles which are of general validity for the whole of Arabic syntax, such as that embodied in عشرون درهمًا, and the case we have just examined is a good example of of the inner consistency of Sībawayhi's analysis.

The problem just dealt with is yet another reminder that the technicalities of the *Kitāb*, let alone of Arabic grammar as a whole, are not the same as the technicalities of Western grammar. One has to sympathise with Jahn, who fully admitted that when compared with the rest of the Arab grammarians,

> Sībawayhi was even more tyrannical than the tyrants themselves, i.e., he diverged even further from our way of deducing and constructing,[45]

though this is hardly enough to excuse the liberties he took in his translation. Indeed, to judge by the context of these words in his preface, he seems to imply that his own translation bears the responsibility for that state of affairs. We must conclude that when Sībawayhi refers to our "present tense" as ما هو الآن فيه [46] or [309] فعل متّصل في حال ذكرك إيّاه [47], for example, it is not because he was incapable of devising a single term to replace these periphrastic definitions, but because he saw no need to do so. In addition, to allot specific meanings to the verb forms would have upset his functional scheme. His linguistic acuity was sharp enough to have seen the need for terms denoting tenses if they were necessary to his functional/structural system, but the fact is that they are not.[(a)] It is, therefore, a mistake to accuse him of deficiencies, which is to judge him by standards not his own. It is particularly futile to accuse him of lacking terminological items which, because they are second nature to a European, are assumed to be indispensible to the Arabs.

The Arabs never, in fact, developed terms which correspond exactly to our terms "passive," "syllable," "mood," "voice,"[48] "case," (i.e., exclusively of nouns), "clause" and "tense," even after they had become acquainted with the Greeks. Indeed they seem rather to have resisted, instead of gratefully accepting, the riches of Hellenistic science as far as their own native disciplines were concerned. So for *metaphōra*, for instance, which was perfectly familiar as استعارة possibly from at least the time of Abū ʿAmr ibn al-ʿAlā,[49] Abū

45. Jahn, *Kitāb* 2, intro. v.[(b)]
46. *Kitāb* 1, 128/153.
47. *Kitāb* 1, 142/170.
48. But cf. above, p. [57].
49. See Bāqillānī, *Iʿjāz* 108. I am grateful to Mr. Kamal Abu Deeb for this reference.

Bišr offers تأدّى and Avicenna offers نقل,[50] neither of which suggest that the idea of استعارة itself owes much to Greek techniques. It would seem obvious, then, that the safest way to appreciate a work like the *Kitāb* is to let it speak for itself, which has been the principle task of this thesis.

[310] When Sībawayhi is allowed to speak for himself, it becomes apparent that he speaks with the voice of a lawyer, or at least of one who has been trained in a legal background, so that it can be said that his way of thinking, far from being alien and Greek, is typically Muslim, especially since the legal sciences represented in his day the only existing system of abstract thought. It is, therefore, inevitable that the first speculative work of Arabic grammar should adopt the only possible method of speculation which was available at the time.[(a)]

But there are deeper connections between law and grammar.[(b)] English students of law are taught as a matter of elementary fact that

> Many of the disputes in jurisprudence are really arguments concerning the meaning of words,[51]

and this view has also formed the basis of an article by Glanville Williams in which he quotes a judge as saying

> a difference in the mere form of words does in several cases make a difference in law,[52]

though his main interest seems to be in absolute semantics rather than syntax.

It is not surprising, then, that the aims of law should sound so very much like those of the *Kitāb* as I have presented them: it is said that the purpose of the law is

> the equitable maintenance of [the] classes in their own stations and functions[53]

and Glanville Williams has described the law in the following terms:

[311] The law, with its verbal apparatus of 'rights,' 'duties,' and 'wrongs,' is merely a particular application of language as a means of social control.[54]

Given the homogeneity of outlook in the Muslim community it begins to appear unavoidable that grammar should be intimately connected with law, and the only problem is to decide which one influenced the other. Jarmī once said that for thirty years he had been

50. Afnan, *JRAS* 1947, 188.
51. Paton, *Jurisprudence* 51.
52. Williams, *Law Quarterly Review* 61, 78.
53. Gibb, in Khadduri, *Law in the Middle East* 1, 27.
54. Williams, *Law Quarterly Review* 61, 71.

giving *fatwas* on the basis of the *fiqh* in the *Kitāb*,[55] which, if it not gross sarcasm, testifies to the usefulness of the *Kitāb* in the field where it was of most practical value. But apart from this sort of evidence it seems more plausible to assume that grammar was influenced by law and not *vice versa*. The idea that law was influenced by grammar is developed in the context of Roman law by Stein, but his case rests too heavily upon the single borrowing of *kanōn* from rhetoric to law. It is scarcely to be accepted that the Romans, or the Arabs for that matter, devised a system of grammar before they devised their legal system, for it is implicit in the situation described by Stein:

> One of the earliest controversies among the Roman jurists, of which we know, concerned the word 'fruits' ...... once the idea of usufruct caught on questions naturally arose about just what was covered by the term "fruits"[56]

that a fixed legal attitude must have existed in order for it to be applied to the problematical linguistic situation.

Where the law did make borrowings from linguistic studies was in the area of pleading, where rhetoric played an important part. But in Arabic [312] this art of pleading, known as *jadal*, is not mentioned anywhere in the *Kitāb*. *Jadal* is said by de Sacy to be the Arabic name for Aristotle's *Topica*,[(a)] and to have acquired in *fiqh* the meaning of the rules which govern legal argument,[57] which is doubtless to be connected with Theodore Abū Qurra's[(b)] statement that *fiqh* itself is part of rhetoric.[58] A similar view is expressed in the article on *fiqh* by Goldziher and Schacht in the first edition of the *Encyclopaedia of Islam*, but the general proposition that Islamic law is a direct borrowing from Roman law (and hence from Greek rhetoric) has been denied by Vesey-Fitzgerald.[59] It would certainly be expected that, if Islamic law did owe anything, directly or indirectly, to Greek rhetoric, this latter discipline would itself have been given a more expert and knowing welcome by the Arabs when they encountered it in the original texts. We only have to compare Fārābī with, say, Ibn al-'Askarī, to see that in rhetoric, as in grammar, the Arabs had been going their own way all the time. *Jadal* remains an interloper from rhetoric, and is not enough to establish any deeper connection.

On the other hand Arabic grammar continued to evince contacts with law, all of them too late, however, to suggest that Sībawayhi had anything to do with them. The device known as *istiṣḥāb al-ḥāl*, defined by Goldziher as the method by which "an existing certainty is not suppressed by a subsequent doubt,"[60] is explicitly used in a gram-

55. Zajjājī, *Majālis* 251, Baġdādī, *Ḫizāna* 1, 179.
56. Stein, *Regulae juris* 28.
57. De Sacy *Anthol. gram.* 472.
58. See Walzer, *Oriens* 6, 128 (= Walzer 1962, 97).
59. Vesey-Fitzgerald, *LQR* 67, 81–102.
60. Goldziher, *Wiener Zeitschrift für die Kunde des Morgenlandes* 1887, 233.

matical argument in the *Inṣāf* of Anbārī.[61] Weil, who translates the term as "the law of holding fast to the basic principle"[62] nevertheless fails to connect it specifically [313] with jurisprudence except by the usual accidental legal metaphor of his translation. We also find in grammatical works discussions of such legal problems as the nature of *nabīḏ*,[63] and Ibn Ya'īš treats some grammatical alternatives in the light of their legal consequences.[64] It is also noteworthy that the *Inṣāf* often uses the idea of *ijmā'*, which might, when compared with the arguments of Sībawayhi, be considered a retrograde step in the history of speculative grammar.[(a)] But in these cases the Arabs themselves clearly recognised that they were infringing upon another, independent discipline, though it was one with which they felt that grammar had much in common, and these occasional borrowings from the law are quite different in kind from the major borrowing which took place in Sībawayhi's time.[(b)]

The borrowing itself, which may have been an unconscious absorption of legal methods both by Ḫalīl and by Sībawayhi, appears to me to have been worth proving by the evidence of the preceding chapters. It has, as one extra proof of a less scientific kind, the advantage that it makes the *Kitāb* comprehensible, which it certainly is not if it is approached as a work of the Hellenistic type. In view of Ḫalīl's reputation as a prosodist and phonetician it is doubtful whether he would have developed the ideas which Sībawayhi attributes to him in the *Kitāb* as far as that work actually takes them, and for this reason alone Sībawayhi deserves Jahn's title of "Father of Arabic grammar."[(c)] The debt to his master is fully paid by Sībawayhi's own acknowledgement of it, but the credit for the achievement of the *Kitāb* must go exclusively to Sībawayhi, who was the first, and I believe the only Arab grammarian to have investigated and explored [314] the workings of Arabic as a living language in terms of an ethical process.

The greatest virtue of this ethical approach is the authority it gives to grammatical prescriptions, for we may well refuse to speak in a certain way merely because we are told to, but we would have to provide sterner objections to speaking in a way that is morally "right" and "good," as in the case of the *lām al-istiġāṯa*, of which Sībawayhi says

> All this has the meaning of surprise or seeking help, otherwise it is not allowed (لم يجز).[65]

The story of the boy who cried "Wolf!" provides the most powerful evidence of the firm basis of social behaviour upon which such a linguistic rule is founded, and points a moral, too, for readers of the *Kitāb* as a whole. Unlike many students of the language, Sībawayhi

61. Anbārī, *Inṣāf* 303.
62. Id. intro. 9.
63. Suyūṭī, *Muzhir* 1, 59f.
64. Ibn Ya'īš, *Šarḥ al-Mufaṣṣal* 1, 11f.
65. *Kitāb* 1, 277/320.

was only concerned with realities, actual speech in actual contexts, where linguistic acts could be seen to have social consequences. We have only have to compare the use of the term *jamīl* as a synonym of *ḥasan* with a specimen sentence from the *Kitāb* which says "I want you to speak nicely or shut up"[66] أريد أن تنطقَ بالجميل أو تسكتَ to see at once how closely linguistic and social behaviour were linked for Sībawayhi.[(a)] We find, and this can be confirmed by reading the works of the later grammarians, that the sense of reality which breathes through the *Kitāb* is a reflection of Sībawayhi's true interest in the way Arabic works, while [315] his heirs offer little more than a spectacle of academic self-indulgence as they wrangle over the corpse of what had been, to Sībawayhi, a living body of language. It has happened before, and I can think of no better conclusion than these words, which were written about the ancestors of our own European grammarians: [(a)]

> L'histoire de la grammaire au moyen âge montre par un exemple frappant qu'en cultivant une science, comme en traitant une question particulière, les hommes peuvent s'engager dans une voie qui les écarte de plus en plus de la vérité, et s'en trouver plus éloignés, au bout de plusieurs siècles de travail, que ceux qui les avaient précédés.[67]

Summary

[328] No critic of the *Kitāb* has explained why the *Kitāb* was written, though it seems that a work of this kind can only be apologetic in nature. From the *Rīsāla* which introduces the *Kitāb* we know that Sībawayhi intended the *Kitāb* to be all his own work.

Subsequently grammar became a different discipline, as is shown by the list of terms of later grammar which are not found in the *Kitāb*. Conversely some terms in the *Kitāb* have not yet acquired their later meanings, and *sabab*, *ʿilla* and *taqdīr* are used to illustrate this.

The *Kitāb* is best translated literally, as is the practice in this thesis. It is a work which is certainly based on axioms which are systematically applied, but one major inconsistency is the use of *ṣifa*, *waṣf* and *naʿt* indiscriminately.

The fate of the *Kitāb* is obscurity and neglect, for grammar soon became an academic game, and logical ideas, symbolised by the change in the meaning of *isnād*, began to intrude. When judged by these standards, the *Kitāb* is distorted, as an examination of an error by Rabin demonstrates. Arabic [329] grammar to this day lacks many ideas considered essential in Western grammar.

The connection between law and grammar is inherent, and evidence is given that Arabic law and grammar remained close.

---

66. Id. 1, 382/430.

67. Thurot, *Notices et extraits* 506.

Sībawayhi's achievement was to combine his deep interest in the realities of lana guage with a sound, legally based system of analysis. But his fate is not unique, and the same happened to him as befell the founders of European grammar.

Addenda to Chapter Seven

[289] (a) The work even lacks a title and may indeed be one of the earliest "books" in Islām. The title may come from the fact that Sībawayhi twice refers to "the book," *al-kitāb* (Troupeau 1976, 1, 32/42, 286/329). In 2, 340/312, there is mention of a *kitāb al-fi'l,* presumably as a subsection of the book. In 1, 389/438 the statement *fī l-kitābi mahmā taqūlu* occurs (not listed in Troupau): it is presented as an incorrect (*qabīḥ*) utterance, taken by Sīrāfī (Jahn §246 n. 5) to mean something like "written down is whatever you are saying," with *taqul* being the correct form, i.e., "whatever you might say."

There are also forward and backward references which clearly indicate that Sībawayhi carried the entire work in his head. For example in *Kitāb* §495 he announces (2, 310/284) that the topic of the *ḥurūf al-qalqala* ("exploded" consonants, see Bakalla 1982, 152) "will also be explained under assimilation, *in šā' allāh,*" which does indeed take place in §565, which begins 142 pages later in the Derenbourg edition. Similarly in §185 1, 315/359 he lists the exceptive particles (*ḥurūf*) and then declares "I shall explain the circumstance of these particles one by one *in šā' allāh,*" which he proceeds to do over the next fourteen pages, then starts another topic (pronouns) with the same declaration. There are also references to "sections" (*fuṣūl*) of the work, e.g., 2, 265/248 "what we have already mentioned in these sections," though in some instances they look like a gloss. A single reference to a *kurrāsa* "fascicle" of the manuscript could also be a gloss, even though it is in the first person, 1, 427/478.

In one case (1, 411/463, not listed in Troupeau, because it is part of the data and not a technical term) *al-kitāb* appears in an example, illustrating that *inna* and *anna* cannot co-occur, so it is "bad" (*qabuḥa*) to say **inna annaka ḏāhibun fī l-kitābi* or **qad 'araftu anna innaka fī l-kitāb*. It is not clear whether Jahn §262, n. 11, or his source Sīrāfī, recognise this as a reference to Sībawayhi's own *Kitāb*, which seems most likely, viz. "the construction *inna annaka ḏāhibun* is not in the *Kitāb.*" If, as is also possible, it is in fact an interpolation, see [302] (a), it might show how "the Book" became the title of this work *sui generis*, as biographers have observed.

[289] (b) Suleiman 2006 discusses the rejection of Sībawayhi by contemporary language reformers, one of whom calls him a deluded criminal. This is, of course, a battle which has been going on for centuries, most notoriously in the doctrinally inspired assault of Ibn Maḍā' (the patron saint of language reformers, d. 592/1196) on the very notion of grammatical causality. Curiously Šūbāšī, one of the authors discussed in Suleiman 2006, may himself have committed a solecism in the title of his work *Long live the Arabic language! Down with Sībawayhi!* where "long live" in the Arabic has the form *li-taḥyā* instead of the apocopated *li-taḥya* of correct Classical Arabic.

[290] (a) See [174] (a) on the occasions where the present writer has disregarded this principle.

[290] (b) Another neglected figure who must be mentioned here is Astarābāḏī, see Larcher 2014 and above, [221] (a).

[291] (a) *Kitāb* 2, 474/424, regarding the unassimilated patterns in doubled verbs, e.g., *urdud, yardud*. Elsewhere Sībawayhi asserts that the Ḥijāzī dialect is older and superior to the Tamīmī dialect, id. 2, 37/41. Apart from declaring a general preference for the Tamīmī forms over the Ḥijāzī, see [50] (a), he is not greatly interested in individual dialects: Rabin 1951, 7, states that Sībawayhi "had no hesitation in reducing differences largely to a schematic opposition of Hijaz and Tamim," and that the collection of dialect data was of only marginal interest to Sībawayhi. Levin 1994 disagrees with this latter point at some length, and shows how carefully and assiduously Sībawayhi did collect such data. Rabin's first proposition, however, remains on the whole valid.

[291] (b) More precisely, it has already been argued above, [136]ff, that Sībawayhi's data were derived from the same shared pool of linguistic material on which all the early scholars, in law, Ḥadīṯ, Qur'ān, based their reconstruction of the ideal form of Islam.

[291] (c) Johnson himself says in his dictionary that "every quotation contributes something to the stability or enlargement of the language."

[291] (d) In Fück's time there was no challenge to Ibn Ḫaldūn's idea that grammar arose to correct the faults in the speech of the newly Arabicised Muslims of various linguistic origins. The main disadvantage of this notion is that it gives no place to the state of spoken, i.e., uninflected neo-Arabic, partly because it assumed that the Arabs all spoke inflected Arabic of the Classical type.

The state of colloquial Arabic, and the origins of the dialects, have generated much debate, but as far as the *Kitāb* is concerned, we can trust Levin 1994 (see [290] (a) above), who presents an abundance of evidence that all the data collected by Sībawayhi directly and indirectly from the mouths of the Bedouin were of the fully inflected variety.

[292] (a) The annotated translation by Versteegh 1995 of Zajjājī's treatise is an invaluable account of what has come to be regarded as an autonomous work by Sībawayhi, though this has no documented confirmation. Nevertheless, the first seven chapters of the *Kitāb* continue to appear in translation as a single unit, e.g., Troupeau 1973–4, Bohas/Carter 2004, Kouloughli 2004, Larcher 2004–2005, and a special section of *Langues et littératures du monde arabe* has been dedicated to it (see Bohas/Kouloughli 2004).

[293] (a) On these hierarchies see above [192] and note (a), also [123] (b) on the role of definiteness/indefiniteness in predication.

[293] (b) In fact there are only three abstract nouns of this type at all in the *Kitāb*, viz. *'ubūdiyya* "servitude" (1, 421/472), *jabariyya* "power," and *taqdumiyya* "boldness in battle" (both in 2, 382/348), suggesting that this suffix had not yet begun to proliferate as it did later in the Islamic sciences.

On the topic of abstract nouns it must be said that Macuch 1982, 21 is not a very plausible account of the reproduction of Greek *philosophia* as *falsafa(h)* in Arabic, claiming that it is a "shortening" of the Syriac/Greek original, from which a verb *falsafa* was then derived. This is wrong way round: the noun *falsafa(h)* is derived from the denominative verb *falsafa*, the latter itself derived directly from *faylasūf*. This is a regular Arabic procedure, cf. *ḥamdala* "to say *al-ḥamdu li-l-lāhi*," verbal noun *ḥamdala(h)*.

[293] (c) There may well be more (for example *ḍamīr al-faṣl*), but to seek them out would by definition take us away from the topic of this thesis. Peled 1999, 61f observes that the number of "brand new technical terms" is "markedly small." It is worth emphasising that the *Kitāb*, apart from some rarely used items such as *jins, ṣinf, naw'* and *'araḍ*, lacks almost the entire scholastic vocabulary and structure, not to mention the terminology of philosophy and logic, cf. Carter 2004, 142f.

[294] (a) Troupeau 1976 has fourteen times, but this can be reconciled with my nine as follows: his first instance (1,278/320) is not *sabab* in the meaning of "cause" but in the meaning of "semantic link"(see [258]–[286]); of the remaining thirteen, my example from 1,371/417 quotes only one of the four occurrences of the word on that page, and my example from 1,383/430 quotes only one of the two instances, so my total of 9 quoted + 4 not quoted matches his 13, after eliminating 1,278/320 (and his 1,385 must be corrected to 1,383).

[295] (a) This is not well put: of course Sībawayhi is interested in grammatical causation, but only as the effect (*'amal*) of the speaker or of parts of the utterance upon each other, see [78] (a): but he does not treat it as an issue of logical causality (*sabab*) or reason (*'illa*). Systematic questions about the *'illa* "reason" for grammatical phenomena were not raised until more than a century after Sībawayhi, "why is the agent of the verb in independent case?," why is *ḍamma* the marker of the independent case/mood? etc. etc., and the best starting point is Versteegh 1995, to which should be added Suleiman 1988, developed into a monograph 1999b.

The position of the present work remains unchanged as far as Sībawayhi is concerned: while we can assume that he was aware of linguistic causality, he did not make any significant use of the terms *sabab* and *'illa* in that sense, and when they do appear in the *Kitāb*, are mostly of phonological and syntactical import respectively, as illustrated in these pages.

[295] (b) Troupeau 1976 actually lists twenty-seven occurrences including two plurals for "reason," and thirteen for *'illa* in the sense of phonological defect. This is a serious deficiency in the present work, but in defence I will say that the ambiguity of the term, "reason" or "defect," is not definitively resolved by Troupeau's classification, and the remarks below, [296] are still valid, to the extent that Troupeau's choices between the two meanings do not all coincide with those of this thesis. Nevertheless there is still much work to be done.

[295] (c) This footnote was omitted from the original text.

[296] (a) See Baalbaki 1979 on "suppletive insertion." Twenty-four occurrences of *taqdīr* are listed in Troupeau 1976, but he does not separate its applications into phonological and syntactical, calling them both "supposition, supposé." His list makes it easy,

however, to confirm that all the instances of *taqdīr* in volume two involve giving *hamza* the phonological status of *'ayn*, i.e., as a full (not weak) consonant. This suggests it might best be translated literally, from the notion of *qadr*, as "assigning the value of one thing to another," which would also be appropriate in syntactical contexts. Curiously we also learn from Troupeau that no such verb (*qaddara*) is used in the *Kitāb*.

[296] (b) The German translates as "by reason of its weakness"; in fact the Arabic *min* itself provides the sense of "because of," so this criticism is not deserved.

[297] (a) "to explain grammatically," "to produce the sentence in this way," and "the construction of both sentences is the same."

[298] (a) All translation of grammatical terms is an exercise in comparative linguistics (or metagrammar, to adapt a term from Peled 1999), which can become a a form of intellectual imperialism. Clearly there is no justification for arbitrarily equating phenomena in the object language with categories in the observer's native system no matter how strong the apparent similarity (cf. Carter 1989, 1993). Needless to say, equations such as "subjunctive" for *manṣūb*, "subject" for *fā'il*, "genitive" for *majrūr*, "regens" for *'āmil*, "sentence" for *kalām* and so on are distortions of the Arabic concepts, *pace* Guillaume, see below.

It is admittedly difficult to avoid this, and the present thesis has failed on several counts, freely using "subject" for *mubtada' [bihi]*, "preposition" for *ḥarf jarr*, "object" for *maf'ūl*, "inflection" for *i'rāb*, "particle" for *ḥarf*, etc., the excuse being that they do not seriously distort our perception of the items to which they refer. For *manṣūb* we should have left "direct" to the French, and it is now to be replaced throughout by "dependent" as a quasi-antonym of "independent" *marfū'*. "Definition" and "indefinition" for *ma'rifa* and *nakira* are misleading, and are replaced by "definiteness" and "indefiniteness."

General reviews of the topic are in Mosel 1975, 1980, Baalbaki 1989, 2008, Carter 1993, Peled 1999, Guillaume 2001, of which the last two cover the whole period of mediaeval grammar.

Peled makes the valuable point (57) that some of the "metagrammatically intuitive" terminology of the *Kitāb* would have been used by both speakers and analysts, that is, are both technical (linguistic) and lay (extralinguistic) terms.

Guillaume has a similar view, see [154] (a), but takes issue with the assertion of Carter 1995, 50 that technical terms should be translated as literally as possible, and quite rightly points out that this is in practice impossible. His solution is an adroit intellectual conjuring trick, to replace "translation" with "transposition," by which device *'amal*, for example, can be rendered "rection" by simply replacing one metaphor with another. One result of this is that the terminology of the host language inevitably will acquire special meanings when applied to the target language, which is a price Guillaume is prepared to pay.

[298] (b) To the untranslatables we should add *tanwīn*. It is common practice not to translate terms unique to the object language: no-one is perturbed by "tilde" or "um-

laut," and indeed the latter is marked as a loan word by the loss of its German upper case initial letter.

[299] (a) See [264] (b).

[299] (b) See Sezgin, *GAS* 1, 5, 15, 27 for works of this title in Qur'ān studies, and *GAS* 9, index p. 388 for grammatical works. Cf. also [205] (a) on *waqf.*

[300] (a) For *iltibās* "involvement" is now preferred, see Carter 1985a, 57 and *passim.*

[300] (b) Above, [247] and [257] respectively.

[301] (a) This is an oversimplification: in addition to the *waṣf/naʿt* pair (see next note) we can observe at least two sets of terms which contain apparent duplications, namely the terminology of predication, see [70] (a), and the case/mood names, which in some contexts are used interchangeably with those of the vowel names, see [164] (a).

As already speculated in [164]-[167], some of these duplications might be accounted for as having been introduced in historically different periods. Talmon 1987a, 1997, 2003 and Versteegh 1993 are especially informative about the terminological uncertainty which preceded the *Kitāb*: what we cannot do, however, is track any movements in detail. We can go no further than a general assumption that terminology was not settled before Sībawayhi's time, and that he may have had a choice, or simply have accepted the ideas of his teachers without standardising their terminology.

[301] (b) Mosel 1975, 287–92 discusses the overlapping terminology *ṣifa, waṣf, naʿt* (and the verb *waṣafa*), concluding that *ṣifa* is used only when the antecedent is a noun, with *waṣf* roughly synonymous, except that *waṣf* may also refer to the qualifying role of the *ḥāl*; accordingly the verb *waṣafa* is used to refer to both kinds of qualification, and extends to predication in general. Given that the *ṣifa* may also be a relative clause, Mosel's term "descriptive adjunct" (1980, 27, though she does not discuss *naʿt* there) is very practical.

As for *naʿt*, Mosel 1973, 289 demonstrates with parallel passages that it is used in exactly the same contexts as *ṣifa*, though to this we would have to add the qualification (not emphasised here) that *naʿt* can denote a *ḥāl*, but is not used for relative clauses, unlike *ṣifa*. No clear reason is offered for this duplication, beyond a tentative suggestion that Sībawayhi had not yet stabilised his terminology. That being so, the remarks made above in note (a) remain valid.

In spite of the indeterminacy of the nomenclature, we can observe that the *ṣifa/naʿt* are defined by their functions and are not members of a specific form class; we may compare this with the categories of *ẓarf*, see Mosel 1975, 345–62 and the *ḥāl*, ibid., 258–80. For this reason these elements do not appear as "parts of speech" when these are defined by the grammarians, cf. [208] (a).

[302] (a) This is a rather sloppy paraphrase of Ibn Jinnī's verdict on Sībawayhi's place in grammatical science, which is worth reproducing more fully: "Suffice it to mention in this regard the story of Sībawayhi, who assembled in his *Kitāb*—which filled a thousand leaves—a wholly original science and a composition which went beyond all that had been heard or seen before. Yet it is rare for any quotation (*ḥikāya*) to be attributed to him, or

tradition (*riwāya*) to be connected with him, except for isolated rarities with no importance or value," going on to say that Sībawayhi was trusted so much by his successors that his truthfulness was never questioned, hence there are no stories about him. In other words, the contents of the "Book" survived but not the person of the author, and Sībawayhi remained outside the *isnād* system by which knowledge was transmitted personally, probably because the *Kitāb* itself became the ultimate source of data and theory.

[302] (b) The *Rasā'il* of Ibn al-Mu'tazz were inaccessible, so no further detail can be provided. However, the lines can be translated as:

> If I wished, I could be like Zayd with his inheritance calculations, or Nu'man when other legal devices fail, or Ḫalīl as a prosodist and possessor of insights, or Kisā'ī with his grammar and his grammatical causes."

Zayd here is al-Ḍaḥḥāk (d. ca 45/666, Sezgin, *GAS* 1, 401) and Nu'mān is Abū Ḥanīfa (*GAS* 1, 409 and see [135]f), early jurists famous for their skills in determining inheritances and devising subtle legal evasions respectively; al-Ḍaḥḥāk here is not the same as the Abū 'Āṣim al-Ḍaḥḥāk involved in an incident with Abū Ḥanīfa, see [146]f.

[302] (c) Transmission and reception of the *Kitāb*. Humbert 1990, 1993 and especially 1995 gives a very detailed coverage of what is known about the life of Sībawayhi, and the manuscript tradition of the *Kitāb*, examining more than seventy manuscripts. One fascinating discovery is that there were two separate manuscript traditions, an "Eastern" one associated with Zamaḫšarī and a "Western" (i.e., Andalusian) one associated with Rabāḥī, and that there were minor textual variants in the very first and last folios of the manuscript so that the reader could quickly check which tradition it belonged to (Humbert 1995, 57f, 104).

The *Kitāb* did not immediately achieve its lofty status, but was in occultation for a few decades until it was brought to prominence by Mubarrad, see Bernards 1997. For a reception of a different kind, in our times, see Suleiman 2006 and [239] (b).

There is still no critical edition of the *Kitāb*. Derenbourg relied mainly on an 18th-century copy, and the Būlāq edition simply reproduces that of Derenbourg. The Hārūn edition, which is still not critical, differs in places from Derenbourg (example in Levin 1985, 124 n. 35), but little has been done on the text itself, apart from a correction in *Kitāb* §143 suggested by Bellamy 1968, who points out that even in the early centuries the Arab scholars had had their own textual problems to wrestle with (cf. Talmon 1984, 698). More work needs to be done to determine how much of the text is actually interpolated gloss or commentary. A whimsical article on the fifty interpretations of the opening words of the *Kitāb* is in Carter 2012b.

As for commentaries proper, that is not a topic for the present work, apart to mention that seventy-six authors of commentaries are listed by Sezgin in *GAS* 9, 1984, 58–63 and Suppl., where it will be apparent that hardly any of them have been published, and, needless to say, more will be found.

[303] (a) There is little point in trying to translate such a monster. A more simple example is found in the same work, showing how any element (though not under all conditions) in a basic sentence such as *aʿṭaytu zaydan dirhaman* can be topicalised, e.g., *anā aʿṭaytu zaydan dirhaman, zaydun aʿṭaytuhu dirhaman, al-muʿṭī zaydan dirhaman anā, allaḏī aʿṭaytuhu zaydan dirhamun* and so on. These exercises in topicalisation are perhaps designed to test the principle of falsifiablity which had intruded into grammar by Mubarrad's time, see [298] and Carter 1995, and contrast [217] above, where truth and falsehood are explicitly excluded from Sībawayhi's grammatical criteria. Goldenberg 1988 (2007), 67–69 outlines the practice as it developed after Mubarrad.

[303] (b) It is possible to find other virtues in [Ibn] al-Anbārī (d. 577/1181) to offset this rather superficial judgement: he was a devoted historian of his discipline, and a perceptive writer on the close interdependence of legal and grammatical theory.

[303] (c) Called "the Caliph of the Grammarians" *al-Farrāʾ Amīr al-Muʾminīn fī l-naḥw*, according to Baġdādī, *Taʾrīḫ Baġdād*, cited by the editors of *Maʿānī l-Qurʾān*, intro. 9, without precise attribution. This is as close as the "Kūfans" could come to matching the "Baṣrans," whose founding work, the *Kitāb*, earned the title "the Qurʾān of grammar," see [304] and n. (b)

[303] (d) For a complete list of all Farrāʾ's terminology see Kinberg 1996. The question of "Kūfan" and "Baṣran" schools does not strictly belong in this thesis, as they are a post-Sībawayhian phenomenon: the rare references to anonymous "Kūfans" (and there are none at all to "Baṣrans" except to al-Ḥaṣan [al-Baṣrī], see Troupeau 1976) do not justify the assumption that theoretical differences among grammarians were substantial enough to speak of "schools" in Sībawayhi's time, *pace* Talmon in [17] (a).

Even after Sībawayhi their allegedly distinctive terminologies are of no diagnostic value, as terms are used indiscriminately by grammarians of both schools, see Carter 1973b. The emergence of systematic grammar from the environment of Qur'anic exegesis is set out in detail by Versteegh 1993, and Talmon 2003 proposes the existence of an "old Iraqi school," but these back-projections come with the same caveats as the origins of the Ḥadīṯ and early legal thinking, cf. [17] (a).

[304] (a) *hal rakibta l-baḥr?*

[304] (b) Curiously this same honour was also accorded earlier to Ḥammād ibn Salama, see Sezgin *GAS* 9, 43 for sources, and above [134]–[136] on his connection with Sībawayhi.

[305] (a) The discussion here has now been overtaken by a number of special studies of *isnād*, on which see [70] (a).

For other aspects of predication see [202] (*jumla* and *kalām*); [58] (sentence types); [123], [219] (definiteness); [123] (b) (copula issues).

[305] (b) Derenbourg notes the reading of the Paris MS A but rejects it without comment. Hārūn 2, 126 follows Būlāq, who follows Derenbourg, but Jahn, n. 3 on §132, prefers the MSS A and B (St. Petersburg) reading, which we have also adopted here, following

Sīrāfī's commentary on this line (MS Atif Effendi 2548, 189b 7). Secondary sources seem to be unaware of the variant.

[306] (a) See [44]f. and [45] (b) For "phonological" here "morphophonological" would be more appropriate.

[306] (b) Here as elswhere read "dependent" for "direct" denoting the *naṣb*, see [298] (a).

[308] (a) Heard from a Bedouin, "As for [being] the son of a Muzanī woman, well, I am the son of a Muzanī woman." See Carter 2015, 38.

[308] (b) "Man sah ein, dass Sibawaihi den Tyrannen noch übertyrannte, d.i. von unserer Art zu deduciren und construiren noch weit mehr abwich." Once again, an over-hasty reading of Jahn has led to a probable misinterpretation: these views are Jahn's paraphrase of his critics, who disparaged his *Kitāb* translation just as they had also done with his edition of Ibn Ya'īš. There is only one "tyrant" here, Ibn Ya'īš; nevertheless, the statement does reflect a widely held position on Sībawayhi.

[309] (a) Troupeau 1960–63 has gathered all the various periphrastic expressions for time and tense (though without indicating the page numbers in the *Kitāb*). The tenses as defined in the opening chapter of the *Kitāb* scarcely match our own neat and tidy tripartite system: although the system is clearly aspectual in nature, the chief stumbling block for the Western observer is that the imperative, imperfect and unmarked future forms are all lumped together in one category, while the marked future is not mentioned at all as a verb class, because it is formed by preposing *sawfa* or prefixing *sa-* to the imperfect. Later grammarians simply imposed the imported tense system upon the verb, cf. Versteegh 1995, 65f, 140f.

It is worth mentioning, in this light, that the examples of the *muḥāl* utterance involving tense in [232], viz. *ataytuka ġadan* and *sa-ātīka amsi* are not purely a lexical issue but rather a formal, morphological one: the adverbial qualifiers here are inconsistent with the temporal implications of the verb forms, so they can never make any sense to the listener.

[310] (a) May this fine specimen of *petitio principii* be forgiven after the toils of the previous three hundred pages.

[310] (b) The secondary sources quoted in the following pages could probably be updated, but would still be saying the same thing, so they will not be augmented here. See also below, [313] (b).

[312] (a) Originally inserted as "*Tropika*"!

[312] (b) Corrected from the erroneous Ṯābit ibn Qurra.

[313] (a) Troupeau 1976 lists only two occurrences of this notion, once as a verb and once as a participle.

[313] (b) Since this was written it has become clear that the interaction of grammar and law was more profound that the impression given here. In Carter 2003 it is shown that certain elements of legal theory were consciously adopted by grammarians, reflecting their legal *maḏhab*.

Given the very close interdependence of the "Islamic sciences" as outlined in Larcher 2000, it is perhaps useful to nominate a few monographs in which the linguistic foundations of this relationship have been given the attention they deserve, viz. (in chronological order), Weiss 1992, Larkin 1995, Gwynne 2004, Vishanoff 2011, Zysow 2013. These also supply rich bibliographical resources for further exploration.

[313] (c) Jahn, *Kitāb* 1, vii.

[314] (a) Another example from the *Kitāb* (1, 231/270), in data for deflected relative clauses supplied by Ḫalīl: *mā anā bi-l-laḏī qā'ilun laka sū'an* and its variant *mā anā bi-l-laḏī qā'ilun laka qabīḥan* "I am not the one to be saying bad things to you." Here the ethical terms are used literally, while a couple of lines above Sībawayhi has typically used *ḥasan* and *qabīḥ* in their technical sense, i.e., structurally correct or incorrect in the context of these very expressions, cf. [154] (a) on the metalanguage continuum.

These sentiments echo such Qur'anic injunctions as Sūra 17, 53 (quoted above [115]), *qul li-'ibādī yaqūlū llatī hiya aḥsanu* "say to my servants they should say that which is best," that is, speak nicely to the unbelievers.

It goes without saying that speaking good Arabic was a religious obligation, and those who mastered it were assured of a superior station in Paradise, see Fück 1955, 16.

[315] (a) "The history of grammar in the Middle Ages is a striking example showing how, in cultivating a science, as also in dealing with a particular issue, people can set off on a path which takes them further and further from the truth, so that they find themselves, at the end of several centuries of effort, even further away from it than those who had gone before them."

Bibliography

Abbot, N., *The Rise of the North Arabic Script and Its Kur'anic development, with a Full Description of the Kur'an Manuscripts in the Oriental Institute*, Chicago, 1939.

'Abd al-Ḥamīd, *Rasā'il*, in *Jamharat rasā'il al-'Arab*, ed. A. Z. Ṣafwat, Cairo, 1937, 2, 432–555.

Abū Ṭayyib, 'Abd al-Wāḥid ibn 'Alī al-Luġawī, *Marātib al-naḥwiyyīn*, ed. M. Abū al-Faḍl Ibrāhīm, Cairo 1955.

Abū Yūsuf, al-Qāḍī, (1), *Kitāb al-Ḫarāj*, Būlāq, 1302.

Idem (2), *Kitāb al-Ḫarāj*, 3rd ed., Cairo, 1382.

Ackrill, J. L., *Aristotle's Categories and De Interpretation*, Oxford, 1963.

Afnan, S., "The Commentary of Avicenna on Aristotle's Poetics," *Journal of the Royal Asiatic Society*, 1947, 188–90.

Idem, *Philosophical Terminology in Arabic and Persian*, Leiden, 1964.

Aġānī, see Iṣfahānī.

Amīn, A., *Ḍuḥā al-Islām*, 6th ed., 3 vols., Cairo, 1961.

Anbārī, Abū al-Barakāt ibn al-Anbārī, *[Kitāb al-Inṣāf fī masā'il al-ḫilāf bayn al-naḥwiyyīn al-Baṣriyyīn wa-l-Kūfiyyīn], Die grammatischen Streitfragen der Basrer und Kufer*, ed. G. Weil, Leiden, 1913.

Idem, *Nuzhat al-alibbā' fī ṭabaqāt al-udabā,'* ed. M. Abū al-Faḍl Ibrāhīm, Cairo [1967].

Aristotle, *Ethica Nicomachea, in The Works of Aristotle, translated into English under the Editorship of W.D. Ross*, vol. 9, Oxford, 1925.

Arnaldez, R., *Grammaire et théologie chez Ibn Ḥazm de Cordoue, essai sur la structure et les conditions de la pensée musulmane*, Paris, 1956.

Baġdādī, 'Abd al-Qādir ibn 'Umar, *Ḫizānat al-adab wa-lubb lubāb lisān al-'Arab*, 4 vols., Bulaq, 1299.

Baġdādī, al-Ḥāfiẓ Abū Bakr Aḥmad ibn 'Alī al-Ḫaṭīb, *Ta'riḫ Baġdād aw Madīnat al-Salām*, 14 vols., Cairo/Baghdad, 1931.

Bāqillānī, Abū Bakr Muḥammad ibn al-Ṭayyib, *I'jāz al-Qur'ān*, ed. S. Aḥmad Ṣaqr, Cairo, [1954].

Beck, E., "Der 'uṯmānische Kodex in der Koranlesung des zweiten Jahrhunderts," *Orientalia* (NS) 14, (1945), 355–73.

[317] Beck, E., "Die Partikel *iḏan* bei al-Farrā' und Sībawayh," *Orientalia* (NS) 15, (1946), 432–38.

Idem, Review of W. Reuschel, *Al-Ḫalīl ibn-Aḥmad, der Lehrer Sībawayhs, als Grammatiker*, *Orientalia* (N.S) 29 (1960), 352–54.

Beeston, A. F. L., Review of W. Reuschel, *Al-Ḫalīl ibn-Aḥmad, der Lehrer Sībawayhs, als Grammatiker*, *Bulletin of the School of Oriental and African Studies* 25 (1962), 343–47.

Bergsträsser, G. G., *Bergsträssers Grundzüge des islamischen Rechts*, ed. J. Schacht, Berlin/Leipzig 1935.

Besthorn, R., "Aristotles og de arabiske Grammatikere," in *Festskrift til V. Thomsen fra Disciple*, Copenhagen, 1894, 166–72.

Bloomfield, L., *Language*, 3rd ed., London, 1957.

Brockelmann, C., *Geschichte der arabischen Litteratur*, 2 vols., Leiden, 1943–1949, Supplement, 3 vols., Leiden, 1937–1942.

Idem, "Beitrage zur Geschichte der arabischen Sprachwissenschaft," *Zeitschrift für Assyriologie* 13 (1898), 29–46.

De Sacy, Baron S., *Alfiyya*, see Ibn Mālik.

Idem, *Anthologie grammaticale arabe, ou morceaux choisis de divers grammairiens et scholiastes arabes*, Paris 1829.

Idem, *Grammaire arabe*, 3rd ed., revised L. Machuel, Tunis, 1905, (essentially a reprint of the 2nd ed., Paris 1831).

Dieterici, F., *Ibn ʿAḳīl's Commentar zur Alfijja des Ibn Mālik, aus dem arabischen zum ersten Male übersetzt*, Berlin, 1852.

EI[1], *The Encyclopedia of Islam*, 1st ed., 4 vols. and supplement, ed. Th. Houtsma and others, London/ Leiden, 1913–1938.

EI[2] *The Encyclopedia of Islam*, 2nd ed., ed. H. A. R. Gibb and others, Leiden/London, 1960–2009.

Ewald, G. H. A., Review of Silvestre de Sacy, *Anthologie grammaticale*, *Göttingische gelehrte Anzeigen* 1830, 801–9.

Fākihī, ʿAbdullāh, *Ḥudūd al-naḥw*, ed. A. Sprenger, Calcutta, 1849.

Fārābī, Abū Naṣr Muḥammad ibn Muḥammad, *Iḥṣāʾ al-ʿulūm*, ed. A. G. Palencia, 2nd ed., Madrid/ Granada, 1953.

Farrā,ʾ Abū Zakariyyā Yaḥyā ibn Ziyād, *Maʿānī al-Qurʾān*, 3 vols., ed. A. Y. Najātī and M. ʿA. al-Najjār, Cairo, 1955–1973.

[318] Fischer, J. B., "The Origin of Tripartite Division of Speech in Semitic Grammar," *Jewish Quarterly Review* (N.S.), 53 (1962–63), 1–21, and 54 (1963–64), 132–60.

Fischer, W., Review of W. Reuschel, *Al-Ḫalīl ibn-Aḥmad, der Lehrer Sībawayhs, als Grammatiker*, *Zeitschrift der deutschen morgenländischen Gesellschaft* 113 (1963), 271–73.

Fleisch, H., "Esquisse d'un historique de la grammaire arabe," *Arabica* 4 (1957), 1–22.

Idem, "Observations sur les études philologiques en arabe classique," *Oriens* 16 (1963), 134–44.

Fleischer, H. L., *Kleinere Schriften*, 3 vols., Leipzig, 1885–1888, repr. Osnabrück, 1968.

Flügel, G., *Die grammatischen Schulen der Araber. Erste Abteilung, die Schulen von Baṣra und Kūfa und die gemischte Schule*, Leipzig, 1862.

Fück, J., *Arabīya, Untersuchungen zur arabischen Sprach- und Stilgeschichte*, Berlin, 1950.

Fyzee, A. A. A., *Outlines of Muhammadan Law*, 3rd ed., Oxford, 1964.

Gibb, H. A. R., *Arabic Literature, an Introduction*, 2nd ed., Oxford, 1963.

Idem, "Constitutional Organization, the Muslim Community and the State," in *Law in the Middle East*, ed. M. Khadduri and H. J. Liebesny, vol. 1, Washington, 1955, 3–27.

Idem, *Studies in the Civilization of Islam*, ed. S. J. Shaw and W. R. Polk, London, 1962.

Glazer, S., "A Noteworthy Passage from an Arab Grammatical Text," *Journal of the American Oriental Society* 62 (1942), 106–8.

Goldziher, I., "Beiträge zur Geschichte der Sprachgelehrsamkeit bei den Arabern," *Sitzungsberichte der kaiserlichen Akademie zu Wien*, 1871, 207–51.

[319] Idem, "Das Prinzip des *istiṣḥāb* in der muhammedanischen Gesetzwissenschaft," *Wiener Zeitschrift für die Kunde des Morgenlandes* 1 (1887), 228–36.

Idem, *Muhammedanische Studien*, 2 vols., Halle a. S., 1889–1890.
Goshen-Gottstein, M., "Structure Analysis in Medieval Arabic Linguistic Theory," *Preprints for the 9th Int. Congress of Linguists*, [1962], 365–71.
Gottheil, R., and Worrel, W. H., *Fragments from the Cairo Geniza in the Freer Collection*, New York, 1927.
Ḥadīṯī, Ḫadīja, *Abniyat al-ṣarf fī Kitāb Sībawayhi*, Baghdad, 1965.
Idem, *Kitāb Sībawayhi wa-šurūḥuhu*, Baghdad, 1967.
Hartmann, M., "Zum *Kitāb* des Sībawayhi," *Zeitschrift für Assyriologie* 11 (1896), 63–68.
Ibn Abī al-Wafā' al-Qurašī, 'Abd al-Qādir, *Al-Jawāhir al-muḍī'a fī ṭabaqāt al-Ḥanafiyya*, 2 vols., Hyderabad, 1332.
Ibn Fāris, *Kitāb al-Ṣāḥibī fī fiqh al-luġa*, ed. M. Chouémi, Beirut, 1963.
Ibn Ḥajar al-'Asqalānī, Šihāb al-Dīn, *Tahḏīb al-tahḏīb*, 6 vols., Hyderabad, 1325.
Ibn Jinnī, Abū al-Fatḥ 'Uṯmān, *Al-Ḫaṣā'iṣ*, ed. M. 'A. al-Najjār, 3 vols., Cairo, 1952–1956.
Ibn Ḫaldūn, *Al-Muqaddima*, Cairo, n.d.
Ibn Ḫallikān, *Wafayāt al-a'yān*, trans. MacGuckin de Slane, 4 vols., Paris/London, 1842–1871.
Ibn Maḍā' al-Qurṭubī, *Kitāb al-Radd 'alā l-nuḥāh*, ed. Shawqī Ḍayf, Cairo, 1947.
Ibn Mālik, Jamāl al-Dīn Muḥammad, *Alfiyya*, ed. Silvestre de Sacy, Paris/London, 1833.
Ibn al-Muqaffa', *Al-adab al-Kabīr*, in *Al-adab al-Ṣaġīr wa-l-adab al-Kabīr*, ed. Beirut, 1960.
Idem, *Al-adab al-Ṣaġīr*, see previous item.
Idem, *Kalīla wa-Dimna*, (C) ed. Cairo, n.d., foreword by Muḥammad Tawfīq 'Izz.
Idem, (S) *Kalīla wa-Dimna*, ed. Louis Cheikho, Beirut 1905.
Idem, (Y) *Kalīla wa-Dimna*, ed. Ḫalīl al-Yāzijī, Beirut, 1884.
[320] Idem, *Risāla fī l-saḥāba*, in *Jamharat rasā'il al-'Arab*, ed. A. Z. Ṣafwat, Cairo, 1937, 3, 25–47.
Ibn al-Mu'tazz, *Rasā'il Ibn al-Mu'tazz fī l-naqd wa-l-adab wa-l-ijtimā'*, ed. M. 'Abd al-Mun'im al-Ḫafājī, Cairo, 1946.
Ibn al-Nadīm, *Fihrist*, Cairo n.d.
Ibn Qutayba, Abū Muḥammad 'Abdullāh ibn Muslim, *Kitāb al-Ma'ārif*, ed. Saroit Okasha (Ṯarwat 'Ukāša), Cairo, 1960.
Ibn Sa'd, *Kitāb al-Ṭabaqāt al-kabīr*, ed. E. Sachau and others, 8 vols., Leiden, 1905–1915.
Ibn Ya'īš, *Šarḥ al-Mufaṣṣal*, 10 vols., Cairo, n.d.
Ibrāhīm Muṣṭafā, "Le premier grammairien arabe," *Actes du XXIe Congrès des Orientalistes*, Paris, 1948.
Iṣfahānī, Abū al-Faraj, *Kitāb al-Aġānī*, 24 vols., ed. Cairo 1927–74.
Izutsu, T., *Ethico-religious Concepts in the Qur'an*, Montreal, 1966.
Jāḥiẓ, Abū 'Uṯmān 'Amr ibn Baḥr, *Al-Bayān wa-l-tabyīn*, ed. 'Abd al-Salām Hārūn, 4 vols., Cairo, 1948.
Jahn, G., see under Sībawayhi.
Idem, *Zum Verständnis des Sībawayhi*, Berlin, 1894, (issued with vol. 2 of the *Kitāb*).
Jurjānī, 'Abd al-Qāhir, *Dalā'il al-i'jāz fī 'ilm al-ma'ānī*, ed. M. R. Riḍā, Cairo, 1961.
Ḫalaf al-Aḥmar, *Muqaddima fī l-naḥw*, ed. 'Izz al-Dīn al-Tanūḫī, Damascus, 1961.
Ḫwārizmī, *Liber Mafātīḥ al-'olūm, explicans vocabula technica scientiarum tam Arabum quam peregrinorum*, ed. G. van Vloten, Leiden, 1895.
Kitāb, see under Sībawayhi. References to the *Kitāb* give the page of the Derenbourg edition, followed by that of the Būlāq edition.
Köbert, R., "Gedanken zum semitischen Wort- und Satzbau," *Orientalia* (NS) 14 (1945), 273–83.
Kramers, J. H., *Analecta Orientalia*, 2 vols., Leiden. 1954–1956.
Krenkow, F., "The Beginnings of Arabic Lexicography till the Time of al-Jauhari, with Special

Reference to the Work of Ibn Duraid," *Journal of the Royal Asiatic Society*, Centenary Supplement, 1924, 255–70.

[321] Loucel, H., "L'origine du langage d'après les grammairiens arabes," *Arabica* 10 (1963), 188–203, 253–81; 11 (1964), 57–72, 151–87.

Maḫzūmī, M., *Madrasat Kūfa wa-manhajuhā fī dirāsat al-luġa wa-l-naḥw*, 2nd ed., Cairo, 1958.

Idem, *Al-Ḫalīl ibn Aḥmad al-Farāhīdī, a'māluhu wa-manhajuhu*, Baghdad, 1960.

Margoliouth, D. S., "The Discussion between Abū Bišr Mattā and Abū Sa'īd al-Sīrāfī on the Merits of Logic and Grammar," *Journal of the Royal Asiatic Society* 1905, 79–129.

Idem, "Omar's Instructions to the Kadi," *Journal of the Royal Asiatic Society* 1910, 307–26.

Massignon, L., "Réflexions sur la structure primitive de l'analyse grammaticale en arabe," *Arabica* 1 (1954), 3–16.

Idem, "Notes sommaires sur la formation des noms abstraits en arabe et l'influence des modèles grecs," *Revue des Études Islamiques* 8 (1934), 507–12.

Merx, A., *Historia artis grammaticae apud Syros*, Leipzig, 1889.

Mez, A., *The Renaissance of Islam*, trans. S. K. Bakhsh and D. S. Margoliouth, Patna, 1937.

Mubārak, M., *Al-Rummānī al-naḥwī fī ḍaw' šarḥihi li-Kitāb Sībawayhi*, Damascus, 1963.

Mubarrad, Abū al-'Abbās, *Kitāb al-Muqtaḍab*, ed. M. 'Abd al-Ḫāliq 'Uḍayma, 4 vols., Cairo, 1964–1968.

Nāṣir al-Dīn Asad, *Maṣādir al-ši'r al-jāhilī wa-qīmatuhu al-ta'rīḫiyya*, Cairo, 1956.

Nicholas, B., *An Introduction to Roman Law*, Oxford, 1962.

Paton, G. W., *A Text-book of Jurisprudence*, 2nd ed., Oxford, 1951.

Pellat, C., *Langue et littérature arabes*, Paris, 1952.

Idem, *Le Milieu Baṣrien et la formation de Ǧāḥiẓ*, Paris, 1953.

Qifṭī, Jamāl al-Dīn, *Inbāh al-ruwāh 'alā anbāh al-nuḥāh*, 4 vols., ed. M. Abū al-Faḍl Ibrāhīm, Cairo, 1950–1973.

[322] Qudāma ibn Ja'far, *Naqd al-ši'r*, ed. Kamāl Muṣṭafā, Cairo, 1963.

Quṭrub, Ibn al Mustanīr, *Kitāb al-Aḍdād*, ed. H. Kofler, *Islamica* 5, (1932), 241–84, 385–461, 493–544.

Rabin, C., *Ancient West-Arabian, a Study of the Dialects of the Western Highlands of Arabia in the sixth and seventh Centuries A.D.*, London, 1951.

Reckendorf, H., *Arabische Syntax*, Heidelberg, 1921.

Rescher, O., "Studien über Ibn Ǧinnī und sein Verhältnis zu den Theorien der Baṣrī und Baġdādī," *Zeitschrift für Assyriologie* 23 (1909), 1–54.

Reuschel, W., *Al-Ḫalīl ibn-Aḥmad der Lehrer Sībawayhs, als Grammatiker*, Berlin, 1959.

Robins, R. H., *General Linguistics, an Introductory Survey*, London, 1964.

Ṣafwat, Aḥmad Zakī, *Jamharat rasā'il al-'Arab*, 4 vols , Cairo, 1937.

Ṣāliḥ al-Aštar, "Ibn Hišām anḥā min Sībawayhi," *Revue de l'Académie arabe de Damas* 40 (1965), 295–309.

Schacht, J., *The Origins of Muhammadan Jurisprudence*, Oxford, 1959.

Segal, J. B., *The Diacritical Point and the Accents in Syriac*, Oxford/London, 1953.

Sezgin, F., *Geschichte des arabischen Schrifttums*, 12 vols., Leiden, 1967–2000.

Šaybānī, Muḥammad ibn al-Ḥasan, *Juz' min al-Amālī li-l-šayḫ Muḥammad ibn al-Ḥasan al-Šaybānī*, Hyderabad, 1360.

Idem, *Kitāb al-Jāmi' al-Ṣaġīr fī l-fiqh*, on the margin of Abū Yūsuf, *Kitāb al-Ḫarāj*, Būlāq, 1302.

Idem, *Kitāb al-Maḫārij fī l-ḥiyal*, ed. J. Schacht, Leipzig, 1930.

Idem, *Al-Muwaṭṭa' li-l-Imām Muḥammad ma'a l-ta'līq al-mumajjad 'alā Muwaṭṭa' Muḥammad*, ed. 'Abd al-Ḥayy al-Laknawī, Karachi, n.d.

Šarīšī, Abū al-ʿAbbās al-Qaysī, *Šarḥ Maqāmāt al-Ḥarīrī al-Baṣrī*, ed. M. ʿAbd al-Munʿim al-Ḫafājī, 4 vols., Cairo, 1952.

Sībawayhi, Abū Bišr ʿAmr ibn ʿUṯmān ibn Qanbar, *Le Livre de Sībawayhi, traité de grammaire arabe par Sibouya, dit Sībawayhi, texte arabe*, ed. H. Derenbourg, 2 vols., Paris, 1881–1889.

Idem, *Sībawayhi's Buch über die Grammatik, übersetzt und erklärt von G. Jahn*, 2 vols., Berlin, 1895–1900.

[323] Idem, *Al-Kitāb*, with Šantamarī, *ʿAyn al-ḏahab min maʿdan jawhar al-adab fī ʿilm majāzāt al-ʿArab*, 2 vols., Būlāq, 1316–1318, repr. Baghdad, 1965.

Idem, *Al-Kitāb*, ed. ʿAbd al-Salām Hārūn, Cairo, 5 vols., 1966–1977, repr. several times.

Sīrāfī, Abū Saʿīd al-Ḥasan ibn ʿAbdullāh, *Kitāb Aḫbār al-naḥwiyyīn al-Baṣriyyīn*, ed. F. Krenkow, Paris/ Beirut, 1936.

Stein, P., *Regulae juris, from Juristic Rules to Legal Maxims*, Edinburgh, 1966.

Suyūṭī, Jalāl al-Dīn, *Buġyat al-wuʿāh fī ṭabaqāt al-luġawiyyīn wa-l-nuḥāh*, 2 vols., ed. M. Abū al-Faḍl Ibrāhīm, Cairo, 1964–1965.

Idem, *Kitāb al-Iqtirāḥ fī ʿilm uṣūl al-naḥw*, 2nd ed., Hyderabad, 1359.

Idem, *Al-Muzhir fī ʿulūm al-luġa wa-anwāʿihā*, 2 vols., ed. M. A. Jād al-Mawlā, ʿA. M. al-Bajāwī and M. Abū al-Faḍl Ibrāhīm, Cairo, n.d.

Ṭabarī, Abū Jaʿfar Muḥammad ibn Jarīr, *Das Konstantinopler Fragment des Kitāb Iḫtilaf al-Fuqahā,*' ed. J. Schacht, Leiden 1933.

Tawḥīdī, Abū Ḥayyān, *Al-Baṣāʾir wa-l-ḏaḫāʾir*, ed. A. Amīn and A. Ṣaqr, Cairo, 1953.

Idem, *Kitāb al-Imtāʿ wa-l-muʾānasa*, 3 vols., ed. A. Amīn and A. al-Zayn, Cairo, n.d., repr. Beirut, 1967.

Idem, *Kitāb al-Muqābasāt*, ed. Ḥ. al-Sandūbī, Cairo, 1929.

Ṯaʿlab, Abū al-ʿAbbās, *Majālis al-ʿulamā,*' ed. ʿAbd al-Salām Hārūn, 2 vols., 2nd ed., Cairo, 1960.

Thurot, G., Notices et extraits de divers manuscrits latins pour servir à l'histoire des doctrines grammaticales au moyen âge, Paris, 1868, *Notices et extraits des manuscrits de la Bibliothèque Royale*, vol. 22, pt. 2.

Troupeau, G., "Le commentaire d'al-Sīrāfī sur le chapitre 565 du *Kitāb* de Sībawayhi," *Arabica* 5, (1958), 168–82.

Idem, "À propos des grammairiens cités par Sībawayhi dans le *Kitāb*," *Arabica* 8, (1961), 309–12.

Idem, "Deux traités grammaticaux arabes traduits en latin," *Arabica* 10 (1963), 225–36.

Trumpp, E., Über den arabischen Satzbau nach der Anschauung der arabischen Grammatiker," *Sitzungsberichte der bayrischen Akademie*, 1879, 2, pt. 2, 309–98.

Vesey-Fitzgerald, S. G., "Nature and Sources of the Sunna," in *Law in the Middle East*, ed. M. Khadduri and H. J. Liebesny, vol. 1, Washington, 1955, 85–112.

Idem, "The Alleged Debt of Islamic to Roman Law," *Law Quarterly Review* 67 (1951), 81–102.

Walzer, R., "New light on the Arabic translations of Aristotle," *Oriens* 6, (1953), 91–142 (also in Walzer, R. *Greek into Arabic. Essays on Islamic Philosophy*, Oxford, 1962, 60–113).

[324] Wehr, H., "Der arabische Elativ," in *Abhandlungen der Geistes- und Sozial-wissenschaftlischen Klasse der Akademie der Wissenschaft und der Literatur in Mainz*, 1952, Heft 7, Wiesbaden, 1953.

Weil, G., "Zum Verständnis der Methode der moslemischen Grammatiker, ein Beitrag zur Geschichte der Wissenschaften in Islam," in *Festschrift für Eduard Sachau*, ed. G. Weil, Berlin, 1915, 380–92

Weil, *Inṣāf*, see Anbārī.

Weiss, J., "Die arabische Nationalgrammatik und die Lateiner," *Zeitschrift der deutschen morgenländischen Gesellschaft* 64 (1910), 349–90.

Williams, Glanville,"Language and the Law," in *Law Quarterly Review* 61 (1945), 71–86, 179–95, 293–303, 384–406; 62 (1946), 387, 406.

Yāfi'ī, Abū Muḥammad 'Afīf al-Dīn, *Mir'āt al-jinān wa-'ibrat al-yaqẓān*, 4 vols., Hyderabad, 1337–39.
Yāqūt, Šihāb al-Dīn, *Iršād al-arīb ilā ma'rifat al-adīb*, 7 vols., ed. D. S. Margoliouth, 2nd ed. London, 1923–1931, repr. Baghdad, n.d.
Zajjājī, Abū al-Qāsim, *Al-Īḍāḥ fī 'ilal al-naḥw*, ed. M. Mubārak, Cairo, 1959.
Idem, *Majālis al-'ulamā'*, ed. 'Abd al-Salām Hārūn, Kuwait, 1962.
Zakī, Aḥmad Kamāl, *Al-Ḥayāt al-adabiyya fī l-Baṣra ilā nihāyat al-qarn al-ṯānī al-hijrī*, Damascus, 1961.
Zamaḫšarī, *Al-Mufaṣṣal fī l-naḥw*, ed. J. F. Broch, Christianiae, 1879.
Zubaydī, Abū Bakr, *Ṭabaqāt al-naḥwiyyīn wa-l-luġawiyyīn*, ed. M. Abū al-Faḍl Ibrāhīm, Cairo, 1954.

The following works are listed for the sake of completeness, although they are not referred to in the thesis, either because they were unobtainable or irrelevant:

'Abd al-Wahhāb Ḥammūda, "Ḥawla baḥṯ awwal man waḍa'a al-naḥw," Majallat Kulliyat al-Ādāb, Jāmi'at Fu'ād al-Awwal 13 (1951), 133–44.
Aḥmad Aḥmad Badawī, *Sībawayhi, ḥayātuhu wa-Kitābuhu*, 2nd ed., Cairo n.d.
Praetorius, F. *Zum Verständnisse Sibawayh's*, Halle a. S., 1895.
Schaade, A., *Sibawayh's Lautlehre*, Leiden, 1911.
Sibawayhi, *Al-Kitāb, a Well-known Work in Arabic Grammar by Imam Abu Bashar Amar al-Sibawayh*, (Arabic text) ed. Mawlvi Kabir-uddin Ahmad, Calcutta, 1887.

Works Cited in the Addenda

Abboud, P. 1979. Sībawayhi's Notion of Grammaticality. *Al-'Arabiyya* 12, 58–67.
Al-Nassir, A. A. 1993. *Sibawayh the Phonologist*. London and New York.
Anṣārī, Aḥmad Makkī. 1972. *Sībawayhi wa-l-qirā'āt*. Cairo.
Auroux S. *et al.* (eds.). 2000. *History of the Language Sciences, 1*, Berlin, New York.
'Awwād, G. 1978. *Sībawayhi, imām al-nuḥāḥ fī āṯār al-dārisīn ḫilāl iṯnay 'ašar qarnan*. Baghdad.
Ayoub, Georgine. 1990. De ce qui 'ne se dit pas' dans le livre de Sībawayhi: la notion de *Tamṯīl*, in Versteegh/Carter, 1–15.
——. 2015. Some Aspects of the Relation between Enunciation and Utterance in Sībawayhi's *Kitāb*. A Modal Category: *wājib/ġayr al-wājib*, in Marogy/Versteegh, 6–35.
Baalbaki Ramzi. 1979. Some Aspects of Harmony and Hierarchy in Sībawayhi's *Kitāb*. *ZAL* 2, 7–22 (also in Baalbaki 2004, no. II),
——. 1981a. A Possible Early Reference to Sībawayhi's *Kitāb*. *ZDMG* 131, 114–18 (also in Baalbaki 2004, no. III).
——. 1981b. Arabic Grammatical Controversies and the Extant Sources of the Second and Third Centuries A.H., in W. al-Qāḍī (ed.), *Studia Arabica et Islamica. Festschrift for Iḥsān 'Abbās*. Beirut, 1–26 (also in Baalbaki 2004, no. XI).
——. 1982. *Tawahhum*, an Ambiguous Concept in Early Arabic Grammar. *BSOAS* 45, 233–44 (also in Baalbaki 2004, no. XII).
——. 1985. The treatment of *Qirā'āt* by the Second and Third Century Grammarians. *ZAL* 15, 11–32 (also in Baalbaki 2004, no. VI).
——. 1989. A Contribution to the Study of Technical Terms in Early Arabic Grammar: The Term

aṣl in Sībawayhi's *Kitāb*, in A. K. Irvine *et al.* (eds.), *A Miscellany of Middle Eastern Articles, in Memoriam Thomas Muir Johnstone 1924–1983*. London, 163–77 (also in Baalbaki 2004, no. IV).

——. 1995. The Book in the Grammatical Tradition. Development in content and methods, in George Atiyeh (ed.), *The Book in the Islamic World*, New York, 123–39 (also in Baalbaki 2004, no. I).

——. 1999a. A Note on a Controversial Passage in Sībawayhi's *Kitāb*, *ZAL* 37, 9–12.

——. 1999b. Coalescence as a Grammatical Tool in Sībawayhi's *Kitāb*, in Suleiman 1999a, 86–106 (also in Baalbaki 2004, no.V).

——. 2004. *Grammarians and Grammatical Theory in the Medieval Arabic Tradition*. Aldershot, Burlington.

——. (ed.). 2007. *The Early Islamic Grammatical Tradition*. Aldershot, Burlington.

——. 2008. *The Legacy of the Kitāb. Sībawayhi's Analytical Methods within the Context of Arabic Grammatical Theory*. Leiden, Boston.

Bakkā, M. K. 1989. *Manhaj Kitāb Sībawayhi fī l-taqwīm al-naḥwī*. Baghdad.

Bakalla, M. Ḥ. 1979. Sībawayhi's Contribution to the study of Arabic phonetics. *Al-'Arabiyya* 12, 68–76.

——. 1980. Some Phonetic Observations in Sībawaihi's Book of Arabic Grammar, in His *Introduction to Arabic Language and Literature*. Taipei, 25–45.

——. 1982. *Ibn Jinnī, an Early Arab Muslim Phonetician. An Interpretative Study of His Life and Contribution to Linguistics*. Taipei.

——. 1983. *Bibliography of Arabic Linguistics*. 2nd ed. London.

Belguedj, M. S. 1973. La démarche des premiers grammairiens arabes dans le domaine du syntaxe. *Arabica* 20, 168–85.

Bellamy, J. A. 1968. A Difficult Passage in Sībawayhi. *JAOS* 88, 239–43.

Bernards, M. 1997. *Changing Traditions. Al-Mubarrad's refutation of Sībawayhi and the Subsequent Reception of the Kitāb*. Leiden, New York, Köln.

Bezirgan, N. A. 1979. Some Logical Rules in *al-Kitāb*. *Al-'Arabiyya* 12, 77–82.

Bobzin, H. 1981. Zum Begriff der Valenz des Verbums. *Historiographia Linguistica* 8, 329–44. Republished in C. H. M. Versteegh *et al.* 1983, 93–108.

——, Kees [C. H. M.] Versteegh (eds.). 1985. *Studies in the History of Arabic Grammar, Proceedings of the First Symposium on the History of Arabic Grammar* (= ZAL 15). Wiesbaden. Cited as *ZAL* 15.

Bohas, G. (ed.). (1993). *Développements récents en linguistique arabe et sémitique*. Damascus.

——, Carter, M. G. 2004. Prolégomènes au *Kitāb* de Sībawayhi. *Langues et littératures du monde arabe* 5, 43–59.

——, J.-P. Guillaume, D. E. Kouloughli. 1990. *The Arabic Linguistic Tradition*. London and New York.

——, Kouloughli, D. E. (eds.). 2004. À propos du préambule au *Kitāb* de Sībawayhi, *Risālat Kitāb Sībawaihi. Langues et littératures du monde arabe* 5, Lyon.

Brockett, S. 1988. Qur'ān Readings in *Kitāb Sībawayhi*. *Occasional Papers of the School of Abbasid Studies, St. Andrews*, 2, 129–206.

Brown, J. 2009. Did the Prophet Say It or Not? The Literal, Historical and Effective truth of Ḥadīths in Early Sunnism. *JAOS* 129, 259–85.

Buburuzan, R. 1993. Exclamation et actes de langage chez Sībawayhi. *Revue Roumaine de Linguistique* 38, 421–37.

Carter, M. G. 1972a. Les origines de la grammaire arabe. *REI* 40, 62–97 (Eng. trans. in R. Baalbaki 2007, 1–26).

——. 1972b. Twenty dirhams in the *Kitāb* of Sībawayhi. *BSOAS* 35, 485–96.
——. 1973a. An Arab Grammarian of the Eighth Century A.D. *JAOS* 93, 146–57. (Arabic translation by Muḥammad Rašīd al-Ḥamzāwī appeared in *Dawliyyāt al-Jāmiʿa l-Tūnisiyya* 22, 1983, 223–45).
——. 1973b. *Ṣarf* et *ḫilāf*, contribution à l'histoire de la grammaire arabe. *Arabica* 20, 292–304.
——. 1974. Two Works Wrongly Attributed to Early Arab Grammarians. *Islamic Quarterly* 18, 11–13.
——. 1979. A Grammatical Experiment That Failed. *Arabica* 26, 267–73.
——. 1980. Sībawayhi and Modern Linguistics. *Histoire, Epistémologie, Langage* 2, 21–36.
——. 1981. The Use of Proper Names as a Testing Device in Sībawayhi's *Kitāb*. *Historiographia Linguistica* 8, 345–357. Republished in C. H. M. Versteegh *et al.* 1983, 109–20.
——. 1983. Language Control as People Control. *Al-Abhath* 31, 76–84.
——. 1985a. The Term *sabab* in Arabic Grammar. *ZAL* 15, 5366.
——. 1985b. When Did the Arabic Word *naḥw* First Come to Denote Grammar? *Language and Communication* 5, 265–77.
——. 1987/88. Arab Linguistics and Arabic Linguistics. *ZGAW* 4, 205–18.
——. 1989. The Arabic and Medieval Latin Grammatical Terms for "Governing," in K. D. Dutz (ed.), *Speculum historiographiae linguisticae, Kurzbeiträge der IV. Int. Konf. zur Geschichte der Sprachwissenschaften* (ICHoLS IV), Trier, 24.-27. August 1987. Münster. 29–36.
——. 1990. *Qāḍī, qāḍi, qāḍ*, Which Is the Odd Man Out? in Versteegh/Carter, 73–85.
——. 1991. The Ethical Basis of Arabic Grammar. *Al-Karmil* 12, 9–22.
——. 1993. Probleme bei der Übersetzung von Fachsprache am Beispiel des Arabischen, in A. M. Frank *et al.* (eds.), *Übersetzen, verstehen, Brücken bauen. Geisteswissenschaftliches und literarisches Übersetzen im internationalen Kulturaustausch*. Berlin, 130–41.
——. 1994. Writing the History of Arabic Grammar. *Historiographia Linguistica* 21, 385–414.
——. 1995. Predication Tests, Copula, and a Link with Aš'arism, in A. Fodor (ed.), *Proceedings of the 14th Congress of the Union Européenne des Arabisants et Islamisants*. Pt. 1, Budapest, 23–36.
——. 1996. Sībawayhi. *Encyclopaedia of Islam*. 2nd ed., vol. 9, 524–31.
——. 1997. Copula in Arabic grammar, in W. Madelung *et al.* (eds.), *Proceedings of the 17th Congress of the UEAI*. St. Petersburg, 37–45.
——. 1998a. Another Khalīl, Courtier, Teacher and Sage, in K. C. Ryding, 16–43.
——. 1998b. The Term *muḍāriʿ* in the *Kitāb* of Sībawayhi, in K. Dévényi, T. Iványi (eds.), *Proceedings of the Arabic and Islamic Section of the 35th International Congress of Asian and North African Studies (ICANAS)*. Part One, Linguistics, Literature, History. Budapest, 3–14.
——. 2002. Patterns of Reasoning: Sibawayhi's Analysis of the *ḥāl*, in K. Dévényi (ed.), *Proceedings of the 20th Congress of the Union of European Arabists and Islamicists, Part One, Linguistics, Literature, History*. Budapest, (= *The Arabist*, vol. 24–25), 3–15.
——. 2003. Legal Schools and Grammatical Theory, in S. Evstatiev (ed.), *Arabistika i Isliamoznanie. Tom 2. Studi po sluchai 60-godishnata dots. d.f.n. Penka Samsareva*. Sofia, 177–83.
——. 2004. *Sībawayhi*. London, New York.
——. 2006. Approaches to the Technical Terms of Arabic Grammar, in B. Michalak-Pikulska, A. Pikulski (eds.), *Authority, Privacy and Public Order in Islam. Proceedings of the 22nd Congress of L'Union Européenne des Arabisants et Islamisants*. Leuven, Paris, Dudley, 459–67.
——. 2007. Pragmatics and Contractual Language in Early Arabic Grammar and Legal Theory, in Ditters/Motzki, 26–44.
——. 2011. Indirect Questions and Reported Speech: A Problem for Arabic Grammatical Theory, in A. A. Avram *et al.* (eds.), *A Festschrift for Nadia Anghelescu*. Bucharest, 118–33.

——. 2012a. Sentence Types in Grammar, Law and Philosophy, in G. Contu (ed.), *Centre and Periphery witin the Borders of Islam. Proceedings of the 23rd Congress of L'Union Européenne des Arabisants et Islamisants*. Leuven, Paris, Walpole MA, 313–25.
——. 2012b. The Parsing of Sibawayhi's *Kitāb*, Title of Chapter 1, or Fifty Ways to Lose Your Reader, in Marogy, 101–18.
——. 2015. The Grammar of Affective Language in the *Kitāb*, in Marogy/Versteegh, 36–65.
Danecki, J. 1978. Early Arabic phonetical Theory. Phonetics of al-Ḫalīl ibn Aḥmad and Sībawaihi, *Rocznik Orientalistycny* 39, 51–56.
——. 1985. Indian Phonetical Theory and the Arab Grammarians, *Rocznik Orientalistycny* 46, 127–34.
Dayyeh, H. 2012. The Relation between Frequency of Usage and Deletion in Sībawayhi's *Kitāb*, in Marogy, 75–98.
——. 2015. *Ittisāʿ* in Sībawayhi's *Kitāb*: A Semantic *ʿilla* for Disorders in Meaning and Form, in Marogy/Versteegh, 66–80.
Diem, W. 1974. Nomen, Substantiv und Adjective bei den arabischen Grammatikern, *Oriens* 23–24, 312–332 (Eng. trans. in Baalbaki 2007, 279–99).
——. 1981. Bibliographie/Bibliography, Sekundärliteratur zur einheimischen arabischen Grammatikschreibung. *Historiographia Linguistica*, 8, 431–86. Republished in C. H. M. Versteegh *et al.* 1983, 195–250. Supplements by Versteegh in *ZAL*, 10, 11, 12, 14, 16 (1983–87).
Ditters, E., Motzki, H. (eds.). 2007. *Approaches to Arabic Linguistics. Presented to Kees Versteegh on the Occasion of His Sixtieth Birthday*. Leiden, Boston.
EALL: Versteegh C. H. M. et al. (eds.). 2006–2009. *Encyclopedia of Arabic Language and Linguistics*. 5 vols., Leiden, Boston. Also available online.
EI². *Encyclopaedia of Islam:* references are to the 2nd ed. (see original bibliography); a 3rd edition is now being produced online.
Endress, G. 1986. Grammatik und Logik. Arabische Philologie und griechische Philosophie im Widerstreit, in B. Mojsich (ed.), *Sprachphilosphie in Antike und Mittelalter*. Amsterdam, 163–299.
Fischer, August, Bräunlich, E. 1945. *Schawāhid-Indices. Indices der Reimwörter und der Dichter der in den Schawāhid-Kommentaren und in verwandten Werken erläuterten Belegverse*. Leipzig, Wien.
Fischer, Wolfdietrich. 1985. The Chapter on Grammar in the *Kitāb Mafātīḥ al-ʿUlūm*. *ZAL* 15, 94–103.
Goldenberg, G. 1988. Subject and Predicate in Arab Grammatical Tradition. *ZDMG* 138, 39–73 (also in Baalbaki 2007, 301–335).
Grunebaum, G. von. 1961. *Medieval Islam*. 2nd ed. Chicago.
Guillaume, J.-P. 1985. Fragments d'une grammaire oubliée: relations prédicatives non-assertées, verbe déclaratif et verbes modaux d'après Sībawayhi (première partie). *BEO* 35, 19–35.
——. 1986. Sībawayhi et l'énonciation, une proposition de lecture. *Histoire, Epistémologie, Langage* 8, 53–62.
——. 1988. Le discours tout entier est nom, verbe et particule: Élaboration et constitution de la théorie der parties du discours dans la tradition grammaticale arabe. *Langages* 92, 1988, 25–36 (Eng. trans. in Baalbaki 2007, 261–77).
——. 1993. Une lecture énonciative du *Kitāb* de Sībawayhi, in Bohas, 41–5.
——. 2001. La lexique technique de la tradition grammaticale arabe: questions de traduction. *Orbis, Supplementa* 17, 591–605.
——. 2004. Nouvelles élucubrations sur l'apport et le support. *Langues et littératures du monde arabe*, 69–79.

Gutas, D. 1999. *Greek Thought, Arabic Culture. The Graeco-Arabic Translation Movement in Baghdad and Early 'Abbāsid Society (2nd-4th/8th-10th centuries)*. London, New York.

Gwynne, Rosalind W. 1990. The *a fortiori* Argument in *naḥw*, *fiqh* and *kalām*, in Versteegh/Carter, 165–177.

——. 2004. *Logic, Rhetoric and Legal Reasoning in the Qur'ān. God's Arguments*. London/New York.

Ḥadīṯī, Ḫ. 1975. *Sībawayhi, ḥayātuhu wa-kitābuhu*, Baghdad.

Haldar, Alfred. 1973. Bemerkungen zur frühen grammatikalischen Bearbeitung der semitischen Sprachen, in M. A. Beek *et al.* (eds.), *Symbolae biblicae et mesopotamicae Francisco Mario Theodoro di Liagre Böhl dedicatae*. Leiden, 169–179.

Ḥannā, J. Ḥ. 1984. *Mu'jam šawāhid al-nāḥw al-ši'riyya*. Riyadh.

Hārūn, 'A. S. 1972–3. *Mu'jam šawāhid al-'arabiyya*. 2 vols. Cairo.

Hnid, M. 2012. Spatial Language in the *Kitāb* of Sībawayhi—The Case of the Preposition *fī*/in, in Marogy, 59–74.

Humbert, G. 1990. Remarques sur les éditions du *Kitāb* de Sībawayhi et leur base manuscrite, in Versteegh/Carter, 179–94.

——. 1993. Un témoignage fossile du *Kitāb* de Sībawayhi, in Bohas, 121–39.

——. 1995. *Les voies de transmission du Kitāb de Sībawayhi*. Leiden, New York, Köln.

[Ibn] al-Anbārī. 1957. *Asrār al-'arabiyya*, ed. M. B. al-Bayṭār. Damascus.

Ibn Durayd. 1958. *al-Ištiqāq*, ed. 'A. S. Hārūn. Cairo.

Ibn Qutayba. 1900. *Adab al-kātib*, ed. M. T. Grünert. Leiden (pagination also in margin of ed. M. D. 'Abd al-Ḥamīd, Cairo 1963).

Iványi, T. 1991. *Qad yaǧūz fī š-ši'r*: on the Linguistic Background of the So-Called Poetic Licences in Sībawayhi's *Kitāb*, in K. Dévényi, T. Iványi (eds.), *Proceedings of the Colloquium on Arabic Grammar, Budapest 1–7 September 1991* (= *The Arabist* vol. 3–4), Budapest, 201–16.

Jum'a, Ḫ. 'A. K. 1980. *Šawāhid al-ši'r fī Kitāb Sībawayhi*. Kuwayt.

Kasher, A. 2009. Sībawayhi's *tanwīn-naṣb* principle revisited. *ZAL* 51, 42–50.

——. 2012. The Term *maf'ūl* in Sībawayhi's *Kitāb*, in Marogy, 3–26.

Khoury, R. G. 1993. *Chrestomathie de papyrologie arabe, Documents relatifs à la vie privée, sociale et administrative dans les premiers siècles islamiques*. Leiden, New York, Köln.

Kinberg, N. 1996. *A Lexicon of al-Farrā''s Terminology in His Qur'ān Commentary With Full Definitions, English Summaries, and Extensive Citations*. Leiden, New York, Köln.

King, D. 2012. Elements of the Syriac Grammatical Tradition as These Relate to the Origins of Arabic Grammar, in Marogy, 189–209.

Kouloughli, D. E. 2002. On Locative Sentences in Arabic, *ZAL* 41, 7–26.

Larcher, P. 2000. Les relations entre la linguistique et les autres sciences dans la société arabo-islamique, in Auroux *et al.* 1, 312–318 (Eng. trans. in Baalbaki 2007, 337–48).

——. 2004–2005. Une formulation ancienne de la théorie grammaticale arabe: la *Risālat al-Kitāb* de Sībawayhi. http://aracapag. hypotheses.org/301.

——. 2007. Les origines de la grammaire arabe, selon la tradition: description, interprétation, discussion, in Ditters/Motzki, 113–34.

——. 2014. *Linguistique arabe et pragmatique*. Beirut, Damascus.

Larkin, Margaret. 1995. *The Theology of Meaning. 'Abd al-Qāhir al-Jurjānī's Theory of Discourse*. New Haven CT.

Law, Vivien. 1990. Indian Influence on Early Arab Phonetics—or Coincidence? in Versteegh/Carter, 215–27 (also in Baalbaki 2007, 121–33).

Leemhuis, F. 1973. Sībawaih's Treatment of the D Stem. *JSS* 18, 238–256.
Levin, A. 1979a. Sībawayhi's View of the Syntactic Structure of *kāna wa-axawātuhā*. *JSAI* 1, 185–213 (also in Levin 1998).
——. 1979b. The Meaning of *ta'addā l-fi'l 'ilā* in Sibāwayhi's *al-Kitāb*, in J. Blau *et al.* (eds.), *Studia Orientalia Memoriae D. H. Baneth Dedicata*. Jerusalem, 193–210 (also in Levin 1998).
——. 1981. The Grammatical Terms *al-Musnad, al-Musnad ilayhi* and *al-Isnād*. *JAOS* 101, 145–67 (also in Levin 1998).
——. 1986. The Medieval Term *kalima* and the Modern Linguistic Term Morpheme, Similarities and Differences, in M. Sharon (ed.), *Studies in Islamic History and Civilization in Honour of Professor David Ayalon*. Leiden, Jerusalem, 423–46 (also in Levin 1998).
——. 1992. The Authenticity of Sībawayhi's Description of the *imāla*. *JSAI* 15, 74–93 (also in Levin 1998).
——. 1994. Sībawayhi's Attitude to the Spoken Language. *JSAI* 17, 204–43 (also in Levin 1998).
——. 1995. The Fundamental Principles of the Arab Grammarians' Theory of *'amal*. *JSAI* 19, 214–232 (also in Levin 1998, Baalbaki 2007, 205–223).
——. 1998. *Arabic Linguistic Thought and Dialectology*. Jerusalem.
——. 2000a. Sībawayhi, in Auroux *et al.* 1, 252–263.
——. 2000b. The Meaning of *Ḥarf ǧā'a Li-Ma'nan*. *JSAI* 24, 22–48
——. 2007. Sībawayhi's View of the *ẓarf* as an *'āmil*, in Ditters/Motzki, 135–148
Machuel, L. 1908. *Vocabulaire des principaux termes techniques de la grammaire arabe*. Tunis.
Macuch, R. 1982. Greek Technical Terms in Arab Sciences. *Graeco-Arabica* 1, 11–34.
Mahdi, M. 1970. Language and Logic in Classical Islam, in G. E. von Grunebaum (ed.), *Logic in Classical Islamic Culture*. Wiesbaden, 51–83 (also in Baalbaki 2007, no. 7).
Marogy, A. E. 2004. Inversion, Definiteness and Case Assignment in Arabic Nominal Structure. The Classical Theory. *Al-'Arabiyya* 37, 77–99.
——. 2010. *Kitāb Sībawayhi. Syntax and Pragmatics*. Leiden, Boston.
——. (ed.). 2012a. *The Foundations of Arabic Linguistics. Sībawayhi and Early Arabic Grammatical Theory*. Leiden, Boston.
——. 2012b. Zayd, 'Amr and 'Abdullāhi: Theory of Proper Name and Reference in early Arabic Grammatical Tradition, in Marogy 2012a, 119–134
——, Kees [C. H. M.] Versteegh (eds.). 2015. *The Foundations of Arabic Linguistics II. Kitāb Sībawayhi: Interpretation and Transmission*. Leiden, Boston.
Meisami, J. S., Starkey, P. (eds.). 1998. *Encyclopedia of Arabic Literature*. 2 vols. London.
Mosel, U. 1975. *Die syntaktische Terminologie bei Sībawaih*. 2 vols. Munich.
——. 1980. Syntactic Categories in Sībawayhi's *Kitāb*. *HEL* 2, 27–37
Naffāḫ, A. R. 1970. *Fihris šawāhid Sībawayhi*. Beirut.
Nāṣif, 'A. N. 1979. *Sībawayhi imām al-nuḥāh*. 2nd ed. Cairo.
Noy, A. S. 2012. Don't Be Absurd: The Term *muḥāl* in Sībawayhi's *Kitāb*, in Marogy, 27–58.
Owens, J. 1990. *Early Arabic Grammatical Theory. Heterogeneity and Standardization*. Amsterdam.
Peled, Y. 1992. *'Amal* and *ibtidā'* in Medieval Arabic Grammatical Tradition. *Abr-Nahrain* 30, 146–71.
——. 1999. Aspects of the Use of Grammatical Terminology in Medieval Arabic Grammatical Tradition, in Suleiman, 50–85.
——. 2007. Problems in the medieval Arabic Theory of Sentence Types, in Ditters/Motzki, 149–88.
Rundgren, F. 1976. Über den griechischen Einfluß auf die arabische Nationalgrammatik. *Acta Universitatis Upsaliensis* N.S. 2, 119–44 (Eng. trans. in Baalbaki 2007, 75–99).

——. 1990. On a Grammatical Term in Sībawayh and What It Has to Tell Us, in E. Keck et al. (eds.), *Living Waters, Scandinavian Orientalistic Studies presented to Professor Dr. Frede Lökkegaard ...*, Copenhagen, 327–38.

Ryding, K. C. (ed.). 1998. *Early Medieval Arabic. Studies on al-Khalīl ibn Aḥmad*. Washington, DC.

Saad, G. 1979. Sībawayhi's Treatment of Transitivity. *Al-'Arabiyya* 12, 83–8.

Sara, S. 2007. *Sībawayh on ʔimālah 'Inclination'. Text, Translation, Notes and Analysis*. Edinburgh.

Semaan, K. 1968. *Linguistics in the Middle Ages, Phonetic Studies in Early Islam*. Leiden.

Suleiman Y. M. 1988. The Notion *'illa* in Arabic Linguistic Thinking. *British Society for Middle Eastern Studies Bulletin* 22–32 (also in Baalbaki 2007, no. 11).

——. 1990. Sībawayhi's "Parts of speech" according to Zajjājī: A New Interpretation. *JSS* 35, 245–63.

——. (ed.). 1999a. *Arabic Grammar and Linguistics*. Richmond.

——. 1999b. *The Arabic Grammatical Tradition. A Study in ta'līl*. Edinburgh.

——. 2006. Arabic Language Reforms, Language Ideology and the Criminalization of Sībawayhi, in L. Edzard, J. Watson (eds.), *Grammar as a Window onto Arabic Humanism, a Collection of Articles in Honour of Michael G. Carter*, Wiesbaden, 66–83.

Talmon, R. 1982. *Naḥwiyyūn* in Sībawayhi's *Kitāb*. *ZAL* 8, 12–38.

——. 1984. A Problematic Passage in Sībawayhi's *Kitāb* and the Authenticity of *aḫbār*. *JAOS* 104, 691–701.

——. 1985a. An Eighth-Century Grammatical School in Medina: The Collection and Evaluation of the Available Material. *BSOAS* 48, 224–36.

——. 1985b. Who Was the First Arab Grammarian? A New Approach to an Old Problem. *ZAL* 15, 128–45.

——.1987a. *Musnad, musnad ilayhi* and the Early History of Arabic Grammar: A Reconsideration. *JRAS*, 208–22.

——. 1987b. Schacht's Theory in the Light of Recent Discoveries concerning the Origins of Arabic Grammar. *SI* 65, 31–50 (also in Baalbaki 2007, 101–20).

——. 1988. *Al-kalām mā kāna muktafiyan bi-nafsihi wa-huwa l-ǧumla*: A Study in the History of the Sentence-Concept and the Sībawayhian Legacy in Arabic Grammar. *ZDMG* 138, 74–98.

——. 1990. *Kitāb Muqaddima fī l-naḥw al-mansūb 'ilā Ḫalaf al-Aḥmar, Dirāsa wa-fihris muṣṭalaḥāt*. *Al-Karmil* 11, 129–99.

——. 1993a. *Ḥattā* + Imperfect and Chapter 239 in Sībawayhi's *Kitāb*: A Study in the Early History of Arabic Grammar. *JSS* 38, 71–95.

——. 1993b. The Early 'Non-Sībawayhian" Views of *'Amal* in Kernel Sentences. *ZAL* 25, 268–88.

——. 1997. *Arabic Grammar in Its Formative Age, Kitāb al-'Ayn and Its Attribution to Ḫalīl b. Aḥmad*. Leiden, New York, Köln.

——. 2003. *Eighth-Century Iraqi Grammar. A Critical Exploration of Pre-Ḫalīlian Arabic Linguistics*. Winona Lake, IN.

Troupeau, G. 1960–63. La notion de temps chez Sībawaihi. *GLECS* 9, 44–46.

——. 1973–74. La *Risālat al-Kitāb* de Sībawayhi. *Mélanges de l'Université Saint-Joseph* 40, 323–38.

——. 1976. *Lexique-index du Kitāb de Sībawayhi*. Paris.

——. 1981. La logique d'Ibn al-Muqaffa' et les origines de la grammaire arabe. *Arabica* 28, 242–50 (Eng. trans. in Baalbaki 2007, 27–35).

——. 1985. Les livres des définitions grammaticales dans la lexicographie arabe. *ZAL* 15, 146–51.

'Uḍayma, 'A. Ḫ. 1975. *Fahāris Kitāb Sībawayhi wa-dirāsa lahu*. Cairo.

Ullmann, M. 1966. *Untersuchungen zur Raǧazpoesie*. Wiesbaden.

Versteegh, C. H. M. (Kees). 1977. *Greek Elements in Arabic Linguistic Thinking*. Leiden.
——. 1978. The Arabic Terminology of Syntactic Position. *Arabica* 25, 261–81.
——. 1980. The Origin of the Term *qiyās* in Arabic Grammar. *ZAL* 4, 7–30.
——. 1981. A Dissenting Grammarian: Quṭrub on Declension. *Historiographia Linguistica* 8, 2/3, 403–429. Republished in C. H. M. Versteegh *et al.* 1983, 167–93.
——. 1983–87. supplements to Diem 1981 in *ZAL* 10, 85–89; 11, 84–86; 12, 86–89; 14, 79–81; 16, 130–33.
——. 1987. Die arabische Sprachwissenchaft in H. Gätje (ed.), *Grundriß der arabischen Philologie*, vol. 2, Literaturwissenschaft. Wiesbaden, 148–76.
——. 1990a. Freedom of the Speaker? The Term *ittisāʿ* and Related Notions in Arabic Grammar, in Versteegh/Carter, 281–93.
——. 1990b. Grammar and Exegesis: The Origins of Kūfan Grammar and the *Tafsīr Muqātil*. *Der Islam* 67, 205–42 (also in Baalbaki 2007, no. 3).
——. 1993. *Arabic Grammar and Qur'anic Exegesis in Early Islam*. Leiden.
——. 1995. *The Explanation of Linguistic Causes. Al-Zağğāğī's Theory of Grammar. Introduction, Translation, Commentary*. Amsterdam.
——. 1997. *The Arabic Linguistic Tradition*. London, New York.
——. 2000. Grammar and Logic in the Arabic Grammatical Tradition, in Auroux *et al.* 1, 300–306.
——, Carter M. G. (eds.). 1990. *Studies in the History of Arabic Grammar II. Proceedings of the 2nd Symposium on the History of Arabic Grammar, Nijmegen, 27 April—1 May 1987*. Amsterdam.
——, et al. (eds.). 1983. *The History of Linguistics in the Middle East*. Amsterdam (reissue of *Historiographia Linguistica* 8, 1981).
Vishanoff, D. 2011. *The Formation of Islamic Hermeneutics. How Sunni Legal Theorists imagined a Revealed Law*. New Haven CT.
Vollers, Karl. 1893 The System of Arabic Sounds as Based upon Sibaweih and Ibn Yaïsh, in D. Morgan (ed.), *Transactions of the Ninth International Congress of Orientalists, held in London, 5th-12th September 1892*, vol. 2, 130–54.
——. 1906. *Volkssprache und Schriftsprache im alten Arabischen*. Straßburg.
Wansborough, J. E. 1977. *Quranic Studies. Sources and Methods of Scriptural Interpretation*. Oxford.
——. 1978. *The Sectarian Milieu. Content and Composition of Islamic Salvation History*. Oxford.
Watt, J. W. 1993. Grammar, Rhetoric and the *Enkyklos Paideia* in Syriac. *ZDMG* 143, 45–71.
Weipert, R. 1992. Ergänzungen zu den bibliographischen Teilen von Band I und II, in W. Fischer (ed.), *Grundriß der arabischen Philologie*, vol. 3, Supplement. Wiesbaden, 269–74.
Weiss, B. G. 1992. *The Search for God's Law. Islamic Jurisprudence in the Writings of Sayf al-Dīn al-Āmidī*. Salt Lake City.
Yaʿqūb, I. B. 1992. *Al-Muʿjam al-mufaṣṣal fī šawāhid al-naḥw l-šiʿriyya*. 3 vols. Beirut.
Zajjāj. 1963–65. (attrib.). *Iʿrāb al-Qur'ān*. ed. I. Abyārī. 3 parts, Cairo.
Zysow, A. 2013. *The Economy of Certainty. An Introduction to the Typology of Islamic Legal Theory*. Atlanta.

Index of Arabic Terms and Proper Names

The page numbers are those of the original thesis. This index does not include persons named in the addenda, though they can usually be traced through the topic of the note in question. All entries are under the Arabic term, when there is one, with cross-references from their English equivalent.

J

K

L

M

N

O

P

Q

Index of Qur'ān Quotations

Index of Poetic Quotations

9781937040581